Emerging Issues in
Primary Education

Emerging Issues in Primary Education

Edited by

Malcolm Clarkson

 The Falmer Press

(A member of the Taylor & Francis Group)
London · New York · Philadelphia

372.941.
EME

UK The Falmer Press, Falmer House, Barcombe, Lewes, East Sussex, BN8 5DL

USA The Falmer Press, Taylor & Francis Inc., 242 Cherry Street, Philadelphia, PA 19106-1906

First published 1988

Library of Congress Cataloguing in Publication Data is available on request

ISBN 1 85000 395 5
ISBN 1 85000 396 3 (pbk.)

Jacket design by Caroline Archer

Typeset in 10½/12 Bembo by
Mathematical Composition Setters Ltd, Ivy Street, Salisbury

Printed in Great Britain by Taylor & Francis (Printers) Ltd, Basingstoke

Contents

Contents

Foreword

Primary Education: Current Issues is intended to complement the reader, *New Directions in Primary Education*, first published by Falmer Press in 1982 and subsequently reprinted on a number of occasions. *New Directions* was concerned to identify trends for primary education in the 1980s and was addressed to 'serious students of primary education, not laymen'. It attempted to open up issues, revealing complexity, avoiding dogmatism and encouraging speculation regarding future developments. Judging from its reception, it appeared to meet the needs of tutors and students for a collection dealing in a sophisticated way with significant issues in primary education. Most of the issues it identified are still current but developments have occurred apace since the beginning of the 1980s both in relation to those particular issues and to others.

This new volume of commissioned papers and extracts is intended to update and highlight new facets of the topics identified in *New Directions* and to discuss other issues which have either arisen or increased in salience since 1980–81. Like *New Directions*, the book provides a variety of viewpoints on the issues it considers. It does not assume that any one interest group has a monopoly of truth or insight. It offers no detailed set of prescriptions or answers. It sets out to inform, rather than supersede, readers' professional intelligence.

1
Introduction:
Primary Education—
Current Issues

Introduction

It is both a truism and a cliché that we live and work in changing times. No doubt our professional predecessors in primary and, for that matter, elementary education would recognize the situation and the thoughts and feelings it engenders. It may well be that contemporaries tend to exaggerate the extent of changes which they are experiencing directly, as compared with the circumstances facing their predecessors. Be that as it may, the reality as experienced currently by those of us involved in primary education is one of shifts—in perspectives, in power and influence, in sources of professional satisfaction and dissatisfaction, in the very ground on which the enterprise rests. To use a geophysical analogy, living on an educational 'fault-line' which is regularly experiencing a series of tremors with the anticipation of more to come is a dangerous, though exciting, context in which to work. To cope cognitively and affectively with the situation requires well-developed self-knowledge, considerable professional intelligence, cool foresight (as well as an informed memory) and a degree of optimism, though optimism tempered by an appreciation of reality. The papers in this book are intended to contribute, in however small a way, to an increase in readers' professional understanding of some of the major issues confronting primary education and thereby to an enhanced sense of the possibility of promoting, modifying or, at the very least, softening the consequences of current shifts and those that are to come.

The first paper sets the contemporary national (and to some extent, international) scene as a backcloth for the developments and issues featured in other sections. It both widens and updates the analysis advanced in the author's paper 'Primary education: 1974–80' in *New Directions in Primary Education* (Falmer Press, 1982). Although only in a sketchy, preliminary way, English primary education is put in a wide cultural and geographical context—a perspective long overdue (and needing much further development) in an area of educational discourse too long characterized by the attempted 'cocooning' of primary education from contemporary cultural trends and by xenophobia in the light of possible international comparisons. The issues raised relate to a wide range of concerns: the reconceptualization of primary education, the structure of the primary curriculum, the redefinition of its components, differentiation, age-related objectives, curricular policy-making and staff deployment and development. The author's identification with one particularly powerful group within the education service, HM Inspectorate, may well have influenced (unduly?) his choice of issues and his delineation of their salient features; other papers in the book take up many of these issues (and others) and present more detailed and rather different analyses. Re-echoing the concerns which underlie the compilation of this book, Colin Richards concludes that recent developments and issues have made it 'even more necessary than ever for those involved in primary education, individually and collectively, to clarify aspirations, to learn from the experience of their pursuit, and so to redefine issues, modify practice and renew those aspirations' (p 21).

Michael Golby provides an alternative introductory perspective, rooted in philosophical ideas but one which is also concerned with how teachers might critically review current practice with a view to evaluating its relevance, though not necessarily in the light of the kinds of issues identified in the previous paper. He views contemporary practice as a complex amalgam of past traditions, representing 'a number of differing, perhaps even contradictory, impulses in primary education' (p 30). He argues that change in such practice does not come about through the application of education theory 'conducted away from the scene of the action in disregard of its subtlety and origins' (p 30) nor from the imposition of blue-prints from 'official' or other sources. Change, he believes, results from the deliberations of practitioners, either individually or collectively (perhaps in collegial settings?), as they consider their aspirations, the means used to pursue them and the effects of their efforts; through such consideration of ends, means and their interplay, elements of old traditions may be reassessed, even discarded, and new elements incorporated, albeit in an evolutionary rather than transformatory way. The ideas contained in this book are intended as contributing elements to this process of professional deliberation; they are not a substitute for it.

Primary Education in England: An Analysis of Some Recent Issues and Developments[1]

Colin Richards

Challenge

Children in primary schools grow physically at a fairly rapid rate; this physical growth is marked and incontrovertible. During their time in primary school, they develop intellectually, socially and emotionally; this development is not so clear cut nor as easily recognizable as physical growth but is real enough in the vast majority of cases. Partly because of teachers' close association and identification with young children, notions of 'growth' and 'development' have been very much part of professional thinking in, and about, primary education itself. The assumption of growth and development in school children has been complemented by parallel assumptions of growth and development in the primary sector of education.

Very occasionally, children's physical development is markedly stunted and medical action is required; in a minority of cases, their intellectual development is considerably retarded and remediation is necessary, but for the most part, professional assumptions about children's growth are not seriously challenged. However, since the mid-seventies, professional assumptions of growth in primary education *have* been challenged. As an enterprise, primary education has not continued to grow, child-like; its growth, in terms of numbers of pupils and teachers has been arrested, even in some senses reversed. Whether, as a result, its development as an enterprise has stagnated or regressed is more problematic and thus controversial. The underlying argument in this paper is that development has continued and continues.

Professional assumptions rest partly on close identification with children, but also in part from experience of living through periods of time with their own particular configurations of circumstances. The sense of loss and unease felt by many teachers in primary education during the last decade results from a challenge to their assumptions forged during a unique period of time (1944–1974) when all of them were children in primary schools, teachers in primary schools or, in many cases, both. Two quotations from MacLure's book on the work of school architects, *Educational Development and School Building* (1984), provides pointers to current attitudes. The first provides a broad-brush picture of the first twenty-five years of post-war education:

> The period was one of unparalleled expansion in England and Wales. For a quarter of a century after the end of the Second World War, the social, economic and demographic conditions were uniquely favourable for educational development. It began with a strong political concensus behind the new Education Act which raised expectations and promised wider opportunities for every-one. On this basis, the education system was reconstructed and modernized ... the concensus did not last: it crumbled in the 1960s, about the time the demographic trend turned down. The optimism and the expectations faded with the on-set of a recession which ended the longest period of sustained prosperity the modern world has known. (p. ix)

It is important to note MacLure's words: '*unparalleled* expansion', 'conditions *uniquely* favourable', 'the *longest* period of *sustained* prosperity'. For those currently involved as teachers or advisers in primary education, their formative years in a professional sense occurred in a period which was economically and educationally aberrant. The loss of morale, which has characterized primary education, though not all primary schools, over the last decade (but particularly from 1980 to 1987) has arisen partly through the straightened circumstances of the time but partly from the atypicality of the previous period to which so many teachers have been, and to some extent still are, unwitting prisoners. In a second quotation, MacLure refers to changes in attitudes, thinking and practice required of school architects post-1975, once the period of unparalleled expansion had come to an end:

> To move out of the familiar thoughtforms of expansion and into the more austere disciplines of contraction and to do so creatively was by no means impossible but it called for a major effort of the imagination as well as a careful review of progress. (p. 265)

As far as primary teachers are concerned, the period since 1975 has witnessed considerable self-examination as the results of successive national surveys by HM Inspectorate have revealed the extent of the gap (inevitable to some degree) between aspiration and realization, between rhetoric and reality—soul-searching further promoted by local education authority curricular reviews and school self-evaluation activities. In some cases, unprofitable nostalgia has been the only result of such experiences. However, in others, realization of shortcomings has led to determination to tackle issues through policy formulation and implementation—at national, local authority and school levels. Sometimes as a result of such initiatives and sometimes independent of them, many schools have continued to develop their conception of an appropriate primary education and have adapted to changing circumstances through the exercise of professional intelligence and imagination. Such schools have risen to the challenge presented by MacLure: development has continued despite, or in some cases even, spurred on by 'the more austere disciplines of contraction'.

The Wider Context

Issues in English primary education in the 1980s, the particular focus of this paper, need to be set in a wider temporal and geographical context if their significance is to be properly gauged. During the last two decades, a number of inter-connected factors (demographic/cultural/economic/ technological) have helped shape Western European societies and have, in turn, influenced provision and response in primary education. They have made it more difficult for primary education to pursue and fulfil its long-established purposes; more significantly still, they have made it necessary for those involved in primary education to review these purposes, to seek what elements of provision need to be reaffirmed, which redefined and which down-played, and to review the means through which purposes are enacted and elements provided. This process has been a Western European phenomenon, not unique in its scale or intensity to England.

Demographic changes result from the complex interplay among economic, social and cultural trends and the decisions of many millions of people. The most significant feature of the demographic situation in Western Europe has been the sharp decline in the number of births since 1965—a decline which began to affect the number of children in primary schools during the seventies. As Table 1 illustrates, countries suffered differentially from decline in primary school populations: some states such as the Federal Republic of West Germany and Austria experienced a 30 per cent fall from 1970 to 1982, others such as the United Kingdom, 20 per cent, and others such as Denmark and Norway less than 10 per cent. Although exact international figures are not available, many countries experienced further decline into the mid-eighties; in England, for example, the number of full-time pupils in maintained primary schools fell from 3,970,197 in January 1980 to 3,372,318 in January 1985.*

* In England, rolls are expected to rise, although slowly, in the late-eighties and early nineties.

Table 1   The number of pupils enrolled in primary education in a sample of
Western European countries (UNESCO, *Statistical Yearbook*, 1984)

Austria	1970	531,934
	1979	420,935
	1982	367,691
Belgium	1970	1,021,511
	1980	842,117
	1982	780,408
Denmark	1970	443,031
	1980	434,635
	1982	420,064
France	1970	4,939,683
	1980	4,610,361
	1982	3,914,450
Federal Republic of West Germany	1970	6,344,774
	1980	5,044,424
	1982	4,500,991
Ireland	1970	520,122
	1979	418,247
	1981	420,871
Italy	1970	4,856,953
	1979	4,506,566
	1982	4,215,841
Netherlands	1970	1,462,376
	1980	1,333,342
	1982	1,201,512
Norway	1970	385,628
	1980	390,186
	1982	372,705
Sweden	1970	615,331
	1980	666,079
	1982	658,127
Switzerland	1970	500,492
	1980	450,942
	1982	415,478
United Kingdom	1970	5,866,349
	1979	5,133,710
	1981	4,685,572

In England perhaps the most obvious changes resulting from falling rolls have been institutional ones in the form of school closures and amalgamations. The number of primary schools has fallen from 20,942 in 1973 to 20,454 in 1980 and 19,068 in 1985. In addition, though exact figures are not available, there have been a very large number of amalgamations usually involving the amalgamation of separate infant and junior schools, but also the combining of separate infant schools or separate junior schools. Such changes have resulted in a sharp decrease in the number of separate infant schools—institutions long established within the English system and often regarded as providing many exemplars of interesting practice in the education of young children. In the management of local education authorities, school size has become a critical factor, not just in terms of the numbers of pupils in very small rural (and urban) schools but in terms of schools having the necessary range and mix of teacher experience and expertise to provide the kind of broad, redefined primary curriculum discussed later in this paper. Internally within schools, falling rolls have resulted in an increase in mixed-age classes which have produced considerable pedagogic problems for teachers not accustomed to them. Very significantly too, reorganization has led to many teachers having to work in institutions covering a wider age range or having to be redeployed to other schools. In consequence, institutional and age-range loyalties have been weakened and teachers' professional identities reshaped. While reorganization has meant enforced mobility for some staff, for others it has reduced opportunities for movement consequent on promotion. Stresses and strains in the form of professional and personal problems of readjustment have severely tested the high quality of interpersonal relationships generally characteristic of English primary education.

During the last twenty years societies in Western Europe have witnessed considerable *changes in the patterns of domestic life* which have influenced the upbringing of children, their social and emotional development and, less directly, their ability to cope with the range of demands resulting from attendance at primary school. As the Council of Europe's Steering Committee on Population (1982) reports 'Better education and vocational training, increased opportunities for employment outside the home, the possibility to plan family size effectively and responsibly and the elimination of the fear of unwanted pregnancy have made many more women more independent' than previously. Moves towards greater equality between the sexes have resulted in a blurring of the distinctions between the roles of men and women, both within the home and within the work place. Since 1965 there has been a great increase in the proportion of women in the labour force (currently about 42 per cent in the United Kingdom) and, more recently, with the steep rise in male unemployment, an increase in the number of men at home. In many homes, men and women are sharing responsibilities and tasks to a greater degree than formerly; relationships are becoming more fluid and less predictable, as couples negotiate and then renegotiate their roles in the family situation. An increasing number of children live in 'one-parent families' or in a number of different domestic situations as their parents remarry or live with other partners after their divorce. In Britain, the effects of such changing patterns on young children's development and receptivity to the intellectual and interpersonal demands of primary schools have not been documented in research terms. The challenge of responding appropriately to the notion of equality of curricular opportunity for both girls and boys has been recognized by policy makers and researchers and in many schools but is providing a difficult and complex one with implications for both the formal and the 'hidden' curriculum and for pedagogy at primary as well as secondary levels.

Changes in domestic patterns are but one aspect of a more pervasive cultural phenomenon which has been recognized in Western Europe—the development of increasingly pluralistic societies where variations in individual and group values, beliefs and lifestyles are acknowledged, though not universally welcomed or encouraged. *Cultural pluralism* of a limited kind is not a new phenomenon since class and regional variations have long been established, but significant in recent decades are the extent to which established views, expectations and assumptions have been openly and widely challenged and the added pluralistic dimensions to cultural life which have resulted from the settlement of ethnic minority groups from former European colonies. Broadfoot (1985) describes this weakening of the normative concensus underpinning society:

> The cultural 'roots' of education policy—like other areas of social life—are increasingly unstable. Affluence, rising expectations, the media, technical innovation and modern forms of communication, the decline of religion and the success of modern science, have all broken up the traditional life-world of more strictly constrained life choices. As the horizons for self-identity are pushed out to embrace a broadening range of alternative forms of life and a myriad of possible futures, traditions are robbed of their authority. They lose their normative force. The more multi-cultural societies become, the more there is a corresponding weakening of consensus. (p. 276)

The challenge facing primary schools in societies such as England, which are both multi-racial and culturally diverse, is to value and respond to diversity amongst the children and at the same time to foster a sense of social cohesion through the pursuit of common aspirations and values.

Economic factors have been, and seem likely to remain, particularly potent influences on developments within educational systems. In the 1960s high rates of economic growth, low inflation and political and public confidence in education as a major investment in future economic growth resulted in a general expansion of educational systems in Western Europe, involving, at the primary stage, improvements in teacher–pupil ratios, accommodation, resources and support services for children and teachers. However, the late 1970s and 1980s have been characterized in economic terms by reductions in manufacturing output and a steep rise in unemployment (in the United Kingdom, for example, the percentage of the working population who were unemployed rose from 6.8 per cent in 1980 to 13.5 per cent in 1985). Education systems have shared in the general depression, as many governments in Western Europe stressed greater value for public money and instigated reductions in public expenditure. Parallel with these developments, many states reduced expenditure on primary education as a percentage of total public current expenditure on education (Table 2); falling pupil enrolments in the primary sector contributed to such governmental savings. In England and Wales, the period of financial constraint at both national and local education authority levels has had its effects, not primarily on staffing ratios which continued to improve until 1984, but on other aspects of primary education. Some of the partial effects, direct or indirect, of financial constraint are documented in HM Inspectorate's expenditure report based on visits to 1,600 maintained primary and secondary schools in the autumn term of 1985: though stressing that 'links between resources and quality are not straightforward' and pointing out the 'marked need for efficient and effective management of people and resources at every level' and 'for improved leadership', the report identifies a statistically significant association between satisfactory or better levels of appropriate resources and work of sound quality, and between unsatisfactory levels of resources and poor quality work (DES, 1986d, p. 6). It goes on:

> Of the resource factors associated with work judged less than satisfactory in the primary schools visited, the most frequently identified was unsatisfactory or unsuitable accommodation ... this was followed, in descending order, by the inadequate provision of books, either in number, quality or appropriateness; the lack of sufficient equipment; inappropriate furniture; and poor quality or unsuitable school-produced teaching materials. Of the non-resource factors identified as adversely affecting the quality of work in primary schools, the most commonly referred to was teaching groups containing pupils with a very wide range of ability or of mixed age. Together, these factors were affecting some 1,270 lessons or just over a quarter of the total. (p. 15)

Technological changes, particularly the development of micro-processing and robotics, are influencing the context and, to an increasing though limited extent, the content of the primary curriculum in England and elsewhere in Europe. In recent years, micro-technology has been held responsible for a significant proportion of the growing unemployment in Western Europe; it seems set fair to be a major influence on the incidence of paid employment in the future, on the kinds of competencies required of those in paid employment, and on the patterns of work and leisure, enjoyed, or endured, by the majority of the population. The availability of cheap micro-computers has direct implications for teaching in primary classrooms and is necessitating an examination of the most fruitful uses to which these powerful tools can be put, and of the kinds of capabilities and attitudes children need to acquire if they are to interact profitably with micro-computers.

Table 2   *Total current expenditure on primary education as a percentage of total public current expenditure on education in a sample of Western European countries* (UNESCO *statistical Yearbook*, 1984)

Austria	1970	29.6
	1980	17.9
	1982	16.2
Belgium	1970	24.7
	1980	25.3
	1982	24.8
France	1970	23.8
	1979	17.4
	1980	21.5
Federal Republic of West Germany	1975	18.3
	1979	16.6
	1980	16.0
Ireland	1970	42.8
	1979	36.0
	1980	26.1
Italy	1970	28.4
	1979	29.2
Netherlands	1970	20.8
	1980	19.2
	1981	19.2
Norway	1970	47.5
	1980	49.3
Sweden	1970	42.7
	1980	44.6
	1982	34.9
United Kingdom	1970	26.4
	1979	26.9
	1980	26.2

English Primary Education and the Primary Curriculum

Against the backcloth of economic, technological, demographic and cultural changes outlined in the previous section, what issues have been developing specifically in English primary education? The first is a highly generalized but very significant development—concerned with changes in the way primary education and the primary curriculum are being thought about and discussed. Until the mid-seventies, discussion about primary education was characterized by a kind of two-party oppositional 'politics'—between adherents of what has variously been termed as the 'developmental', 'progressive' or 'liberal romantic' perspective on the one hand and the 'elementary', 'utilitarian' or 'conservative' perspective on the other. It is possible to characterize the two perspectives briefly and without undue distortion. The 'liberal romantic' view of primary education, exemplified most clearly but not totally in the Plowden Report (CACE, 1967), starts from, and constantly refers back to, the individual child when developing educational principles. It celebrates self-expression, individual autonomy, first-hand experience, discovery learning and personal growth. Compared with other perspectives, it advocates a much more equal partnership of teacher and taught with teachers, to some extent at least, learning 'alongside' children; it emphasizes the processes of learning rather than its products; and it offers children a relatively high degree of choice (though still somewhat circumscribed) in the type, content and duration of activities. The 'elementary' tradition in contrast views the curriculum as a repository of essential subject matter and skills which need to be handed down or transmitted by teachers in an orderly, systematic way. It stresses products rather than processes, reception rather than discovery learning, social and intellectual distance rather than partnership between teachers and children. It offers children little or no discretion in the content or style of the learning they undertake.

Since the mid- or late-seventies, a third perspective 'liberal pragmatism', has become increasingly prominent in professional discussion of primary education. This holds a middle ground position, viewing the curriculum as a set of learning experiences largely, but not entirely, determined by teachers but respecting to some extent both the individuality of children and the importance of cultural transmission. Advocates of liberal pragmatism advocate a broad curricular grounding for all children, in part preparatory for secondary education, but a grounding which takes account of the fact that children learn through both first-hand and second-hand experiences, which uses children's knowledge and interests as starting points and contributions to on-going work but which shapes and refines children's experience along teacher-structured lines. The approach seeks to be both liberal, in giving a broad range of experience through a variety of teaching and learning styles, and pragmatic in building on and extending much current practice. It is characterized too, by a concern for planning and policy-making at school and local authority levels, for systematic progression and continuity between and within schools and for evaluation and assessment of children's learning at each level from the class to the education system nationally. The last ten years have witnessed the gradual formulation, refinement and public expression of this view of primary education; the perspective has set, and continues to set, the agenda for discussion and policy-making in English primary education.*

* Alternative perspectives on changing modes of thought related to primary education are provided by Golby (1982) and Blyth (1984).

As a result of the influence of liberal pragmatism and its concerns for planning and policy-making, the primary curriculum is coming under increasing scrutiny—not just the teaching and learning activities offered within it, but the very way it is conceptualized. Despite this development the long-established subject-based framework for the curriculum is alive and well and living in the minds and, to some extent, the practices of many policy-makers and teachers, the result in part of their own primary and secondary education. Its attraction is very strong, as witnessed by the fact that even the Plowden Report (CACE, 1967), while acknowledging that children's learning did not fall into neat subject compartments, went on to discuss the curriculum under separate subject headings. To some teachers, subjects appear to be almost 'natural' components of any curriculum; to others who acknowledge their 'artificial' and social construction, they are extremely convenient categories for curriculum analysis and review; to others they are an irrelevance and a reactionary irrelevance at that. The newer frameworks for discussing the primary curriculum, discussed in this section, are attempts to define, and trace inter-relationships among, the constituent elements of a primary curriculum to which all children should be introduced—elements drawing on, but going beyond, established subjects.

HM Inspectorate's report of the national primary survey (DES, 1978) is one such attempt. It distinguishes skills and attitudes recurring in various parts of the curriculum and analyzes the work of primary children under five headings: (a) language and literacy; (b) mathematics; (c) science (experimental and observational); (d) social studies; and (e) aesthetic and physical education. As judged by the recently published findings of a DES survey (DES, 1986d), this framework has become an established part of the curricular policies adopted by a number of local education authorities. In an essay published in 1984, Blyth offers a six-fold categorization, 'not subjects or, necessarily, forms of understanding or endeavour, but rather six elements in children's lives' (p. 53) which need to be incorporated into what he terms an 'enabling curriculum': (a) growth, health and movement; (b) communication (through a variety of codes—linguistic, numerical, graphical, electronic, physical); (c) interpretation of the social and physical world; (d) vision and imagination; (e) feeling, expression and appreciation, especially through the arts; (f) values and attitudes.

Recently, HM Inspectorate have put forward, as a basis for discussion, a six-fold framework for the analysis, review and development of the curriculum—primary as well as secondary (DES, 1985e). This comprises: (i) general aims: (ii) areas of learning and experience; (iii) elements of learning; (iv) cross-curricular issues; (v) general characteristics of the curriculum; (vi) assessment. Central to this framework are 'two essential but complementary perspectives': nine areas of learning and experience (aesthetic and creative, human and social, linguistic and literary, mathe-matical, moral, physical, scientific, spiritual and technological) in, and through, which children's understanding and competence are to be developed and four elements (knowledge, concepts, skills and attitudes) which constitute the bases for the planning and selection of teaching and learning experiences within each of the nine areas. The discussion document has met with general approval from local education authorities and from national professional associations; its discussion in many schools has unfortunately been hindered by industrial action; its reception by tutors in institutions of higher education has been mixed, some commending its basis in cultural analysis and the usefulness of its framework as an analytic tool, others critical of some of its distinctions as epistemologically suspect.

Whether through the primary survey's five broad categories, Blyth's six elements or HM Inspectorate's nine areas, primary schools are being challenged to consider the structure of the whole curriculum and to do what some have done already, *ie.* readjusting emphases, widening curricular opportunities and so moving away from what Alexander (1983) terms 'the two curricula syndrome' whereby mathematics and English are given far greater importance, far greater time allocation, many more resources, more systematic planning and more considered evaluation and assessment than other parts of the curriculum. Acceptance of the view that, for example, all nine areas of learning and experience are essential to children's education leads at the very least to schools' review of the human, temporal and material resources devoted to constituent parts of the curriculum to see whether there are any unjustifiable imbalances which need to be redressed. Issues such as priority, range and balance within the curriculum are now having to be addressed systematically and explicitly. Their consideration inevitably involves the making of practical judgments concerning the extent to which aspirations are currently being realized and the exercising of value judgments regarding desirable re-emphases or alterations to existing practice. The uncertain nature of both these kinds of professional judgment does not obviate the necessity of making more nor of involving all teaching staff and governors (and perhaps also non-teaching staff) as the ILEA Report (1985) suggests in their discussion and resolution.

Such review is made even more necessary by the ever-broadening range of curricular demands being made on schools. Aspects of health education (*eg.* DES, 1986b), environmental education, political education (*eg.* Harwood, 1985, 1986), education for family life (*eg.* DES, 1985c), world studies (*eg.* Fisher and Hicks, 1985), technology (*eg.* Williams, 1985; Williams and Jinks, 1985), information technology (*eg.* Wagstaffe, 1988) and industry education (*eg.* Jamieson *et al.*, 1984), to name but some, are pressing their claims as offering worthwhile, particularly relevant experiences to children at an age where their attitudes are being formed and basic views of the physical and social world established. Equally, the increasing recognition of the fact of discrimination on the basis of gender and/or race leading in some local education authorities and schools to explicit policies to counter racism and sexism is also placing demands on teachers to reappraise teaching methods, forms of organization and programmes of work in all curricular areas. The 'over-loading' of the primary curriculum can only be prevented if schools reject an 'additive' model of curriculum design (whereby new areas are simply tacked on to existing work) and instead adopt a thorough going review, perhaps taking several years, of their programmes of work using criteria such as those proposed by HM Inspectorate (1985) to see which established elements need to be retained, which de-emphasized and which perhaps omitted entirely and which new elements ought to be incorporated, not necessarily as discrete entities but perhaps as facets or dimensions to existing areas of work. In relation to the problem of overload, it is important to stress, and hopefully it is comforting for primary schools to acknowledge, that 'A single activity can contribute to several areas of learning. When learning to cook, for example, 6-year-olds can extend their vocabulary and oral skills; learn to recognize simple mathematical relationships; be trained in hygiene; and improve their manual dexterity' (DES, 1985, para. 34).

As yet a further dimension to this re-examination of the curriculum, the nature of the 'basic skills' developed in primary schools are being redefined to include a range of higher level capabilities previously considered by some schools to be applicable for only a minority of children. *The Curriculum from 5 to 16* (DES, 1985e, para. 100) offers a tentative classification of such redefined 'basics' which need to be practised and refined by all children during their time in primary school. The national primary survey (DES, 1978) helped set this trend in train; successive middle school surveys (DES, 1983, 1985b) have continued it. It is being argued that individually, in small groups or through whole class discussion, primary children of all ages need to be given more opportunities to pose questions, to offer explanations, to predict and to speculate. They need greater encouragement to test their ideas through conducting experiments, designing structures, inventing artefacts or undertaking enquiries; through selecting and evaluating evidence and through establishing tentative conclusions, patterns or generalizations. Such higher-level capabilities based, for their proper application, on understanding related to particular areas of learning and experience are regarded as the heart of successful primary practice. They are not easy to foster in the crowded ecological setting of the primary classroom as HM Inspectorate's surveys and other research studies indicate but are characteristic of teaching and learning in some schools.

The development of a wide range of approaches is a challenge not only to practitioners, but also to researchers who have examined teaching and learning in primary classrooms over the last decade, but who, according to Simon (1985) have not yet developed adequate pedagogic theories to account for or to guide practice. Nowhere is this lack more evident than in relation to the related issues of match (DES, 1978; Bennett *et al.*, 1984) and differentiation, *ie.* providing children with learning experiences which take due account of their varying characteristics and yet which are guided by a common set of principles and purposes which transcend these differences. In his paper which links the neglect of pedagogy in England with the issue of differentiation, Simon argues that:

> To develop effective pedagogic means involves starting ... from what children have in common as members of the human species; to establish the general principles of teaching and, in the light of this, to determine what modifications of practice are necessary to meet specific individual needs. If all children are to be assisted to learn, to master increasingly complex cognitive tasks, to develop increasingly complex skills and abilities or mental operations, then this is an objective that schools must have in common; their task becomes the deliberate development of such skills and abilities in all their children. And this involves importing a definite structure into the teaching, and so into the learning experiences provided for the pupils. Individual differences only become important, in this context, if the pedagogic means elaborated are found not be appropriate to particular children (or groups of children) because of one or other aspect of their individual development or character. In this situation, the requirement becomes that of modifying the pedagogical means so that they become appropriate for all; that is, of applying general principles in specific instances. (page 99)

If progress is to be made on the elucidation of general principles of teaching and learning and on appropriate forms of differentiation, researchers have not only to focus more on learning and on the curriculum in the classroom context but also to involve teachers much more as collaborators and 'critical friends' in the research enterprise. More than this, more teachers need to be encouraged to take a research stance towards their practice: systematically enquiring into it and its effects and making their findings known to fellow practitioners inside and outside the research community. Despite the claims made by some of its proponents, this 'teacher as researcher' movement, a development of the 1970s, is a frail plant requiring careful nurturing in the bracing climate of the 1980s if it is to make a major contribution to understanding classroom practice and developing the professionality of teachers.

As outlined in paragraph 81 of *Better Schools* (DES 1985a), another current development is the attempt to define more closely the kinds of skills and understandings children should be able to exhibit, bearing in mind the diversity of abilities and rates of development which obtain amongst 11-year-olds. The difficulty of this exercise is readily acknowledged: 'It will be no short or easy task to move towards a more precise definition of attainment targets' (para 81). The aim is to establish at national level sets of reasonable expectations in different curricular areas, which 'at school level

... can and should be finely tuned to accommodate particular classes and indeed pupils' (DES, 1986a, para 24). Papers in the HMI series *Curriculum Matters*, findings from the Assessment of Performance Unit (APU), accounts of 'good practice' by HM Inspectorate and specially commissioned research in the area of primary mathematics are different strands of this process of clarification. This work is being paralleled in local authorities such as Croydon where expectations of performance at primary level have been made explicit (Croydon, 1985). The effort at a more precise definition is based on the belief that this will help all concerned to assess the effectiveness of policies and practice at national, local and school levels; will encourage teachers to have appropriately high expectations of children and will help motivate the pupils. It needs to be stressed that the aim is *not* to produce a highly specific set of minimum attainment targets to be reached by all pupils—a 1980s equivalent of the Revised Code of the last century.

Two other major curricular issues, continuity and consistency, could feature specifically in an overview such as this but can, for convenience, be subsumed in a last overall issue—the emergence of the curriculum as an object of policy at national, local, and, increasingly, school levels. Nationally, central government has an explicit policy, *ie*. to secure 'a broad agreement about the objectives and content of the school curriculum' and is pursuing this through seeking consensus in four areas: the purposes of learning at school; the contribution of each main subject area or element to the curriculum as a whole; the organization and content of the 5–16 curriculum; and statements of expectations of pupils' performance, as discussed in the previous paragraph. A number of general aims have been agreed (DES, 1985a, para 44); a number of fundamental principles enunciated (breadth, balance, relevance and differentiation); a discussion paper on the organization and content of the 5–16 curriculum issued (DES, 1984b); and other work undertaken including the publication of the *Curriculum Matters* series. In the area of science, a definitive policy statement has been issued (DES, 1985d) setting out an overall approach and priorities and, at the primary level, broad criteria for the selection of content, areas of study in which children's understanding of scientific concepts should be developed and factors important in the successful implementation of primary science. Through these initiatives it is hoped to achieve a measure of continuity and consistency nationally such that all pupils 'have access to a curriculum of similar breadth and balance irrespective of their level of ability, the school they attend or their social circumstances' (DES, 1985e, para 3).

With the passing of the 1986 Education Act local education authorities too are being required to have curricular policies to inform the execution of their duties, especially in relation to such matters as staff development, the deployment of the teaching force and the advisory service and the achievement of a continuous 5–16 curriculum. Judging from a recently published report (DES, 1986c) at least five-sixths of authorities have already drawn up curriculum policy statements or plan to do so, some covering the 5–16 curriculum as a whole and some dealing separately with primary and secondary curricula. Finally, schools are being urged to formulate policy statements embodying their general educational intentions and establishing appropriate expectations relating to the wide range of their children's abilities, aptitudes and educational needs (DES, 1983, 1985b). Such an approach to curricular policy-making demands conscious and co-ordinated planning by primary practitioners; it does not deny the importance of individual teacher flair or opportunism but assumes that these are not sufficient to secure children's entitlement to a broad, balanced and relevant primary education. Concerted action by primary staff, along the lines discussed in the next section, is being recommended.

Staff Development and Deployment

The curricular trends discussed in the previous section are necessitating the re-examination and the reinterpretation of the task of primary teachers in relation both to their 'own' classes and to their colleagues. Several major findings from the national primary survey (DES, 1978) have provided the foundation from which this reappraisal has developed: (i) the effectiveness of a broad curriculum involving the application of basic skills to other areas (para 8.29); (ii) the lack of sufficiently consistent coverage for important aspects of the curriculum, thereby putting a broad curriculum 'at risk' in some schools (para 6.09); (iii) the beneficial influence of some post-holders on the quality of work (paras 4.5 and 7.36).

In many schools, ways are now being sought of tapping the curricular and pedagogic expertise of individual members of staff (not just post-holders) for the benefit of the school as a whole in order to develop and keep under review a redefined curriculum which provides consistent coverage of important areas and elements and which encourages the development and application of higher-level 'basic' skills. Such attempts are based on the beliefs: that it is no longer reasonable to expect class teachers to cope individually and unaided with the range of demands now being made on them, and that individual self-sufficiency is undesirable in any case in view of the importance of continuity of experience and reasonable consistency of approach from class to class within the same school. In the light of such beliefs, four aspects of the primary teacher's role are undergoing re-examination: curriculum co-ordination, class-teaching, collaboration with parents and involvement in school-wide review and policy-making. Progress in this reinterpretation varies from school to school and from aspect to aspect.

Since the publication of the primary survey, many local education authorities and heads, with the encouragement of the DES and HM

Inspectorate, have made considerable efforts to develop the role of curriculum co-ordinators or consultants in primary schools. Increasingly, not just post-holders are involved; there is often an expectation that all, or almost all, members of staff, including relatively inexperienced teachers,will take on a co-ordinating role for an aspect of the curriculum. Job descriptions for co-ordinators are commonplace and, in some cases, arrangements are in hand for reviewing progress in relation to the discharge of responsibilities so described. In some, though not all, schools such co-ordinators are now regarded as central to curricular review and development: formulating and monitoring programmes of work, giving advice, managing resources, keeping in touch with developments in their curricular area, providing advice on the school's needs for in-service education, and, less often, running school-based in-service sessions, offering exemplars of classroom practice which colleagues can observe and discuss, and working alongside teachers in the class situation. Fulfilling a co-ordinating role requires a range of demanding skills (Campbell, 1985) as well as sensitive support from headteachers, access to outside advice, ideas and facilities, and most particularly, time during the school day to observe the work being done and to guide and support other teachers in the class context. Headteachers have a key role to play in helping establish the legitimacy and value of the co-ordinator's role, particularly through encouraging and persuading class teachers to welcome advice from their peers as an accepted part of normal, professional practice. Developing co-ordinators' subject-matter expertise and their knowledge of how children might engage with that subject matter is also very important, if the programmes of work they devise and the advice they offer are to be soundly based. Developments in initial teacher training, involving students studying a subject or area of the primary curriculum for two years at a level appropriate to higher education, are intended to develop this expertise and confidence among new entrants to the primary teaching profession (DES, 1984a).

Although some progress has been made in clarifying the nature of the co-ordinating or consultancy role and in enhancing its standing, there is far less clarity, and more apprehension, among teachers generally concerning the implications of recent curricular thinking for the place of the class teacher. Some have foreseen the dismantling, or at the very least, the weakening, of the class-teacher system, particularly in the upper part of primary schools. It needs to be stressed that the long-standing and valued tradition that one teacher should be responsible for ensuring that his/her class receive a curriculum adequate in range and depth is not seriously 'at risk', but the way this responsibility is to be properly exercised and supported *is* being reinterpreted in the light of the changes and developments outlined earlier. It is being argued that the class-teacher system needs strengthening through sensitive deployment and development of the expertise which already exists on primary school staffs by means of a variety of ploys, varying from the one-off occasion, through temporary short-term arrangements to more permanent long-term procedures, all subject to modification as circumstances change. Support for the class teacher could take one or more of a variety of forms, depending on the individual and the area of the curriculum in question: occasional advice from a co-ordinator or other member of staff with specialist knowledge; a detailed scheme of work identifying concepts, skills, subject matter and attitudes to be developed and giving guidance on organization, methodology, differentiation and assessment; attendance at in-service courses run by outside agencies or by school personnel; co-operative teaching with one or more colleagues; help for a period from an advisory teacher; a co-ordinator working alongside a colleague for a time to help introduce a new aspect of work; or, in some cases, perhaps most often (but not necessarily only) with older children, a member of staff with specialist knowledge teaching someone else's class a particular aspect of the curriculum for a month, a term or a year, provided the class teacher retains overall responsibility for the work of the class, including the links that would need to be made between his/her own work and that of the specialist. Ideally, as a class teacher, an individual member of staff would have access to support such as this in each area of the curriculum except the one for which he or she had co-ordinating responsibility; in that area, he/she would be expected to provide support to colleagues.

The fostering of collaborative rather than individualistic modes of working is also illustrated by moves involving the renegotiation of home-school relationships so that parents are not only informed about, but also actively involved in their children's *school* education in a way which complements the more general educative influence they can exert through the many experiences of family life, including the fostering of particular interests and hobbies. This renegotiation is particularly manifest in those schools which are collaborating with parents so that children's learning in class is deliberately reinforced and enriched by experiences at home jointly planned, at least in part, by teachers and parents. The most obvious sign of this partnership in children's home learning is the proliferation of schemes involving parents systematically in their children's reading following the startlingly positive effects of such practices, particularly in socially disadvantaged areas, noted in researches such as those by Hewison and Tizard (1980) Tizard, Schofield and Hewison (1981) and by Widlake and Macleod (1984). Similar parental involvement schemes are now being launched for mathematics. Of course, parental involvement in children's school learning through provision of experiences at home has long occurred on an *ad hoc* basis; the harnessing and co-ordination of such activities are increasingly being seen as an extremely valuable supplement to schools' efforts. To be optimally effective, such co-ordination needs the long-term commitment of the whole staff and is thus a policy matter for schools; it also requires the development of a subtly different range of skills as teachers take on the role, however limited, of adult educationist, albeit with a primary education

19

focus. Such collaboration also has far-reaching implications for the kinds of learning activities provided in school time and to which parental activities are to be related: for example, more of the same at home might well be unproductive in the long term, despite its short-term reinforcing effects. Home-school co-operation in relation to the teaching of reading and, increasingly mathematics, is a particularly topical exemplar of a more general phenomenon—the increasing involvement of parents in the work of the education service, not just in England but in Western Europe more generally.

Perhaps the most difficult to realize of the four role adjustments called for by recent developments relates to the development of what Campbell (1985) terms 'collegiality'—participatory decision-taking by the staff as a whole. Primary teachers have traditionally seen themselves as relatively autonomous in their classrooms but having little influence on the school as a whole (Taylor *et al.*, 1972): teachers first and members of a school's staff second. They are now being asked to take a collaborative rather than individualistic approach to their work—not just in relation to curriculum planning and review but in terms of decisions relating to issues such as the identification of the school's INSET needs under the new INSET grant arrangements, links with parents and the wider community, and liaison with other schools and outside agencies. This 'collegial' approach may be manifest in the formulation and endorsement of policies for particular areas of the curriculum or in relation to issues such as anti-racism or anti-sexism; it may take the form of school self-evaluation activities using local education authority materials or schemes such as GRIDS (MacMahon *et al.*, 1984) to tackle issues springing directly from the felt concerns of staff; it may lead to the production of school development plans such as those advocated in the ILEA report on primary schools (ILEA, 1985). The development of collegiality has implications for the in-service education of teachers who will need greater understanding of inter-personal and group processes to participate effectively and has implications for the role of heads whose basis of authority may increasingly rest, not on their formal position, but on their skills in facilitating colleagues' participation and in helping them solve problems and resolve conflicts (Coulson, 1988). In some areas, the concept of collegiality is being extended to other schools in the locality, as groups of schools meet to develop and co-ordinate their work and to engage jointly in in-service education. As Campbell points out, the collegial school may still be more of an image than a reality, though a significant number of schools are developing along these lines.

Conclusion

The issues raised in this paper bear witness to the fact that during the last decade, despite MacLure's 'disciplines of contraction', policy and practice in English primary education have continued to develop—in response both to outside forces and to the education system's own dynamic. The issues highlighted are not the only ones affecting, or likely to affect, primary schools; for example, changes in the initial training of teachers or issues related to equal opportunities are not discussed here in detail but are likely to prove influential in many schools. The task of the primary teacher has never been easy, either for novitiates aware of their shortcomings or for experienced practitioners aware of the inevitable gap between professional aspiration and achievement. Recent developments and issues have served to make that task even more demanding but have, helpfully, highlighted the impossibility of individual self–sufficiency in discharging it. They make it even more necessary than ever for those involved in primary education, individually and collectively, to clarify aspirations, to learn from the experience of their pursuit, and so to redefine issues, modify practice and renew those aspirations. It is, however, important to set high expectations for professional development as well as for the development of pupils, despite the inevitability of a degree of disappointment when these are not fully met. As Stenhouse pointed out, 'Success can be achieved only by lowering our sights. The future is more powerfully formed by our commitment to those enterprises we think it worth pursuing, even though we fall short of our aspirations ... we shall only teach better if we learn intelligently from the experience of shortfall, both in our grasp of the knowledge we offer and of our knowledge of how to offer it' (Rudduck and Hopkins, 1985, pages 125–6).

Note

1   This paper was written before the government's announcement that it intended to establish a national curriculum. (Ed.)

References

ALEXANDER, R. (1983) 'Training for primary class teaching: an agenda for progress', *Primary Education Review*, 16.

BENNETT, N. *et al.*, (1984) *The Quality of Pupil Learning Experiences*, L. Erlbaum Associates.

BLYTH, W, (1984) *Development, Experience and Curriculum in Primary Education*, Croom Helm.

BROADFOOT, P, (1985) 'Changing patterns of educational accountability in England and France', *Comparative Education*, 21:3.

CAMPBELL, R, (1985) *Developing the Primary School Curriculum*, Holt Rinehart and Winston.

CENTRAL ADVISORY COUNCIL FOR EDUCATION (ENGLAND) (1967) *Children and Their Primary Schools* (The Plowden Report), HMSO.

COULSON, A, (1988) 'An approach to headship development through personal and professional growth'. This volume.

CROYDON (1985) *Primary Education in Croydon*, Croydon.

DEPARTMENT OF EDUCATION AND SCIENCE (1978) *Primary Education in England*, HMSO.

DEPARTMENT OF EDUCATION AND SCIENCE (1983) *9–13 Middle Schools*, HMSO.

DEPARTMENT OF EDUCATION AND SCIENCE (1984a) *Initial Teacher Training: Approval of Courses*, Circular 3/84, HMSO.

DEPARTMENT OF EDUCATION AND SCIENCE (1984b) *The Organization and Content of the 5–16 Curriculum*, HMSO.

DEPARTMENT OF EDUCATION AND SCIENCE (1985a) *Better Schools*, Cmnd 9469, HMSO.

DEPARTMENT OF EDUCATION AND SCIENCE (1985b) *Education 8–12 in Combined and Middle Schools*, HMSO.

DEPARTMENT OF EDUCATION AND SCIENCE (1985c) *Home Economics from 5–16*, Curriculum Matters Series 5, HMSO.

DEPARTMENT OF EDUCATION AND SCIENCE (1985d) *Science 5–16*, HMSO.

DEPARTMENT OF EDUCATION AND SCIENCE (1985e) *The Curriculum from 5–16*, Curriculum Matters Series 2, HMSO.

DEPARTMENT OF EDUCATION AND SCIENCE (1986a) *English from 5–16: The Responses to Curriculum Matters Series 1*, HMSO.

DEPARTMENT OF EDUCATION AND SCIENCE (1986b) *Health Education from 5–16*, Curriculum Matters Series 6, HMSO.

DEPARTMENT OF EDUCATION AND SCIENCE (1986c) *Local Authority Policies for the School Curriculum*, HMSO.

DEPARTMENT OF EDUCATION AND SCIENCE (1986d) *Report by HM Inspectors on the Effects of Local Authority Expenditure Policies on Educational Provision in England, 1985*, HMSO.

FISHER, S. and HICKS, D, (1985) *World Studies 8–13—A Teachers' Handbook*, Oliver and Boyd.

GOLBY, M, (1982) 'Micro-computers and the primary curriculum', in GARLAND, R. (Ed.), *Microcomputers and Children in the Primary School*, Falmer Press.

HARWOOD, D. (1985) 'We need political not Political Education for 5–13 year olds', *Education 3–13*, 13:1.

HARWOOD, D. (1986) 'To advocate or to educate?', *Education 3–13*, 14:1.

HEWISON, J and TIZARD, J (1980) 'Parental involvement and reading attainment', *British Journal of Educational Psychology*, 50.

ILEA, (1985) *Improving Primary Schools*, ILEA.

JAMIESON, I. et al (Eds.) (1984) '*We make kettles: studying industry in the primary school*, Longman.

MacLURE, S. (1984) *Educational Development and School Building: Aspects of Public Policy 1945–1973*, Longman.

MacMAHON, A. et al, (1984) *Guidelines for Internal Review and Development in Schools: Primary School Handbook*, Longman.

RUDDUCK, J and HOPKINS, D. (Eds.) (1985) *Research as a Basis for Teaching: Readings from the Work of Lawrence Stenhouse*, Heinemann.

SIMON, B (1985) 'Why no pedagogy in England?' in *Does Education Matter?*, Lawrence and Wishart.

STEERING COMMITTEE ON POPULATION (1982) *Conclusions*, European Population Conference, Council of Europe, Strasbourg.

TAYLOR, P *et al*, (1972) *Purpose, Power and Constraint in the Primary School Curriculum*, Macmillan.

TIZARD, J., SCHOFIELD, W. and HEWISON, J. (1981) 'Collaboration between teachers and parents in assisting children's reading', *British Journal of Educational Psychology*, 52.

WAGSTAFFE, A (1988) 'Emerging issues in micro-computing', this volume.

WIDLAKE, P. and MACLEOD, F (1984) *Raising Standards: Parental Involvement Programmes and the Language Performance of Children*, Community Education Development Centre.

WILLIAMS, P. (1985) *Teaching Craft, Design and Technology Five to Thirteen*, Croom Helm.

WILLIAMS, P. and JINKS, D. (1985) *Design and Technology 5–12*, Falmer Press.

Traditions in Primary Education

Michael Golby

Traditions are alive and well in our primary classrooms; indeed, it is impossible to conceive of primary practice as such without relying upon the notion of traditions. This fundamental point, which is philosophical in nature, will be illustrated by reference to a classroom recently observed. From this description there should emerge both a clearer idea of the important sense in which traditions are inescapable and the extreme potency of existing traditions in primary schooling. From this basis will be mounted a discussion of the prospects for development in primary school practice. It will be suggested that development is best conceived on an evolutionary model rather than as the application of principles or theories generated in ignorance of the origins of present practice. Conceptions of curriculum planning promulgated in the orthodox perspective of recent official documents are of little use to curriculum developers and it is urgent that support be found for more deliberative approaches.

The physical configuration of a classroom (as of the school which contains it) is a reflection of longstanding and developing ideas about what is to go on inside it. The classroom itself had historically to be invented to supersede the 'open plan' environment of monitorial teaching. So too, earlier, did the school come into being as a protected and specialized environment within which children were to be treated specifically as pupils, rather than say as labourers or sinners, as would be appropriate in workplaces or churches. If schools and classrooms came about at specific historical moments and have continuously developed since—all for reasons which can be identified, although of much complexity—we can assume they will continue to develop in future. The past is not a series of mistakes that has yielded a modern enlightenment. All ages make their best and sincerest accommodation to their circumstances. A sense of the evolution of classrooms and schools goes with a sense that their future is in human hands, though not in the hands of any individual or group. A feeling for the presence of the past in the present may help us to contribute, with due humility, to the making of the future. This view of things, it is worth noting, is distinctly 'non-rational' in the sense that it stresses the negotiated and social nature of change in educational practice. In doing so it places attempts to derive future directions from a priori principles in a larger context. More will have to be said of this later in this chapter.

I wish to illustrate the living nature of a variety of traditions within quite ordinary everyday practice by referring to an afternoon I recently spent in a primary classroom. The classroom observed, which was for thirty-two five, six and seven-year-olds in a primary school, was set up physically as illustrated in the diagram.

Some features of this situation, observable simply from the classroom diagram and in advance of any account of the teaching carried on within it, are as follows:

(i) The teacher's desk has a frontal position standing centrally and commanding the blackboard. This reflects a continuing subscription to the idea, if not to the practice, of instructional teaching in which the teacher is the fount of knowledge. She needs to have in clear line of sight every individual learner whose work she can literally oversee.

(ii) Pupils, however, are to be seated in groups. The common octagonal desks place children in many different physical attitudes towards the teacher and to one another. Not all the children will be for all of the time in eye contact with the teacher. If the centrality of the teacher's desk implies instruction (though it does not entail it) then the grouping of the children implies interaction, perhaps even cooperation, among them (though it by no means entails these things).

(iii) Mathematics and reading have occupied a considerable amount of classroom space. The physical equipment of activity materials (rods, scales, workcards, books) has been concentrated in specific spaces to allow access for children who must necessarily occupy and use this space sequentially and in small numbers. This entails that not all the children will be doing the mathematics required by the apparatus, or using the class library books at once and therefore that there will be complexity in the use of time by the pupils individually and collectively. Equally, it entails that the teacher will be deploying her time selectively among the children as they work in these, and other, areas of the classroom. So the instructional situation implied by the teacher's desk and blackboard is contradicted by the physical space given to mathematics and books. A 'mixed economy' of classroom activity seems to be suggested by these arrangements.

(iv) The computer (BBC B) has found access to the classroom and it has been located within an area otherwise reserved for mathematics

Figure 1

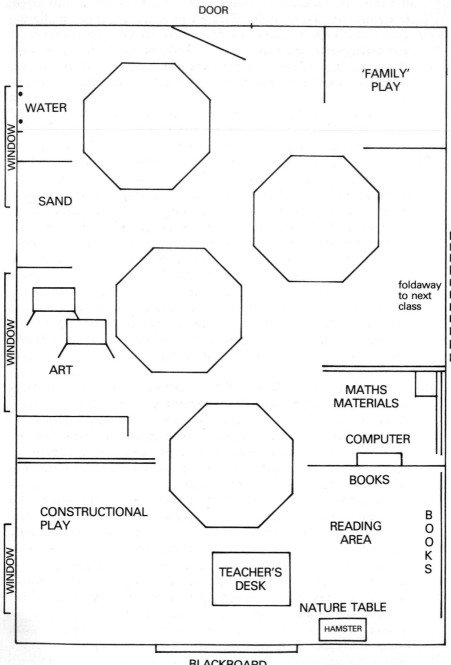

material. Following the national drive to introduce computers sponsored by the Microelectronics Programme of the Department of Trade and Industry, computers will be existing in various niches in classrooms and schools. Their physical location itself might tell us a lot about the take up of the micro even in advance of knowledge of its use. Here there is an affinity, on the face of it, with the secondary school practice whereby micros and computing generally have become a province of many mathematics departments.

(v)   Play has a physically peripheral status, being located at the margins of the available space. Though the various forms of play are closely differentiated they all occur away from the central spine of the classroom occupied by the desks. It would be quite conceivable to locate play activities, or some of them, in the centre and group desks around the walls. Is it too fanciful to suggest that desk work is to occupy the central role in class and play to be a recourse from its demands? Constructional play is located close to the desk, perhaps so that the teacher can keep a closer eye on these activities which may pose a greater physical danger than those elsewhere. The family, like families outside in the real world, retains a seclusion and privacy at the furthest remove from the centre of power, in the 'family' play area. The forms of play are diverse, a mini curriculum in themselves, containing elemental materials in the shape of sand and water, socializing opportunities in the 'family play' area and imaginative and motor activity with constructional toys and bricks.

(vi) Art has found a territory in this classroom. Like play it is at the margin and its claim on classroom priorities, though made, is nicely balanced with that of elements of 'play', with which it may be equated. The art work seems to be confined to painting and opportunities for other work in the expressive area not apparent. This reflects an assumption that painting is the staple or core form of artistic expression for young children.

(vii) The natural world gains access to this classroom in the shape of a pet hamster and a nature table containing books and specimens and children's work in relation to them. Here we are most forcibly reminded that what is present is on the scene at the expense of everything else which could have taken its place. The natural world represented here is the world of nature study not the world of physics. It may approach botany and zoology but it nowhere becomes experimental nor even scientifically detached and dispassionate. The disciplines of the laboratory do not enter this classroom in any form; but those of the observer, the artist and the carer for 'nature' do.

In these arrangements for learning within the four walls of a classroom may be seen a curriculum-in-waiting. The selection which is made here has been made not on abstract principles nor from formal professional debate. Rather, this curriculum-in-waiting has been precipitated out of diverse initiatives and innovations over the years. The 'three Rs' curriculum of the elementary school lives at the core; expressive and developmental aspects of the child's nature are recognized in the various opportunities for play and artistic expression; the social aspect of learning stressed by Dewey's 'project method' is recognized in the provision for children to be in groups; the hamster and the nature table uphold a metaphysical idea of the educational importance of the natural world long associated with progressive education.

The curriculum selection in this classroom must also be viewed in the light of what is not present. Primary French and i.t.a. are not visible and this will be no surprise to those up to date with primary education, though fifteen years ago it would have been a different story. Not every innovation proposed and strongly supported by outside agencies, as both primary French and i.t.a. were, survives. Equally, not every longstanding practice continues either. There is no map of the world in the room, no biblical texts, no cane.

It would be possible to overrate the significance of some of these physical dispositions. Perhaps I have done so and perhaps I have added rather more interpretation than is fully justified. What the description is intended to do is to raise the idea that none of this is at all accidental. What is in the classroom, and where it is, is so in every case for a reason, or set of reasons. Like the classroom itself, a human invention that came into being at a certain time through an act of educational imagination, the arrangement of desks and equipment has derived from longstanding beliefs and assumptions deep in the practice of the teachers and staff concerned. That these are not purely idiosyncratic matters of private or personal taste is evidenced by the fact that this classroom, though unique, is typical. Many other classrooms like it could have been depicted. None would have been identical but they all would have had much in common with this example. What we see in the example is a physical manifestation of a set of traditions making up modern practice in primary education. Of course, there will be differing emphases from school to school, classroom to classroom, local education authority to local education authority and from one end of England and Wales to the other. There will also be differences, probably more important ones, from one end of the age range to the other and this example is from the lower end of the primary span of 4+ to 12+. Yet what arrangement of furnishings, fittings and materials are we likely to find elsewhere which would not be of a piece with the beliefs and assumptions manifest in the classroom I have depicted? Any piece of personal eccentricity or local enthusiasm would be likely to be shortlived. And I suggest this because I wish to assert that primary practice is a complex social tradition or set of traditions made up of an historical flow of ideas laid down at different times and for different contemporary purposes. The task of the educationist is to critically review these traditions for their present relevance; it is not to discard them wholesale as outdated nor cling to them as a heritage defying change. Above all, these traditions—so far represented only in tables and chairs and equipment in physical juxtaposition—cannot be ignored. There is no other intelligible or safe approach to curriculum development than to respect the origins and development of the constituents of present practice. There is no 'rational' way to proceed except by relating present needs to the potential for development within classrooms such as this.

Having described the classroom with the intention of raising questions about how what is there came to be there, and how what is not came to be excluded, I can now go on to describe how this physical situation came into use during one particular afternoon. This may yield further clues to the chemistry of the classroom which we must understand if we are to engage in responsible curriculum development rather than innovation without change.

Even more strongly than in describing physical appearances one is aware that subjective biases and ideological presuppositions threaten the validity of descriptions of social phenomena. Some things can unproblematically be said, however. For example, girls and boys entered together in an informal and unceremonious fashion. No salutations or marching. It is assumed here, as it has not always been assumed, that primary education will be co-educational. The board school buildings standing today with their confident archways proclaiming 'Boys' and 'Girls' entrances remind us of this. How far this presumption in favour of co-education entails a common curriculum which does not differentiate on grounds of gender would constitute a research project in itself. But it was noticeable that several girls (and no boys) made immediately for the family play area. Choice or prescription? Questions later of the teacher revealed that initial activities during the afternoon were of a generally 'free' nature subject to two conditions. The children should have finished their morning's work and they should 'get a balance' over all the available 'choosing activities' over a period of time. The teacher had an idea where children's preferences were, what they needed to be encouraged into and moved on from.

As the afternoon wore on it was apparent that children were having to complete their morning's work in mathematics, reading and writing, before moving to their 'choosing' activities. The octagonal table at the back of the class remained well occupied for the better part of the afternoon. This, I learned, was the table where the 'not so quick' children worked. Though children had no set desks they were clearly grouped in a general way by 'ability' and this was manifesting itself in empty places at the table immediately in front of the teacher.

Throughout the afternoon the teacher was on her feet and in fact never occupied her central chair and desk. She perambulated the classroom spending short periods of time with individual children and occasionally offering a quietening word to those involved in play. She was followed for much of the early part of the afternoon by a comet's tail of children with spelling books at the ready. Only very occasionally did she deal with more than one child at a time. Her relation to the play was very largely non-interventionist, a watchful eye. At the end of the afternoon she read a story in the reading area and after dismissing the children had a parent to talk to.

When the curriculum represented in the physical configuration of the classroom came into active being during the afternoon, additional understanding became available of the underlying mixture of assumptions by which it worked. The primacy of mathematics and literacy; the individualistic nature of the curriculum despite the octagonal tables; the use of a concept of 'ability', based on mathematics and literacy, as a principal organizing device; the importance of play as a 'natural' occupation of children to be allowed its own development; the relationship to parents as one worth devoting time to; all of these were undeniably apparent in this ordinary afternoon's work. This can I think be said without too much worry about observer subjectivity or self-confirming observations.

More subjectively, I was left with an overwhelming sense of the complexity of what was going on, a complexity vastly beyond the bland description I have given. And also of the typicality of this situation in representing a number of differing, perhaps even contradictory, impulses in primary education. How far does traditional educational theory help us to sort out and gain control of situations like this? How far has the recent spate of curriculum documents helped? These are questions I should now turn to before going on to speculate about future directions.

Too much, the greater part, of educational theory is conducted away from the scene of the action, in disregard of its subtlety and origins and in terms of crude dichotomies. It was long ago remarked by O'Connor (1957) that in education the term 'theory' is little more than a 'courtesy title' (p.110). His reasons concerned the futility of trying to approximate theories in education to those in science. This is of course a very narrow view of theory as something that can be valid in scientific activity only and is elsewhere a vanity. Certainly, we theorize in politics and art, in morality and religion. What is wrong with educational theory is not that it cannot be scientific but that it has not attempted to understand the daily practice of teachers before going on to judge and make recommendations about that practice. Theory must start from practice though there is no reason why it should end there. Theory should be thought of as a critical commentary upon practice and not as some body of knowledge from which practice may be derived by the application of principles, a 'top-down' model. The implications of this view for the relationship between teaching on the one hand and theorists and researchers on the other, and between schools and teacher training institutions, are considerable and deserve fuller analysis. For the moment, however, we must register the failure of educational theory to help us understand the daily complexity of teaching life, saturated as it is with the presuppositions of our predecessors.

The principal way in which the failure of educational theory has been demonstrated is its tendency to deal in over-simple categories of an 'either-or' nature. Darling (1978) observes

> The progressive/traditional classification of educational thought is seductively simple. There are several ways in which its widespread, and generally unthinking, adoption may appear to have unfortunate effects.
>
> To begin with, it legitimizes a confrontation style of educational debate in which abuse of the other side is common, and the re-examination and refinement of one's own views is not. The opposition is rarely given credit for having a case which is even *prima facie* respectable, either intellectually or morally, and this is coupled with a refusal to admit even minor difficulties or weaknesses in one's own position.
>
> It further suggests that while there is little or no common ground between the opposing sides, each side speaks with a single voice. The extent of the differences of opinion within each group is not fully appreciated by its members because (a) the more energy devoted to attacking the opposition, the less attention is spent on observing one's own side; and (b) the defence of one's own group is facilitated by a degree of self deception about the unity of the group's views.
>
> The polarization effect obscures the possibility that one may, without inconsistency, side with the traditionalists in some circumstances and the progressives in others. Instead of discussing whether teachers should use either discovery methods or instruction, it might be more fruitful to consider whether each method does not have some merit. The crucial question would then become: 'In what circumstances is one method more appropriate than the other?' It seems likely that teachers are more adept at this kind of thinking than theorists. (p.158)

Darling goes on to suggest the extension of the classification to include a 'radical' position. This draws attention to some useful distinctions to be made, for example that there exists a breed of thinkers who are so progressive as to call for the end of schooling, the deschoolers. There is an obvious distinction between the thought of Sir Alec Clegg and John Holt or Ivan Illich. The importance of progressivism has been that it has been taken up by the 'educational establishment—inspectors, advisers and college lecturers plus some concerned politicans' (*ibid*, pp. 159). Yet, what is required, it seems to me, is not still more theorizing among contending educational positions nor still more research (of which more later) but a closer understanding of practice itself. This will involve teachers much more closely than hitherto in the production of theory, although not necessarily as final arbiters of the significance of what they do. Because educational theory has been the commodity of superior progressivist non-practitioners it has brought into a dangerous disrepute all forms of analysis of educational practice. It is urgent that theory should be rehabilitated.

One specific reason for this urgency is that the 'curriculum debate' since the Ruskin speech of October 1976 has yielded very little understanding of the primary curriculum. What has occurred is that a traditional vocabulary for curriculum discussion has been strengthened. This is a vocabulary of 'standards' and 'specialization', of 'subjects' and 'assessment' which has all but supplanted those 'Plowden' views of the curriculum characterized by an emphasis on 'interests' as a curriculum starting point and 'growth' as a prevailing metaphor, which were gaining some ground in the sixties and seventies. The emphasis on written statements of aims (with the assumption that the curriculum is the means taken to achieve those aims) places teachers in a contractual and instrumental relationship to those who regard themselves as clients, whether parents, governors, local education authorities or central government. Of course, which of these constituencies is properly to be regarded as the 'client' is part of the incoherence of this position and the reason why endless formulations and reformulations of the powers and make up of governing bodies can never be fully satisfactory. Two results ensue from this way of conceiving the curriculum and the teachers who 'deliver' it. Firstly, and most importantly, the child as a principal client is entirely overlooked, subjugated to a process conceived by others. Connected with this is the fact that in some circumstances teachers are the child's safeguard against exploitation and miseducation. Secondly, the curriculum is conceived in the terms dictated by the common sense among the dominant interests of the day. The 'world of work' is thus overrepresented in the secondary school rhetoric (if not yet in the practice) and its correlate 'busyness' in the primary school. A melange of ideas supporting traditionally subject-based curricula, didactic methodology, standardized testing and discipline has been solidified since the Great Debate. Its effect on the primary school has been to wither the confidence and values of many progressively trained teachers. It is of course a moot point how far these values ever penetrated into classroom practice. The Plowden Report was optimistic on this point and the Primary Survey (1978) and subsequent HMI pronouncements have tended, on the contrary, to allay post-Tyndale anxieties about unbridled and undisciplined 'playway' approaches. HMI have said in various places that much of primary practice is too routine and unimaginative. Whatever the take-up of progressive values we can be sure that much further thinking and experimentation are necessary if we are to see primary teaching based soundly on a knowledge of children's learning and on a considered educational philosophy. There is a developing body of research on children's learning, notably that of Donaldson (1978), Tizard and Hughes (1984) and Hughes (1986). The prevailing context for educational development over the past ten years, at least, has not allowed teachers and those who support them to capitalize on insights such as these for, as I have said, the child has been subservient to social goals and moral panics about disorder. The child has been a spectre at the curriculum feast. It is surely time to reinstate the child and the meaning children make of school to the centre and not periphery of our educational debates.

Two linked and debilitating aspects of technology stand in the way of this rebirth of humanistic understanding. On the one hand, a technology of educational research has been harnessed to a saloon bar orthodoxy about the curriculum. This has reinforced narrow conceptions of teaching as a process of matching tasks to children's abilities in a context of control. Efficiency has become the chief educational virtue. On the other hand, industriousness and busyness have become educational values in themselves. The meaning of classroom tasks to children and the significance of reflection, discourse, the inner life and the posing of alternatives have been banished from view. The connection of these revived conceptions of the classroom as workplace and the teacher as task-master to the 'world of work' cannot be mistaken, as Willis has shown in the secondary context.

What more precisely are the objections? Research will only produce answers to the questions it poses. Both HMI, in their newly acquired survey research posture, and the professional educational research community have responded to the political and social climate by asking narrowed questions. Annex B of the Primary Survey (1978), to take a major example, is a schedule of questions reflecting a view of what is important in the curriculum. Here no questions about the overall coherence of the curriculum and the thinking underlying it are to be found. Large scale survey research reduces complexity, attends to surface features only, looks for the measurable aspects of behaviour rather than its invisible causes, drives towards generalizations and fails to identify originality. That is its nature. Leaving aside the subjectivity at the heart of the observational judgments individual HMIs contributed to the massive enterprise of the survey, the pool of data collected was all collected to a preformed agenda which assumed a post-elementary school curriculum (drills and frills). The reassurance yielded by the survey spoke only to those interested in standards, control and efficiency. The climate it set for subsequent inspections and reports was of value to progressives only in so far as it provided some protection for their continued operations. That may be no small benefit in a hostile world and perhaps it is unrealistic to hope for more from HMIs. If that is so, it is doubly unfortunate that professional researchers have in the main followed the trend. Funded research is bound to the questions the policy makers wish to ask. So *The Quality of Pupil Learning Experiences* (Bennett *et al.*, 1984) contains nothing on quality beyond the idea of 'matching'. Quality is equated with the demand tasks make of children. It contains nothing on the nature of learning beyond the idea that it is something acquired through striving over 'cognitive dissonance'. It has no analysis at all of the idea of experience assuming this can be unprob-lematically 'provided' into terms intended by a teacher without any contribution from the child. Now, quality must raise question of value. What is the worth in educational terms of the tasks with which children are presented? Is learning to be distinguished from behavioural response as something which cannot be engineered in a subject but has to be actively pursued? (Langford, 1968). What is the contribution of a learner's past to the experience he or she can have in the present? (Clark, 1979).

Perhaps fundamental to research of this kind is its denial of contexts, its reliance upon what is seen in the present. For example, do the tasks seen in the classroom fit into an overall activity which gives them a meaning and purpose? It would be hard to conceive of any classroom regime as simply a succession of disconnected tasks. What holds them together in a mean-ingful sequence? We cannot expect further observation to answer this question satisfactorily for ultimately it becomes a matter of the point of the whole curriculum sequence itself. This is in the nature of a rationale or explanation which cannot be read off from events conclusively but must derive from understanding the intentions of the teacher. The teacher's understanding of what he or she is doing is thus ineradicably part of the evidence, just as children's understanding of what they are doing is part of the evidence too. This does not mean that what teachers or children say is final and conclusive, only that the diverse ways in which judgments may be formed on these matters cannot be expelled from educational research, however much we would like it to be scientific. The positivistic tradition maintained in the psychological input to training courses, has obvious strengths. It is a pity it has not been matched in recent years by a growth in interpretive studies such as those of Sharp and Green (1975), Armstrong (1980) and Rowland (1984). Is it too much to hope that funds may be forthcoming from official quarters in a more liberal dawn for research which is less tied to conservative orthodoxies on the curriculum?

Perhaps the most obvious candidate for such studies is the use made of the micro-computer in primary schools. This machine is the very emblem of the modernity cult. How will it be incorporated into the primary curriculum? It could go the way of programmed learning, an earlier manifestation of scientific arrogance in relation to teaching. It could become a new means of enslaving pupils to meaningless tasks, an aspect of innovation without change the more dangerous because the more effective. Or it could introduce qualitative changes in pupils' opportunities to access information, test hypotheses, develop original ideas and interact with experts. Only if the machinery is seen in a clear context of educational ideas can the latter occur. Perhaps the principal idea to hold on to here is that the pupil must be in control. There are studies, such as Hughes (1986), which show the beginnings of how this may be possible and we urgently need to develop such work at classroom level. Otherwise the very real danger is that the computer will become an educationally irrelevant toy. Because of the seductive modernity of microelectronics generally we too easily fall into the trap of believing its introduction can be a panacea. The enormous enthusiasm of many teachers for micros is a mixed blessing here for energies expended in one area may not be well distributed across the whole curriculum. What can the micro do which enables us to pursue our educational goals more effectively? What new potential for learning is opened up by the judicious use of the technology? These seem to be the essential questions. Above all, two considerations seem fundamental. We should remember that the present state of the art is primitive and there is no real virtue in learning programming techniques which will be redundant in a short time. Education must provide the deeper structures to our thought and feeling; mere techniques need to be seen in that light and taught for their instrumental value. They have no intrinsic value any more than assembling computers has for the South Korean (female) factory operative.

Secondly, as technologies what is provided by micros is essentially the rapid processing of information. Teaching will always involve information processing but it is also deeply concerned with information *getting*. The vicarious experience to be had at the console must be complemented and preceded by the experience of investigative activity. Investigating the potential of the micro itself which is an enormously compelling activity, is separate from understanding the significance of what is put into it in the first place. Only if that is understood is it logically possible to understand what new significance our data may acquire from the processing. This vicariousness of micro-technology is the same vicariousness as that of the book. I do not underestimate books as I do not underestimate micros. But I would be reassured if I believed that teachers made the most of books as a learning medium. Research in this area should look for uses of micro-technology which extend good practice. This will in all likelihood be undramatic practice, quietly effective, a long way removed from the bloated expectations of the more uncritical exponents of micro-technology.

What then of future directions for primary education? There are of course obvious problems in telling the future. Of it nothing can be known. By contrast, what we *can* know is something of how the present situation came into being, what our present desires are, how children learn and what is possible for us in the here and now. So instead of predicting the future, an activity full of wish fulfilment and pervaded by vested interests, it is better to take a considered view of where we are and how we may help to shape the immediate trends. Global discussions of educational ideologies are less helpful than a close understanding of the present. Joan Tamburrini

(1986) suggests that 'an understanding of recent findings on developmental research and their implications is far more useful to a teacher than those slogan–like prescriptions' (p. 35). This is an aspect of a truly deliberative approach, which essentially reviews the existing traditions for their adequacy to present and forseeable conditions and modifies them accordingly. This may appear unadventurous and culpably gradualist to more radical and revolutionary educationists yet I believe it is the only realistic way to proceed. It does not succumb to neophilia (by worshipping technology for instance) nor supposes that everything is alright. It does not patronize the past by assuming our predecessors have left us nothing of value nor refuses to test promising new ideas. It does not regard curriculum as an applied science consisting of predicting the future and then preparing for it. This approach eschews generalities and proceeds circumspectly, constantly keeping under review both the means and ends of practice which are seen to be totally intertwind (Westbury and Wilkof, 1975). It is practical rather than rational, seeing curriculum as an evolving form of life not a blueprint to be changed at will.

Viewed in this light, what help have recent developments given the deliberative teacher? The answer is I think very little. The 'orthodox perspective' (Southworth, 1985) has been reinforced by a torrent of curriculum documents. This perspective is characterized by an emphasis on the written word as a form of guideline to curriculum activity and aims as essential ingredients within a means–end model of teaching. Teachers are viewed as operators of a 'delivery system' whose chief commodity is 'subjects'. Work and play are separated. Learning is regarded as something achieved through instruction, most efficiently in age groups or 'classes' rather than in more naturalistic social groupings, 'family groupings' for example. Children, insofar as they are seen at all, are seen as individual learners detached from the wellsprings of their social being in family and community. There is no conception of teaching as other than instruction and control and no account of the relation between the school and the outside world. This is a true description of Baker's curriculum in the 1987 consultative document (DES, 1987).

I submit that the situation in the classroom I described at the outset is a natural result of our collective failure to resolve the tensions within current practice. It is not that a final resolution into unsullied perfection is ever going to be possible. That we have no right to hope for. What we can reasonably expect is that the framework for professional practice could be a little more tolerant of the idea that there are values within the educational community which deserve the respect, the space and the resources to be more fully worked out. More generous support for the development of practice is required and it is to be hoped that collaboration with parents and others at ground level in governing bodies and in the many developing schemes for parental participation will foster a more deliberative approach. It would be unnecessarily apocalyptic to say that ten years of curriculum 'debate' has stultified the primary school for ever. As Southworth (1985) observes 'The sheer quantity of documents which are bombarding schools at the present may force schools into submission and easy acceptance' (p. 48). But let us hope that the contents of this book may play their part in releasing ideas for the consideration of teachers and others concerned with the practical business of improving practice.

References

ARMSTRONG, M (1980) *Closely Observed Children*, Chameleon.

BENNETT, S. N. *et al* (1984) *The Quality of Pupil Learning Experiences*, Lawrence Erlbaum Associates.

CLARK, C (1979) 'Education and behaviour modification', *Journal of Philosophy of Education*, 13.

DARLING, J. (1978) 'Progressive, traditional and radical: A realignment', *Journal of Philosophy of Education*, 12.

DEPARTMENT OF EDUCATION AND SCIENCE (1987) *The National Curriculum 5–16: A Consultative Document*, HMSO.

DONALDSON, M. (1978) *Children's Minds*, Fontana.

DEPARTMENT OF EDUCATION AND SCIENCE (1978) *Primary Education in England and Wales* (The Primary Survey) HMSO.

HUGHES, M. (1986) *Children and Number*, Blackwell.

LANGFORD, S. G. (1968) *Philosophy and Education*, Macmillan.

O'CONNOR, D. J. (1957) *An Introduction to the Philosophy of Education*, Routledge and Kegan Paul.

ROWLAND, S (1984) *The Enquiring Classroom*, Falmer Press.

SHARP, R and GREEN, A. (1975) *Education and Social Control: A Study in Progressive Primary Education*, Routledge and Kegan Paul.

SOUTHWORTH, G. (1985) 'Perspective on the primary curriculum', *Cambridge Journal of Education*, Lent.

TAMBURRINNI, J. (1986) 'Trends in developmental research and their implications for infant school education: In place of ideologies' in DAVIS, R. (Ed) *The Infant School: Past, Present, and Future*, Bedford Way Paper 27, University of London.

TIZARD, B. and HUGHES, M. (1984) *Young Children Learning*, Fontana.

WESTBURY, I. and WILKOF, N. (Eds.)(1975) *Science, Community and Liberal Education*, Chicago University Press.

2
General Curriculum Issues

Introduction

As a concept 'curriculum' is essential to an understanding of the educational enterprise. The meaning of that concept is neither precise nor agreed: it is both unclear and contested. No one definition secures, or is ever likely to secure, general agreement. However, some formulations are likely to achieve greater currency than others because of the source from which they come. One such formulation is that provided by HM Inspectorate in their overview document *The Curriculum from 5-16*:

> A school's curriculum consists of all those activities designed or encouraged within its organizational framework to promote the intellectual, personal, social and physical development of its pupils. It includes not only the formal programme of lessons, but also the 'informal' programme of so-called extra-curricular activities as well as all those features which produce the school's 'ethos' ... Teaching and learning styles strongly influence the curriculum and in practice they cannot be separated from it. (p. 7)

Recently, powerful voices, both professional and political, have criticized primary education for focussing *unduly* on teaching and learning styles and for failing to give adequate attention to the issues of curricular content embodied in those 'activities' and of standards of learning and their assessment. The content and outcomes of primary education are now centre-stage. The perennially important issues of breadth, balance, relevance, differentiation and progression are being discussed more urgently than ever and their implications drawn out more precisely than hitherto. Some important general curriculum issues—range, consistency, process versus content, continuity—feature in the companion volume *New Directions in Primary Education* and though still very relevant are not explicitly considered here in any detail. This section focusses specifically on rationales for the primary curriculum and on the emergence of the curriculum as an object of policy at national and local levels.

In the first extract, Alan Blyth examines a number of theoretical bases for the primary curriculum and links them to currently expressed viewpoints; readers could, with profit, do the same in relation to future curriculum formulations. Before putting forward his own rationale, he distinguishes three theoretical approaches:

(i) An approach through 'forms of understanding and endeavour', *ie.* broad categories of mental activity to which primary children are to be introduced.

(ii) A 'process' approach whereby children construct their own understanding rather than receiving it as a form of understanding and endeavour.

(iii) A 'social imperatives' approach concerned less with individual children's knowledge and understanding and more with the capabilities to be developed to meet the needs of society.

He then gives his own view of the curriculum ('planned intervention in the interaction between development and experience') and provides a rationale in terms of enablement ('to equip the child not just with skills and content or even values and attitudes and understandings, but with the capacity to choose and to accept and cope').

The second contribution focusses on the HMI overview document referred to in the opening paragraph, a formulation rooted primarily in the first of Alan Blyth's theoretical approaches. Colin Richards argues that *The Curriculum from 5–16* suggests an approach to thinking about, designing and reviewing the whole curriculum which could help resolve issues related to the content and outcomes of primary education. The paper is put in its political/administrative/educational context; the main points of its rationale are highlighted and some of its implications for primary teaching drawn out in terms similar to those put forward in section 3 of this book.

The HMI document has been published to stimulate professional discussion about the whole curriculum; it does not represent, though it hopes to inform, government policy. In contrast, the long extract from the White Paper *Better Schools* does review a number of policy initiatives undertaken by central government in pursuit of its aim to secure 'a broad agreement about the objectives and content of the school curriculum'. According to *Better Schools*, a number of general aims have been agreed; the fundamental principles of breadth, balance, relevance and differentiation enunciated; consultation undertaken on the organization and content of the 5–16 curriculum, and work undertaken in relation to defining the kinds of skills and understandings children should be able to exhibit at the end of the primary stage. In addition, the paper sets out the government's view of the distribution of responsibilities for the curriculum at national, local and school levels: the importance attached to curricular policies comes over clearly.

Whereas *Better Schools* is concerned primarily with national responsibilities and initiatives and Jim Campbell's chapter later in the book focusses on curriculum policy-making at school level, Harold Heller's contribution forces on the LEA. He argues that the notion of LEA policies represents a qualitative change in the local management of the education service arising from a range of formidable political and social pressures, which he briefly reviews. He examines the development of curricular policies in three local education authorities—varying considerably in style. He concludes that curricular policies are more easily developed in those authorities with traditions of forward planning and with officers and advisers willing to take on interventionist roles. He identifies a long 'game-plan' in which central control of the curriculum will be eventually asserted—possibly with structural modifications removing education from local authority control.

Joan Dean's contribution argues for curriculum continuity throughout the 5–16 span, and for commitment to tackle it from teachers, schools and local education authorities. She argues that it is possible to create greater continuity without insisting on uniformity and believes that a national curriculum might help, provided it is complemented by discussion at school level amongst families of 'receiver and feeder' schools. She outlines the strategy which, if followed, could make children's school experience somewhat less discontinuous than it often is at present. Her conclusion is particularly hard-hitting:

> We have given lip service to the idea of continuity for many years.
> It will only happen if our commitment is sufficient to give it a high
> level of priority. There is a very real need to do so.

The sixth extract illustrates the difficulties encountered in providing the kind of broad, balanced, differentiated and progressive curriculum called for both by central government and by HMI. It summarizes the findings of an important research project into the quality of the learning environments provided in a number of infant classrooms (for a comment on this project see page 34). It focusses particularly (and valuably) on the nature of classroom tasks—their planning and presentation, their curriculum content, the intellectual demands they make on children and their appropriateness or match to children's attainments. Further such studies are required in a range of curricular areas and age-groups. The curriculum as actually experienced by primary children is still grossly under-researched.

Judith Whyte's article discusses the effects of gender in primary education—a developing focus of interest prompted by a concern to promote equal opportunities for all. She summarizes gender differences in performance at the primary stage and argues that schools tends to reinforce and exaggerate differences between girls and boys—not by direct teaching, but through a 'hidden curriculum' of informal comments and assumptions. She believes that 'it is in the child's picture of the social world that the primary-based teacher can do most to promote change' (p 113).

A parallel concern for equal opportunities underlies Keith Kimberley's contribution. This addresses the issue of how the education system, and in particular the school curriculum, should respond to the ethnic/racial/cultural diversity within British society. He advocates a multicultural education 'based on a rethinking of all that is taught in relation to its appropriateness and contribution to the development of a more equal and less discriminating society'. He concludes: 'The important issue in the continual remaking of the curriculum is whether it functions to highlight and analyze the underlying inequalities which are such crucial features of contemporary life, or whether its construction ensures that such uncomfortable contradictions are suppressed'. Where does primary education stand in relation to illumination or suppression?

Along with recognition of the deleterious consequences of discrimination based on gender or race, there has been increasing concern not to discriminate on the grounds of supposed disability, unless that discrimination can be justified on educational grounds. Ann Lewis focusses on provision for children with special educational needs in mainstream primary schools following the 1981 Education Act. The latter is described as 'the most significant change concerning special educational needs in recent years' but its implications are believed not to have filtered through yet to the majority of primary schools. The paper reviews developments and raises a range of curriculur issues (such as consistency, continuity, breadth and match) and staffing considerations—relevant to primary education generally but discussed here with special needs particularly in mind.

Bases for the Primary Curriculum

Alan Blyth

[Blyth distinguishes three theories of curriculum and relates the primary curriculum to each of these]

First, there are theories based on the nature of knowledge or, more adequately, understanding. One such theory is lucidly and cogently expressed in the writings of Hirst (1974). The essential point in such theories is that there are forms or styles of understanding which are independent of individual knowers and which are also each conceptually independent of the others, with truth-criteria of its own. Thus, for example, empirical or scientific understanding is something that constitutes one part of everybody's experience but it is also distinct from other forms. A list of such forms of understanding would normally include, alongside empirical or scientific understanding, modes that are mathematical, logical, literary, historical, aesthetic, moral and religious, with a distinct social-scientific mode possibly constituting yet another. It is a list such as this, with its necessary liability to slight modifications in detail, that will be implied in the subsequent discussion. The forms will however be deliberately styled as *forms of understanding and endeavour* rather than of knowledge, since they represent broad categories of mental activity and not mere cognition.

A curriculum based on this kind of assumption must necessarily have a timeless character, since the 'forms' themselves are considered to reflect, in large measure, the structure of mind. Therefore, it must show what Eggleston (1977) terms a 'received perspective'. It must also include, for everybody, some introduction or 'initiation' into all of the forms of understanding and endeavour that figure in whatever list is preferred, at any particular moment, by a particular writer. The slight variability that is

Reproduced from BLYTH, W. A. L. (1984) *Development, Experience and Curriculum in Primary Education*, Croom Helm.

implied by this subjectivity of definition is not a serious flaw in the argument for a curriculum based on *forms*, for the measure of agreement between writers is high, and indeed could be raised higher through the outcome of a sustained programme of research using techniques such as factor analysis or cluster analysis to distinguish between the basic components. Some limited studies on these lines have already been undertaken. It could, of course, emerge that the forms themselves appear to change over time, as cultural conditions alter; but the forms approach in its stronger embodiment would not permit of such change; and in any case any change that did become evident would be very slight from year to year, or even from century to century.

The relevance of forms of understanding has become established in official policy, notably in the documents issued by Her Majesty's Inspectorate in England and Wales on the secondary curriculum (DES, 1977). At the primary stage, however, the forms-of-understanding approach appears to falter somewhat. It seems more realistic to speak of historical or scientific understanding at the age of 16 than at the age of 6. Even in physical and aesthetic activities the separate consideration of forms of endeavour may seem a trifle pretentious for infants. Yet Ashton's (1975) survey of aims in primary education made use of this kind of categorizing, while Dearden (1968) has enunciated a classic case for basing consideration of the primary curriculum on forms of understanding. For if the forms really are logically distinct and independent of individual interests, then they must also be independent of development. In one sense they must also be independent of experience, since they imply an *a priori* assumption that experience will lead toward a commonly agreed view of knowledge and experience as it 'is'. Their claim to determine curriculum, even for the youngest, depends on the belief that human knowledge is, and must be, like that.

Another feature of the usual lists of forms of understanding is that they bear quite a close relationship to subjects. Language, history, science, mathematics, physical education, moral education, religious education, art and craft—all seem very close to one or other of the forms, although others, 'fields' such as geography and (in some formulations) some of the social sciences, straddle them. It is, however, important to remember that the forms are much more than a refurbished description of subjects. For the assumption is not that subjects suggested forms, but rather that forms have gradually, in the course of human history, given rise to subjects and to disciplines, and to the whole articulated structure of the traditional curriculum and its modifications. There could be slow modifications in subjects, as in the forms themselves, in the course of long historical periods, and rather different versions in different cultures, but within the dominant modern Western culture, they are regarded as valid, and that is sufficient for most practical purposes: so the argument goes.

Granted these features of the forms approach to curriculum, it is not surprising that primary education is one of the areas in which it has been challenged. One of the ways in which a challenge can be mounted is to envisage curriculum as something wholly derived from the nature of the learner rather than from the forms of understanding or endeavour ... there is a more promising approach which regards understanding as constructed anew by every learner, with the accumulated intellectual achievements of mankind as a principal part of the available cognitive resources rather than as an imperative that must be obeyed when curriculum is developed. This will be termed, as is now the custom, a *process* approach, and has something in common with Eggleston's 'restructuring perspective' (1977). On this analysis anyone who chooses to disregard these achievements may be an idiot, but he is not a transgressor. Each individual constructs his intellectual world in basically the same way as the creative artist or scientist or thinker who is at the margin of intellectual advance. The formulation of hypotheses and experiments, the active means of discovery or verification are characteristic of the early primary years in their own way, just as they are characteristic of the community of scholars and scientists. Re-discovery proceeds by the same means as discovery. So, as Blenkin and Kelly (1981) indicate with particular lucidity, though Dewey would have agreed, the proper approach to the primary curriculum in a scientific culture should be through learning by discovery, not through an exploration of prespecified forms. Moreover, the curriculum itself should be shaped according to research, not only on its components as was once the case, (Fleming, 1946) but on its very basis (Kelly, 1981).

There is nothing startingly new in this claim. It has been characteristic of the progressive tradition in education, especially primary education, during the past half-century, and it informs much of the Plowden Report (CACE, 1967), which is widely regarded as representing that tradition, though the report itself is much less bold and consistent than its critics sometimes assert. It can be readily accommodated to both development and experience, for it allows the individual's discovery of knowledge to be proportioned to his development and responsive to his experience. It can comprehend an integrated day in the infant school and a pattern of partial differentiation into broad subject-areas at the upper primary or middle-years level. Even at the primary stage, however, it may imply some of the practical difficulties identified with the integrated curriculum by Bernstein (1975), including in particular the professional demands it makes upon teachers. But the principal point remains that it cannot meet the objections of those who, having considered all aspects of the question, still feel that the specific claims of forms of understanding and endeavour are too powerful to be set aside.

There is also a third approach to curriculum that receives widespread support. It may be called the *social-imperatives* approach. Unlike the first two, it is concerned less with individual knowledge and endeavour and more with the needs of society. The relationship between individual and social aims is one of the perennial issues in education, and this approach is one of its recent manifestations. The emergence of the modern secular state has been accompanied, almost inevitably, by schemes for the education of suitable citizens. A sequence can be traced from pre-revolutionary and revolutionary France and the newly independent USA, through the builders of national systems in nineteenth-century Europe, to twentieth-century regimes of the Right and Left in Europe and beyond. Much of the writing on this theme has been of a trivial, polemic or merely administrative nature, but there have been examples of coherent philosophical thought about education and social needs which have risen above the level of most of this literature. They include Durkheim's vision of secular moral education, Kerschensteiner's programme for technical understanding, and designs for different kinds of political education by writers as different as Gentile and Gramsci. Not all of these have spelled out the content of the curriculum in detail; not all of them have indicated what pedagogy would be appropriate. Some have done both, and all have implications for both.

In contemporary writings there are two main threads in the social-imperatives approach. The first is concerned primarily with technical competence and know-how. It lies behind many of the calls for more science and technology in the curriculum. Though, of course, science also figures prominently in the forms and process approaches, technology lags behind in both, and it is its direct instrumental value that brings it into prominence in this third approach. Indeed, some of the call for emphasis on an agreed core curriculum in English education, which would bring it closer to other systems, is derived from this kind of instrumental competence. The other thread is frankly political and ideological, and is seen at its most conspicuous in a Marxist state where compulsory and exclusive political education is invariably introduced, and almost as visibly in a fundamentalist Islamic state, though it exists widely in other societies too, even in those which officially deny it. The relationship between these two kinds of social-imperatives curriculum is significant. Few societies with overt political curricula omit technological elements; indeed in Marxist-Leninist education there is often a polytechnical element introduced for social and political reasons. Meanwhile, in Western societies a technological emphasis may be accompanied by official displeasure towards overt political education. All of these considerations apply to primary as well as secondary education, though in the process they may result in a relative depreciation of the importance of primary education as such.

A further modification of this social-imperatives approach to curriculum should also be mentioned, particularly in view of the recent impact that this modification has made. In this modification the construction of knowledge is itself seen, particularly by Marxists and phenomenologists, as essentially the work of social groups. More than that, the intellectual products of scientists and scholars are regarded as the result of social processes rather than as objective achievements. If the primary curriculum is viewed from this angle, it is not enough to conceive it 'in terms of activity and experience', as the 1931 Primary School Report put it (Consultative Committee of the Board of Education) or even to opt for one form of social imperative, because this would only result in, for example, a bourgeois curriculum in the middle-class school, a proletarian curriculum in a working-class school, and a curricular conflict where the cultures are mixed. Other social divisions, for example between town and country, might result in other constructions of understanding and endeavour. Important though it is to recognize the strength of social influence in the building of knowledge, and the difficulty of defining a single social imperative, it is hard to see how this approach can contribute substantially to the making of curricula, for either it implies accepting social differentiation of the curriculum as inevitable, or it involves reinforcing the claims of one social imperative as against others. This might mean imposing middle-class values, as existing formal education is alleged to do, or it might mean substituting working-class values and imposing those, as some might like to do; or winnowing the culture of any community to define and build on the best of its own values as Midwinter (1975) once recommended. It is by no means certain that any of these policies would prove either practicable or defensible.

There are, of course, other ways of classifying approaches to curriculum. Richards (1982, Part 1), for example, writing in particular of the primary curriculum, selects four 'ideologies', liberal romanticism, educational conservatism, liberal pragmatism and social democracy, as informing recent thinking about the primary curriculum. The first two of these have something in common with the process and forms-of-understanding approaches respectively, though in the case of educational conservatism much more emphasis is laid on cultural heritage. Liberal pragmatism implies some blend between the two. Social democracy embodies one, but only one, form of social imperative. Kohlberg and Mayer (1972) divide approaches to curriculum into three: progressive, culture-transmission and romantic. This departs rather further from what is suggested here, for the first two both embody something of the process approach, while forms of understanding are rather precariously combined with culture transmission (as in Richards's educational conservatism), and social imperatives are left rather adrift. It would, of course, be possible to cite many other instances of curricular classification, but these two seem especially pertinent to the present discussion. The decision to use the classification based on process, forms of understanding and social imperatives is made because they seem particularly appropriate to a discussion of curriculum in relation to development and experience.

[*Blyth goes on to develop his concept of 'the enabling curriculum' which draws on but transcends the approach based on 'process', 'social imperatives' or 'forms of understanding'.*]

The role of curriculum considered [here] is that it is *planned intervention in the interaction between development and experience*. This is to be taken to mean that curricular experience is planned intervention between development and general experience. For the sake of simplicity, henceforth the nicety of meaning will be overlooked and 'experience' will denote 'general experience' while 'curriculum' will be used as shorthand for curricular experience....

....If the terminology is kept simple, the relationships are far from simple. For there is an ongoing interaction between development and curriculum, and between experience and curriculum, as well as between development and experience. The difference between curriculum and the other elements is the obvious one, that development and experience are continuous whereas curriculum is substantially confined to the place and time of formal education. This does not mean that its importance is proportionately reduced. The pressures of society throw into relief what goes on in school; curriculum as a whole, unlike development or experience as a whole, is designed to make a positive impact on children; and curriculum is fashioned in such a way as to interact positively with development and experience and to maximize their value for children.

As we have already seen, many of the most far-seeing among those who emphasize the importance of development in education stress, as Montessori did, the necessity of curriculum as a means of optimizing development. Similarly, many of the ablest and most thoughtful advocates of experience in education stress that curriculum is itself a major component of experience. As Dewey said of education: 'It is that reconstruction or reorganization of experience which adds to experience, and which increases ability to direct the course of subsequent experience' (Dewey, 1916, p. 76). Thus curriculum is both a part of experience and a means of extending experience.

In fact, curriculum is essential to both development and experience.

There is one further important consideration. In the preceding discussion, there was some danger of regarding the curriculum as static, or at any rate of giving priority to the curriculum as it appears at the later primary stage. But primary education has to be considered as a whole, and begins at a chronological age when, on any showing, development and experience preclude the clear differentiation of the curriculum into forms. To begin with, it must be much more of a totality. Differentiation into separate kinds of activity is itself a part of the curriculum process at the primary stage. More than that, it is something that forms part of guided discovery. For this reason the emphasis on the process approach to curriculum at the primary stage is further strengthened. Whatever arguments might be applied in secondary or even in later primary education, the primary curriculum as a whole has to take account of what happens at the very start.

Hitherto, some of the characteristics of a worthwhile primary curriculum have been indicated: its relation to development and experience, its prime but not exclusive dependence on the process model, and its modification according to age. It has already been defined as a balanced intervention in the interaction between development and experience, with the proviso that the interaction takes place between all three elements. What is needed now, before the discussion is taken further, is a more succinct term for the kind of curriculum that is to be elaborated.

The term I suggest is: the *ENABLING CURRICULUM*.

If we are to speak of an enabling curriculum, then it is necessary to say what it enables, and why it enables more than would be the case if it were not introduced.

The verdict about what this curriculum enables must depend on the approach that has been advocated [here]. Thus, first, it has to be a curriculum that enables development and experience to take place beneficially. It must provide additional equipment that arises through development beyond the powers of the human organism as such, development that can arise only through the stimulus of a systematic process of construction of reality strengthened by awareness of widely-accepted forms of understanding and endeavour. It must also provide opportunities for the expansion and reflective scrutiny of experience, within a social context that ensures that development and experience are social as well as individual.

Beyond this, it must also enable each individual to become a person with an emerging set of values and ideals. Development and experience do not necessarily imply this, so, if it is a desirable goal, it must fall to the enabling curriculum to promote it. Of course, the emerging set of values and ideals must itself reflect the general value-system within which the curriculum is to operate, which is for the present purposes a democratic one, designed to function within the various contexts that have been considered. A curriculum designed to operate within a quite different framework of values might also be termed 'enabling', but if this were to apply where only a 'forms' approach, or a social–imperatives approach, was adopted, then its enablement would be much more limited in scope. It would be less productive, and less democratic, in its interaction with development and experience in general.

Even so, an enabling curriculum envisages two further outcomes. First, it does not simply condition development and experience, within however congenial a context. Based as it is on chosen values, it also enables choices to be made. Choices have to be made, in any life situation, and choices made in the light of development and of experience are usually more wisely made than those made, as it were, at random. An enabling curriculum is intended to go beyond this again.

It is intended to reveal more clearly the conditions within which choices have to be made, and the influences which bear upon the chooser. Having stripped off much of the surrounding opacity, it leaves the chooser and the choice face to face. Then, the chooser depends on the emerging set of values and ideals. For it is the ultimate strength, as well as the perversity, of

personal autonomy that choices must eventually be made without dicta-
tion. In a democratic ideology, autonomy and not automation must be the
intention, and the curriculum must enable but not compel. The most that
an enabling curriculum can do is to leave the doors and the options open:
this it should do, and it is a great deal to do.

Secondly, an enabling curriculum must enable *acceptance*. This may seem
to contradict the enablement of choice, but in fact it places choice in
perspective. It is not false humility or social quietism, but a recognition
that, in our existential situation, individuals must accept limitations, not
least in themselves. It sets in perspective the aim often suggested for
education, that all children should be enabled (sic) to develop their powers
to the utmost of which they are capable. For such an aim can only be
achieved if it includes the power of acceptance of limitations, constraints,
frustrations, disappointments, betrayals, accidents, illnesses, disasters and
deaths. It may be unfashionable to emphasize this, but a curriculum that has
nothing to say to these experiences, in the face of which development
usually also remains silent, is a disabling mockery. Too often, primary
education has been envisaged for an unreal world created by wishful-
thinking adults who prefer to sweep the unpleasant and the tragic,
vicariously, under the carpet while claiming that in doing so they are
'protecting' children. A truly enabling curriculum has to enable those who
meet it in the interaction between development and experience to accept
reality in all its ugliness as well as all its beauty and potential.

Before the argument is taken further, it would be useful to indicate how
this enabling curriculum relates to some terms which are more familiar in
discussions of the primary curriculum. One of these is *progressive*. The
enabling approach has much in common with the mainstream of progressive education, whose opponents might well assume that it is little more
than a variant on that theme. But the usual contention of advocates of
progressive education is that it should be more self-consciously linked
with children's active learning and also with a mildly socialist orientation
generally. The commitment of an enabling approach to forms of understanding might also be viewed with some suspicion. Much the same might
be true of the term *child-centred*. An enabling curriculum is intended to be
more than child-centred. It takes account also of differences in social
situation, and here again the acceptance of forms of understanding may act
as a mark of distinction between an enabling and a child-centred approach.
At first these distinctions may seem trivial and tedious, but they do in fact
embody quite an important distinction between the typical embodiment of
educational reformism and what is recommended here. For in the enabling
curriculum the process approach has the principal, but not the only, place.
[Every] attempt will be made to use a consistent terminology about the
enabling curriculum, even if it sometimes involves a tendency to be
repetitive.

There will certainly be objections to this enabling curriculum, especially perhaps from those who are sincerely convinced of the primacy of forms of understanding and endeavour as such, and of the predominant significance of subjects and disciplines. Almost as many objections could be raised by those who, from whatever point of view, accord first place to social imperatives. There will also be others, of a philosophical cast of mind, who will contend that this enabling curriculum may not in fact do the enabling that is expected of it, and that other types of curriculum might in fact be found to do the enabling at least as well as, or even better. They may maintain that it represents just the kind of wishful and soft-centred extrapolation from selected research findings and from edited experience that has plagued English primary education ever since Plowden, modified only by a touch of existentialist pessimism. Still others will cavil at the mixture of 'forms' and process that is is advocated and may wish to substitute something more sturdy and homogeneous; this position might be adopted by Blenkin and Kelly (1981) with their radical empiricist model, or by Egan (1979) with his essentially developmental approach, or by those such as Kirby (1981) who adhere more closely to the child-centred tradition. Much that is advocated in this enabling curriculum corresponds to the central tenets of one or more of these approaches, so that they are more likely to criticize it for lack of clarity and homo-genity—a curricular fudge-and-mudge, an embodiment of Richards' 'liberal pragmatism' (Richards, 1982, Part I)—than to regard it as embody-ing the spirit of reaction. Certainly it would gain if upheld by empirical verification, which would be a lengthy and complex business. In default of such confirmation, it is presented as a relatively appropriate way of intervening beneficially in the interaction between development and experience. What is more: it tallies with much that Richards calls for in his advocacy of a well-grounded, 'fine-grained' curriculum consistency (Richards, 1982, part 2).

References

ASHTON, P. *et al* (1975) *The Aims of Primary Education: A Study of Teachers' Opinions*, Macmillan.

BERNSTEIN, B. (1975) *Class, Codes and Control: 3 Towards a Theory of Educational Transmissions*, Routledge and Kegan Paul.

BLENKIN, G. and KELLY, V. (1981) *The Primary Curriculum*, Harper and Row.

CENTRAL ADVISORY COUNCIL FOR EDUCATION (England) (1967) *Children and Their Primary Schools* (The Plowden Report), HMSO.

DEARDEN, R. (1968) *The Philosophy of Primary Education*, Routledge and Kegan Paul.

DEPARTMENT OF EDUCATION AND SCIENCE (1977) *Curriculum 11–16: Working Papers by HM Inspectorate: A Contribution to the Current Debate*, HMSO.

DEWEY, J. (1916) *Democracy and Education*, Macmillan.

EGAN, K. (1979) *Educational Development*, Oxford University Press.

EGGLESTON, J. (1977) *The Sociology of the School Curriculum*, Routledge and Kegan Paul.

FLEMING, C. (1946) *Research and the Basic Curriculum*, University of London Press.

HIRST, P. (1974) *Knowledge and the Curriculum*, Routledge and Kegan Paul.

KELLY, V. (1981) 'Research and the primary curriculum', *Journal of Curriculum Studies*, 13, 3, pp 215–25.

KIRBY, M. (1981) *Personal Values in Primary Education*, Harper and Row.

KOHLBERG, L. AND MAYER, R. (1972) 'Development as the aim of education', *Harvard Educational Review*, 42, 4, pp 449–96.

MIDWINTER, E. (1975) *Education and the Community*, Unwin Education.

RICHARDS, C. (Ed) (1982) *New Directions in Primary Education*, Falmer Press.

The Curriculum from 5–16: Background, Content and Some Implications for Primary Education

Colin Richards

Introduction

The school curriculum matters. Through it, pupils develop their under-standing of, and competence in, ways of knowing regarded as valuable in our society. Those professionally engaged in the education service and others with a personal interest in it attest to the importance of the curriculum. But such general assent is not sufficient to give direction to the formulation of policy or the improvement of practice. To do this, closer agreement is required as to the purposes informing the curriculum and as to the ways in which such intentions might be realized in schools and classrooms. This article examines the context, content and some impli-cations of *The Curriculum from 5 to 16* (1985) (hereafter referred to as CM2)[1], a discussion document from HM Inspectorate. As part of the felicitously named 'Curriculum Matters' series, it suggests an approach to thinking about and designing the whole curriculum which might help to clarify and develop broad agreement concerning objectives and content. By focussing here on its implications for primary education, this article runs the risk of blunting one of the most important thrusts in the document—the provision of a common framework intended to promote communication and planning within and across the phases but without riding roughshod over legitimate differences in approach.

Context

During the last decade, primary education has had to contend with a formidable range of issues. Perhaps the most dramatic has been the large contraction in the numbers of primary-aged children, which has brought in

Reproduced from *Education 3–13*, 14, 1, 1986, pp. 3–8.

its wake closures, amalgamations, staff re-deployment, mixed aged classes and a host of professional and personal problems which demographic statistics have obscured, but which have loomed large in the day to day life of schools and education offices. The last ten years have witnessed continuing financial constraint with concerns for greater cost-effectiveness and with considerable repercussions on the funding of schools. Good 'house-keeping', always important in the primary sector, has become even more crucial and time-consuming. Growing public interest in schooling has led to schools being publicly accountable in ways and to a degree not previously encountered. Mechanisms and procedures for discharging accountability have had to be reconsidered and to some extent reconstituted. These developments have taken place at the same time as other major factors have affected British society and, directly or indirectly, primary schools: changing family patterns, the development of micro-technology, the growth in unemployment and the increasing recognition of discrimination on the grounds of gender and race. This changing social and economic context has made it important to review the primary curriculum and the way it is realized in schools to see what elements need to be reaffirmed, which redefined and which omitted.

This process of reappraisal to which CM2 is intended to contribute is already under way in a considerable number of schools. Professional development has been stimulated by a variety of factors including local education authority curricular reviews, school self-evaluation schemes, the programmes of work of the former Schools Council, the activities of the School Curriculum Development Committee and the provision of in-service education of both an award and non-award bearing kind. Publications such as *Primary Practice* (1983)[2], the Cockcroft Report (1982)[3] and HMI surveys of primary (1978)[4], first (1982)[5] and middle (1983)[6] schools have raised issues concerned with curriculum planning, breadth, differentiation, assessment, continuity, staff deployment and teacher education which have promoted discussion and action at local authority and school levels and in institutions of higher education.

The concern to reappraise the content and quality of education has also been shared by successive Secretaries of State for Education and Science and for Wales as part of the duty laid upon them by the 1944 Education Act to 'promote the education of the people of England and Wales'. Chapter 2 of the White Paper (1985) *Better Schools*[7] reviews a number of initiatives in this respect and reiterates the government's concern to reach a 'broad agreement about the objectives and content of the school curriculum' which can become the basis of the curricular policies of the Secretaries of State, the local education authorities and the schools. What is being sought is *not* unanimity within the education service, but a broad measure of agreement; *not* agreement about the *detailed* organization and content of programmes of work in schools but general assent to the purposes of education, the range of knowledge and skills to be included in the curriculum and the kinds of understandings and qualities children are to be helped to develop, or to acquire. *Better Schools* states:

> The definition of agreed objectives for the curriculum, in principle encompasses four strands: the purposes of learning at school; the contribution of each main subject area or element; the organisation and content of the 5–16 curriculum as a whole; and what is to be attained at the end of the primary phase and of the compulsory years in the secondary phase. The objectives apply also where the age ranges of schools do not correspond with the typical pattern. (Page 13)

The publication of CM2 seeks to stimulate professional debate concerning the first three of these four strands and so inform the Secretary of State's national curricular policy. It is in part a response to the call made in his Sheffield speech of January 1984 for an open discussion aimed at clarifying and developing the objectives of the 5–16 curriculum.

Content

The document provides both a language in which to discuss the curriculum and a framework in which to plan it. Its use of non-emotive terms such as 'areas of learning and experience', 'concepts', 'skills' and 'attitudes' is intended to facilitate communication about the curriculum, which might otherwise be impeded by participants' preoccupation with 'subjects' and 'content' on the one hand and with 'children's needs and interests' and 'processes of learning' on the other. Use of such a common language, however ill-defined it may be around the edges, may help clarify areas of agreement as well as indicate more precisely areas of disagreement. Such a language may well be an essential pre-requisite for establishing curricular continuity both within and between primary and secondary phases.

To use a cartographic analogy, the document also provides a kind of curricular map or chart which aids analysis and planning. Projected on a small scale, it provides an overview of the large area of the school curriculum, outlines its shape, gives some indication of its contours, draws attention to its prominent features and traces some inter-relationships among them. It indicates the regions to be explored and illustrates some of the means which could be employed, but it does not provided directives as to the routes to be followed, the organisation to be adopted or the precise equipment to be used. Its status needs to be made clear; it is provisional rather than definitive—subject to revision in the light of discussion and exploration and to evolution in the light of changes over time.

A six-fold framework for curricular review and development is offered, comprising (i) general aims, (ii) areas of learning and experience, (iii) elements of learning, (iv) cross-curricular issues, (v) general characteristics of the curriculum and (vi) assessment. It is important to stress that the framework is concerned with the factors that need to be borne in mind when appraising and designing a curriculum, *not* with the ways in which teaching and learning should be organized, whether in terms of subjects, broad areas, topics, activities or any combination of these:

> It is for individual schools to decide how the curriculum is to be organized for teaching purposes, but each of these ways of organizing the work in primary schools has to be assessed in terms of its fitness for purpose (p 9).

(i) General Aims

The document reaffirms the need to have educational aims which underlie and give guidance to the day to day work of schools. In particular, the goals of education outlined in the Warnock Report (1978)[8] and the aims proposed in *The School Curriculum* (1981)[9] are endorsed as providing the kind of broad guidance required to give a general orientation and thrust to a school's activities. CM2 argues for the importance of helping develop pupils' autonomy, rationality and self-confidence so that they 'grow up to become competent, confident, rational and self reliant adults who can manage their own lives and play their part in society' (p 3). Such long-term purposes are best served in the present by approaches to teaching and learning which stress enquiry, questioning and challenge, which give enjoyment and satisfaction from the successful completion of tasks and which encourage children to use their imagination. In this way, the present is not to be sacrificed to the future, nor the imagination to the intellect, nor intrinsic satisfaction to instrumental considerations. In Aspin's (1981) terms[10] education is as much concerned with the 'possibilities of the present' as 'the cares of the morrow'. The purposes outlined in CM2 are avowedly pragmatic, derived from professional concerns with curricular policy and practice rather than finely argued educational theory with its base in epistemology, ethics, metaphysics or whatever. Underlying the arguments in the publication is a concern to achieve unity of purpose throughout the 5–16 age span so that all pupils of whatever race or gender have 'access to a curriculum of similar breadth and balance, irrespective of their level of ability, the school they attend or their social circumstances' (pp 3–4). Chapter 6 of the primary survey (1978) indicates the scale of the problems facing primary education in providing that access.

(ii) Areas of Learning and Experience

Though important, general aims need to be 'cashed out' in harder currency, if the task of transacting the curriculum with children is to proceed. CM2 argues that in pursuit of such aims, primary and secondary schools should involve all children in each of nine areas of experience and learning at all stages from 5–16. This approach to the curriculum through areas of experience and learning has been worked on through co-operation between HMI, local education authorities and secondary school teachers, but is here presented with a developmental perspective to stress the importance of each stage building on the foundation laid in earlier ones. Within the document, the areas are discussed in alphabetical order—deliberately so since *all* are regarded as essential to a child's education, though the relative emphasis given to each may properly vary somewhat at different stages in the educational process. The areas are (a) aesthetic and creative, (b) human and social, (c) linguistic and literary, (d) mathematical, (e) moral, (f) physical, (g) scientific, (h) spiritual and (i) technological. The characteristics of each area are offered 'not as definitive statements but as a basis for further discussion in schools' (p 17).

'They constitute a planning and analytical tool' (p 16) which school staffs or individual teachers might use to assess their current or proposed curricular provision before making modifications (either additions or, just as importantly, deletions). For example, if particular areas were missing or poorly represented in the work undertaken with particular classes or age groups of children, alternative provision could be made, perhaps in the form of new topics to be introduced in project work, or new processes to be introduced into creative activities, or new subjects to be put on the timetable. General acceptance of the view that children should have their understanding and capabilities developed in all nine areas during their primary education would have far-reaching implications; it would present a tremendous challenge for individual schools, let alone individual teachers, to meet.

(iii) *Elements of Learning*

To provide analytical 'bite' to planning based on areas of learning and experience CM2 introduces the notion of 'elements of learning'. These constitute the bases used to select what it is that children should be introduced to within each of the nine areas. Four major elements are distinguished: (a) knowledge (ie subject matter to be taught or learnt), (b) concepts (which, singly or in networks, enable children to organize knowledge and experience), (c) skills (many different kinds of capability related to the performance of tasks) and (d) attitudes (including dispositions and qualities of character). Further documents in the Curriculum Matters series aim to relate these to particular subjects or aspects of the curriculum. CM2 does not discuss exactly how such elements might be incorporated into the curriculum planning process, but one possible way would be for schools (the whole staff or a working party) to (a) analyze an area of learning and experience in terms of significant concepts and skills, aided by local authority statements, Curriculum Matters publications and other published material, (b) consider the kinds of subject matter which could illuminate the concepts and involve the development of skills and (c) select and organize particular content which is comprehensible, interesting to the children and useful, either in terms of contributing significantly to their current understanding of the particular area or in terms of ready application in other contexts. Thinking about the primary curriculum in terms of skills, concepts, attitudes and subject matter is not new; what is significant is the advocacy by HMI of this self-conscious, analytical approach to curriculum planning for all primary schools.

(iv)   Cross-Curricular Issues

An earlier section in this article briefly referred to developments within British society which have impinged on the work of primary schools. Such factors have given rise to a number of cross-curricular issues which complicate still further the tasks of curricular planning and review but which, if neglected, render the curriculum at the very least less vital and at the worst almost irrelevant. Environmental education, health education, political education and education for economic understanding are examples of such cross-curricular concerns which, though sometimes taught separately, 'are more frequently and often more appropriately mediated through topics, subjects, groups of subjects or the general life of the schools' (p 13). But most fundamental of all is the issue encapsulated in the Swann Report's (1985) title 'Education for All'[11]. Equal opportunities for both boys and girls and for children from ethnic minority and majority communities presuppose a unity of purpose and a consistency of provision which apply irrespective of the size, type and location of the schools children attend. Curriculum planning and review have a part to play in achieving this more consistent provision.

(v)   Characteristics of the Curriculum

The fifth component in the proposed framework comprises a set of broad criteria which can be applied when appraising the whole school curriculum or just one of its constituent parts. The criteria reflect issues of perennial importance in curriculum design and to be applied and acted upon require professional discussion and decision-making involving not only the consideration of factual matters, but the making of value and other judgments. The criteria are more than rhetorical devices; they raise very significant questions relating to the curriculum as planned by teachers and as experienced by children. These criteria are:

(a)   Breadth
Are all primary children being appropriately taught in all nine areas of learning and experience and being introduced to the

four elements of learning associated with them? Are children being given a broad range of activities within an area and within its component parts?

(b)   Balance

Is each area of learning and experience and each element given appropriate attention in relation to the others and to the whole curriculum as experienced by the child? What constitutes 'appropriate attention'? Over what period of time is this balance to be sought? Are the activities within an area of experience reasonably balanced? Are children experiencing a balanced range of teaching and learning approaches? The value judgments implicit in 'balance' cannot be avoided but need addressing directly.

(c)   Relevance

Is the curriculum relevant in terms of (a) improving children's understanding and competence in each area, (b) increasing their understanding of themselves and the world in which they live including the influences which bear on them, (c) developing their self-confidence and (d) equipping them with the knowledge and skills needed for adult living?

(d)   Differentiation

Does the work provided allow for differences in the abilities and other characteristics of children of the same age and yet at the same time does it have an overall unity of purpose which transcends individual differences?

(e)   Progression and Continuity

Within the primary school, is the work in each aspect of the curriculum reflecting and building on work done previously? Externally, do primary schools take adequate account of the influences to which their entrants have already been exposed and of the expectations entertained of their children by the schools to which they will transfer in due course?

Such general criteria and the challenging questions they entail need to be applied not only to the curricular policies and practices of individual schools but also to curricular policy statements emanating from whatever source.

(vi)   Assessment

In addition to putting forward the broad criteria for curriculum evaluation outlined above, CM2 provides some guidance on assessment which, it argues, 'is inseparable from the teaching process' (p 51). Assessment is seen as serving two complementary purposes: (a) to improve children's learning through diagnosis of their strengths and weaknesses, discussion and self appraisal and the more effective matching of work to children's capabilities, and (b) to improve the curriculum through helping teachers to see how far their intentions are being realized and thus in what ways their teaching approaches may need modification. Although acknowledging that much assessment must be largely impressionistic in the crowded world of the classroom, it argues that assessment can be improved by getting expectations clearer (the Curriculum Matters series and the APU surveys should help here), by refining observation in the classroom and by judicious use of more objective forms of testing, which should be very closely related to the work in hand.

Some Implications

CM2 offers a fresh perspective on the curriculum, including a redefinition of what is 'basic' to primary education. Its argument that children should engage in a carefully devised, adequately justified and widely defined curriculum related to all nine areas of learning and experience offers a formidable professional challenge, already being taken up in a number of schools but with very significant implications for the self-sufficiency of the individual class teacher and the individual school.

The approach in CM2 demands conscious planning and evaluation from primary practitioners. It does not deny the importance of intuition or of 'tacit knowledge' when working with children, nor the significance of teachers' opportunism in capitalizing on children's interests aroused by those unexpected events which can prove so productive in primary classrooms. But it does assume that both intuition and opportunism are not sufficient to secure children's entitlement to a broad, balanced and relevant primary education.

The suggested approach places very great demands on class teachers, demands which, unaided, most cannot be expected to meet fully. A collaborative, rather than individualistic, approach to curriculum planning and review is implied—collaboration dependent upon teachers' deepened understanding of the areas of learning and experience and of how children might engage with them and upon the sharing of this expertise to teachers' mutual benefit and that of the children they teach. A key indicator of, and contributor to, this 'collegial'[12] approach to decision-making would be the formulation of curricular policies arrived at through staff discussion and setting out educational intentions and broad expectations relating to teaching and learning in various aspects of the curriculum or areas of learning and experience. Such policies would not deprive class teachers of all discretion in curricular matters, since the policies would not precisely prescribe content or methodology, but would be binding in a way that old-style schemes of work never were. Another manifestation of a collegial approach would be the preparation of what the 'Thomas Report' (1985)[13] terms 'school development plans', where primary schools 'set up arrangements to review where they are in relation to the many aspects of their internal and external environment, and to make plans for working on some of them ... [such] a plan should be operated by all teachers for it is a contract between the head and staff to which, in the end, all must subscribe' (pp 76–7). Work on particular areas of learning and experience believed to be less than adequately represented in the school's curriculum would be a suitable focus for such a development plan.

Far from devaluing the work of class teachers, collegial approaches, paradoxically perhaps, would increase their standing by fully recognizing the formidable range and levels of demand now being made upon them and by involving them, not just in the planning of the work of their own classes, but in the establishment of a school-wide curricular framework. The long-standing and valued primary tradition that one teacher should be responsible for ensuring that his/her class receive a curriculum adequate in range and depth is not in dispute, but the way this responsibility is to be properly exercised and supported is at least open to reinterpretation in the light of the changes and developments outlined earlier in this article. Support could take one or more of a variety of forms depending on the individual class teacher and the area of learning and experience in question: occasional advice from a post-holder or other member of staff with specialist knowledge; a detailed scheme of work setting out elements of learning and giving advice on organization and methodology; school-based workshops or attendance at in-service courses organized by other agencies; a post-holder working alongside a colleague for a time, to introduce a new aspect of work, or perhaps more useful, to help her/him introduce it; or, in some cases, perhaps most often with upper juniors, a member of staff with specialist knowledge teaching someone else's class a particular aspect of the curriculum for a month, a term or a year, provided the class teacher retains overall responsibility for the work of the class, including the links that would need to be made between her own work and that of the specialist.

What is being discussed is not the dismantling of the class-teacher system, but its strengthening through sensitive deployment and development of the expertise which already exists on primary school staffs by means of a variety of ploys, varying from the one-off occasion, through short-term procedures, to more established long-term arrangements, all subject to renegotiation as circumstances change. Paragraphs 772 and 773 of the Plowden Report (1967)[14] could be cited in support of more flexible patterns of staff deployment to bring children into contact with teachers who have particular expertise.

A shortage of space precludes detailed consideration of the implications of CM2 for the self-sufficiency of the individual primary school, but such are the expectations of primary schools that most would need additional support to implement it effectively. Such assistance could take a variety of forms including: the formulation of local education authority curricular policies and guidelines and the management of the teaching force in the light of these; the establishment of 'clusters' of schools for the development and co-ordination of their work, as outlined in the Thomas Report; the deployment of advisory teachers to support work in particular areas of experience and learning; the provision of in-service education targetted on the needs of whole schools rather than simply individuals; the improvement of staffing levels to enable reductions to be made in the contact time of primary teachers; and the development of the skills of curriculum management at all levels. Such developments would still provide plenty of scope for individual schools' discretion on curricular matters but would help ensure greater consistency of curricular provision from one school to another across an authority. In this way, the concept of 'collegiality' might be extended beyond the individual school to encompass others in the locality.

Conclusion

In a speech in November 1985, Eric Bolton, Senior Chief Inspector, remarked on the lack of a sustained debate about, and scrutiny of, the curriculum in primary schools. He argued 'It is difficult to identify sufficient common ground, or at least sufficient common language, to begin to discuss the primary curriculum nationally, let alone carry out the kind of scrutiny and development required to develop a primary curriculum framework and agreed objectives' (p 13)[15]. The publication of CM2 is an attempt to provide such a common language and to provide some common markers to enable the search for a framework to proceed. The success or failure of the document and others in the Curriculum Matters series will rest on the response they receive from those striving to improve still further the education they provide. That 'sustained debate' is already beginning; do join it.

Notes

1 DEPARTMENT OF EDUCATION AND SCIENCE (1985) *The Curriculum from 5 to 16*, Curriculum Matters 2, An HMI Series, HMSO.
2 SCHOOLS COUNCIL (1983) *Primary Practice*, Working Paper 75, Methuen Educational.
3 DEPARTMENT OF EDUCATION AND SCIENCE (1982) *Mathematics Counts*, HMSO.

4   DEPARTMENT OF EDUCATION AND SCIENCE (1978) *Primary Education in England*, HMSO.
5   DEPARTMENT OF EDUCATION AND SCIENCE (1982) *Education 5 to 9*, HMSO.
6   DEPARTMENT OF EDUCATION AND SCIENCE (1983) *9–13 Middle Schools*, HMSO.
    DEPARTMENT OF EDUCATION AND SCIENCE (1985) *Education 8 to 12 in Combined and Middle Schools*, HMSO.
7   DEPARTMENT OF EDUCATION AND SCIENCE (1985) *Better Schools*, Cmnd 9469, HMSO.
8   DEPARTMENT OF EDUCATION AND SCIENCE (1978) *Special Educational Needs*, HMSO.
9   DEPARTMENT OF EDUCATION AND SCIENCE (1981) *The School Curriculum*, HMSO.
10 ASPIN, D. (1981) 'Utility is not enough: The arts in the school curriculum' in WHITE, J. *et al.*, (Eds) *No, Minister*, Bedford Way Papers 4, University of London, Institute of Education.
11 DEPARTMENT OF EDUCATION AND SCIENCE (1985) *Education for All*, HMSO.
12 See CAMPBELL, R. (1985) *Developing the Primary School Curriculum*, Holt, Rinehart and Winston, chapter 10.
13 ILEA (1985) *Improving Primary Schools*, ILEA.
14 CENTRAL ADVISORY COUNCIL for EDUCATION (ENGLAND), (1967) *Children and Their Primary Schools*, HMSO.
15 BOLTON, E. (1985) 'Assessment: Putting the horse before the cart', *Times Educational Supplement*, 22 November.

Curriculum Policy-Making: National

Department of Education and Science

30. Addressing the North of England Conference in Sheffield in January 1984, the Secretary of State for Education and Science proposed a programme of measures relating to the school curriculum in the interest of raising standards. Consultations with the government's partners in the education service and with other interests have shown that there is widespread acceptance of the need to improve the standards achieved by pupils, and of the proposition that broad agreement about the objectives and content of the school curriculum is a necessary step towards that improvement.

31. Such broad agreement, explicitly formulated, would enable the partners in the education service to take the necessary action together. It would also have other important advantages:

(1) it would be clear what tasks society expects our schools to accomplish. The schools' performance could then be more fairly judged against agreed expectations about those tasks;

(2) it would mean that parents, employers and the public would have a closer understanding of the purposes for which they were being asked to support the work of the schools and would thus be better placed than they are now to co-operate with the schools in achieving common aims. Despite many constructive local and national initiatives, schools and employers continue to understand each other's purposes and needs imperfectly; and employers have made it clear that they would welcome a clearer agreement about the schools' objectives;

(3) it could become an important means of raising teachers' expectations of their pupils' performance, which would then be reflected in their

Reproduced from *Better Schools* (1985) HMSO, pp. 4–12, 13–15, 17–21, 26.

approaches to teaching and assessment. It could also help to remove preconceptions based on pupils' sex or ethnic origin;

(4) it would help to secure that in our national school system variations to suit local circumstances do not allow school standards in any locality to fall below an acceptable level;

(5) it is a prerequisite for monitoring progress over time in the achievement of higher standards of performance.

32. The government acknowledges the magnitude of the task it is setting itself and its partners. Objectives cannot be agreed for all time. Even initial agreement will take several years to accomplish, although some objectives may be settled sooner. It will be carried out through policy statements (such as the recent statement on science education in schools) issued by the Secretaries of State after consulting all concerned. Alongside these, but not normally coinciding in time, there will be HMI publications designed both to inform and to stimulate discussion. In particular, publications in the recently inaugurated Curriculum Matters series will build up a general description of the objectives of the curriculum as a whole for all children of compulsory school age, and the contribution which individual areas and subjects can make towards those objectives. They will examine individual subjects and curricular elements in more detail, considering where appropriate such matters as teaching approaches, and proposing objectives to be attained at the ages of (in particular) 11 and 16.

The Distribution of Responsibility for the Curriculum

33. The formulation of national objectives for the curriculum necessarily starts from current policies and practice, both of which already often serve purposes which are explicitly stated. The government wishes to base these objectives on the best practice currently adopted by LEAs and schools.

34. The objectives are intended to have practical effect by becoming the basis of the curricular policies of the Secretaries of State, the LEAs and the schools. Curricular policy at each of these three levels would thus be directed towards the same objectives. But the application of the objectives is different at each level because the functions of the Secretaries of State, the LEA and the school, though interrelated, are separate from each other, and are exercised over a progressively more limited geographical area. The Secretaries of State, the LEA and the school each need a curricular policy in order to discharge their respective functions in accordance with their judgments. The Secretaries of State are accountable to Parliament for the performance of the education service at all levels. Their curricular policy informs not only the exercise of their statutory duty 'to promote the education of the people of England and Wales and the progressive development of institutions devoted to that purpose, and to secure the

effective execution by local authorities, under [their] control and direction, of the national policy for providing a varied and comprehensive educational service in every area'; but also the exercise of the statutory functions which give expression to this general duty, for example in relation to the supply and training of teachers and the determination of proposals from LEAs and governing bodies of aided schools about the pattern of school organization. The LEA's curricular policy informs the exercise of a wide range of its functions, particularly in relation to such matters as the provision of schools, the deployment of its teaching force and its advisory service. The school's curricular policy informs the organization and delivery of what is offered to the pupils. It is one important means through which the school can plan the optimal disposition of its human and other resources, assess its own performance, and promote an understanding of common aims with parents and employers. Since the functions of the Secretaries of State, the LEA and the school interrelate, the policies adopted at each level influence, and are influenced by, those adopted at the others. LEAs, for instance, have an important role seeking to promote good practice by spreading successful approaches from one school to another.

35. It follows from the separate but interrelated functions of the Secretaries of State, the LEA, and the school that the curricular policy of each may contain features not found in that of one or both of the others. For example, it would not be appropriate for either the Secretaries of State of the LEA to determine the detailed organization and content of the programme of the pupils of any particular school. That should be a matter for the headteacher and his staff, and that this should be so would be acknowledged in the curricular policy of the Secretaries of State and the LEA...

36. ...It also follows from the different functions of the Secretaries of State, the LEA and the school that the common objectives are applied with differences of emphasis and balance to reflect local circumstances and are pursued by a variety of routes in accordance with local judgment. For example it would not in the view of the government be right for the Secretaries of State's policy for the range and pattern of the 5–16 curriculum to amount to the determination of national syllabuses for that period. It would however be appropriate for the curricular policy of the LEA, on the basis of broadly agreed principles about range and pattern, to be more precise about, for example, the balance between curricular elements and the age and pace at which pupils are introduced to particular subject areas (e.g. a foreign language). Within the authority, the curricular policy of each school would reflect the policy of the LEA, for example through the staff and other resources made available to it by the LEA, but would develop, in the detail needed for the work of the school, the strategies by which the school intended to secure an appropriate curricular range and pattern in the programmes of its pupils. Such strategies would

reflect the school's own priorities in accordance with its traditions, its ethos and its view of the needs of its pupils in the light of parental and other expectations.

37. The establishment of broadly agreed objectives would not mean that the curricular policies of the Secretaries of State, the LEA and the school should relate to each other in a nationally uniform way. In the government's view such diversity is healthy, accords well with the English and Welsh tradition of school education and makes for liveliness and innovation. Some conflict of view in the working out and application of national, local and school curricular policies may therefore be unavoidable. It is important that the statutory framework should facilitate the satisfactory resolution of such conflicts where they arise. That is the purpose of the government's plans, described in chapter 9, to redefine the curricular responsibilities of the LEA, the governing body and the headteacher of county, controlled and maintained special schools. The government does not propose to introduce legislation affecting the powers of the Secretaries of State in relation to the curriculum.

38. Broadly agreed objectives for the curriculum, once formulated, will need to be reviewed from time to time in the light of how they have stood the test of practical application and to take account of changes in our society and in the role assigned by it to our schools. Such reviews will need to involve all the partners in the education service and its customers. The adaptation over time of jointly adopted objectives is a joint task....

★   ★   ★   ★

The Scope of Broadly Agreed Objectives

43. The definition of agreed objectives for the curriculum in principle encompasses four strands: the purposes of learning at school (paragraph 44); the contribution of each main subject area or element (paragraph 54); the organization and content of the 5–16 curriculum as a whole (paragraph 56); and what is to be attained at the end of the primary phase and of the compulsory years in the secondary phase (paragraph 80). The objectives apply also where the age-ranges of schools do not correspond with the typical pattern.

(i) The Purposes of Learning at School

44. A possible list of the purposes of learning, closely following that offered in 'The School Curriculum', is:

(1) to help pupils to develop lively, enquiring minds, the ability to question and argue rationally and to apply themselves to tasks, and physical skills;

(2) to help pupils to acquire understanding, knowledge and skills relevant to adult life and employment in a fast-changing world;

(3) to help pupils to use language and number effectively;

(4) to help pupils to develop personal moral values, respect for religious values, and tolerance of other races, religions, and ways of life;

(5) to help pupils to understand the world in which they live, and the interdependence of individuals, groups and nations;

(6) to help pupils to appreciate human achievements and aspirations.

There is room for legitimate disagreement about the priority to be attached to each element in this list, and the relationship between them. LEAs and schools have generally reflected the content of this list in their own formulations of basic aims. The government takes that as evidence that, at the most general level, there is very little disagreement that these are indeed the purposes of school education.

45. The government believes, and its belief is embodied in certain national programmes, that these purposes require that the curriculum offered to each pupil, from whatever background, should reflect a number of fundamental principles. Those set out below have commanded wide-spread assent during the consultations of the last twelve months:

(1) the curriculum in both primary and secondary schools should be broad: as a whole and in its parts it should introduce the pupil to a wide range of areas of experience, knowledge and skill. The HMI surveys 'Primary Education in England' and 'Curriculum and Organisation of Primary Schools in Wales' both pointed conclusively to the fact that the teaching of language and mathematical skills in isolation or in a purely theoretical way was less effective than when they were associated with a wide-ranging programme of work which also included art and craft, history and geography, music, physical education, and science. This principle applies in respect of every pupil: it leaves no room for discrimination in the curriculum on grounds of sex;

(2) the curriculum should be balanced: each area of the curriculum should be allotted sufficient time to make its specific contribution, but not so much that it squeezes out other essential areas;

(3) the curriculum should be relevant: all subjects should be taught in such a way as to make plain their link with the pupils' own experience and to bring out their applications and continuing value in adult life. Related to this is the need for a practical dimension to learning, reflected both in the balance between subjects and in the content and teaching of subjects themselves. Most pupils take well to practical and other work which they believe will help them to get on in the modern world, whose technology they find stimulating rather than daunting. The curriculum should be devised and taught so as to harness such excitement and enthusiasm. These requirements are at

the heart of the Technical and Vocational Education Initiative (TVEI, described in paragraph 50), which explores how what is learned at school from age 14 can be more effectively related to the demands of working life; and of the Microelectronics Education Programme, whose aim is to help schools to prepare pupils for a society in which the new technology is commonplace and pervasive. The government thinks it important that the relevance of the curriculum should also be enhanced, as is happening increasingly, by local initiatives which bring schools and employers together in shared activities;

(4) there should be careful differentiation: what is taught and how it is taught need to be matched to pupils' abilities and aptitudes. It is of the greatest importance to stimulate and challenge all pupils, including the most and least able: within teaching groups as well as schools the range of ability is often wide. The Cockcroft Report ('Mathematics Counts') pointed to the 'seven-year difference' at age 11 in attainment in mathematics, and similar differences may be expected in other subject areas. Such differences need to be reflected in classroom practice. The government is supporting development work to promote this principle through the Lower Attaining Pupils' programme, which investigates how differentiation is best developed and applied across the curriculum for pupils within the chosen target group. It is thus closely concerned with teaching approaches. Similarly, for pupils (including the most able) aiming for the 16 + examinations and beyond, the General Certificate of Secondary Education (GCSE, see chapter 3), with differentiated papers and questions, will encourage and test success at different levels of attainment.

★   ★   ★   ★

52. The principles in paragraph 45 have important implications at all levels as curricular policies are given expression in curriculum content and teaching methods. They underlie the discussion of the curriculum for the primary and secondary phases which follows, and they are at the heart of successful classroom practice in the primary phase as well as the secondary (though they may be applied differently in each case). The fact that their application is here and later usually expressed in relation to subjects should not be misinterpreted. In the government's view every element of the primary and secondary curriculum and every area of learning within it is concerned with the development of positive personal qualities and attitudes; and that curriculum can validly be analyzed and described in a number of ways for professional and other purposes. But much curricular content is, for many purposes, and especially in the secondary phase, most conveniently described by reference to the body of knowledge and skills

associated with a particular subject. Such a description implies no particular view of timetabling or teaching approach. Nor does it deny that learning involves the mastery of processes as well as the acquisition of knowledge, skills and understanding. The government believes that these two aspects of learning are not in opposition to one another. When it comes to practice, there is much common ground among those who may hold widely divergent curricular philosophies. It is not in dispute that the purposes of education at school go beyond learning the traditional subjects. Nor is it generally denied that the acquisition of both practical and intellectual skills is often impossible except on the basis of factual content and that certain essential skills entail an understanding of specific factual material.

53. Subjects themselves change and develop. Moreover subject boundaries are not rigid and need to be approached flexibly. Some subjects are deliberately taught in connection with others, particularly in the primary phase; some elements or aspects of a subject arise naturally in the course of teaching another subject; the amount of time devoted to any subject relative to other subjects varies in accordance with the age and ability of the pupils and the pace of their progress. Pupils' timetables need not be, though particularly in secondary schools they often are in practice, structured by reference to subjects. What is at issue is neither whether particular elements of the curriculum appear overtly or are 'hidden' nor the labels which appear in the timetable (which are in any case variable in the secondary phase and may not exist in the primary phase), but the place within the curriculum which the content and processes associated with subjects should occupy in substance.

(ii) The Contribution of Each Main Subject Area

54. The second strand in the definition of objectives concerns the contribution of each main subject area both to the development of positive personal qualities and attitudes and to intellectual and practical skills, understanding and knowledge ... The task of giving a complete account of the contribution which each curricular element makes to the 5–16 curriculum as a whole will need to be accomplished through the policy statements and the HMI publications described in paragraph 32.

55. Religious education has its special contribution to the education of all pupils, and should be given the significance which it deserves within the curriculum. The place of religious education is governed by statute: the government has no plans to propose changes in the provisions of the Education Act 1944 relating to religious education and collective worship in schools, provisions which have stood the test of time. Within the statutory framework an introduction to the Christian tradition remains central to the religious education provided in our schools. The govern-

ment looks to LEAs and schools to ensure that the statutory requirements are met.

(iii) The Organization and Content of the Curriculum

56. The third strand is the organization and content of the 5–16 curriculum as a whole. The demands which arise from the four principles outlined in paragraph 45 in relation to the knowledge, understanding and skills to be acquired, the processes to be mastered, and the personal qualities and attitudes to be developed greatly exceed, in aggregate, the time available for teaching and learning, particularly during the secondary phase. It is therefore essential to eliminate in both the primary and the secondary phase material and practices which do not use that time to good effect. The removal of such clutter takes a variety of forms—the avoidance of unplanned repetition within and between subjects; the dropping of work which, though once important, is now outdated, for example the science teaching which has failed to incorporate more recent concepts and technological developments; much better planning by the LEA and the schools of the transition between schools to avoid curricular discontinuity or needless repetition; and improved planning of courses and syllabuses within each school for the same purposes.

57. The time so saved could in principle be used in two ways. It could assist a redistribution of the balance between the elements which make up the curriculum so that each may, to a greater extent than now, make its particular contribution without leaving insufficient time for all other essential elements to make their particular contribution. For any subject area there is a minimum period for which it has to be offered to enable the pupil to gain a lasting benefit; that minimum depends on the area of learning itself, on how closely it can be related to and reinforced by other areas of learning, and on the pupil and his stage of development. The time gained can also be used more effectively by improving what is offered to pupils within the area of learning in question, without altering the amount of time devoted to that area, by concentrating on the essential aspects of what that area is best able to contribute to the pupils' total education.

58. It is evident that even when such changes are made and curricular planning optimizes the interrelation of areas of learning, schools will still have insufficient time for teaching all that it is in principle desirable for them to teach. Choices will need to be made and priorities determined. In the government's view, both of these matters fall properly for determination at the level of the LEA and the school, within a framework set by national, LEA, and school curricular policies.

59. As a step towards achieving that framework, the Secretaries of State issued, in September 1984, a discussion paper 'The Organisation and Content of the 5–16 Curriculum' which set out provisional views. Taking account of the comments received, the government believes that it is now timely to offer a statement of national policy on the broad issues raised, and

to pursue discussions in the light of it. These discussions will need to take account of the concurrent process of formulating, on the basis of consultation, statements of policy about the contribution of each main curricular element towards the totality of the curriculum.

The Primary Phase

60. Children develop quickly during their time in primary schools. The primary phase should help pupils to get the most out of the process of growing up and should build on their natural enthusiasm during this period of rapid change. To this end, the primary phase should help pupils to learn to understand themselves, their relationships with others and the world around them; should stimulate their curiosity and teach them to apply it purposefully and usefully; and should develop the foundations for later learning and those personal qualities and attitudes which, if acquired during the primary phase, provide a sound base for what follows. The principles set out in paragraph 45 should apply throughout this phase, and should be so applied that learning becomes, and remains, a pleasure.

61. Teaching in the primary phase is organized very flexibly, allowing any given curriculum to be delivered in a variety of ways. Although the curriculum which the primary schools seek to deliver is largely a common one, they use widely differing language to describe it. Such descriptions can validly seek to begin by relating what is taught to the development, for example, of values and attitudes or of particular understanding, competence and knowledge. In the light of its consultations, the government believes that there is wide agreement that the content of the primary curriculum should, in substance, make it possible for the primary phase to:

— place substantial emphasis on achieving competence in the use of language (which, in Wales, may be Welsh as well as English; but which does not normally encompass foreign languages);
— place substantial emphasis on achieving competence in mathematics, in accordance with the recommendations of the Cockcroft Report;
— introduce pupils to science;
— lay the foundation of understanding in religious education, history and geography, and the nature and values of British society;
— introduce pupils to a range of activities in the arts;
— provide opportunities throughout the curriculum for craft and practical work leading up to some experience of design and technology and of solving problems;
— provide moral education, physical education and health education;
— introduce pupils to the nature and use in school and in society of new technology;
— give pupils some insights into the adult world, including how people earn their living.

62. What has been set out above does not fully describe the tasks of primary schools: they have in addition to cope with a range of other needs of pupils, not least those arising from their home circumstances. A primary curriculum on these lines would be both broad and relevant. A reasonable balance between its elements may best be achieved by including what pupils should know, understand and be able to do in each area of learning in the statement of the school's curricular aims, and carefully and regularly monitoring both the substance of what is taught and pupils' progress against that statement. Plainly the content of the curriculum cannot be divorced from the teaching approaches employed. To take one important aspect of these, teachers in almost all primary school classes have to teach a broad curriculum to a very wide spread of ability. They need to ensure that the pace of learning is as suited to the brighter children as it is to the average or the less able. The importance of differentiation will become increasingly apparent as pupils get older. Teaching the broad curriculum outlined in paragraph 61, and doing so with the necessary differentiation, places formidable demands on the class teacher which increase with the age of the pupils. Older primary pupils (including those in middle schools) need to benefit from more expertise than a single class teacher can reasonably be expected to possess; this has consequences for staffing and the deployment of staff within a school, including the use of teachers as consultants.

63. A general acceptance of the objectives set out in paragraph 61 will have two further advantages. Experience has shown that the adoption of appropriately varied teaching strategies and schemes of work which reflect all these objectives enables pupils of all abilities to progress more quickly in achieving each one of them, including those relating to language and mathematics. Furthermore, teachers have a framework for so arranging the elements in the 5–11 curriculum that there is both coherence and progression in what is offered; and there is less risk that teachers will be professionally isolated in their work.

64. These principles should be capable of application in the great majority of primary schools. The main constraints lie in the number of teachers and their collective qualifications and skills, and in the size of the school. The smaller the school, the more serious these constraints are likely to be.

The Transition from the Primary to the Secondary Phase

65. The 5–16 curriculum needs to be constructed and delivered as a continuous and coherent whole, in which the primary phase prepares for the secondary phase, and the latter builds on the former. These requirements are essential whether or not the transition from one phase to the other involves a change of school. In educational terms the transition does not represent a radical departure but merely a step in a progression from

teaching mainly or entirely by the class teacher to a situation in which the pupil needs to be taught by many specialist teachers. It is in the pupil's interest that the progression should be gradual, so that he can accommodate to a multiplicity of adults to whom he looks for guidance and does not lose sight of the coherence of his programme through the fragmentation of its delivery. In the government's view, older pupils in the primary phase should begin to be systematically introduced to teaching by members of staff with expertise in an area of the curriculum other than that which the class teacher can offer. Moreover, while it is important in the secondary phase to secure match between the teachers' subject qualifications and experience and the teaching programme, there are advantages in not exposing the youngest secondary pupils immediately to the full range of individual specialist teaching. However this change is phased, curricular continuity and progression are essential. Their achievement requires much detailed organization and effort by the LEA and the schools concerned whatever the age of transfer between schools may be ...

★   ★   ★   ★

...(iv) Levels of Attainment

80. The fourth strand in the definition of objectives relates to levels of attainment. It is the government's longer-term aim to raise pupil performance at all levels of ability so as to bring 80–90 per cent of all 16-year-old pupils at least to the level of attainment now expected and achieved by pupils of average ability in individual subjects, ie the level associated with grade 4 in the CSE examination; and to do so over a broad range of knowledge, understanding and skills in a number of subjects. A necessary step is to define more precisely what is meant by the desired level of attainment at age 16 for pupils of differing abilities. A much clearer and more precise definition than exists at present will be available when the new GCSE examinations are established, as chapter 3 explains. These examinations will provide a point of reference for attainment at age 16, but only in relation to the knowledge, understanding, skills and competence which the examination courses are designed to develop. Attainment targets are needed also in relation to matters not tested by the GCSE and, in relation to all aspects of the curriculum, for the end of the primary phase.

81. A more precise definition, based on the government's longer-term aim, of what pupils of different abilities should understand, know and be able to do, will assist with the formulation of the curricular policies of the Secretaries of State, the LEA, and the school; will help all concerned to assess the effectiveness of policies and practice; will encourage teachers to have high expectations of pupils (and so help to bring about their realisation); and will help to motivate the pupils. It will be no short or easy task to move towards a more precise definition of attainment targets. These

cannot be simply expressed if they are to apply to the whole ability range of pupils; and the type of definition and the degree of its precision are bound to vary between elements of the curriculum. A start on the necessary work is being made in the HMI publications described in paragraph 32 and, for age 16, in the development of grade criteria for the GCSE. The work will be supported by the findings now in course of publication from the surveys conducted by the Assessment of Performance Unit (APU) of pupil performance in English, mathematics and science at age 11 and 15 (and, for science, also at age 13), and by an account which HMI will publish ... of good work done by primary pupils in a number of areas of learning. This information will show schools and others what pupils at all levels of ability can actually achieve and will therefore throw light on what they might be expected to achieve as policy and practice develop.

Curriculum Policy-Making: Local

Harold Heller

This chapter will look at curriculum policy from the local education authority (LEA) perspective, arguing that the very notion of whole LEA (or of whole school) policy represented a qualitative change in the local management of the education service, arising from profound political and social pressures manifest in the 1970s. It will try to clarify the origins and implications of these forces and examine some particular instances of curriculum policy implementation, both as evidence of this historical process in English education and as paradigms of wider innovation processes. It will conclude with some forecast of possible trends in LEA policies as they are likely to impinge on the primary sector over the next few years.

The Emergence of Curriculum Policy

Like many English institutional frameworks, the 1944 Education Act is greater than the sum of its parts. By this I mean that a mere legislative analysis of its original shape and subsequent addenda and amendments would not convey very much of its influence on the subsequent forty years of educational achievement. Indeed, a notional Martian observer might, on the basis of a perusal of the Act alone, reconstruct a system that we would find it hard to recognize. Gaps, compromises or omissions were amply compensated by the broad consensus which had emerged around its formulation and which enabled implementation to proceed with a rare degree of general support for some twenty years. Anthony Crosland's landmark circular (10/65) set a new direction with its thrust towards non-selective forms of secondary schooling; indicating that the consensus which had sustained the Act in its tripartite and ostensibly meritocratic mould was beginning to dissipate.

The curriculum is one of the key areas where the Act's collusive understatement managed for an even longer period to command support (or, at the least, an agreement not to question the matter too closely). Section 23 of the Act gives the LEAs clear responsibility for control of the 'secular curriculum' in its schools, while the model articles of government (Section 8) elaborate a highly abstract notion of delegated control and interlocking responsibilities, whereby the LEA carries strategic control: '... shall determine the general educational character of the school and its place in the local educational system'; the governors carry a planning role at unit level: '... shall have the general direction of the conduct and curriculum of the school'; while the head is cast in the role of operational manager: 'shall control the internal organization, management and discipline'. All this is bound and underpinned by systems of consultation between head and governors (8(c)i) and head and Chief Education Officer (8(c)iv).

This idealized model of curriculum delivery was, of course, well suited to the meritocratic consensus implicit in the post-1944 settlement. A relatively unchanging curriculum framework would allow for clear and open preparation in the primary phase for the differentiated schooling to be offered after the age of eleven. The primary curriculum, insofar as it was critically examined, was conceived as a known range of skills and activities largely defined by reference to later stages of the educational process. While individual teacher style and methodology might vary, the scope for personal or school discretion as to goals and content was limited. In this 'steady state' period curriculum policies and mechanisms could remain either implicit or bureaucratized, as in the model Articles already cited.

The second half of the 1960s and the 1970s were to introduce a high degree of turbulence into the systems finding expression in conflict and debate over 'the curriculum' which now took on a fresh significance and political salience.

There were many threads to this convergence. At the professional level can be cited the lengthening of the teachers' certificate courses and the early growth of the graduate (BEd) route into primary education; the development of teachers' centres; the adventurous phase of the Schools Council—all tending to create a climate of critical exploration of curriculum issues. Politically, the sociological evidence[1] was now firmly suggesting that the apparently egalitarian post-war dispensation had not only failed to narrow, but might even have widened, inequalities of life-chances for children; an accompanying sense of economic decline and political drift led to greater demands for accountability as policy options in education seemed to come at ever higher cost. Structurally, the reforms of local government of the 1965–74 period all argued for larger units which would be able to take the strategic control over the curriculum implied in the 1944 Act, but also be in a position to enact and evaluate policy through, for example, a body of education advisers with a wide range of general and specialist skills[2]. Managerially, the fashion for management by objectives (MBO) had migrated from the USA and was in vogue in Whitehall during the late 1960s; it was associated with the move to 'corporate management' in the new and larger local authorities, leading to attempts to impose systematic policy planning and review procedures even at school level. These, and similar, trends can be seen to have promoted the notion of curriculum from an inert to a dynamic status by the middle of the 1970s.

Thesis and Antithesis—Plowden and Tyndale

For the majority of practitioners such factors have lower impact than the front of stage debates which are conducted largely in educational discourse. For primary teachers and for LEAs the Plowden Committee's (1967) report[3] seemed to epitomize the changing nature of primary education through the 1960s and to mark a change of direction for the future. As with similar such large and weighty commissions the ensuing debate is often more about what they are perceived to have said or implied than about a critical evaluation of the document's text. Plowden became associated with notions of 'child-centredness' and heuristic learning; with less formal and more imaginative styles of teaching and learning and with a developmental approach to the curriculum. It seemed also to lead towards more organic and cooperative forms of teacher activity, with the notions of groups and teams offering a range of experiences to young children, in distinction to the cellular and solitary environments of traditional primary classrooms.

The reaction to this Plowden stereotype took time to mature and manifested in two broad forms, the professional and the political. The years 1975–76 may be taken as a critical period when resistance to the Plowden philosophy took both powerful and cogent expression. Professional voices ranged from the 'objective' research of Neville Bennett (1976)[4] to the populist rhetoric of Cox and Boyson (1975–1977)[5]. Political scepticism followed in the wake of the William Tyndale episode where accounts of ideological distortion and incompetent practice seemed to bear dramatic witness to Black Paper assertions[6]. The sense of Nemesis was rounded with the scene of a Labour Prime Minister, at a trade union college, unequivocally condemning such curriculum excesses and inadequacies[7]. The scene was set for a major contest over control of the curriculum where the protagonists were not merely the three local partners described in the 1944 Act (LEA, governors and head) but, additionally, central government acting initially thought the DES (and later prepared to circumvent the bureaucratic delays and impotence of that agency by invoking intervention through the MSC at secondary and tertiary levels)[8].

A Question of Control

That this thrust was a feature of the developing system rather than an idiosyncratic or partisan bias is borne out by its steady emergence across the period of both Labour and Conservative governments in the 1970s and 1980s. One further corollary of the apparent failure of the educational theorists to vindicate the grand promises of educational reform was the ever more vocal demand of the 'clients' to have greater influence over both process and product of schooling. A well orchestrated campaign by industry to draw attention to apparent deterioration in the basic attainments of school leavers arose in the late 1970s (impregnable to the well-documented evidence that, with the rapid expansion of higher education places they were drawing on a very different stratum of pupil ability than ten years earlier).

Parents too were officially recognized as having a steering role with the publication of the Taylor Committee's (1977) report on the government of schools[9]. These trends began to take on more formal and less exhortatory shape in the 1980s with a series of Education Acts legislating for greater accountability over the work of schools and giving the local community greater access to control. Central government's incursion seemed an uneasy blend of stick and carrot. The torrent of curriculum papers, ostensibly working for consensus among the partners in the curriculum was viewed by teachers and LEAs with much suspicion, whether through the broad statements of policy (like Circulars 6/81 and 8/83) or in the series of Curriculum Matters, launched late in 1984 as a strategic follow-up to the pivotal Sheffield speech on the curriculum by Sir Keith Joseph in the early part of that year. Such suspicion was not eased by an apparent (and it would seem, ill thought through) bias towards the definition of learning objectives at specific age milestones. If this stick was, for the moment, only being waved over the rump of teachers and LEAs, its menace was registered with recalcitrant hostility. At the same time juicy carrots were preferred which all but the most obdurate (or asinine?) were unable to withstand.

A succession of central initiatives and projects were launched in areas of curriculum cherished by the government (and, in many cases, fully endorsed by professional judgment). The scale and range of such initiatives, however, soon enlarged to the point where the local authorities claimed with some justice that since the funding came from the global rate support grant pool, local expenditure decisions were being preempted by central action. Worthy programmes like the Low Attaining Pupils Project were soon augmented by more controversial central priorities (TVEI being the most costly and politically sensitive: although, at the time of writing, nearly all the initially hostile LEAs have capitulated).

This central lever of change and direction in the curriculum has now been institutionalized through the Education Support Grants mechanisms and the new in-service grant arrangements which will give the DES considerable influence over the funding of priorities, and while there has been political opposition to this trend it is hard to see any alternative government voluntarily relinquishing these very real opportunities to have some guiding influence over the shape and direction of the curriculum. Indeed, it may be argued that the relative impotence of government in the post-war, post-Butler Act settlement was viable only while the broad consensus held. The unmistakeable evidence of economic and political decline and the polarization of recipes for its remediation seems to dispose any likely government to find some point of leverage in the country's system of education and training.

The national demand for greater consistency of approach and outcomes had a professional as well as a political source. As the reachback effect of 11 + selection was removed from the nation's primary schools in the 1960s and 1970s HMI were clearly observing the consequential reaction. That this was a mixed picture should be no surprise: that the results were often spectacularly inferior to the idealization which many theorists held out as the promise of the newly liberated primary curriculum seems equally unsurprising from our current vantage point.

The already quoted work of Bennett and his associates was augmented by the diligent, often pedestrian but largely persuasive national surveys carried out by HMI in the mid and late-1970s [10] These less glamorous accounts of primary practice served to underline some basic points of principle that appeared to have been discounted as the rapid expansion of pupil numbers over the last decade had led to an explosion of new equipment, plant and curriculum ideas. Nor should it be overlooked that this expansion had accelerated the growth of the teaching profession which was now a much younger and less experienced force, capable of rapid promotion at an early age, and produced by a training system which had itself undergone unprecedented and often unsystematic growth.

This chapter is not the occasion to explore these fundamental changes in the structure and composition of the primary teaching force in the 1970s; its interaction with the abolition of selective procedures at 11 and with the larger national trends outlined above will, I believe, have causal links with the picture observed both by Bennett and by the national Inspectorate.

Some of these basic points of principle have now been well assimilated into conventional practice; the HMI concept of 'match'; the notion of appropriate teacher intervention and balanced style; the underlining of the need for continuity and progression; the demand for a consensus of teacher expectations and goals; the danger of neglecting specialized teaching altogether—these would not now appear alien concepts.

By paradox, however, as these messages were being filtered and disseminated through the system in the late 1970s the underlying context to their picture was radically changing. If some of the failures and excesses described were the result of too rapid change and expansion, the new infrastructure was one of decline and concentration. The sharp downturn in birth-rates reinforced by the economic crisis engendered by the oil shocks combined to reverse the influences at school and classroom level and to step up power at LEA and DES level. Jobs in primary schools were at a premium; tenure in particular schools was diminished; the quality of new entrants rose perceptibly; the teacher training system was ruthlessly purged. It may be argued, somewhat crudely, that with this reversal of employment and resource power, curriculum control at school and classroom level was equally challenged and redirected.

With these complex and interwoven factors as a backcloth, I will now exemplify the development of LEA curriculum policies by looking at three LEAs of significant and similar size which took different approaches to the emerging needs of the primary curriculum.

A View from the LEAs

The three LEAs whose primary curriculum strategies are described below are known, with varying degrees of familiarity to the present writer. The fact that one of these is profiled with greater prominence is a function of the writer's deeper acquaintance with that model rather than a commendation of practice in that LEA.

All three would be considered medium to large authorities, with populations above half a million; thus they would conform to the original DES specification for LEAs large enough to guarantee wide coverage of curriculum issues through advisory services and in-service resources of adequate size and scope.

The historical sketch given above will have indicated some of the stimuli—both explicit and implicit—which brought LEAs to the relatively novel point in the late 1970s and early 1980s of planning and implementing whole authority curriculum policies. The following accounts may be read as case-studies both of that historical process and of the possible trends emerging in the context of curriculum control.

Farmshire

This authority covers a wide tract of country with some very scattered rural settlements; it also contains some larger towns with concentrated centres of schooling. The reorganization of 1974 saw considerable boundary adjustments in the area and Farmshire traded a good deal of territory and population with its neighbours, gaining substantially in net terms. It had to move from a fairly unitary traditional 'shire county' to a more diverse and less coherently manageable LEA. This brought both political and educational changes which were still being manifested more than ten years after reorganization.

The results of the pre-1974 position of a scattered population and a traditional shire county culture were seen in educational policies that can best be described as a mixture of the paternalistic and the 'laisser-faire'. These factors tended to elevate the influence of the local community in school policies, since the county administration was often overstretched and the County Education Committee would be very sensitive to local pressures and needs (since their own power base would often rest on the assertion of such local identities).

These same factors were conducive to the growth of paternalism as a management style in such counties as Farmshire, particularly in the years of influence, prestige and relative prosperity for the education service which were terminated with the growth of larger authorities and the deliberate subjugation of the 'big-spender' committee, education, by the new corporate management of the 1970s.

Typically, this style of management was built on larger-than-life personalities who imposed themselves very powerfully on the educational constituency, largely through a personal dominance which operated on and through headteachers. This power was often benevolent; frequently innovatory; but also, at times, arbitrary. It was often exercised in personal interventions or commitments but was rarely based on a systematic analysis of need.

Interventions in the curriculum domain were rare, and the notion of 'curriculum policies' would have been alien to the style. Thus, schools were to be supported, exhorted or chastised depending on their propensity to attract attention at county hall; while the desired state of grace for a school could be described as virtuous anonymity.

In these circumstances curriculum development strategies were often highly dependent on local initiatives. Teacher's centres were usually part-time and volunteer led; advisory services in this era were composed of sets of (often gifted) individuals supporting 'good practice' but rarely in a position to generalize to the rest of such scattered LEAs. The amplifier effect of curriculum change to be observed in more compact authorities was rarely present.

For Farmshire, the changes of 1974, although powerful, needed assimilation. The advent of closer corporate control over education's administration at local level; the centralist thrust of DES curriculum initiatives (through Circulars 6/81 and 8/83); and the changes in political and demographic makeup were being felt forcibly by the mid 1980s. A more 'dirigiste' management style had emerged with a streamlined administration and advisory service dedicated to more consciously efficient management. One corrolary was a reexamination of curriculum policies to assess whether the mixture of fairly bland generalized statements at county level together with the permissive interpretation of school-level policies still met the practical needs of the service.

Adapting to this changed world was not easy, but many in Farmshire were becoming uncomfortable with the clear evidence of unacceptably wide variations in quality of curriculum thought, vision and delivery in the primary schools and were addressing ways in which this might be alleviated.

It was, however, by no means taken for granted that the kinds of solutions adopted by more interventionist LEAs (and illustrated below) would be either desirable or effective in the circumstances of Farmshire. The problem had, nevertheless, been sensed and appreciated; alternative possibilities were being explored and their consequences reviewed. If the action and implementation stage was still to be reached, there was little doubt (at the time of writing) that a transition from the *laisser-faire* culture of the past was underway, stimulated not only by the powerful political pressures and changes already outlined but also by a shared sense of professional dissatisfaction with the present state of the curriculum in primary schools.

Middleton

This LEA while similar in size to Farmshire differs in several characteristics. Its composition is more mixed in economy, with a good deal of light industry and some pockets of heavy manufacture. In recent years these have been hit by recession, while its more agricultural base has enjoyed the modest prosperity seen more widely in Farmshire.

As a local authority it has had a much more consciously managerial outlook, venturing into the fields of performance-review and having bought the services of external management consultants to enhance its efficiency.

Even before this advent of managerialism and corporatism characteristic of many of the larger new conservative controlled local authorities at the time of the first Thatcher government, the education authority had shown itself to be both adventurous and interventionist in its curriculum policies. This had been especially evident in the authority's innovatory work on the in-service training and professional development of teachers. In this field Middleton had carried out several experiments on design and delivery on INSET, and, partly, no doubt, in the wake of national recognition of its pioneering work had assimilated into its working programmes through the 1970s a high demand from teachers for professional development together with a set of mechanisms for its exploitation. These included a very high profile for INSET, and the elevation of the work to priority level among advisers, whose working brief was much more collective and systematized than in Farmshire. This developmental work was also heavily supported by an integrated teachers' centre and higher education network which was actively and consciously involved in the assessment and satisfaction of school needs. A key element was the personal commitment of the chief education officer, who had national and international perspectives and involvement in the field of school development. As with much innovation, these initiatives were thus soundly protected and seen as valued by those of high status in the LEA. The message about values was therefore clear not only to members, officers and advisers but also to schools and teachers.

The effect of this INSET activity in Middleton was to prepare schools as organizations for the curriculum policy stage which flowed from the DES initiatives of the early 1980s. In a sense this pattern may be seen as atypical. Elsewhere (as in Farmshire) individual schools were allowed or encouraged to debate the curriculum but rarely to look at the underlying organizational conditions which would facilitate the introduction and implementation of whole-school policies. Where LEAs, as here, had been encouraging the development of 'thinking schools' there was a state of 'cultural readiness'[11] which was likely to lead to more rapid and thorough-going change. In making its response to Circular 8/83 Middleton chose to build on this earlier work (including the consultation which had led to the production of an LEA view of the curriculum in the late 1970s). However, in these new conditions of policy formation it chose an initially centralist strategy by establishing a small working party of elected members with a single teacher representative. Professional guidance took the form of the most senior officers and advisers. The 'political' flavour of this strategy can be sensed from the statement that the early sessions of the working party were dominated by the question of '... how there can be achievement of balance between national, local and individual need'.

As far as the primary sector was concerned the working party decided to take advantage of the LEA's existing strengths to further its goals and converted the INSET programme for 1982/3 to developmental and consultative work concerned with curriculum 'issues, principles and practices'. One of the outcomes of the considerable in-service initiative of that year was the production of a booklet offering *Principles for the Primary Curriculum*. The following year's primary INSET programme for heads and deputies was similarly constrained by the curriculum policy imperative, and was devoted to guidance on implementation not only of the principles document but also of draft guidelines being produced by the advisory service with teachers. The emerging materials will be used in the authority's 'School Focussed Teacher Education' programme.

This is, of course, only a partial and limited view of a complex and many-layered process undertaken in Middleton. It does, however, illustrate not merely a more deliberate and interventionist form of policy-making but the significance of the pre-existing local 'culture' and of the importance of key individuals (as with Middleton's chief education officer). Because the INSET experiments of the 1970s had been well established and rooted, it was possible to begin the LEA phase of policy with a small, political group, in the understanding that dissemination and detailed guidelines would receive full involvement at school level. Had the structures and mechanisms for professional development not been so securely established it could be argued that such a 'top-down' model might have led to conflict or non-participation by the teaching force.

Furthermore, in such a climate of accountability and performance-review, it might be claimed that the formation of strategic principles and priorities for the curriculum was the legitimate responsibility of elected members.

Steeland

This authority had been substantially reorganized first in 1968 and then again in the national 1974 shake-up. The effect of the first change had been to allow it to form new structures and mechanisms in the late 1960s which would equip it to confront, more proactively, some of the challenges which followed the later reorganization.

Steeland had experienced as severely as any LEA the cyclical fortunes of the UK economy. A period of hectic growth and investment in heavy and traditional production industry in the 1960s and early 1970s had given way to downturn and decline in the decade that followed. The absence of any real light industry or white-collar occupations turned this 'de-industrialization' into massive and chronic unemployment, with the collapse of apprenticeships offering less than 10 per cent of schools leavers any prospect of jobs. By way of paradox, this bleak scenario did as much to liberate schools towards fresh thinking as it served to demotivate them in offering a curriculum notionally directed towards the goal of work.

Among the results of the 1968 reorganization had been a structure of officer and adviser deployment and responsibility which made planning at LEA level a first and natural priority. The advisory team had been created in 1968 as a generalist force, each carrying cross-curricular responsibilities and heavily involved in the appointment and development of staff, with a conscious policy of succession-building through intensive INSET, and, after 1974, a high level of management development for staff in schools.

In the mid 1970s Steeland was led by a committee chairman of unusual drive and foresight who encouraged forward planning and experiment at a high level of risk. His national contacts led him to encourage officers and advisers to anticipate what he foresaw as a government thrust to gain access to the control lever of the school curriculum. Thus, in 1977, the advisory service launched a process of curriculum review and renewal which was to last many years and to have beneficial effects far beyond the immediate scope of the exercise. An early decision was to eschew the (to many attractive) notion of advisers setting up small groups of 'expert' or 'progressive' practitioners to produce guidelines in each of the main subject disciplines. The traditions of a generalist advisory service and the already visible benefits of wide teacher involvement in developmental work led to a complex but well-networked review programme, in which, unlike Middleton, there was no small commanding group. The design was to produce an interactive, cross-phase and cross-curricular model with a high premium on wide debate and negotiated documents.

In all, some twenty-two separate writing groups were commissioned, and all schools were given an invitation to volunteer names—as were the teaching unions. (All nominations to the groups were accepted.) Three kinds of groups were established:

Three phase groups (deliberately cutting across the LEA's transfer ages).
Five special interest groups, to take account of special needs and interests (e.g. Assessment; special needs pupils).
Fourteen curriculum groups, broadly covering the defined subject disiplines, but with a 3 to 19 age remit.

At the outset the phase and special interest groups were asked to produce a statement of principles to circulate to all other groups and to stimulate initial debate. This was also designed to avoid any narrowing of perspective by the subject groups.

Each group (which numbered 15–18 teachers, with a small support of officers and advisers) launched its work with a three day residential programme and met thereafter regularly over approximately eighteen months. Intervisiting and communication between groups was encouraged, but each was perceived as autonomous. The resulting sets of guidelines were reported to the education committee; endorsed and circulated to all schools as a stimulus for curriculum planning and not as any master-plan. When, therefore, DES circulars 6/81 and 8/83 were received the process of curriculum review and exploration was well launched and Steeland could then move to the dissemination phase which, after the success of the review (as much in its process aspects as in its products) was patterned on the same principle of 'trusting the teachers'. The teachers' unions with officers and advisers then formed a planning group to move from curriculum review to policy development.

It was soon agreed that in conformity with the 'house-style' what would be offered centrally would be an 'enabling framework' and that the detailed and specific planning would need to be demonstrated at school and governing body level.

The group decided to adopt the HMI eight 'areas of experience'[12] as the best general statement of contemporary educational goals and to attach to this a simple cycle of evaluation principles as its guidance to schools. With the agreement of the education committee, each school was asked to begin to review its own curriculum policy in the light of these principles. First, however, the planning group was to organize several LEA-wide seminars for heads and governors to exemplify the significance of the principles. This too was achieved by the active involvement of a further large group of teachers, which produced stimulating and relevant presentations illustrating the areas of experience in a cross-age and cross-curricular style. The whole was prefaced with a film of LEA schools using the theme 'communication' to draw out those linking themes which vitalize and synthesize the service. After this 'sentisization' the process went back to each school where staffs were encouraged to produce coherent statements and make presentations to their own governing bodies.

This is a hurried account of a process that lasted some six years and merely to use it to demonstrate how an LEA satisfied the bureaucratic demands of the DES would be to abuse the reader's tolerance. It may be more useful to highlight some of the implications for schools and the LEA which seemed to the writer to emerge both from this process and its aftermath. It may be particularly relevant to instance some of those 'unintended consequences' which often confront the innovator (the line between Sod's Law and serendipity is very fine).

Involving a wide range of teachers in a participative and developmental process can produce enormous individual and collective professional growth.

Those who come through such a process are likely to form the next generation of professional leaders.

As leaders of schools they will tend to repeat the model of participative development which they themselves have experienced with the LEA.

Schools led in this fashion are more likely to respond creatively and positively to new demands, risks and challenges.

Cooperation between teachers and the LEA in such developments does not eliminate dispute and conflict but may make it easier to negotiate resolutions to other difficulties.

The task of designing, implementing and monitoring curriculum policies at the level of the individual school is much more complex than is often implied, and, in many respects, the structures and cultures of English schools increase the difficulty.

The LEA's role is not merely to set the boundaries and framework for curriculum policy, but to be a continuing stimulus to debate within schools. Inspection and close evaluation are often oppressive and unhelpful to the school: a more useful role to fulfil may be that of the 'critical friend'.

Conclusions and Conjectures

This paper has, somewhat arbitrarily, looked at three case-studies of curriculum policy making in LEAs of similar size. No claim is made that these are typical cases or exemplify national trends. What they do serve to underline, however, is that the traditional description of the English education system as 'a national service locally administered' is at best a platitude and more probably an anachronistic evasion.

It has been argued that the consensus around the goals and values of the 1944 Education Act began to evaporate at a time of national decline and loss of faith in post-war collective institutions: the coincidence of some egregious cases of waywardness in a small number of schools served to fuel demands for greater control of a rambling and increasingly costly service.

It was unsurprising that the curriculum, as the core-process of the school, should have attracted the attention of governments anxious to appease populist sentiment and gain some purchase over the system.

The case-studies will have shown that, as a mechanism for control, the LEA is a crude lever. It seems likely that the politician's fantasy of a detailed and written curriculum which can be checked and tested will not have been banished by the DES initiatives described above.

There is evidence in the manner and content of the 'Curriculum Matters' series by HMI that a long 'game-plan' is being worked out, in which central control of the curriculum will eventually be asserted (of course, more in sorrow than in anger) because of the apparent inability of the local partners to satisfy 'reasonable' expectations of minimum and consistent standards of achievement. Whether this will demand some major structural upheaval (such as the severing of education from local government, through the establishment of direct authorities more accountable than now to central government) must remain speculation.

At the local level the case-studies serve to show that curriculum policies are most easily developed in coherent LEAs with a tradition of forward planning and officers and advisers unafraid to set a lead through intervention.

However, evidence from elsewhere tends to confirm the view emerging from these studies that curriculum policy is not an independent function that can be called up on demand but is part of a cycle of activities which presupposes reflective and self critical professional development at all levels of the service.

Notes

1 See, for example, the accounts of longitudinal studies of children which began to emerge in the 1960s. *All Our Future* (1968) by Douglas, Ross and Simpson, had its picture of continuing inequalities confirmed by the later studies produced by the National Childrens' Bureau.
2 The evidence submitted to the Maud Commission on Local Government (1969) by both DES and the AEC argued for LEA populations of around half a million to sustain such support services.
3 CENTRAL ADVISORY COUNCIL FOR EDUCATION (ENGLAND) (1967) *Children and their Primary Schools* (The Plowden Report), HMSO.
4 BENNETT, S. N. *et al.* (1976) *Teaching Styles and Pupil Progress*, Open Books.
5 COX, C. and BOYSON, R. *Black Papers* (1975 and 1977).
6 Report of the public enquiry 'The Auld report' ILEA (1976).
7 James Callaghan's Ruskin College speech *Education*, 22 October 1976.

8   See, for example, the letter to all LEAs of January 1983, from David Young, Chairman of MSC, inviting bids for TVEI funds.
9   DES (1977) *A New Partnership for Our Schools*, HMSO.
10   See, in particular, the HMI primary survey of 1978.
11   A good summary of the key conditions for institutional change is given by Warren Bennis in *Organisation Development*, Addison-Wesley (1969) pp. 70–5.
12   DES (1977) *Curriculum 11–16* (The Red Book), HMSO pp.3–8.

Continuity

Joan Dean

Jeremy was a summer born child and would therefore have only two years in the infant school. His father was in the army and his mother, who was a former teacher, was aware that her son would face the problems of frequent moves and changes of school which were an inevitable part of army life. Since he was a very bright little boy, she encouraged his interest in books and reading to the extent that by the time he entered school he was reading fluently. She explained all of this to the head of the school when she went to enrol Jeremy and received a disapproving and discouraging answer. 'The school' she was told, 'much preferred that parents left the teaching of reading to them and in any case the busy teacher of the reception class children would not have time to deal with one child whose needs were very different from the others. Jeremy would just have to fit in with the school programme.' Consequently Jeremy went through an entirely unnecessary programme of introductory reading work. He rapidly concluded that school was boring and that it didn't take much effort to succeed.

On transfer from infant to junior school Jackie was reading at an average level for her age group although she was below average in intelligence. She was beginning to write quite well after a slow start although her phonic knowledge was inadequate. In number she had problems in spite of much effort by her teachers. In the junior school she went into the class of a teacher who had previously taught 11-year-olds, but because of changes brought about by falling rolls was now teaching 8-year-olds. Though a good teacher in many ways, he found difficulty in adjusting to this change. In particular he had had very little experience of teaching children who had not yet established basic skills. The records which came with the children gave general opinions rather than specific information about what the children did and did not know, and since the head believed in delegating and letting people find their own feet, it was well on in the year before Jackie's problems were even appreciated and the work generally did not meet her needs.

Southwick School drew on ten middle schools for 8–12 year olds. The largest group came from Northurst and numbered about forty. The other schools were scattered over a wide area and a few children came from each. The head of the intake year dutifully visited all the middle schools and found out what she could about the children and there was a good link for some departments with Northurst but it was clearly impossible for all departments to link with all the middle school teachers involved and almost as difficult for the middle school teachers to link with all the secondary schools involved.

In French an LEA graded objectives scheme helped to create some continuity for those children coming from schools who had adopted the scheme, but even here the variety of levels at which children entered the secondary school made it difficult for teachers to take up where the middle schools had left off. In other subjects it was even more difficult and teachers generally dealt with the problem by starting everyone from the beginning. Consequently there were a number of children who made no real progress in their first year in the secondary school because they were simply going over work which had already been covered in the middle school.

Jeremy, Jackie and all the children entering Southwick School experienced discontinuity which could well have serious consequences for their development and learning. None of the schools involved was a bad school and none of the teachers was a poor teacher. In Jeremy and Jackie's classes there were children who flourished and there were children who entered Southwick and made excellent progress in their first year there. Yet these are not isolated cases. There are many occasions when there is a lack of appreciation of what children have achieved at a previous stage at home or at school. There are also occasions where teachers learn to deal with new situations at the expense of the children they teach. There are situations when teachers are critical of what happened previously and miss the strengths of the past experience. There are teachers who do not build on what has gone before; teachers who start their pupils all over again from the beginning without noting what has been done; teachers who mistrust their previous colleagues and are not interested in what they say, and so on.

There are also discontinuities in the treatment of children. Anyone looking at 7-year-olds in an infant school or 8-year-olds in a first school in July, will be conscious of their independence and confidence as the oldest children in the school. This is even more evident at the top of the junior or middle school. Much is expected of them and many live up to these expectations. In September they are the 'little ones' again and very often expectations are far lower. It is, for example, salutory to note the extent to which primary children are expected to work unsupervised and the rarity of this expectation in the secondary school below the sixth form.

Discontinuity may also be fostered by the organization within the LEA. Staffing and resource provision for primary and secondary schools may not be viewed as a continuum but may be decided separately using different criteria, sometimes by separate committees. LEA administrators and advisers may also have separated responsibilities and while this does not necessarily lead to a lack of continuity it can do so if it is no one's responsibility to see education as a whole.

This is not to suggest that different stages of education should operate in the same way. Change can stimulate and is part of a child's growing up. It becomes a matter for concern when the change is so great that it interferes with the child's learning, as it did with Jackie or when the complexity of the organization or the unwillingness to use the information available about children leads to starting everyone from the beginning. Education is a continuous process for each child and we need to make the curve of continuity a smooth one from teacher to teacher, class to class and school to school.

Issues of continuity received fairly limited attention in the HMI primary survey of 1978, *Primary Education in England*. Consideration of continuity was not included in the schedule of observation and did not appear in the conclusions. It was therefore presumably a matter for incidental observation. There was one particularly interesting finding, however, which suggested that while there was a reasonable amount of attention given to continuity within many schools, the emphasis at transition tended to be on easing the problems for the child with 'the importance of continuity in the curriculum of the schools...largely overlooked'. This would seem to be important and to give cause for concern.

Since the publication of the primary survey there have been some important studies of continuity. Part of the ORACLE study which was reported in Galton and Willcocks (1983) *Moving from the Primary Classroom* described the way in which while a teacher's style tended to remain constant, the pupil's style of learning tended to change with the teacher, so that children who were attention seekers with one teacher might change style and work in a more concentrated fashion with another. The study is particularly interesting on the changes between primary and secondary schools. It found a substantial increase in the amount of whole class teaching in the secondary schools and an increase too in the time spent on task. In spite of this there was a drop in progress for a substantial number of children. In the last year in the primary school 91 per cent of the children in the survey made progress, but in the first year of the secondary school only 69 per cent made progress and the others either stood still or fell back. Study of the pupils making losses shows a higher proportion of boys than girls. 'Fewer than half the boys in the sample made gains on the tests of basic skills during their first year in the transfer school and 45 per cent fell below their feeder school score. In contrast over three-quarters of the girls made gains and a fraction under 15 per cent made losses.'

A study by Andy Stillman and Karen Maychell (1984) reported in *School to School* described a study of educational continuity in the Isle of Wight which includes some information also about mainland schools. The Isle of

Wight has a middle school system where pupils transfer to high schools at 13. This particular age of transfer perhaps creates a greater need for continuity than the earlier ages since pupils are that much nearer to public examinations and the time for the secondary school to discover what individual pupils can do is limited.

The picture the study revealed is the expected one. There was a certain amount of effort to create continuity with meetings of teachers both from primary and middle schools and from secondary and middle schools to discuss continuity in different areas of curriculum. These meetings were beset with the familiar problems that the schools for the older children did not wish to be seen to dictate to the teachers from the feeder schools and the teachers from the feeder schools were sensitive to this possibility. There was a tendency to discuss content before discussing the subject in broader terms and meetings were not always well led, partly because of the sensitivity of the situation. Information in records passed from one stage to the next were often differently structured by the different contributory schools and it was therefore not possible to use them for purposes of comparison of pupils. Gradings in particular had no agreed meaning and were therefore of limited use.

Both middle and secondary schools were shown to have stereo-typed views of each other which led to a lack of trust between them. The secondary schools suggested that the teaching offered in middle schools was inadequate and that there was a need to start again from scratch when pupils entered the secondary school even though this was agreed to lead to a loss of interest on the part of the pupils. The study examined a number of the views held by secondary schools about the previous stage of education and found them to be mostly without foundation. The study also found that teaching immediately prior to transfer in the island schools was very similar to that immediately following transfer—a finding which would probably be different where the age of transfer was lower.

This study suggests that there is a need for a great deal of liaison work with primary and secondary teachers in particular and that LEAs need to take a leading role if we are to overcome the sensitivities involved. There should be some fundamental thinking about curriculum which could guide decisions about content and there is also a need for different schools feeding a particular school to have some agreement between them so that children do not enter the secondary school with vastly different experiences.

One of the clearest things to emerge from the Isle of Wight study is the amount which needs to be done if there is to be real continuity from school to school. It requires a major commitment on the part of schools at all levels and the middle schools or junior schools have the particular problem that they have to liaise with other schools at both ends. Such a commitment would be difficult to ensure at the present time when numerous other developments are concerning teachers.

Findings of this kind strengthen the case for the introduction of the national curriculum. We have not so far found a way to provide adequate continuity for all children in a situation where each school is responsible for the curriculum it offers. To achieve this, we would need to be prepared to spend a great deal more time in discussion and planning. It is perhaps easier to have a curriculum imposed nationally.

The concern which many of us feel about the introduction of a national curriculum is that it may be devised in such a way that schools lose the impetus that the freedom to experiment has given the best of them. A national primary curriculum needs to be more concerned with understanding and skills in the different aspects of curriculum than detailed content, although content is the raw material from which understanding, skill and the ability to use knowledge can be developed.

In 1978 the Primary Survey suggested that we have a great deal of work to do in clarifying our thinking and establishing a sense of direction in subjects such as science and environmental studies even within schools, let alone between stages of education. Since then LEA Guidelines have been published in many subjects and at a national level the recent HMI publications following *The Curriculum 5–16* (DES, 1985) have started us on this process.

If goals are seen in fairly broad terms there is no reason why they should be limiting. It might, for example, be possible to agree that all junior or middle schools contributing to a particular secondary school or schools should undertake a local study which involved field work, including some historical, geographical, sociological and scientific work and attempted to develop some agreed skills and concepts. A group of schools working together at this could develop a variety of approaches and materials from which teachers could select, and these would be the common ground on which the secondary school could build without too much limitation for anyone and this could equally well apply at an LEA or national level. The advantage of this kind of approach is that it gives an opportunity to set different goals for different children while providing some common ground for everyone. It is perhaps worth remembering that within the schools of any LEA there will probably be a few children at the end of the primary stage who could take a school leaving examination in some subjects and others who still have serious difficulties in reading and basic number.

Unfortunately such goals do not sit easily with the idea of tests and benchmarks. A curriculum whose effects can be measured easily is likely to be a limited curriculum although benchmarks of performance will provide a much firmer base for a secondary school taking children from a range of primary schools. We need to remind ourselves constantly that a child's development and learning are more than the acquisition of skill, knowledge and understanding, however. We live in a fast changing society and this has important implications for education; implications which we have only partly understood and accepted at present. Knowledge itself is changing and there is no longer any way that schooling can equip a child with knowledge for all that lies ahead. What we know is that (s)he will have to change, adapt and learn afresh and this means that the ability to meet new situations and challenges is important. (S)he needs confidence to meet the unknown, strategies to tackle new problems and the ability to deal with new knowledge. All of this suggests that the process of learning at school and the way a child structures what (s)he knows are very important. Much of this learning takes place as a by-product of acquiring content. Perhaps it needs to be more clearly in our minds than formerly. Certainly we need to assess progress towards goals of this kind and deliberately build into what we do the development of the skills which enable a child to become an independent learner.

There is also a need to look at personal and social development as a continuous process. We need to work together to find ways of helping children to develop desirable qualities for learning such as curiosity, persistence and inventiveness. We also need to foster other qualities, such as understanding of others, capacity for taking responsibility, ability to form and maintain relationships, as well as providing social skills such as the ability to express needs and views, to question and to enquire, to work with others to agreed ends and to cope with wide variety of social situations. Individual teachers often help children to develop in these ways, but a policy is needed which ensures that the development of these abilities is continuous from year to year and from school to school.

Demands for particular kinds of behaviour also create discontinuity. It can be salutory to follow a particular child for a day in a large secondary school to see the variety of demands made upon him or her and the ways in which (s)he needs to adjust to different teachers. This is less of a problem at the primary stage, but we could often help children more over this kind of adjustment if we talked about it with them and looked at what is involved in assessing each situation for the child. It is the child with most difficulty in learning who is often most confused over adjusting to different adults. Security to some extent depends upon knowing one's boundaries. Children begin to feel secure when they know what is required of them, what is and what is not allowed and the teacher's likely reactions. While a measure of insecurity can be stimulating, too much can be counter-productive and a child may spend time working out what the teacher wants and guessing the right answers rather than concentrating on the material under consideration.

There would certainly seem to be a need for a longer term view of education and greater emphasis on continuity than we have at present and the national curriculum would seem to be the simplest solution to this problem. There will still remain a need for teachers and schools to talk and work together to ensure continuity but there would be rather less to discuss.

The national curriculum, whatever its nature, will undoubtedly bring improved continuity for children. However, it will still be necessary for teachers to work with each other and agree to do things in certain ways. Each teacher will still need to see that his/her work fits into the overall pattern for each child. Teachers will still need to keep records for the benefit of others and use the records others have written. This is all time-consuming, often difficult and will still require a professional appreciation of the need for continuity.

The most important factor for continuity within the school is probably the extent to which teachers work together and think about long term planning. Children are in an infant school for two or three years, in a first school for three, four or five and in a junior or middle school for four years. However it is rare for the school to plan as far ahead as this, looking at the way in which teacher knowledge and skill can be built up and planning developments sufficiently far ahead to build up resources. It is true that it is not possible to predict levels of staffing or capitation so far ahead but this makes long term planning even more important. If a key member of staff may leave and not be replaced, it is doubly important to see that others are developing skills which would enable them to take over. If resources may be increasingly difficult to acquire, then their purchase needs to be planned over a longer period. Every school staff needs to discuss continuity and long term planning and will still need to do this when there is a national curriculum. Teachers are more likely to feel commitment to common plans when they have been involved in decision and policy making about curriculum and resources. Such discussions foster teacher development and help to ensure a more continuous education for each child.

The development of a national curriculum would involve a different way of looking at work within the individual school. At present written schemes of work in primary schools tend to be drawn up through staff discussion of content with perhaps some discussion also of how it might be taught. If the bones of the curriculum were given then the discussion would need to centre on the way in which it could be implemented. This might be an easier task which would make good use of the professional skills of teachers. The danger is that teachers would no longer feel the need to discuss curriculum or to be concerned with continuity from school to school.

Whatever the changes on the national scene, discussion needs to go on among 'families' of feeder and receiving schools if curriculum continuity is to be achieved. Although parental choice has made the number of schools from which any secondary school receives children more numerous, there are for most secondary schools a number of feeder schools from which the majority of their children will come and with whom good relationships can be built up. There should be inter-visiting, exchange of ideas and information and a following up of individual children. The national curriculum statement will need to be supported with copies of schemes and syllabuses need to be exchanged and discussed as well as records. It can also be valuable to exchange teachers for a time so that each school comes to understand the other.

Record keeping is an essential ingredient in making education continuous. We need to give thought to how we can provide records for each child which give teaching information which is easily accessible and useful rather than expressions of opinion about potential. If one teacher is to be able to take on from where the last teacher left off with an individual child or a group of children, what (s)he needs to know is what the child or group has or has not done, knows or does not know. (S)he needs to know what has been tried and with what success and where there have been problems and difficulties. If a school is wanting to group children on entry, then information about reading ages and potential is useful but it is of limited value in helping a teacher to decide what to teach and how to teach it.

It is in the early years of schooling that teachers perhaps come nearest to recording this kind of information, but as the child grows older, it becomes more difficult to identify what (s)he does and does not know and the practice tends to change to one of recording grades and adding brief comments. It is even rare to find a record of the courses and books used, yet this could very often be duplicated for a group of children and individual variation recorded. Our record systems at the later stages of education seem more concerned with sorting and grouping children than with seeing that each is getting a continuous education matched to his/her needs.

This is not to deny the need to grade for some purposes, but to suggest that what many schools do at present is of limited value because insufficient thought is given to the child's long term needs and the kind of information which is useful for a whole range of purposes. Grading, for example, would be of more value if it were used to identify areas of concern within a subject. It is of limited teaching value to know that overall, Gillian has a C for English, but if the record indicates that Gillian's ability to write in creative and personal ways is A and she tends to be only of average ability in more factual writing, the receiving teacher has useful information to work on, especially if the meaning of the grading system has been carefully considered and agreed.

Continuity is what is or is not experienced by the individual child. (S)he is the one who experiences the discontinuity of demands by different teachers and different schools. His/her parents may have an awareness of what is happening which is different from that of the teachers. We can learn a good deal from talking with children and their parents about what has happened to them. It can also help if we encourage both children and their parents to see and plan ahead and make a point of explaining our goals to them more frequently than we sometimes do. There are many occasions when, by not making our goals explicit, a school or a teacher loses the advantage of harnessing the child's desire to learn and the parent's desire to provide support.

But it is not only the teachers and the schools that need to be committed and concerned with continuity. The LEA needs to have a commitment to long term planning and continuity and the extent of this commitment will be reflected in the way it attempts to provide resources, particularly teachers, to see children through what has been started, perhaps by building a time lapse into calculations for staffing and capitation where rolls are falling. This is further helped if there is a measure of virement in the use of resources and local financial management should help a good deal. It should perhaps be noted in passing that it is difficult for an LEA to reconcile continuity and parental choice: both seem to be highly desirable but are conflicting.

We also need this commitment nationally. Local and national policies tend to work against continuity when the major parties hold radically different views. The many developments of the past few years have provided schools with much food for thought which needs to be assimilated and interpreted to meet the needs of individual children. Schools therefore need some honest assurance that resources will be available so that they can plan ahead. It may well be better to face and accept a not very generous provision which can be maintained than to be buoyed up with promises which prove impossible to fulfil.

We have given lip service to the idea of continuity for many years. Continuity will only happen if our commitment is sufficient to give it a high level of priority. There is a very real need to do so.

References

DEPARTMENT OF EDUCATION AND SCIENCE (1978) *Primary Education in England*, HMSO.

DEPARTMENT OF EDUCATION AND SCIENCE (1985) *The Curriculum 5 to 16*, HMSO.

GALTON, M. AND WILLCOCKS, J. (Eds) (1983) *Moving from the Primary Classroom*, Routledge and Kegan Paul.

STILLMAN, A. AND MAYCHELL, K (1984) *School to School*, NFER-Nelson.

The Experienced Curriculum

Neville Bennett, Charles Desforges, Anne Cockburn and Betty Wilkinson

The focus of this study has been on task processes in classes of 6 and 7-year-old children whose teachers were rated as better than average by the advisory service in the education authorities concerned. Working closely with these teachers showed clearly that they were dedicated and conscientious people. Few with experience of working with infant teachers would doubt this description. The questions posed in this study relate to how such dedication is harnessed in attempts to provide appropriate learning experiences for their pupils.

In appraising the quality of learning experiences the demands on the children of the tasks were first ascertained. Although there were often marked differences in the classrooms studied, tasks demanding practice of existing knowledge, concepts or skills predominated. This was particularly apparent in language work where over three-quarters of all tasks set demanded practice. A typical task was a request from the teacher for the class to write a story, usually accompanied by exhortations on neatness and appropriate grammar. Here the demand was for the practice of well-understood routines and rarely did such tasks impart or demand the acquisition of new knowledge. This staple diet of little new knowledge and large amounts of practice was rarely varied to include tasks which required either the discovery or construction or new of different ways of perceiving problems, or the application of existing knowledge and skills to new contexts.

The teachers studied held strongly to the philosophy of individualization and it was therefore expected that differential demands would be intended for children of differing levels of attainment. High and low attaining children certainly received different curriculum content but they experi-

From Bennett, N. *et al.*, (1984) *The Quality of Pupil Learning Experiences*, L. Erlbaum associates, pp. 213–21.

enced similar patterns of task demand. Thus similar ratios of incremental*
to practice tasks were planned for both groups of children. This pattern
was further conpounded by the fact that teachers found it much more
difficult to transform an intended incremental into an actual incremental
task for high attainers. In reality therefore high attaining children received
less new knowledge and more practice than their low attaining peers. This
is the opposite pattern to what might have been expected with the probable
consequences of delays in progress for high attainers and lack of opportunity for consolidation for low attainers (cf. Brophy and Evertson, 1976).

The main reasons for teachers failing to implement intended demands
were twofold; poor or misdiagnosis, and failures in task design. Many
mismatches in demand occurred because the teacher did not ascertain that
the child was already perfectly familiar with the task content. Poor or
non-diagnosis thus underlay the fact that many incremental tasks actually
made practice demands. Task design problems were also relatively frequent. In such cases the requirements for the performance of the task did
not match the teacher's intention.

Little improvement in patterns of task demand happened as a result of
transferring to a junior class or school. Here the pattern changed markedly
as the term progressed. Revision tasks predictably predominated in the
early weeks as the teachers ascertained the base from which to start.
Thereafter incremental and practice tasks were the most prevalent.

Here too there were marked differences in the classrooms studied but in
general there were more incremental and few practice tasks in this term
than in the infant classes. This pattern was more apparent in junior than
primary schools and particularly so in the language area. This would
indicate a quickening pace in knowledge acquistion. However this general
pattern hid the rather surprising trend that the number of incremental tasks
decreased, and practice tasks increased, as the term progressed. Thus
children were rapidly introduced to new concepts and skills early in the
term with little opportunity for consolidation, whereas later in the term
knowledge acquisition fell away to be replaced by more and more practice.

Teachers' task intentions during this term were similar to those found in
infant schools. They planned large amounts of practice and revision for
high attainers and a high input of new knowledge with little opportunity to
practice for low attainers, with the same predictable consequences.

High attainers also experienced, as they had in the infant classes, tasks
which did not make the intended demand. Thus they received 80 per cent
more practice tasks than intended, indicating little extension of concept
acquisition, whereas low attainers experienced equal amounts of incremental and practice tasks which left little opportunity for consolidation. In
number work the pattern was even more notable. Here low attainers
received three times more incremental than practice tasks. The same

---

* Incremental tasks involved in the aquisition of new facts, rules and procedures

problems of mis- or non-diagnosis and task design underlay the mismatching of intention and actual demand.

The quality of a pupil's learning experience is also related to the match between the intellectual demand of tasks and the pupil's attainments. In both number and language work at infant level teachers were able to provide a match on approximately 40 per cent of tasks. About a third were too difficult for the child and a little over a quarter were too easy. This general pattern masks marked differences in the classrooms studied. There was also an indication that teachers in the infant schools were somewhat better at matching than those in infant departments of primary schools. It was also very clear that the quality of matching varied in relation to the children's intellectual standing in the classroom. High attainers were underestimated on over 40 per cent of tasks assigned to them, a pattern similar to that reported by HMI (1978). But an equally clear pattern of overestimation was found for low attainers. Of their assigned tasks 44 per cent were overestimated in both language and number work.

Matching was worse in first term of junior schooling where the proportion of matched tasks in number work fell to 30 per cent. The incidence of mismatching was particularly severe for high attainers since three-quarters of the tasks they received were underestimates. Low attainers again suffered from overestimation, a trend which was more marked in junior schools than junior departments. It was also interesting to find that the quality of matching declined as the term progressed. In the last observation period for example most of the incremental tasks were overestimates and practice tasks underestimates.

Teachers were adapt at recognizing a task that was proving too difficult but were totally blind to tasks whose demands were too easy. The reasons for this are at least twofold. Firstly the teachers' typical management style required them to be seated at the front of the class, and as a result supervision was limited to quick observational sweeps of the classroom. The usual image was of a class working cheerfully and industriously. This, indeed, is the second reason for a teachers' lack of recognition of too-easy tasks. Children always worked in this way irrespective of appropriateness of the task set. From the teachers' point of view, children were busy, and busy work equated with appropriate demands.

Thus in the short term, inappropriate work appeared to have little direct emotional or motivational consequences for children of this age. Although cognitive problems, which manifested themselves in unproductive or confusing learning experiences, were all too clearly apparent in the post task interviews, this cognitive confusion was masked from the teachers by the children's cheerfulness and industry. The teachers avoided the immediate consequences of such confusion by rewarding individual endeavour, and by restricting their considerations of children's work to the product, not the process of such work, a facet taken up later.

Intended classroom learning is embedded in the content of the tasks teachers provide for children. A detailed analysis of the structure of curriculum content was therefore carried out for number and language.

In number, all teachers used some kind of sequenced scheme. Children worked through these schemes 'at their own rate,' although the teachers perceptions of 'rate' in this context appeared to refer to rate of mechanical progress through the scheme rather than rate of understanding. The content of the task, often in the form of work cards, was thus individualized, even though task demand was not. Little teaching was undertaken. Children were usually told to carry on from where they had last left off.

In contrast no sequential schemes appeared to be used in language. Most tasks were generated from the teacher's source of ideas. Most tasks were designed to develop writing skills, the typical approach being to introduce the topic as a class lesson involving discussion prior to its specification as a common class task. There was therefore no differentiation of task demand for children of differing levels of attainment. And as was stated earlier the great majority of such tasks required only the practice of established concepts and skills for higher attainers. Writing was thus characterized by a lack of sequence and a lack of development.

It is also of interest to note that there was a clear differentation in the tasks presented between reading and writing skills. Writing tasks were for the development of writing skills, and reading skills were to be enhanced by phonics and comprehension exercises. As such there was no integrated language approach.

Although different in source, presentation, demand and sequence, number and language tasks had in common a teacher stress on procedural rather than cognitive aims. They were interested in the production and presentation of work rather than in the identification or discussion of cognitive process.

Although an accurate general picture, enormous differences in content provision were observed between classes, and within the classes, studied. In mathematics some classes covered almost twice as many areas as others. Further, the 'work at your own rate' philosophy precluded many low attainers from experiencing a wide range of content met by their more academically advanced peers even in the same classroom. Only half of the low attainers experienced division and money problems for example. The fineness of the sequence of development within any specific area, e.g., subtraction, also varied widely. In some classes the content was covered in a series of giant, sometimes quite mystifying leaps, whereas in others the same operations were developed in finely graded stages.

The width of the curriculum also varied greatly. In some classes a very narrow range of content was covered yet in the same period of time other teachers managed a much wider range with apparent success. These wide differences in provision appear to result from the selection of the particular mathematics scheme used. But within-class differences stem more from the teachers' decisions regarding individualization of instruction. 'Covering the basics' thus has a bewildering variety of meanings, but as yet there is no evidence of what implications these may have for subsequent mathematical understanding. What is clear however is that generic phases such as 'the basics,' 'the four rules of number' or 'own rate' are almost meaningless in practice.

A wide variety of provision was equally evident in language work. But here it was the common and predictable features of writing experiences which attract attention. Teachers had uniform and restricted aims which, in three-quarters of tasks observed, were to practice writing with particular attention paid to quantity and grammar, especially full stops and capital letters. Teacher evaluation focussed on quantity, neatness and grammar irrespective of how the task was specified, or the attainment level of the child.

The children did little to focus the teachers' attention on to their bland and uniform diet. As well as the ubiquitous cheerfulness and industry they were totally clear about how to please their teachers irrespective of their overt demands. Thus, for example, the exhortation to 'write me an exciting story' was clearly interpreted as a request for a given number of lines of neat writing with due attention to full stops and capital letters. And in this interpretation they were correct.

Despite this diet however some progress was made in writing. When this was assessed after six months the children wrote, on average, more words, generated more ideas and used more connectives. They also wrote stories which were judged to be better on quality and organization. On the other hand there was little or no development of those aspects which teachers stressed the most. More than half the children failed to use full stops appropriately and correct usage of capital letters remained almost static. The overt encouragement by teachers for exciting stories appeared to have no impact since no change in imaginative content was recorded over the six month period.

The failure of children to deploy correct grammatical usage when not under the direct supervision of teachers could result form lack of appropriate teaching or it could be that such exhortations were premature. Only future studies will tell.

It was shown earlier that poor, or misdiagnosis, underlay many failures to transform an intended into an actual task demand. Another crucial role for diagnosis is in delineating children's cognitive confusions prior to the provision of adequate explanations. The evidence shows that here too diagnosis is a central problem. The teachers did not diagnose. They reacted to the product of a child's task performance rather than to the processes or strategies deployed in attaining the product. Thus procedural matters, such as taking the child through the rules of carrying numbers or providing spellings, predominated, rather than diagnosis of the nature of the child's cognitive misconceptions. This was usually undertaken at the teachers' desk in an atmosphere of 'crisis' management as teachers' attempted to attend to the queues whilst simultaneously supervising the class visually. Their evident frustration was an obvious consequence, and, given their chosen managerial style, unavoidable. Often the only individual teaching that children received was at the teacher's desk, but teaching within the above context hardly seems designed to enhance individualized learning, although it must be recognized that classes of thirty children impose severe constraints on teachers time and attention.

Nevertheless teachers cannot afford to disregard children's misconceptions. This maxim, together with the all too obvious problems teachers had with diagnosis, led to the development of an in-service course from which it was hoped to gain a better understanding of this from another group of experienced teachers. The ultimate aim was to provide practical advice for teachers which took into account normal classroom constraints.

Through the use of actual case studies and transcripts, followed by training in the use of diagnostic interviewing in their own classroom, teachers came to understand and accept the utility and necessity of diagnosis. Over time they learned to derive tentative hypotheses or hunches about the nature of the children's misconceptions. But they simply could not sustain an analysis of the child's responses. They fell back to direct teaching, stressing procedure rather than understanding.

A number of reasons accounted for this failure. The interviews were conducted within the framework of the typical crisis management style, i.e., that teachers are the providers of instant solutions to a constant stream of problems. As such the interviews got in the way of management. The second reason was that teachers could not stop teaching. There was a constant urge to rush into direct teaching at the first sign of error, before the misconception had been properly diagnosed. The third reason was that conducting a good diagnostic interview requires considerable skill. Teachers are not trained in such skills and find it difficult to acquire them. No doubt accumulated experience is hard to discard. And finally to conduct an effective interview requires an understanding of the processes to be attained, and experience in the manner in which children can, and typically, do, misinterpret processes.

Focussing on classroom tasks, and the influences of teachers, pupils and classroom context on their quality and performance, has brought into sharp relief a number of concerns, some serious, relating to the demands and appropriateness of tasks; to decisions regarding curriculum content; to the adequacy of teacher diagnosis and explanation; and to classroom management strategies. Most of these receive scant attention in the research literature (cf. Rosenshine, 1983) but are central factors in achieving and maintaining the quality of pupil learning experiences.

What has emerged in general terms is an increased understanding of the formidable problems teachers face as they strive to implement the laudable philosophy of individualizing instruction, and the equally formidable array of skills that are required to carry this out effectively. The objective here however is not to criticize teachers for not being perfect but to provide a clear specification of the apparent problems with a view to improvement. What follows therefore is an exploration of ways and means whereby this improvement might be sought whilst recognizing that the issues are complex and interactive. Nevertheless two major problem areas arise, classroom management, and teachers' knowledge and understanding of content and pupils' typical responses to it.

It has been shown that teachers typically adopt what has been termed a crisis management style. This requires that they be all things to all pupils at all times. The consequences of this style include constant interruptions, divided teacher attention, lack of adequate class supervision, lack of opportunity for adequate diagnosis and explanation and, in many instances, teacher frustration. In short, a learning environment which is far from optimal for teacher or taught.

It has been claimed that teachers often sacrifice a concern for learning in favour of a concern for management (Doyle, 1979) and the findings reported here would seem to lend some support for this view. Nevertheless the essence of any good management strategy is to provide a system of rules and procedures which will optimize the main purpose of the work setting. In classrooms therefore management should provide the framework for the teachers' learning intentions. One of the main failings in crisis management style is that it does not allow for the creation, or the flexible use, of time necessary to fulfil these intentions adequately. Evaluations of alternative managerial techniques must therefore recognize these as central criteria.

A number of suggested alternatives emanate from observed practice. The first is the abandonment of dual queues, a system which has been shown to benefit neither the teacher nor the pupils. This need not require the modification of the teachers' stated aim of marking work with children present although the operationalization of this aim certainly requires amendments to cut down the ubiquitous queuing. One method would be the creation of a clear set of classroom rules regarding queuing which could profitably be used in conjunction with changes in the function and operation of groups.

Much of the teachers' time was taken up by their willingness to react to low order requests. In language work for example they were constantly harrassed for spellings. This represents a great deal of wasted time as well as breaks in continuity of working, and is, perhaps, a result of a lack of clarity in teachers' objectives for this kind of work. It seems unlikely that children of this age are capable of error free writing. Teachers must thus decide whether they want error-free work, in which case copy writing would seem more appropriate; or whether they wish for imaginative, expressive writing, in which instance spelling could be neglected in the short term. In the latter case this would provide an opportunity for teachers to acquire a more coherent understanding of patterns of children's errors which are currently masked by ad hoc provision. In the language work observed teacher's intentions appeared to fall awkwardly between these two stools.

Teaching to groups of children rather than to the class or individual is currently prescribed by HMI (1980). This report reiterated the suggestions made in the Plowden Report (CACE, 1967) concerning the utilization of groups since it was recognized that teachers could not be expected to individualize instruction in large classes of children. Unfortunately the use of classroom groups in practice has emerged as no more than a convenient seating arrangement rather than as a specific site for teaching.

Here too teachers need to clarify their aims. The assumption appears to be that simply sitting children together will further intellectual and social development. Research on groups does not support this assumption and neither do the findings reported in this study, where it has been shown that interaction is usually of dubious quality. Classroom groups do have potential as teaching and learning contexts, and many schemes are available (Slavin, 1983), but this potential is far from being realized.

Nevertheless if properly managed teaching to groups, regardless of whether the rest of the class is engaged on the same content area, could hold advantages in terms of extended contact, the opportunity to fine tune task demand and provide adequate diagnosis. A further stage in this process could be the implementation of peer teaching, although more research in normal classroom settings is required in this area.

Teachers would of course benefit greatly from additional assistance in the classroom, but teacher aides in Britain are not common. An increasing number of schools are however inviting the participation of parents in the teaching process both in school and at home with evident success (Tizard *et al.*, 1982). The encouragement of this trend, which might perhaps be extended to suitable unemployed school leavers for example, would create the time necessary for teachers to concentrate on individual pupils.

These suggestions by no means exhaust the possibilities. The purpose here is not to provide comprehensive solutions but to indicate that possibilities do exist for the creation of teacher time. But when created a second step is necessary—the development of teacher skills. In order for adequate diagnosis and explanation to be afforded by teachers additional knowledge and skill in curriculum content areas, and in interacting with individual pupils, is required. Teachers need to be knowledgeable about the schemes available, their differing content, assessment procedures and implications for the management of learning. Crucially they need knowledge of how a wide range of pupils typically respond to this content, their common errors and misconceptions. On the basis of such knowledge they need to develop a range of strategies designed to overcome them.

Attention needs to be drawn to the cognitive complexities of content, rather than concern with mechanical progress; and to the processes whereby pupils arrive at products, rather than to the products themselves. In order to fulfil this change in focus, skills require developing in diagnostic interviewing and the phrasing of explanations. The problems experienced in this study provide a guide in this area although it is likely that training at pre-service level may not meet these same issues. Training at in-service level has the additional difficulty of attempting to overcome established routines.

There is an increasing demand, in Britain at least, that prospective teachers should undertake the academic study of a single specialist subject area for at least two years of their course. If this is interpreted by teacher educators to mean the provision of courses on esoteric academic content and theory then such study is unlikely to have implications or meaning for subsequent classroom practice. The findings of this study would indicate that for the training of teachers of young children additional time should be provided for students to develop their own pedagogic theories based on increased contact with pupils working on typical curriculum contents. A large and regular amount of time spent with different pupils throughout the course developing their knowledge and skills in content, diagnosis and interaction, bolstered by a closer examination of the continuity of learning experiences in the longer teaching practices, seems more appropriate.

At in-service level, skill based courses in this area need to be supplemented by initiatives designed to reduce the isolation of teachers with respect to their decisions on curriculum content. A detailed sharing of information through the exchange of their own case studies with teachers in other schools might be considered, perhaps extended by case conferences of individual children or curriculum decisions within their own school. The current trend towards the creation of posts with specific curriculum responsiblility should help this process with the specialist post holder taking a key role.

The philosophy of individualized instruction has informed the education of young children for many years. We do not doubt the validity of this but, like all ideals, it is easier to theorize about than practise. Nevertheless teachers of this age group have made significant steps towards its successful implementation. Learning environments have been created which are characterized by good social relationships, expert utilization of resources, happy and industrious pupils. What this study has revealed is that a number of cognitive aspects of this environment appear to have been hidden from teachers. These have been carefully specified, and their possible consequences outlined, not to carp or criticize, but as a basis for improvement. Teachers will, we hope, accept them in this spirit, for their information, reflection, maybe even inspiration. For improving the quality of pupil learning experiences is as much their aim as ours.

References

BROPHY, J. and EVERTSON, C. (1976) *Learning from Teaching*, Allyn and Bacon.

CENTRAL ADVISORY COUNCIL FOR EDUCATION, (1967) *Children and Their Primary Schools* (The Plowden Report), HMSO.

DOYLE, W. (1979) 'Making management decisions in classrooms' in DUKE, D. (Ed). *Classroom Management*, University of Chicago.

HMI (1978) *Primary Education in England: A Survey by H.M. Inspectors of Schools*, HMSO.

HMI (1980), *Education 5 to 9*, HMSO.

ROSENSHINE, B. (1983) 'Teaching functions in instructional programs', *Elementary School Journal*, 83.4, pp. 335–52.

SLAVIN, R. (1983) *Cooperative Learning*, Longman.

TIZARD, J. *et al.* (1982) 'Collaboration between teachers and parents in assisting childrens reading'. *British Journal of Educational Psychology*, 52, pp. 1–15.

Equal Opportunities in Primary Education

Judith Whyte

'As every schoolboy knows ...' is a common phrase, usually finishing off with some technical or scientific fact about the world. The use of school*boy* draws attention to something we all know, but until recently have not been prepared to admit, that schoolboys' knowledge is different from and more extensive than girls'.

Discussion about the effects of gender in education has focussed on the secondary level, on choice at 13s and the way girls are avoiding physical sciences, technical crafts and—worryingly—the newer subjects like control technology or computing.

Why should primary teachers be concerned? After all, girls do so much better than boys during the junior years. They learn to read and count sooner, and their general intellectual achievement is superior right up to the age of 11. Once, we assumed that girls and boys had different innate abilities, but that explanation has gradually come to seem less convincing as we see that, under certain conditions in schools and society, girls achieve just as well as boys. It is *attitudes* to learning, formed early in life, which appear to determine what kinds of knowledge girls and boys acquire later on.

It is especially difficult to uncover the roots of problems which grow over a long period. Two examples of sex difference in achievement illustrate what I mean:

(i) Adult literacy tutors are often amazed to find how many highly successful men, active in public life, have kept secret for years the fact that they have never learned to read.

(ii) A girl with science passes is less likely than any boy—even a boy who has never done science at all—to enter a scientific or technical occupation.

Reproduced from *Primary Education Review*, 17, 1983, pp. 5–7.

In the first case, boys who could have learned to read chose not to; in the second, a girl with ability in science may never use it. Attitudes to learning about language and science are formed in the primary school.

Language

Girls get off to a headstart, compared with boys. They speak their first word and first sentence sooner; they appear to be in a state of 'school readiness' about six months earlier than their brothers; they learn to read sooner and faster and throughout the primary school years girls, as a group, excel boys on every aspect of verbal performance.

Children's attitudes to reading are also quite distinctive: girls like to read on their own and they enjoy long, thick books, while boys prefer comics, annuals and shorter books. Poor, or backward readers are more likely to be boys and also to be maladjusted and anti-social, and whereas reading difficulties in girls tend to be associated with low intelligence, the same is not true for boys.

What all this seems to add up to is that boys are not, somehow, strongly motivated to read and so some fail to learn at all. Boys experience greater learning difficulties because so much of the primary school curriculum is language based. It has been suggested that the 'reader role', indeed the 'pupil role' in primary schools is passive and conforming; it runs counter to the expectation of boys that they be active and restless if not positively naughty and disruptive. In consequence, some boys reject reading alto-gether at this stage. On the whole, it is not girls but boys who have problems with reading. Concern with reading development can thus be seen as evidence that boys' performance and achievement is considered to be more important. It may be the underlying reason why so many resources have been devoted to the teaching of reading. It could also explain why so many children's books have been criticized for sex bias. If teachers and publishers are trying to win over boys, then the under-representation of female characters is not surprising. What is less defensible is what has been called the 'cult of the apron': for example, out of fifty-eight books examined in one typical study only twenty-five had a picture of a female in them, and twenty-one of the twenty-five were wearing pinnies. They included a mother alligator, a mother donkey, a mother rabbit and a mother cat, all wearing aprons!

It is the narrow stereotyped view of females in children's books which is potentially so damaging to girls, because sex bias affects not their language ability, but their view of themselves. Very few primary materials show women in work roles outside the home, or girls in active, adventurous, risk-taking or leadership positions. When they do (e.g. Pippi Longstock-ing) boys enjoy reading them just as much as girls. But many books teach children to believe that girls and boys are very different creatures, with almost opposing interests. The war of the sexes may be invisible to us because we take it so much for granted. But children are in no doubt that there exist two, mutually exclusive and frequently hostile groups. A current chant in a Manchester infant playground is 'Boys are fantastic! Girls are elastic!'

Even 5-year-olds know that behind the facade of sexual equality, the unwritten rule is that boys come first. The chant implies that boys are something special, while girls are malleable, adaptable, secondary. The lesson is learned at home: mums and dads, we know, treat boys and girls differently almost from the moment of birth, buy them different toys and provide them with different activities. Far from challenging, schools tend to reinforce and exaggerate these differences, not by direct teaching but through a 'hidden curriculum' of informal comments and assumptions.

A 'Hidden Curriculum' of Sex Role Teaching

School organization segregates children by sex from the very first day. Boys and girls have separate lavatories, cloakrooms and sometimes play spaces. They line up separately, are expected to wear different sorts of clothes, are given different games to play and may even learn different light crafts. Not surprisingly, they soon learn to keep themselves in separate groups whenever they have the choice. Teachers treat them differently, expect different standards of behaviour from the two sexes, and reinforce stereotyped behaviour. For instance, infant teachers assume that girls are better behaved, play more often in the Wendy house, and clean up more readily, while boys play with bricks and have greater physical strength (Chasen, 1975). They encourage their beliefs by for instance complimenting boys, but not girls on their strength, and girls, but not boys on their appearance.

From the earliest age, girls are cuddled and gentled; parents and teachers are harder on boys from the start, as if to indicate that boys must 'stand up for themselves.' Children don't interpret it quite like that; boys think adults don't like them so much, and they believe teachers dislike boys and prefer girls. Perhaps because they have been more sympathetically treated from the start, girls are more eager to please grown-ups.

Observations in a nursery school showed that if a boy hit someone or broke something, teachers were *three* times more likely to notice than if a girl did the same. The boy would get a loud, public telling off while everyone in the room became aware of his naughtiness. Little girls tended to receive a brief, soft rebuke which others could not hear.

Some little boys are upset by such treatment, but the majority become hardened to the experience of teacher–disapproval. The apparent unfairness of it all may even draw boys together in a kind of anti-teacher solidarity.

Girls often escape rebuke, their 'naughty' behaviour fails to get much attention, and so they seek it instead by being 'good.' Girls are significantly more anxious to please the teacher than boys. This is an example of one way teachers' own expectations can become self-fulfilling, as children learn to respond in the way that seems to be expected of them.

So girls are 'officially' in favour, and boys are expected to give more trouble, but this doesn't mean that teachers prefer girls. On the contrary they somewhat despise girls' conformity, and find boys more 'lovable' because they are 'baddies.' When teachers give them more time and attention, the naughty attention-seeking behaviour is reinforced again, in a circular self-perpetuating process which becomes the laid-down pattern of interactions in mixed classrooms.

Learned Helplessness

Teachers' preference for boys may also affect their judgment of pupils' ability. They know that girls do better as a group, but tend to explain away or devalue their achievement—'girls are only good at arithmetic, but weak on concepts'. They are more impressed by the 'brightest' boys in the class, and seem to think that boys are potentially more able:

> Although girls seem to be good at most things, in the end you find
> that it's a boy who's going to be your most brilliant pupil.
> (Clarricoates, 1978).

Just because girls are always assumed to be more highly-motivated, their mistakes and failures are put down to sheer stupidity, while boys in the same position are thought to be just lazy or playing up. In one study teachers attributed boys' failures to 'lack of motivation' *eight* times more often than they did with girls.

One consequence is that boys are less discouraged by failure: they are told and believe that what they need to do is try harder or pay attention next time. This excuse is not made available to girls, and even small mistakes make them feel inadequate. In the long term they will avoid new and difficult work, for fear of being shown up as 'dim.' Hence their over-reliance on verbal skills, in which they still feel sure of themselves.

Boys learn persistence and become more confident; girls are initiated into 'learned helplessness'; their preference for language-based modes of learning does not help them to cope with other modes, e.g. numerical or visuo-spatial, and their tendency to be 'good' deprives them of adult attention. Secondary school teachers are less likely to know girls' names.

Maths and Science

At 11, girls and boys score equally well on a test of science knowledge, but their attitudes are already strongly differentiated: girls are much less interested than boys in physical science topics such as 'how electricity is produced,' 'nuclear power,' 'different kinds of rocks' or 'atoms and molecules' (GIST, Initial Survey, 1981). Even earlier at the age of 7, children see science as an essentially masculine domain. It is unlikely that anyone actually taught those views, so we must suppose they are picked up incidentally; that is why introducing primary science or technology, while a step in the right direction, is not sufficient in itself.

A number of studies have shown that children's stereotypes are most rigid when it comes to occupations. The classic example is the small girl who insisted that women could not be doctors, only nurses, even though her own mother was a qualified GP! That small social fact was completely outweighed by the picture of the world she had gained by other means.

It is in the child's picture of the social world that the primary-based teacher can do most to promote change. More and more women are breadwinners, not always by choice; more and more men are beginning to find pleasure and satisfaction in cooking, child care and looking after the home. We can already see the need for adults of both sexes who are flexible, competent, independent and self-confident as well as caring and sensitive. By expanding our definition of what it means to be 'masculine' or 'feminine,' we may also succeed in fulfilling the important educational aim of broadening the possibilities and opportunities for both girls and boys.

References

CHASEN, B. (1975) 'Sex role stereotyping and pre-kindergarten teachers' in INSEL, P. and HACOBSEN, L. (Eds) *What Do You Expect? An Inquiry into Self-fulfilling Prophecies*, Cummings.

CLARRICOATES, K. (1978) 'Discussions in the classroom—A re-examination of some aspects of the 'hidden curriculum' in primary schools', *Women's Studies International Quarterly*, 1, pp 353–64.

KELLY, A. *et al* (1981) *Initial GIST Survey*, Manchester Polytechnic.

The Curriculum in and for a Multicultural Society: Policy and Perspectives

Keith Kimberley

Changing Perspectives on the Curriculum

Among teachers and those who make policy for schools at the level of local and central government, there seems to be a general consensus that the school curriculum should be related both to the present state of society and to hopes for its future and that curricular aims should be framed within this broad agreement. There is, however, far less agreement on how to read, or interpret, the society in which we live, and open disagreement on the values which should inform the future shaping of society.

Not least difficult for those involved in education in the last two decades has been the problem of deciding on the degree of responsiveness to be accorded to diversity. Consider this key statement on the curriculum from the DES in *The School Curriculum* which brings to the foreground these 'issues' as worthy of special mention:

> First, our society has become multicultural; and there is now among pupils a greater diversity of personal values. Second, the effect of technology on employment patterns sets a new premium on adaptability, self-reliance and other personal qualities. Third, the equal treatment of men and women embodied in our law needs to be supported in the curriculum. (DES, 1981)

Now consider this discussion of the complex patterns of attainment of children of different classes and groups by Mortimore and Mortimore written for the ILEA:

> The policy of the ILEA has been to prepare all pupils and students for life in what has become a multicultural society, and, whilst taking care not to overemphasize cultural diversity, has sought to

Reproduced from GUNDARA, J. *et al.*, (Eds) (1986) *Racism, Diversity and Education*, Hodder and Stoughton.

build on its strengths. This is in line with the argument that what is needed is a multicultural curriculum which 'is a perfectly natural response to the altered nature of British society and, for many teachers, to the cultural composition of the classes they teach'. (ILEA, 1983a)

At one level, the two approaches look similar. They share an assumption which perceives Britain as having *become* multicultural. (This appears to imply that British society was in the past not multicultural until some recent event—presumably the advent in large numbers of visible minorities.) Similarly, they share the use of the term 'multicultural', using it as an umbrella to encompass a variety of dimensions.

At another level, there are substantial differences, as might be expected given the radically different contexts from which the two documents come. By contrast with the DES emphasis on the expression of diversity in terms of *personal* values and the impact of future employment/unemployment patterns on individuals, the Mortimores' paper puts emphasis on the preparation of 'all pupils and students for life in a multicultural *society*'. In this they follow the major shift in thinking of the late 1970s which asserted the importance of reviewing the curriculum for *all* students in *all* schools and which in the 1980s has become an organizing principle in the Swann Report, *Education for All* (DES, 1985). The ILEA document is also distinct from that of the DES in the implicit acknowledgment that, in the real world, the formulation of policy is concerned with difficult problems of selection and balance. For example, 'Whilst taking care not to overemphasize cultural diversity, has sought to build on its strengths' suggests a practical understanding of the curriculum decision-making process.

The difficult and delicate decisions referred to above affect all teachers and it is both the virtue and the vice of a devolved system of responsibilities for the curriculum that much responsibility is located at the level of the classroom. Teachers, at the time of writing, are particularly aware of pressures on them from a variety of sources, which they ultimately have to resolve in terms of the content they select and the approaches they adopt.

There is increasing pressure from central government as it makes moves to define, prescribe and impose a national curriculum. There is pressure from LEAs for schools to give information to meet DES demands for curriculum statements and the LEAs' own policy requirements. In many areas, there is pressure from parents and community pressure groups to which teachers are often uncertain how to respond. Often teachers are called on to decide between rival proposals for content, or between conflicting interpretations of reality. Sometimes they have to choose between contradictory messages from central government, LEA and local community. This is perhaps what Jenkins and Shipman have in mind when they describe the curriculum in terms of 'transactions' at a 'trading post ... on the cultural boundary between generations, between sexes, and between cultures' where 'all the value dilemmas of the pluralistic society find their expression ... This means that the trading post isn't simply on the boundary between generations but also between competing ideologies with society' (Jenkins and Shipman, 1976).

Another way of viewing current concerns is to suggest that the curriculum always has been a point at which conflicting values and competing ideologies in society have been 'magically' resolved—usually in favour of maintaining existing routes to knowledge and privilege. What has changed, perhaps, is the sense of sureness that teachers know what to select from the culture and how to relate what happens in schools to the 'needs' of society. Willey takes this argument further by arguing that:

> The presence of minority ethnic groups in Britain has had the effect of raising questions which have fundamental implications for the very nature of the schooling which is provided. Post-war, black immigration has thrown into sharp relief many of the basic issues inherent in the development of UK education over the last thirty years. (Willey, 1982)

In this view of schooling and hence the curriculum, it is not that society has 'become multicultural' but that the presence of visible and resistant minorities has brought into the open the 'basic issues' which divide society.

Education In and For a Multicultural Society

The difficulties involved in attempts to resolve within the curriculum the conflicting social and economic relationships, attitudes and values which exist in society at large find representation in the very language used. When we talk of educating students 'in and for a multicultural society', the phrase has encoded within it the shifts in perspectives and priorities of recent educational history.

The formula generally used here, 'in and for a multicultural society', has the advantage of ensuring that the debate makes problematic the nature of society itself. It makes the focus for rethinking the curriculum explicit; implies the need for tackling also the institutional structures within which the curriculum is experienced; and raises, though it does not resolve, the tricky relationship between schooling and the 'needs' of society.

The term 'multicultural', despite its useful portmanteau nature, is, however, much limited by its recent history. Classrooms, or schools, have been defined as 'multicultural'. This has meant variously that the teachers thought the self-image of ethnic minority students needed to be supported; that advantage was to be taken of the presence in the classroom of students whose cultural background was different to widen the perspectives of the majority; or, quite crudely, that anyone looking in through the classroom door would see that the class was not predominantly white. Each of these meanings and contexts denies the application of 'multicultural' to *all* classrooms. In the first two of these narrow definitions, 'multicultural' is perceived as a perspective in which the supposed needs of certain ethnic groups provides the organizing principle or, when the implications for all children are considered, it is perceived in terms of how children can benefit from encounters with such 'interesting' bits of custom, language or religion as their fellow students can offer. In the third example, 'multicultural' has become equated simply with being visibly different.

These usages have created considerable confusion and generated the idea that there actually are kinds of education which can be called 'multicultural' rather than a need for responses within education to the historical and continuing diversity of British society. Equally dangerous has been the implication that the only place where change is needed is in schools where specific ethnic 'minorities' are visibly present. Ethnicity has been proposed solely in terms of the ethnicity of 'minorities'. This has had the effect of preventing people seeing the implications for mainstream culture of contact between languages and cultures and hence of recognizing that intercultural contact is reciprocal by nature. Each culture affects and reshapes others with which it comes into contact. Cultures in contact do not remain static but are subject to continual change.

Redefining Multicultural Education

Davis (1981) argues, multicultural education needs to be redefined as the transmission of worthwhile concepts, skills, attitudes, values and principles through the selection of content which is chosen from at least the range of cultures to be found in British society. He is particularly scathing on the subject of 'topics on cultures', asking how any teacher can *do* the West Indies in five weeks and Asian culture in half a term. 'Before teachers do this kind of work they really ought to prepare a five week topic on English culture and having seen the results, should abandon the model' (*ibid*).

This redefinition of multicultural education offers an answer to those who have been critical of its proponents' failure to face up to the racism inherent in prevailing white ethno-centric perspectives, and in the structures of British society, since for Davis worthwhile concepts, skills, attitudes, values and principles are those which are conceptually strong enough to expose and deal with racism and related inequalities based on sex and class in both personal and institutional contexts. A *multicultural* education then becomes a 'good' education for all students in all places, one that is likely to be based on a rethinking of all that is taught in relation to its appropriateness and contribution to the development of a more equal, less discriminatory society.

'A Perspective Emphasising Primarily Equality'

What needs to be emphasized at this stage in the argument is that beyond a certain point the reinterpretation of the multicultural paradigm becomes less satisfactory than its replacement by alternative formulations. This is the view expressed in Berkshire's Discussion Paper (1981) which has also been adopted by the ILEA as 'a policy for equality' (ILEA, 1983,c, d, f). In it the specific criticisms from the black community have been brought together with a more fully developed understanding of what is involved in tackling racism in its structural as well as attitudinal dimensions than was apparent in the late 1970s when the first 'multicultural' policies were framed. What is also apparent in the case of the ILEA is a determination simultaneously to tackle issues concerning class and gender.

In this perspective, the dehumanizing effect of racism on white people, giving them distorted views of their identity, society and history, is put alongside the web of discriminatory policies, practices and procedures which constitute institutional racism for black people. Both the ideological and the structural components, it is argued, must be tackled if racism is to be dismantled.

Richardson (1982) elaborates the implications for the curriculum of this perspective. He emphasizes the problematic nature of the relation between what goes on in school and the direction taken in society.

> Changes in society do not necessarily have to be accepted or welcomed in schools and neither in schools nor in society should changes be considered independently of the distribution of power and, therefore, of questions about whose material interests are being promoted, and whose are being challenged.

Against the DES (1977) Green Paper *Education in Schools* view that the curriculum 'should reflect a sympathetic understanding of the different cultures and races that now make up our society', he proposes an 'Alternative Green Paper' framed in the following terms:

> Our society contains conflicts of interest between social classes, between the sexes, between generations, between the dominant, mainly racist white majority on the one hand and ethnic minorities of Asian or Caribbean background on the other. Within world society as a whole, Britain's ruling élite is part of the North: it is in economic conflict with the South, and actively colludes with and benefits from patterns of repression and exploitation in Third World countries. As part of the West it is in conflict also with the East, and wastes vast sums of money on armaments. The curriculum of our schools should help pupils and teachers and the local authorities to which they belong, to understand the power structures in which they participate as victims or as beneficiaries,

and should help them develop commitment to, and practical skill in working from their various positions towards greater equality, peace and justice, locally, nationally and internationally. (Richardson, 1982)

Policy and Planning

So far the discussion has been in terms of shifts of perception and emphasis and has been of most relevance to the formulation of aims for the curriculum. This next section considers responses being made at the levels of DES, LEAs, and schools.

Department of Education and Science Responses

There is little indication at the time of writing in DES statements on the national curriculum that it is a key priority for those taking stock of the curriculum to analyze ways in which the British version of a multicultural society comes to have such deeply embedded inequalities based on race, class and gender in its daily life, ways of thinking and institutional structures. It will be a matter of continuing importance to see in what ways the Secretary of State for Education responds to the recommendation in *Education for All* that:

> The response of schools, both 'multi-racial' and 'all white', to cultural diversity has to be seen as a central feature of the current debate on the balance and breadth of the school curriculum. The Secretary of State should focus on this issue when considering responses to DES Circular 8/83 and in any further statements that he may make and any agreements that he may seek about the curriculum. (DES, 1985)

Local Educational Authority Responses

The LEAs, as might be expected, do not present a consistent policy position on the appropriate curriculum for a multicultural society ... approaches range from those which see multicultural education as an add-on component to existing arrangements to those which propose a curriculum generated from the principles of equality and social justice. A growing number of LEAs now have publicly available policy documents but only a few of these are as far-reaching in their implications as those adopted by the Royal County of Berkshire and the ILEA.

It is, perhaps, valuable to consider what these two LEAs have to say about curriculum issues as their positions take the argument for change further than central government has yet been prepared to venture and they can be seen as offering an ideological challenge to those LEAs and schools who are reluctant even to begin the process of rethinking the curriculum.

Berkshire's *Education for Racial Equality* (Berkshire, 1983) sets out the values on which the policy is based, the programme of activities which are implied for teachers, the support to be provided, and the arrangements to be made for monitoring progress. The key curriculum question asked is: 'which topics in primary schools and which subjects and syllabuses in secondary schools are most relevant for developing understanding of racial equality and justice?' Teachers are challenged as to when and where in their schools pupils were likely to be learning, directly or indirectly, about concepts or themes such as: diversity, similarity, justice, civilization, migration, racism, colonialism, resistance, interdependence.

A similar, though slightly less intellectually threatening approach is taken in the ILEA's *A Policy for Equality* (ILEA, 1983c, d) which has as one of its components an anti-racist statement together with a set of guidelines for practice. It is recognized in this document that there can be no one blueprint but rather a set of 'principles, directions and methods for development' (ILEA, 1983d). As with the Berkshire policy, ILEA teachers are challenged to sort out their own positions in relation to racism and culture and then to develop a curriculum guided by the following four principles:

(i)   Very young children need both an affirmation of the value of people of all colours and cultures and to be helped towards avoidance of stereotypes and misrepresentations which form at a very early age.

(ii) A wide range of content is important but it is vital that pupils develop analytical skills and can engage in an understanding of cross cultural perspectives and values.

(iii) Pupils and students must have opportunities to gain an historical perspective that is free from ethnocentric biases.

(iv) The whole curriculum must be open to all so that no sort of restricted access is given to some pupils because of stereotyped views of ability (ILEA, 1983d).

School Responses

It is, as yet, one of the most remarkable features of the UK educational system that change can be set in motion in individual schools without having to wait for external directives from DES or LEAs, ... This freedom is accompanied by responsibilities to test out changes that are proposed against the best knowledge available, and to listen to the views of students, parents, governors and others closely involved in the community. An example of this can be seen where concern both to counter the racism experienced by black students and to deter any young people from joining white racist groups has led parents, teachers and other interested people to come together to discuss the ways in which schools can contribute to tackling racism. Some primary and secondary schools have, on this basis, developed policies for tackling racism which have made explicit to all concerned, teachers, students and parents, the value system from which the school is operating...

Conclusion

The important issue in the continual re-making of the curriculum is whether it functions to highlight and analyze the underlying inequalities which are such crucial features of contemporary life, or whether its construction ensures that such uncomfortable contradictions are suppressed. Our success in facing up to the difficulties that have to be tackled will show very clearly in the school curriculum. It makes visible the response that society makes to its diversity either by creating space and giving recognition or by resisting any incursions. It also makes visible, since the curriculum is, theoretically, based on principled choices, the value systems of the society at large. It shows up how far there is real interest in enabling students to develop 'lively enquiring minds'. It reveals the ambiguities of what is meant by the 'instilling' of 'respect for religious and moral values' and 'tolerance [*sic*] of other races, religions and ways of life'. Crucially, it exposes whether the stated intentions of helping students 'to understand the world in which they live' (DES, 1981) extends to *all* the facts—including the uncomfortable ones.

References

BERKSHIRE LEA (1981) 'Education for equality', paper presented to the Advisory Committee on Multicultural Education, Berkshire.

DAVIS, G (1981) 'Assumptions underlying current practices in multicultural education', paper presented to the Research Seminar of the Centre for Multicultural Education, University of London Institute of Education.

DEPARTMENT OF EDUCATION AND SCIENCE (1977) *Education in Schools: A Consultative Document*, HMSO.

DEPARTMENT OF EDUCATION AND SCIENCE (1981) *The School Curriculum*, HMSO.

DEPARTMENT OF EDUCATION AND SCIENCE (1985) *Education for All* (The Swann Report), HMSO.

INNER LONDON EDUCATION AUTHORITY (1983a) *Race, Sex and Class: 1 Achievement in School*, ILEA.

INNER LONDON EDUCATION AUTHORITY (1983b) *Race, Sex and Class: 2 Multiethnic Education in Schools*, ILEA.

INNER LONDON EDUCATION AUTHORITY (1983c) *Race, Sex and Class: 3 A Policy for Equality and Race*, ILEA.

INNER LONDON EDUCATION AUTHORITY (1983d) *Race, Sex and Class: 4 Anti-racist Statement and Guidelines*, ILEA.

INNER LONDON EDUCATION AUTHORITY (1983e) *Race, Sex and Class: 5 Multiethnic Education in Further, Higher and Community Education*, ILEA.

INNER LONDON EDUCATION AUTHORITY (1983f) *Race, Sex and Class: 6 A Policy for Equality: Sex*, ILEA,

JENKINS, D. and SHIPMAN, M. (1976) *Curriculum: An Introduction*, Open Books.

RICHARDSON, R. (1982) 'Culture and justice: Key concepts in world studies and multicultural education' in HICKS, D. and TOWNLEY, C. (Eds) *Teaching World Studies*, Longman.

WILLEY, R. (1982) *Teaching in Multicultural Britain*, Longmans for the Schools Council.

Children with Special Needs in Primary Schools

Ann Lewis

There are broadly, two views concerning the term 'special educational needs' (SEN). One is that SEN refers to learning difficulties and that children with learning difficulties have distinct educational needs. Previously these were thought to be the result of deficits within the child, more recently learning difficulties have been seen as the result of a combination and interaction of factors related to the child, the home and the school. An alternative view is that it is artificial and unhelpful to treat one group of children as requiring different teaching and learning strategies from other children, and the term special educational needs is used generically to encompass all children. This second view stresses that teaching is about observing individual children, matching learning opportunities to the child and critically reflecting on the results. The former view has dominated SEN work in Britain up to the present time and represents the focus adopted in this chapter.

Developments Since 1980

A major, legislative change in this period has been the 1981 Education Act. This Act came into force on 1 April 1983 and defined a child with SEN as a child who 'has a learning difficulty which calls for special education provision to be made for him' (para 1(1)). Section 1(2) of the Act states that a child over 5 years old has a learning difficulty if 'he has a significantly greater difficulty in learning than the majority of children his age; or he has a disability which either prevents or hinders him from making use of educational facilities of a kind generally provided in schools, within the area of the local authority concerned, for children of his age.' The latter part of this statement proposes that a child's needs are seen as relative to the resources normally available to him. It takes into account that a child who has SEN in one LEA or even school, might not exhibit those needs in a different LEA or school. The 1981 Act recognized that learning or behavioural difficulties are not solely the result of factors relating to the child but are also, some would argue only, a function of the school environment. The requirement that children with learning difficulties be assessed in terms of their needs contrasted with previous practice which had been to define children with SEN in terms of categories of handicap.

The Act also requires LEAs to produce a statement on each child thought to have SEN that require access to resources which are not normally available to all children. The formal written statement is 'maintained by the authority showing a child's SEN as assessed by the authority, the special education provision which the authority deems necessary and the school or other arrangements considered appropriate to meet those needs' (Smith, 1985, page ix). Educational psychologists (EPs) have a substantial role in compiling information for statements and the number of EPs has reportedly increased by 20 per cent since the Act came into force (TES, 1986a).

The 1981 Act was an attempt to incorporate a number of themes promoted in the Warnock Report (DES, 1978a) and the Act does represent official recognition of the desirability of integrated education in principle. It can now be asked, given that it is nine years since the publication of the Warnock Report and over four years since the 1981 Act came into force, has the Act led to changes?

At best the 1981 Act has encouraged genuine integration. In some LEAs this was happening in the 1970s and the Act provided a focus and justification for these policies. In rural authorities the incidence of integration was relatively high even before the 1981 Act was passed as the geographical dispersal of the school population meant that transporting children to special schools was too expensive or timely to be feasible. The range of published accounts (for example Hegarty *et al.* 1982) illustrates the diversity of responses to the Act. The overwhelming conclusion from these reports is that integration can work successfully but it requires good resourcing and staff commitment to integration. However there is a need to extend full and part-time integration projects to more schools and to widen the integration projects beyond the personal contacts from which they have, largely very successfully, begun.

It appears that the Act has not been used merely to provide special education cheaply even though it is clearly less costly in the short term for an LEA to provide a mainstream school place than a special school place if no additional resources such as a classroom auxiliary are made to the mainstream school. Recent DES statistics (DES, 1985a) show that the net recurrent institutional expenditure per full-time pupil for 1982–83 was £730 for each primary school pupil, £1015 for those in secondary schools and £3265 for each special school pupil.

Evidence on the overall extent of integration in England and Wales following the passing of the 1981 Act, on the basis of DES statistics, suggests that full-time integration is not as widespread as reports by enthusiasts might suggest. It would seem that children with sensory handicaps (eg hearing impairment) are being integrated on a wider scale than previously. However, many children classified as having moderate learning difficulties and/or behavioural difficulties are still being nominally placed in segregated special schools (Swann, 1985; Lewis, 1986a). It seems probable that although full-time integration has not increased markedly for children from special schools, there is an increasing range and number of partial integration programmes. The phrase 'partial integration programmes' refers to schemes in which children are nominally based in a special school or unit but regularly attend mainstream school classes for part of the week, for example for one half day. Partial integration programmes are providing a valuable transition from a completely segregated system to relative, although not total, integration.

In spite of the support for integration embodied in the 1981 Act it has not been wholeheartedly welcomed. It has been criticized as 'grossly inadequate' (NUT, 1982) for lacking the muscle to enhance educational provision for all children with SEN. Aspects which were omitted from the Act include: provision for children with SEN at pre-school and further education levels, requirements concerning teacher training for children with SEN and additional resources to implement the Act. The Act has also been criticized for an emphasis on those children thought to require SEN statements, that is those traditionally placed in segregated special schools, and a neglect of the large number of children identified as having SEN in primary and secondary schools. Cooke (1985) has argued that a substantial weakness in the Act was the failure to require the establishment of a National Advisory Committee for Children with Special Educational Needs as had been recommended in the Warnock Report (para 16.47).

The Act has also been criticized on quite different grounds by those who feel that a separate Act to make provision for children with SEN is misguided in principle. (For example the Children's Legal Centre (CLC) 1985 'There is clearly a sense in which having separate legislation ... applying only to children and young people with SEN is, in some sense, in itself discriminatory'). Tutt (1986) has warned that the change from 'handicap' to 'needs' still reflects deterministic thinking and an assumption that disability equals need. Tutt argues that whilst 'the concept of needs may be useful in professional discussion, it is totally inappropriate, inadequate and detrimental when allied with the bureaucratic structures of service delivery' (p 30). He supports his argument by drawing parallels between the 1981 Education Act and the 1969 Children's and Young Person's Act. It is argued that in both cases the clients receive a worse rather than a better service and that needs theory focusses attention on the individual and not the situation in which the individual is operating.

There seems to be considerable variation between LEAs in the extent to which the demands of the Act are being met. At worst it has led to, or sustained, complacency, evasion of responsibility and breaking of the law

(CLC, 1985). It is argued in some quarters that the Act has done a disservice to children identified as having SEN. The ending of the old SE procedure and categories of handicap has removed a statutory procedure which gave some obligation to provide special educational placements. Without the label of a specific handicap LEAs may more easily claim that the child's needs are being adequately met in the ordinary classroom. Whether or not this is the case depends on how far individual needs are met without the legal backing of a formal statement.

There is evidence to indicate that some LEAs are abusing the statementing procedure (Sharron, 1985; Fish, 1986). Some are making a policy decision to defer statementing until the age of 7 or 8. This is likely to sharpen an integration/segregation division between infant/first schools or departments and junior/middle schools or departments. Other LEAs have been accused of 'standardizing' statements on children instead of writing statements which reflect each child's needs (Sharron, 1985). In addition as the LEA has a legal obligation to provide educational resources to meet the needs of a statemented child a head may try to have as many children as possible statemented in order to obtain more resources although these resources may not be used for 'statemented' children (Fish, 1986).

The 1981 Act has been the most significant change concerning SEN in recent years. However at present the implications of the Act are barely beginning to filter through into mainstream primary schools. Perhaps it is too soon to expect to see the results of the legislation on a wide scale. Effective change in education is notoriously slow but we are seeing shifts towards greater inter-professional teams in which members of different professional groups (for example educational psychologists, peripatetic services and mainstream teachers) work closely together, a questioning about special education and experiments with different patterns of integration. Concern is, rightly, shifting from arguments about 'integration or segregation?' to 'what is the most effective education for individual children?'.

A second change affecting the teaching of children with SEN in primary schools concerns in-service training. The need to extend training in SEN at both initial and in-service levels was one of the recommendations put forward by the Warnock Report (DES, 1978a). The period since 1980 has seen considerable expansion in both LEA and higher education initiatives related to training for SEN in ordinary schools (SENIOS) in spite of the omission of teacher training from the 1981 Act. Some LEAs have developed authority wide schemes, often for designated special needs personnel in every school (for example Muncey and Ainscow, 1983; Dawson, 1985).

The provision of specific funds from the DES for in-service training of special needs personnel has supplemented LEA initiatives. The DES funding was specifically for one term courses and began in 1983. Funding has been reduced since that date, despite the welcome given to the courses.

There is clearly a considerable need for in-service training as is illustrated by the extent of reservations about teaching children with special needs found in recent research (Hedderley, 1983; Thomas, 1985). Croll and Moses (1985) in research carried out in 1982, found that a substantial percentage of the 423 junior school teachers interviewed were reluctant or refused to integrate children with various handicaps in the ordinary classroom. The percentages of class teachers reluctant or refusing to have children with SEN in the ordinary class ranged from 48 per cent concerning ESN(M) (sic) children and 31 per cent concerning children in a wheelchair, to 16 per cent concerning children with partial hearing. On the other hand nearly 8 per cent and 23 per cent of these teachers were enthusiastic about integrating ESN(M) or partially hearing children respectively. Nearly half of the teachers who were reluctant or refused to have ESN(M) children in their own classes had had this experience. Teachers who had had experience of integrating children with a handicap, whatever the specific handicap, were more enthusiastic about integration of that group than teachers without that experience. Croll and Moses report that the teachers in their survey tended to see the children's difficulties as innate and not as related to the teacher's behaviour. One concomitant of this was a pessimism about the educational potential of the child. If integration is to be carried out effectively there is a need for relevant training to extend: (a) beyond one member of staff in each school even if he/she is the designated SEN postholder (b) to the head and (c) to administrators and advisers.

Changes in initial teacher training have also taken place. A number of DES documents have pointed to the need for more attention to be paid in initial teacher training courses to the teaching of children with SEN and this is included in the criteria for accreditation of teacher training courses (DES, 1984). When the accreditation procedure is complete then, in theory at least, all newly trained teachers will be equipped to cater for children with a wide range of SEN within mainstream classes. When the effects of this, combined with the results of INSET programmes described above, are felt in the schools then the way will be open for an effective increase in integration. It is right that training initiatives precede wide scale integration. If it was otherwise then educationalists would rightly complain of forced and hasty integration into unprepared schools. It remains to be seen how far the training courses described above succeed in promoting effective integration. The ending of most initial special education training (ACSET, 1984) may also promote integration as teachers intending to go into special school teaching will have to spend the early parts of their careers in mainstream schools. These teachers will require special education INSET focussing on knowledge and techniques related to specialized forms of SEN before they transfer to teaching in special schools.

A third change since 1980 related to SEN is the extent to which some of the ideas developed in the special education field have, largely implicitly, been adopted in mainstream education. For example, the goals of education put forward in the Warnock Report on special educational needs (DES, 1978a) have been quoted in a major mainstream curriculum document (DES, 1985b) with the statement that 'these goals apply to all pupils and all types of schools' (p 6). Similarly educational screening procedures of the 1970s which focussed on the early identification of children with learning difficulties have highlighted the importance of matching appropriate work to the needs of individual children. The importance of 'match', first mentioned by HMI in the 1978 Primary Survey (DES, 1978b) is now a central theme of many mainstream curriculum documents.

Thus the major developments since 1980 in connection with children with special needs: the 1981 Act, inclusion and extension of initial and in-service teacher training and the adoption by mainstream education of certain special education developments are all changes which focus on devolving the boundaries between special and mainstream education.

Current Concerns in Relation to Children with Special Needs

A major change in education in England over the past two decades has been the increasing involvement of central government in attempting to influence the direction which schools should take. Recent indications (Patten, 1986) are that the present government aims to increase central control of education still further. The large number of documents concerning the school curriculum produced by the DES and HMI show how both groups have sought to influence curriculum practice although few of these documents have discussed curricular provision in the light of SEN. DES and HMI documents are discussed in several recent publications (Campbell, 1985; Southworth, 1985a and 1985b; Richards, 1986). A number of key themes representing a national agenda for the curriculum and with implications for all spheres emerge from these documents. Some of the common themes will now be discussed and their implications for the curriculum for children with SEN in primary schools considered.

Consistency

Demands for consistency in the school curriculum have been increasing. These imply the need for consistency both within and between schools. Developments such as Croydon's objectives for primary education (Croydon Education Authority, 1985) are one outcome of this concern. These objectives include statements such as the following:

By the end of the infant stage most children should be able to:
    tell the time to within 5 minutes,
    and use the calendar ....
    add, subtract and multiply numbers up to 20 ... (p. 12)

Before leaving primary school at 11 all pupils should have:
carried out basic observation and recording of the weather,
had practical experience of finding out about it
(the local community) (p. 19).

However as Blenkin and Kelly (1983) have pointed out, consistency in aims and objectives does not necessarily lead to consistency in curriculum practice.

Consistency in terms of work across LEAs has been promoted through authority wide initiatives (for example, SNAP (Special Needs Action Programme) in Coventry LEA, (Muncey and Ainscow, 1983); PALMS (Problems in Acquiring Literacy, Meeting Special Needs) in Hampshire LEA (Dawson, 1985). PALMS is a two day course for approximately twenty-five teachers, preliminary activities are carried out over four weeks prior to the course. Day one of the two day full time course focusses on identification of SEN, assessment, match and appropriate teaching programmes predominantly using materials produced within Hampshire LEA. Day two includes work on developing intervention programmes, monitoring, recording, evaluating, language policy, parental involvement, classroom organization and school-based INSET. Post-course work is concerned with the development of school-based INSET, course members are expected to carry out in their own school a similar INSET programme to that which they have just experienced. SNAP similarly aims to train key people (SEN coordinators for each primary school) using materials produced within the LEA. The coordinators then help colleagues in their schools to learn the new approaches. It is not clear whether or not these INSET schemes lead to greater consistency across the LEA in practice, but it seems safe to assume that this is one of the aims of the approaches for their promoters.

Changes in the roles of peripatetic remedial and school psychological services, away from highly individualized client based work and towards systems based approaches also reflect a means of potentially achieving greater consistency in an LEA. In this respect although the changes apparently spring from educational arguments (for example the weaknesses of individual remedial reading tuition, Shearer, 1967; and dissatisfaction with single client child guidance work, Gillham, 1978) they fit closely with the shift in educational politics at both national and local levels. The reversion to a focus on reports on individual children, brought about through the 1981 Education Act, conflicts with attempts by educational psychologists to focus on systems and thereby to increase consistency in an LEA.

In the 1960s and 1970s many LEAs encouraged a range of initiatives and contrasting approaches were explored within individual authorities. This led to a diversity of programmes and enthusiasm for the methods among the teachers by whom they were developed. This diversity has been the envy of American educationalists (for example, Barth, 1980). It is doubtful how far teachers will cooperate with initiatives which originate outside their schools, and even their LEAs. Emphasis should be on approaches to curriculum development such as Campbell's (1985) collegiality model which develop within the school and utilise teachers reflections on their own practice.

Thus consistency is a two-edged sword, it is to be welcomed in that educational practice which hampers learning will, one hopes, be eliminated. However greater consistency across LEAs is likely to lead to conservative practice in education and slow response to change.

Continuity

Calls for continuity in the school curriculum are linked with demands for greater consistency. Continuity implies that there is progression and logical sequence in the curriculum presented to individual pupils as they move through their schooling. A number of the mechanisms being developed to promote consistency will, it is hoped or presumed, also promote continuity, for example, guidelines.

One illustration of this concern is the criticism of work in withdrawal groups for children with learning difficulties unless it clearly relates to work carried out by the class teacher. Remedial reading tuition integrated with the rest of the work of the class was advocated in the Plowden Report (CACE, 1967). Plowden's view reflected research at the time which showed the disadvantages of teaching children with learning difficulties in separate groups, withdrawn from normal classes for part of the day (for example, Shearer, 1967). Both the primary and first school surveys (DES, 1978b and 1982) found a high incidence of withdrawal group teaching; in 41–53 per cent (depending on the age group) of classes and 75 per cent of schools respectively. A review of HMI reports on individual infant and first schools, inspected 1983–1985, illustrates reservations by the inspectorate concerning lack of coordination between remedial and class teachers (Lewis, 1986a).

The use of 'carefully selected and precisely stated teaching objectives' (Ainscow and Tweddle, 1984, p 2) has been strongly advocated in work with children with special needs over the past decade in both special and mainstream schools (Ainscow and Tweddle, 1979; Lewis, 1984). There is research evidence (for example, Freebody and Tirre, 1985) that a step by step approach in which a task is divided into a series of small teaching steps is more effective for children with learning difficulties than a global approach which focusses on a range of skills. However the objectives approach still arouses controversy and is not accepted by all those concerned about children with SEN (Blenkin and Kelly, 1983). Objections have been made on educational (Goddard, 1983) and sociological grounds (Barton and Tomlinson, 1984).

One reason for the increasingly widespread use of the objectives approach in the SEN field may be that it fits closely with the prevailing educational climate. It, in theory at least, focusses on achieving continuity and consistency in practice; matters which lie at the heart of many of the curriculum documents produced by the DES and HMI. A seminal book on the application of the behavioural objectives approach for children with moderate learning difficulties (Ainscow and Tweddle, 1979) cites the need for progression and continuity within the school described, as one of the main arguments for their advocacy of the approach. HMI are not advocating the use of behavioural objectives but they are arguing for greater clarity of teaching intentions.

Breadth

HMI discussion and survey documents from the Primary Survey (DES, 1978b) onwards have expressed a concern with the need for breadth in the primary school curriculum. Breadth both within and across subject areas has been called for. The need for breadth across the curriculum is voiced particularly clearly in a recent document (DES, 1985) in which nine areas of learning and experience are seen as of equal importance. The world of work, CDT and multicultural education are examples of specific fields which schools are being encouraged to incorporate into their curricula. Presumably good teaching in these areas means that all children will receive appropriate teaching. However it is worth emphasizing that the curriculum needs to be planned with all children in mind, including for example the partially sighted, those with severe learning difficulties and the physically handicapped. The CDT curriculum for example would need to include projects which these children could carry out. Work by Kincaid *et al.* (1983) illustrates how science projects can be adapted for children with mild or moderate learning difficulties so that these children are not excluded from this area of the curriculum because, for example, they are unable to tackle abstract problems or to read the workcards.

The curriculum for children with SEN, in both special and mainstream schools has been criticized as being even narrower in range than the traditional mainstream curriculum (Goddard, 1983). Many of the HMI reports on individual special schools and units also illustrate this concern. A large amount of time devoted to the teaching of literacy and numeracy in isolation to children with learning difficulties inevitably means that those children receive a reduced range of activities in other curriculum areas, particularly aesthetic areas and science. For example supplementary reading tuition in primary schools has often been made possible by withdrawing the child from a PE lesson or assembly (Lewis, 1986a). This practice has led children with learning difficulties to receive a narrower curriculum diet than their classmates.

The second aspect of breadth in the curriculum concerns the need for breadth within curricular areas. There has been criticism of narrow teaching of, for example literacy and numeracy, which concentrates on written exercises and neglects oral work and problem solving. Attention has been drawn to this problem in the literature on children with SEN through discussion of psychological models of instruction (*eg.* Haring *et al*, 1978) which emphasize the importance of learners generalizing and adapting skills. Haring *et al.* propose a four stage instructional hierarchy through acquisition, fluency, generalization and application adaptation. Calls for teachers of children with SEN to teach to all levels of the above hierarchy may be seen as demands for greater breadth in the curriculum. If the teaching of mathematics is viewed within Haring *et al's* framework then the learning of, for example, early addition, would encompass the acquisition of early number bonds, fluency in using these, generalizing them through, for example money, time, measuring and weighing activities and applying number bonds in problem solving. Although the starting point is rather different from that of HMI the outcomes in terms of recommendations for teaching are very similar. The two approaches may therefore be seen as complementary responses to the same problem, that is, the focus on too narrow a curriculum for children identified as having SEN.

Match

A recurrent theme in DES and HMI documents is the need for appropriate match, that is the differentiation of work suited to the capabilities of the individual child. This is a concept which is fundamental to primary and special education, indeed for the British Psychological Society (1976) it was the distinguishing feature of special education 'special education is special in so far as it pays particular attention to the match between learner and curriculum' (6.3.)

The application of match is clearly seen in the work on the early identification of children with learning difficulties. This work developed in Britain during the late 1960s and early 1970s. It has been estimated (Lindsay and Pearson, 1982) that by 1982 85 per cent of LEAs used some form of 'early identification' procedure. The term match was not applied in that context however the procedures were essentially about identifying children with SEN as a first stage and, as a second stage, in appropriately matching work to those needs. It is interesting that the former stage of the identification procedure has now been formally abandoned in many LEAs and attention is focussed on the second ('match') stage, (Wedell and Lindsay, 1980; Lewis, 1985), thus drawing attention to the need to amend teaching strategies rather than labelling deficits in the child. If a school has a systematic monitoring programme for all children then early identification procedures are but one element within this, integral to the whole. Some LEAs now have systematic monitoring devices designed for use by classroom teachers at the infant school stage (for example, ILEA's Classroom Observation Profile).

One of the dangers in the current concern with match and differentiation of pupils needs is the possibility that it will be linked with a crude banding of pupils. Mr Stuart Sexton, political adviser to Sir Keith Joseph, was reported (TES, 1983) as saying 'The government is doing its best to encourage setting and streaming at the top end of the primary school'. The dangers of streaming especially for children with learning difficulties who are likely to find themselves labelled as the 'bottom' group are clear from research (for example, Jackson, 1964).

Teacher Expertise

The most effective deployment of teachers, that is the use of teachers in a way which makes maximum use of their particular interests and capabilities, is another recurrent theme in recent HMI and DES publications. One of the mechanisms being suggested to bring this about is an emphasis on the role of the postholder in primary schools. The value of a teacher with responsibility for a curriculum area acting as a consultant to other members of staff has been widely advocated (Campbell, 1985; ILEA, 1985b; Richards, 1986).

The frequency of coordinators for SEN (or 'remedial work') seems to vary substantially between LEAs. In some LEAs (for example, Coventry) every primary school has a named teacher as the special needs coordinator. In some schools this is a scale post, in others responsibility for special needs has been added to a previous responsibility, for example language. In certain schools the named teacher for special needs has no scale post and is, in some cases a part time teacher. Clearly there are considerable disadvantages in the latter. The naming of a SEN coordinator in every school may be a relatively recent development. The primary survey (DES, 1978b) did not cite any postholders for SEN or remedial work in its table of designated scale posts for curricular areas, although these may have been subsumed under language posts.

At its best a good coordinator (or consultant) for any curriculum area, can do much to promote good practice within the school (*ibid*). A SEN consultant should coordinate all SEN work within the school for the full range of SEN including any partial integration programmes, lead revision of relevant school policy, advise colleagues on particular SEN approaches and techniques, liaise with parents and outside agencies working with children with SEN, attend and report back on SEN courses and workshops and, where appropriate, teach children with SEN in collaboration with the class teacher.

Another aspect of the emphasis on teacher expertise and maximizing the use of personnel concerns the use of volunteer helpers in schools. Primary classes, particularly those in infant and nursery schools, now often have several adult volunteers, without formal qualifications or paid posts in the school, working alongside the class teacher (DES, 1978b and 1982). These adults may include parents and retired people (both of these groups may have relevant professional qualifications for work with children in school), YTS pupils, local sixth formers and community service workers. Nursery nurses and non-teaching classroom assistants employed by the LEA also work full-time in classrooms alongside the class teacher. An additional range of support is provided by qualified adults who work intermittently with the class teacher, for example educational psychologists, and school medical services. All of these groups frequently work with children identified as having SEN. Maximization of the use of personnel should extend to providing relevant in-service training for these groups. SEN coordinators could take the lead in this in-service training.

The involvement of a diverse group of classroom helpers, many of whom work with the sub-group of children in the class identified as having SEN, creates a considerable management problem for the class teacher. The teacher is under pressure to be seen to have a clearly organized, systematic and appropriate approach to the teaching of all children but particularly those with whom helpers are working. In some schools a system of daily task cards has been developed for the individual children with whom helpers work. The daily task card is compiled by the teacher and lists the activities and objectives towards which the child is currently working. A helper working with the child collects the card before starting work with the child, commences at the point indicated and makes a comment on how far the child has progressed through the day's activities and objectives when she or he has finished. Another helper or the teacher can then continue from the point indicated. This type of system goes some way towards ensuring that the child benefits from the additional individual or small group help, and that the helpers feel they are working usefully in the classroom and are not being given miscellaneous time-filling jobs.

Implications for the Teaching of Children with SEN

The current concerns in education which have been outlined above and applied to the teaching of children identified as having special needs in primary schools indicate a number of directions which SEN work in primary schools ought to take.

Firstly, primary schools will have to adjust to incorporating children with a wide variety of SEN on a range of partial integration programmes. This will reflect changes in the role of special schools away from the traditional role in which they supplied segregated schooling reflecting a medical model of children with disabilities. Any change of role for special schools will have a knock-on effect on primary and secondary schools. The indications are that the divisive parallel system of special and mainstream schools is being eroded and that pupils identified as having SEN are ceasing to be marginalized. However this does not imply that the end of special schools is in sight. This is clearly not the case.

The consensus of opinion among writers on the future of special schools (for example, Bowers, 1984; Galloway, 1985; ILEA, 1985a) is that the special school should be, and is, taking on an increasing variety of roles. These include the provision of a diverse range of part-time placements, advisory and collaborative work with local schools, assessment functions and SENIOS INSET work. In future there are likely to be partial integration programmes for all but the most profoundly handicapped children. Even children with severe learning difficulties who, prior to 1970, would have been the responsibility of health rather than education departments, are increasingly likely to spend part of their school week in primary schools (Carpenter *et al.*, 1987).

Secondly each primary school will need to develop a curriculum which integrates not children but the curriculum for different pupils. This integrated curriculum (Lewis, 1986b) developed largely within the school and shaped by LEA policy will initially require the SEN coordinator to take on a key role. The integrated curriculum for children with SEN will require:

(i)   an outline of the whole school curriculum;
(ii) focus within this on priorities for children with SEN;
(iii) resources for SEN linked with (ii) above;
(iv) matching of individual children's needs to (i) and (ii); and
(v)   continuous records of progress, reflecting (iv) above.

Thirdly there is a need for greater coordination of SEN services at all levels: within individual schools, within LEAs and across England and Wales as a whole. Many authorities have developed SEN provision in a piecemeal fashion with a variety of schools, units and support services including home tuition. The implementation of the 1981 Act may be the catalyst for a rationalization of services, with optimum, not necessarily total, integration as the goal. This would disentangle the multiplicity of often uncoordinated, SEN approaches and services which burgeoned during the 1960s and early 1970s.

Fourthly parents of children identified as having SEN will, rightly, be in a more powerful position than they have been previously. However there is a danger of a two tier special needs sector developing which cuts across special/mainstream placement arguments. This two tier system will not be based on school placement specifically, although this is related, but on effectiveness of parental pressure to obtain what parents regard as the best education for their child. Many articulate, informed parents are arguing for specific educational programmes for their children. This has occurred in relation to, for example, the dyslexia lobby. These parents are aware of their rights and conscious of the government's legal obligations under the

1981 act. Ironically the dyslexia lobby has used the 1981 Act to support claims for increasing specialist, segregated provision whereas some parents of Down's Syndrome children have used the Act to put pressure on LEAs to provide integrated educational provision for their children (TES, 1986b). However as Pring (1983) has noted 'All children matter, not just those whose parents have learnt to play the market effectively' (p 1).

All parents should have access to a SEN consultant who will outline the available educational alternatives in an unbiased way, neither suggesting that the special school is automatically a 'good' placement nor that the local primary school is necessarily the best option. This role is partly carried out, in many authorities, by an AEO for special education for whom liaison with parents is one of his/her roles. However, realistically such a role constitutes a full time job in an LEA. A voluntary SEN consultancy service has been set up to which any parent in the country may go for advice. This suggests that there is a need for such a service. A National Advisory Committee on Children with Special Educational Needs, as advocated in the Warnock Report but excluded from the 1981 Education Act might partly fill this role.

The professionalization of pressure groups within SEN has developed in recent years, particularly in relation to children with physical or sensory handicaps or severe learning difficulties. Parents of children in these groups are predominantly from 'middle class' backgrounds in contrast to the poorer backgrounds of parents of children in other special education sectors. The professionalization of pressure groups is likely to continue and to accelerate if government spending on education is perceived as declining further. Groups such as RADAR, Elfreda Rathbone Society, AFASIC, British Dyslexia Association and RNID are increasingly involved in issuing publications and running courses oriented to teachers working with children with specific sub-groups of SEN. The result of the development of these pressure groups is likely to be a segmentation of special needs into higher status groups with active and wealthy pressure groups and lower status special needs groups who lack such representation.

Conclusion

Discussion about the teaching of children with SEN since 1980 has inevitably been dominated by the integration debate. An advantage of the sharpened focus which the integration debate has brought to the topic is the way in which it has highlighted the value judgments underlying SEN. However a disadvantage is that is has skewed discussion towards a minority of children with marked physical, sensory or learning difficulties and neglected the vast majority of children with SEN who are now, and have been, in mainstream schools. For the future, let us learn from the rethinking about special education which was occurred and focus on considerations about effective provision for individual children.

Acknowledgement

My thanks to Colin Richards for his facilitative comments on a draft of this chapter.

References

ACSET (ADVISORY COUNCIL FOR THE SELECTION AND EDUCATION OF TEACHERS) (1984) *Teacher Training and Special Educational Needs*, June.
AINSCOW, M. and TWEDDLE, D. (1979) *Preventing Classroom Failure: An Objectives Approach*, Wiley.
AINSCOW, M. and TWEDDLE, D. (1984) *Early Learning Skills Analysis*, Wiley.
BARTH, R. S. (1980) *Run School Run*, Harvard University Press.
BARTON, L. and TOMLINSON, S. (1984) *Special Education and Social Interests*, Croom Helm.
BLENKIN, G and KELLY, V. (1983) *The Primary Curriculum in Action*, Harper and Row.
BOWERS, T (Ed) (1984) *Management and the Special School*, Croom Helm.
BRITISH PSYCHOLOGICAL SOCIETY (1976) 'Summary of evidence presented to the Warnock Committee', *Bulletin of the British Psychological Society*, 29. pp. 1–6.
CAMPBELL, R. J. (1985) *Developing the Primary School Curriculum*, Holt, Rinehart and Winston.
CARPENTER, B., LEWIS, A. and MOORE, J. (1987) 'An integration project involving young children with severe learning difficulties and mainstream first school children', *Mental Handicap*, 14(4) pp. 152–7.
CENTRAL ADVISORY COUNCIL FOR EDUCATION (CACE) (1967) *Children and Their Primary Schools* (The Plowden Report), HMSO.
CHILDREN'S LEGAL CENTRE (CLC) (1985) 'The flaws in the 1981 Act', paper given at the International Congress on Special Education, Nottingham, July.
COOKE, G. (1985) 'Warnock—What now?' *NAPE Journal*, 16, pp. 4–5.
CROLL, P. and MOSES, D. (1985) *One in Five*, Routledge and Kegan Paul.
CROYDON EDUCATION AUTHORITY (1985) *Primary Education in Croydon: A Guide for Parents*, Croydon, Croydon Education Authority and the Voluntary School Authorities in Croydon.
DAWSON, R. (1985) 'Special needs INSET in Hampshire', *Education*, 18 October, pp. 351–2.
DEPARTMENT OF EDUCATION AND SCIENCE (1978a) *Special Educational Needs* (The Warnock Report), HMSO.
DEPARTMENT OF EDUCATION AND SCIENCE (1978b) *Primary Education in England*, HMSO.
DEPARTMENT OF EDUCATION AND SCIENCE (1982) *Education 5 to 9*, HMSO.
DEPARTMENT OF EDUCATION AND SCIENCE (1984) *Circular 3/84*, HMSO.
DEPARTMENT OF EDUCATION AND SCIENCE (1985a) *Statistical Bulletin*, September, HMSO.

DEPARTMENT OF EDUCATION AND SCIENCE (1985b) *The Curriculum from 5–16* Curriculum Matters 2. An HMI series, HMSO.

FISH, J. (1986) Paper on the integration of children with special educational needs, Westhill Conference, Birmingham, January.

FREEBODY, P. and TIRRE, W. C. (1985) 'Achievement outcomes for two reading programmes: an instance of aptitude-treatment interaction', *British Journal of Educational Psychology* 55, pp. 53–60.

GALLOWAY, D. (1985) *Schools, Pupils and Special Educational Needs*, Croom Helm.

GILLHAM, B. (Ed) (1978) *Reconstructing Educational Psychology*, Croom Helm.

GODDARD, A. (1983) 'Processes in special education' in BLENKIN, G. and KELLY, V. *op. cit.*, pp. 248–77.

HARING, N. G., LOVITT, T. C., EATON, M. D. and HANSEN, C. L. (1978) *The Fourth R: Research in the Classroom*, Merrill.

HEDDERLEY, R. (1983) 'Monitoring the integration of the disabled child', *British Psychological Society, Division of Educational and Child Psychology, Occasional Papers*, Vol. 7(1) pp. 31–37.

HEGARTY, S. and POCKLINGTON, K. with LUCAS, D. (1982) *Integration in Action*, NFER/Nelson.

ILEA (1985a) *Educational Opportunities for All*, ILEA.

ILEA (1985b) *Improving Primary Schools*, ILEA.

JACKSON, B. (1964) *Streaming: An Education System in Miniature*, Routledge and Kegan Paul.

KINCAID, D., RAPSON, H. and RICHARDS, R. (1983) *Science for Children with Learning Difficulties* Macdonald Educational.

LEWIS, A. (1985) 'Predictive accuracy in early identification procedures', *Cambridge Journal of Education*, 15, 3, pp. 133–8.

LEWIS, A. (1986a) 'Meeting special needs in infant classes—A discussion of evidence from HMI reports on individual schools', *School Organization*, 6, 2, pp. 245–55.

LEWIS, A. (1986b) 'Integration and the curriculum', *Primary Contact*, 4(1) pp. 1–7.

LEWIS, G. (1984) 'A supportive role at secondary level', *Remedial Education*, 10, 1, pp 7–11.

LINDSAY, G. and PEARSON, L. (1982) *Identification and Intervention: School-based Approaches*, TRC.

MUNCEY, J. and AINSCOW, M. (1983) 'Launching SNAP in Coventry,' *Special Education Forward Trends*, 10, 3, pp. 8–10.

NUT (1982) *The Education Act 1981—A Union Guide*, (Revised edition). Education Department, NUT.

PATTEN, C. (1986) Address to AMMA Conference, Cardiff, April.

PRING, R. (1983) 'Privatization in education; RiCE paper. February.

RICHARDS, C. (1986) 'The curriculum from 5 to 16: Background, content and some implications for primary education; *Education 3–13*.

SHARRON, H. (1985) 'LEA "has ignored Act" on child handicap assessments; *Times Educational Supplement*, 8 March.

SHEARER, E. (1967) 'The long term effects of remedial education; *Educational Research* 9, pp. 219–22.

SMITH, C. (1985) *New Directions in Remedial Education*, Falmer Press.

SOUTHWORTH, G. W. (1985a) 'Perspectives on the primary school curriculum; *Cambridge Journal of Education*, 15, 1, pp. 41–9.

SOUTHWORTH, G. W. (1985b) 'Further perspectives on the primary curriculum; *Cambridge Journal of Education*, 15, 3, pp. 139–47.

SWANN, W. (1985) 'Is the integration of children with special needs happening? An analysis of recent statistics of pupils in special schools'. *Oxford Review of Education*, 11, 1, pp. 3–18.

THOMAS, D. (1985) 'The determinants of teachers' attitudes to integrating the intellectually handicapped; *British Journal of Educational Psychology*, 55. pp. 251–63.

TIMES EDUCATIONAL SUPPLEMENT (1983) 18 March

TIMES EDUCATIONAL SUPPLEMENT (1986a) 14 February.

TIMES EDUCATIONAL SUPPLEMENT (1986b) 17 January

TUTT, N. (1986) 'The unintended consequences of integration', *Educational and Child Psychology* 2, 3, pp. 30–8.

WEDELL, K. and LINDSAY, G. (1980) 'Early identification procedures: what have we learned? *Remedial Education* 15, 2, pp. 130–5.

Recommended Further Reading

BOOTH, T., POTTS, P. and SWANN, W. (1987) *Preventing Difficulties in Learning*, Blackwell/Open University Press.

BRENNAN, W. (1982) *Changing Special Education*, Open University.

CLARK, M. M. and GLYNN, E. C. (Eds) (1980) *Reading and Writing for the Child with Difficulties*, University of Birmingham, Educational Review, Occasional Publications, 8.

DEPARTMENT OF EDUCATION AND SCIENCE (1983) *Young Children with Special Educational Needs*, HMSO.

DESSENT, T. (1987) *Making the Ordinary School Special*, Falmer Press.

GIPPS, C., GROSS, H. and GOLDSTEIN, H. (1987) *Warnock's Eighteen Per Cent*, Falmer Press.

GULLIFORD, R. (1985) *Teaching Children with Learning Difficulties*, NFER/Nelson.

HEGARTY S. and POCKLINGTON, K. with LUCAS, D. (1981) *Educational Pupils with Special Needs in the Ordinary School*, NFER/Nelson.

HODGSON, A., CLUNIES-ROSS, L. and HEGARTY, S. (1984) *Learning Together*, NFER/Nelson.

MALE, J. and THOMPSON, C. (1985) *The Educational Implications of Disability*, Royal Association for Disability and Rehabilitation.

SEWELL, G. (1986) *Coping with Special Needs*, Croom Helm.

VAUGHAN, M. and SHEARER, A. (1985) *Mainstreaming in Massachusetts*, Centre for Studies on Integration in Education, and the Campaign for People with Mental Handicaps.

WELTON, J., WEDELL, K. and VORHAUS, G. (1982) *Meeting Special Educational Needs*, Bedford Way Papers 12, University of London.

WOLFENDALE, S. (1987) *Primary Schools and Special Needs*, Cassell.

3
Aspects of the Primary Curriculum

Introduction

As the quotation in the conclusion to Colin Richards' second paper points out, discussion about aspects or elements of the primary curriculum is bedevilled by the problem of language. Whatever language is used carries with it as 'baggage' connotations and assumptions which some primary educationists find uncomfortable, even distasteful. Currently three 'languages' are available: that of subjects, seen by some as having elementary school or secondary school connotations; that of broad areas (such as language or social studies) probably more acceptable to the majority of primary teachers but believed by some to lack rigour and precision; and that of areas of learning and experience (p 56) proposed by HMI but yet to gain wide currency in primary education. For the purposes of this section, the curriculum is analyzed in terms of broad areas—mathematics, language, science, the arts and the social subjects—but with a significant addition to reflect recent developments: microcomputing of potential application across the curriculum. No attempt is made here to provide comprehensive coverage of the primary curriculum nor does any one paper purport to summarize all the important issues in its field. Together they provide an introduction to many of the important curricular developments of the last five years. Yet again, they demonstrate the range of demands now being made on primary education and the need for collective, rather than individualistic, professional action to meet them.

Hilary Shuard provides a brief critique of much (not all) current provision in primary mathematics which she characterizes as being largely based on a transmission style of teaching whereby 'the children's task is more nearly to find out what the teacher is thinking than it is to think out mathematics for themselves' (p 146). She stresses the importance (and the difficulty for teachers) of children gradually constructing mathematical meaning for themselves by reflecting on and discussing their own experiences, much of it first-hand. She argues persuasively that the new technology of calculators, microcomputers and digital watches implies fundamental alteration in the content of primary school mathematics.

John Pearce contends that language is best conceived not as a school subject nor as a broad area of the curriculum but as the medium for all school activity. Consequently, 'the detail of what children are taught, of lesson content in the narrow sense is trivial compared with the language awareness the teacher brings to structuring and managing her pupils' experience (160)'. His paper outlines what that 'language awareness' entails and how it might be acquired through initial and in-service education. He believes that the key to improving children's language is not through getting them to adhere to the grammatical conventions of an out-dated 'bourgeois era' but through the provision of a range of educational experiences richly informed by teachers' understanding of how language functions.

The third contribution charts the emergence of science in recent years as a key area in the primary curriculum and suggests some of the dangers, as well as opportunities, this presents to science as an investigative activity. Michael Day contends that science has developed quantitatively—in that it is taught in many more primary schools than at the time of the national primary survey—but has now reached a 'quality plateau'. A major part of this paper outlines the way forward through encouraging and sustaining enquiry-based approaches in this area. His concluding speculations are particularly interesting. Will greater concern for content isolate science from its investigative basis? Will science give ground to technology, characterized provocatively by the author as 'this young curriculum cousin of science [which] is very much part of the utilitarian thrust of current government thinking'?

Through his initial cautionary tale André Wagstaff's paper adds to the horticultural analogies which have been so characteristic of discussion about primary education. He goes on to describe how microcomputers have been introduced into English primary schools over the last five years and why the potential of the new technology has yet to be realized in terms of children's learning. Valuably, he analyzes various forms of software and their uses. He stresses the importance of a sense of realism and critical appreciation on the part of practitioners and the necessity to set up support structures if primary teachers are to 'begin to put this powerful resource in its proper perspective and use it to enhance children's learning experiences'. He sees the present period as a 'make or break' time for primary microtechnology.

The fifth contribution is taken from a little read, much neglected report, *The Arts in Schools* published by the Calouste Gulbenkian Foundation. It begins by providing a sobering overall assessment of primary arts education; 'There are many [primary] schools where the arts flourish. In every case, the headteacher and other staff appreciate and support them'. But, it goes on to say 'We share the view of HMI that work in the arts in many primary schools is disappointing' (p. 197). Albeit in general terms, it provides pointers to the aims of arts education at the primary stage, the kinds of provision needed and the way key problems might be tackled. It emphasizes the need for schools to develop the full variety of children's intelligence and capabilities in whatever form, artistic or otherwise, they manifest themselves.

Nowhere is the problem of language more evident than in the area of the curriculum variously described as social studies, humanities, topic work, history, geography etc. Here, the Scottish term 'the social subjects' is employed as a shorthand for social sciences, history and geography—areas employing a range of related skills and sharing many of one another's important organizing concepts. Alastair Ross provides an overview of the considerable documentation and the rather less considerable development work in this area over the last twenty years. He distinguishes three main approaches and speculates on future developments. He is anxious about the possible fragmentation of the area and about its possible redefinition in terms of content or subject matter rather than in terms of skills and concepts related to particular social issues and concerns arising from children's experiences and interests.

Issues for Curriculum Development in Primary Mathematics

Hilary Shuard

Education for Change

The primary children of today, and of tomorrow, will live out their adult lives in the twenty-first century. It is the hope of all teachers that what children learn at school will sustain them into adult life, in a variety of ways. Teachers hope that experiences encountered at school will open doors in children's minds to interests, activities and challenges that can continue to be pursued as the young people grow older. Teachers also hope that what is done at school will prove to be useful learning, which will equip children to live in the world in which they will find themselves.

Foretelling the future is always a chancy business, especially in a world which is changing as rapidly as that of today. Perhaps the only thing we can be sure of is that today's children will continue to live in a world of change, and that the ability to cope with change is the life skill that will be the most important skill to them.

Primary mathematics has an important place in all children's experience of schooling, and it is therefore important to ask how far it contributes to education for change, to useful life skills, and to abiding interests and challenges in people's lives. The curriculum of primary mathematics needs to change in a number of ways. It does not take sufficient account of how children learn, nor does it take sufficient account of changes in technology. But more importantly, it does not take sufficient account of the need to prepare children to live in a continually changing world, and to face the challenges of change.

Reproduced from SHUARD, H. (1986) *Primary Mathematics Today and Tomorrow*, SCDC Publications/Longmans.

Teaching Styles

It is still the case that the major model of teaching employed in primary mathematics is that of *transmission*. The teacher has mathematical knowledge, and his or her task is to convey it to the pupils. This is sometimes done by exposition followed by practice, or it is sometimes done by practical work, in a 'guided discovery' mode, in which the children carry out activities which should enable them to 'discover' what the teacher had in mind. This model of teaching has two consequences; first, it makes the children dependent on the teacher—the teacher knows what is right, and the children's work is validated by the teacher's approval. The children's task is more nearly to find out what the teacher is thinking than it is to think out mathematics for themselves. The second consequence is that this model engenders lack of confidence in many teachers, as they privately acknowledge to themselves that their knowledge of mathematics is inadequate for them to be the fount of all wisdom in the subject to their pupils. This often leads to a very narrow teaching style, in which exploratory activity and open questioning by the pupils are not encouraged.

If children are to learn to face challenges with confidence, they need to become independent thinkers, in mathematics as in everything else. Teachers at Kitamaeno School in Japan ask the children to learn to do everything for themselves—including learning how to learn mathematics. The 'investigations movement' values children's own mathematical thinking, and does not expect a 'right answer', but rather looks for honest individual thinking at the level of which a pupil or a group is capable. The work which is now being done on discussion as a teaching method in mathematics enables teachers to understand their pupils' thinking much more clearly than they could do in the style of 'exposition by question and answer'. Recent work on the learning of mathematics gives evidence for a *constructivist* view of learning in mathematics—children gradually construct meaning for themselves, by reflection on their experiences. They need to be given opportunities to reflect and to develop their thinking to a more advanced level in discussion with others who hold different views.

A most important challenge, therefore, in curriculum development in primary mathematics, is to develop styles of teaching which give full value to children's mathematical thinking, and which enable them to think independently with enjoyment and energy, and to develop good attitudes to mathematical problem solving. This is no easy task—teaching styles are much more resistant to change than is mathematical content. Teachers will need to support one another, using their own discussions as a means of learning, during a period of change, and to work together to explore methods of classroom organization that will enable them to develop their teaching.

A further challenge in the development of teaching styles is provided by the 'seven-year difference'. In a top junior class of mixed ability, some children have a fairly full understanding of most aspects of place-value for whole numbers, some children have had this understanding for several years, and are well advanced in their grasp of the decimal system, and others will not understand place-value, even for whole numbers, for several years to come. Similar differences exist for other age groups, and in other topic areas. All these children need activities which will challenge their thinking at their own level.

Processes

If children are to develop as independent mathematical thinkers, teachers need to know what are the processes of mathematical thinking, and how children learn to use them. Only thus can teachers provide activities and topies for investigation which will help children to become more adept at using these processes. Traditionally, the primary mathematics curriculum has been thought of in terms of mathematical content, rather than in terms of the processes of mathematical thinking. In recent years, many processes have been identified, but little is yet known about the stages at which different children become able to use a process such as classification or generalization, and in what situations they are spontaneously used. Much work will be needed in this area, involving both research into children's mathematical thinking and the development of activities which embody different processes.

New Technology

Another major issue in curriculum development is the impact of new technology on primary mathematics. Calculators have become everyday tools in adult life, and the pencil-and-paper algorithms for the 'four rules' are disappearing fast; people now calculate mentally or use a calculator. In school, the pencil-and-paper algorithms are one of the most important bastions of 'transmission' teaching; children have had to be taught the correct ways of doing these algorithms, even though there is evidence that many children are remarkably resistant to learning them, and prefer their own methods. Now, the algorithms are no longer needed as useful life skills—a calculator is always available for computation which a person cannot do in his or her head. This new context for primary mathematics needs to provoke a complete reassessment of the curriculum in the field of number; at present, calculators are largely being used to support the traditional number curriculum, whose major effort was focussed on the pencil-and-paper algorithms.

The removal of the need for children to learn the pencil-and-paper algorithms as tools for use will enable number work to focus on under-standing of the number system, and on using it for problem solving, both within mathematics and wherever else in the curriculum problems occur. In this way, it will become easier for the style of teaching in primary mathematics to move from the 'transmission' model to a 'constructivist' model. However, the pencil-and-paper algorithms for the four rules have been a major, and necessary, element of primary arithmetic for the last 100 years, and it will not be easy for many teachers to grasp that these algorithms are no longer necessary for use, nor that a valid, useful and exciting primary mathematics curriculum is available without them. The new technology of calculation provides the biggest challenge to the content of school mathematics throughout the whole history of compulsory schooling in this country. It is a challenge that must be tackled if the primary mathematics curriculum is not to become 'the sabre-toothed curriculum'—activities that are only done in school, and which have nothing to do with life.

The calculator is a cheap, personal, portable tool which mechanizes one type of mathematical skill. The same cannot yet be said of the computer. Outside school, it is still largely a desk-top machine, and within school it is still an expensive resource that has to be shared between many children. However, this may change within the next ten years. Portable computers the size of an A4 file are already available, although the size of the display limits their use at present, and the cost is still prohibitive for individual use by most people. It is possible, however, that the next generation of primary children may own portable computers in the way that the present generation own calculators.

Even today's computers have much potential in primary mathematics. Both the Turtle graphics aspects of LOGO, and its potential in control technology, give ways in to independent problem posing and problem solving for primary children. Packages now available can mechanize graph drawing and the handling of data, and children can write very short programs of their own to tackle mathematical tasks. Practice activities, when practice is necessary, can also easily be monitored by the computer. All these uses of the computer can only grow in future years, and will open new mathematical doors to children.

Other new developments, such as the digital watch, may change children's environments in such a way as to modify some of their mathematical concepts, giving a different emphasis from that we now take for granted. When a child's first watch is digital, and when it is worn at a very early age, it is dubious how far that child regards the hours as cyclic, in the way that we who were brought up with analogue watches now do. Teaching approaches will need to take account of these continuing developments. Teachers will continue to need to keep up to date with the new technologies that are coming into children's lives, and to adapt their teaching approaches accordingly.

New styles of teaching, and new technology, will also have their impact on content areas other than number. Logic and algebra may become more accessible through computing, both Turtle geometry and the changing environment may change children's perceptions of shape and space, and the increasing sophistication of society, and the increasing ability to handle large amounts of data, bring a new need for understanding of probability and statistics.

Perhaps the chief danger of the impact of new technology on primary mathematics is that it might displace the simple technology of 'practical mathematics', which has developed greatly in the last thirty years. For many years to come, young children will still need to develop their mathematical concepts through counting real things, grouping them into sets, using structural apparatus, measuring, weighing, making shapes, and many other activities. New technology will not provide substitutes for these real experiences, but it does provide supplementary experiences of its own.

Our Changing Society

Primary mathematics is taught within a society which is itself in a state of rapid change. A new awareness of the sexist nature of much traditional practice, and of the disadvantage suffered by minority groups, needs to be reflected in primary mathematics, as well as in other areas of schooling. Much remains to be done here, as it is still the case that girls and boys seem to perform somewhat differently in mathematics in the primary years, and that mathematics can still seem to children not to be a multicultural subject.

It is also now increasingly realized that parents need to be involved in their children's education, in mathematics as elsewhere in the curriculum, and that the school needs to be accountable to the community and to the parents of its children. No longer can curriculum development—especially in mathematics—take place entirely within the school, without reference to the larger community whose children receive their schooling through that ' curriculum.

And it is this that presents the greatest challenge of all. The attitudes of very many adults to mathematics are extremely negative. They regard it as mysterious, difficult, rule-bound and important. As parents, they are anxious that their children will do well at it, and the only way of doing well at it that many of them know is through the hard grind of learning the rules and practising them. Thus, they think that what they want from their children's schools is pages of sums.

Schools will need to take parents into their confidence and help them to understand the need for new ideas and new methods if their children are to succeed in mathematical thinking. Moreover, parents will themselves need to be involved in mathematical thinking if their attitudes are to change; in a few schools already, parents are working alongside children at investigational mathematics, and calculator games learnt at school are being played at home.

Conclusion

Thus, there are a number of major issues that will need to be tackled in curriculum development in primary mathematics in the next few years. These issues can only be addressed through the enthusiasm and hard work of primary teachers; it remains true that 'curriculum development is teacher development'. However forward-looking many primary teachers are at present—and many are very forward-looking—the world is not standing still, and only by continual cooperative forward movement will all who work in primary mathematics education together be able to meet the challenge of primary mathematics today and tomorrow.

Note

Readers are encouraged to read Hilary Shuard's book in full in order to gain a more complete treatment of the research and sources quoted in this brief extract. (*Ed.*)

Language

John Pearce

Vision and Adjustment

The client was finding her optician a touch unhelpful. She had learned of a new type of lens which gave a continuous change in focus, from distance focus in the upper part to leading focus at the bottom. The optician had had one or two patients who found these lenses uncomfortable and thought this one might have been deceived by advertising: he tried to warn her off: 'Some people find them very difficult to get used to. The edges of your field of vision curve away deceptively ... staircases can be quite dangerous ... some of my patients couldn't adjust to them at all ...'. The patient, for her part, insisted. Within three weeks she found, as she expected, that her brain was compensating for the distortions, which at first had been quite disconcerting. A week or two later she was forgetting she wore glasses at all. Before long she had forgotten there had ever been a distortion problem. This capacity of the brain to adjust what it 'sees' has been investigated by scientists (*eg.* Gregory, 1970) and operates in all walks of life.

The nation asks its whole system of primary education to adjust to new lenses from time to time, too. Many primary schools have forgotten what it was like, in the days before the Primary Survey (DES, 1978) to teach no science. A similar adjustive process occurs, on a smaller scale, whenever a primary school has a change of headteacher. This capacity for adjustment and how to manage it are central concerns in subject leadership. Also, primary teaching is undergoing a slow, sustained adjustment from leadership based solely on status to a leadership based on professional expertise. Most forms of in-service training for primary heads seek to widen their perceptions of leadership to give scope for expertise they do not have themselves. In language this is a particularly important and difficult process.

151

Changing Climates and Fixed Opinions

New Directions in Primary Education, the predecessor to this book, did not include a paper on 'language'. The inclusion of one here is indicative of a changed climate, but less so than the appearance of 'language' in a list which includes several conventional curriculum subjects. For language is not just a subject: like eyesight, we all have experience of it, opinions about it—and little or no consciousness of the lenses through which we see. Ask an ordinary working man what he thought language was, what he used it for, and he would be hard put to find an answer of any kind: most likely he would say he had never thought about it. Press him, and he might readily admit to having difficulties with some of the things one has to use language for, like filling in forms or writing a letter or asking the boss for time off for something very personal. And he would know that there are many different ways of speaking outside his range of experience. But the idea that language operates to structure society itself, or influences our perception of the world, or can be used as an instrument of tyranny over racial or gender groups—all this would strike him as bordering on the unnatural.

Pose the same questions to an 'educated' English person, such as (let us say) a nursing sister, a personnel officer, or a solicitor, and her answer would be very different. Her immediate response to a question about the nature of language would probably be to refer to it as the right way to speak and write; she would define its purposes by referring to communication with other people, by reading or by writing. Press her and she would recognize that, yes, a great deal of language is spoken and listened to, but the reading and writing side is the important part. Unless she belonged herself to a minority group she would probably claim to speak the sort of 'correct', not-very-regional accent of millions of middle-class English people and might be surprised to hear a specialist identify from it much of her background. And if she was typical she would be likely to harbour, but not always to reveal, a belief that there are too many sub-standard accents and ways of speaking around nowadays. The odds are better than evens that her speech is significantly different from that of her father, and possibly that of her mother.

These perceptions about language are strikingly different from those of the specialist scholar. He is vividly aware that language is deeply systematic in almost every respect. English is like a score of other languages in the main features of its word-order and like hundreds of languages in its use, in most of its vocabulary, of a syllabic structure. He knows that there is a large but limited number of ways in which the parts of a sentence can be organized together, but that each of those structures can be used, by drawing on the huge vocabulary of the language, to convey an infinity of meanings. He knows that in English speech the 'tunes' or intonation patterns can convey at least as much meaning as the words they are mapped on, and to convey those meanings in writing may take very different sets of words. The linguist knows that words divide into classes but that in sentences they have functions, and words in some word-classes can operate in a number of functions. He knows that the spelling and punctuation of any language are systematic too—if they were not, nobody would ever learn them, let alone be able to use them. So, too, the immense number of accents in English reflects the vast historical and social complexity of the communities that speak it. Faced with this diversity, knowing that one form of English is a standard language in India, another in Canada, yet another in England, the linguistic scholar discards any notion that one is better than another. Disciplined to listen to speech with an ear finely attuned to its variations, the linguist is liberated from the innocent prejudices and snobberies which inform the attitudes to language that predominate among laymen—who for this purpose include professionals in most other spheres no matter how eminent. [Much of this material is given a non-technical account in Doughty *et al.*, 1972 and Pearce, 1985.]

But language is not quite like the bones and muscles we put in the care of a doctor, or the vehicles and manning and routes we entrust to a traffic manager in a bus system. It is part of us, part of our identity and everyday living, something we do not like to see meddled with or even expertly understood by others. Language may be playing a key part in our own careers. Plenty of public figures now well known in their 'standard' non-regional accents grew up speaking a marked local accent, discarding it as their milieu and its needs changed. This social and geographical movement is normal, and it has lasting and complex connections with language—but those are entangled with attitudes and feelings. Some of us can revert to a childhood accent with ease; others cannot; some of us feel proud of this, others ashamed of it; and all our feelings are related to the fact that some forms of speech carry more prestige than others. Some have adopted what they see as prestigious speech-forms with less than full accuracy, leading to the curious condition the experts call hypercorrection. (For a fuller account, see Doughty *et al.*, 1972 or Trudgill, 1975.)

The speech diversity of Britain is astonishing: the standard book (Trudgill, 1984) has twelve chapters on the large number of accents in English, not to mention nine more on the other languages spoken in this country and nine chapters on problems of linguistic intermixing. The linguistic scholar cannot afford to see this variety as blameworthy or any one accent as 'bad' or 'low'. But typical English people, especially middle-class ones, do tend to see language mainly in terms of correctness. Whenever education enters the discussion, too, it is too quickly forgotten that children's speech-form is very well fixed by the age of 5, and the role of the school is again seen as partly corrective. The linguist does not make the judgment on children's speech that this view takes for granted. This fact opens up a real gulf between scholars and those responsible for social policy. It is a gulf which is the central 'emergent issue' about language in primary education; the only other issue that matters is what we are to do about it; and neither issue is in any degree simple.

The issues are blurred in several different ways. Among teachers and those who train them the subject 'English' is largely if not entirely monopolized by an ideology hostile to the serious study of language, whose adherents believe (quite erroneously) that such study is inimical to the status of literature. Among laymen the topic is distorted by the durable nature of accent prejudice and, above all, by the influence of half-remembered half-knowledge gained at school—with distaste if the subsequent career proved a disappointment, with a quite unjustified trust among those who have achieved success. More recently a further blurring has occurred in the form of political propaganda: so great is the ignorance of language among laymen that there are seemingly votes to be gained by promising to reinstate the claimed traditional virtues of 'grammar' in the school curriculum. The social history of the present century gives to this last development a distinctive resonance. Until shortly after World War II English society generally accepted a set of conventions about public and private life which derived from an elite. This consensus was not so much imposed by the professional class as imitated by others, and applied to modes of dress, table manners, social conventions, acceptable speech, and a wide range of matters in and out of the home. Many historians have called this a 'bourgeois culture', and have pointed to its rapid collapse during the 1950s. It was to survive in the independent and many grammar schools for some decades more, and with it there survived for many who attended such schools the unquestioned belief in 'grammar' and non-regional speech that marked the bourgeois era. In a sense, the current demand to restore such elements to the schools of today is a cultural throwback, a survival. But it exploits a feature of language we tend to forget: in a rapidly changing society, the demands on our language competence also change, leaving us feeling under-prepared and under-skilled. We are in danger of imputing to alleged inadequacies in our schooling many of the problems for which no schooling could have prepared us. We should beware of repeating this in the curriculum we offer our children today.

Current Primary Practice

Against this confused and confusing background, we must expect to find the practice of primary schools to be very varied. There are five main strands to identify, but most primary schools practise a mixture between them. In trying to set out the character of each I risk giving only a caricature, and the range between best and worst in each one is very wide indeed.

1. The reading preoccupation

Primary teaching has set out to achieve proficiency in reading from its earliest days, and still does. The dominant place of reading in the infant school leads to two emphases in the junior school. One is adherence to a numerical scheme or set of levels long after the pupil's competence would justify abandoning it. The belief that reading competence progresses through linear stages in this way is a half-truth at best, but when it imposes a lock-step series of levels of reader on most children over the age of 9 it impedes other learning and will undermine the growth of a spontaneous reading habit. The other emphasis stems from the supposition that being able to read a text and being able to comprehend it are similar skills. The result is an attachment to 'comprehension' as a classroom activity which is almost invariably a gross waste of time—written answers to written questions on written pieces taken out of context maximize the laboriousness, often in the interests of keeping children occupied.

2. The literature and creativity stance

Many teachers have reacted against the reading obsession (as they see it) by encouraging children to move from staged readers to proper books as soon as possible. They share and convey enthusiasm for children's fiction—and let nobody suppose that the last four decades of children's literature have not been a golden age in English writing. They often believe that they should seek to bring children to experience in their own writing the creativity that marks 'real' authors (Benton and Fox, 1985). This stance has advocates who would bring within its purview most of initial literacy teaching, and others who claim that its proper implementation makes all teaching or study of the formal aspects of language unnecessary. At its best the work of such teaching is impressive and moving. As a basis for universal practice it raises many unanswered questions, not least about the cost of the necessary books. [The best source-book is Meek *et al.*, 1977.]

3. The slot-and-filler school

It is not hard to find classrooms where 'English' means a daily period of working through a textbook or work-book. Where the source of the exercises is a large box of printed cards, often containing the text as well as the questions, the work may be nearer to that of our first example, but most such 'laboratories' resemble old-fashioned textbooks in the kind of process they set going for children. In its crudest from this reduces language to the status of mental arithmetic, asking children to fill in a missing word in a sentence, a tedium of little or no instructional power which is nevertheless repeated in some recent computer software. One widely purchased example asks J4 children to fill in twenty missing words in a piece of continuous prose and then tells them 'Now write out *your composition* in your exercise book' (my italics). Many of the same weaknesses occur in primary textbooks that purport to instruct children about spelling, punctuation, sentencing and so on. They have in common the error of supposing that children need to learn the 'how' of writing when the prime need, as the creativity school has realized, is the stimulating of the 'what'.

4. Topic and composition

Many junior school teachers, feeling tentative about what they anxiously call 'creative writing', have evolved a style of work which rests on themes or topics that give rise to occasions for reading and writing. The great strength of this practice is that the writing usually stems from actual observation or genuine knowledge. Its weakness is that the range of styles, contexts and outcomes is apt to be limited, and the writing rarely offers scope for originality or for coming to terms with experience.

5. The oracy school

A more recent arrival, much in evidence in multi-ethnic and inner-city settings, is the practice of developing children's oral skills to the utmost and deriving writing tasks from the oral vitality, the inventive classroom drama and the language diversity on offer. This approach has enthusiastic advocates as a celebration of the ethnic and social identities in a school, integrates well with the creativity school, but leaves some questions about written competencies.

Missing from all five models is that pre-war staple the class reader, which formed an essential complement to the exercises of the course-book, slot-and-filler model. The 'total' scheme that claims to offer a full set of 'levels' of reading books and a full menu of related language activities is also missing: it is not so much a new version of one of these models as a piece of machinery that can be found overlaying several of them. The best of them, Ginn's *Reading 360*, can be found in selective use by the reading-preoccupied teacher, who pushes on through the levels and ignores the language work; and in a coursebook-based regime the Cards replace the exercises but without the oral element so carefully built into them; while some teachers see a similarity to topic work which is really spurious.

All these approaches are incomplete, not because they are bad, but because they lack a coherent, informing perception of language and language-learning. The reasons for this state of affairs were addressed, ineffectively it proved, by the Bullock Report (DES, 1975), but lie in the history of teacher training since the war. It is no part of my purpose to denigrate that history or accuse any of its participants, but it remains a fact that initial training was responsive to new knowledge in the growth period of psychology but almost totally closed against it in the growth period of linguistics. Hence, very few teachers trained for primary work have brought the knowledge, understanding and skills needed to enable them to conduct the language curriculum of their pupils in a coherent and informed way. Even in child psychology there is a gap between textbooks in wide use and the best of recent (and readily available) scholarship.

For example, here is Gorden Wells' Bristol research team's recording of Matthew: he is 7 years old, making a clay model of a diver with classmates, and the teacher includes Amanda and Maxine in her discussion with him:

Amanda: Mrs M., if he put this bit in the belt and this bit in the back with the oxygen, it might look like a real diver.

Matthew: That's what I'm trying to do.

Teacher: Do you think it looks like a real diver at the moment?

Matthew: No.

Amanda: No.

Maxine: Not much. It hasn't got the equipment on it.

Amanda: Yes, but if you put the feet too small it could easily fall down.

Teacher: How do you know about a real diver, Matthew?

Matthew: I read a lot about it.

Maxine: Why? Have you got a book about divers?

Matthew: Two. Two great big annuals of divers at home, and I read 'em... Every night 'fore I go to bed. But I'm in—I'm in the middle of book one and in book two it tells you about deep-sea divers. In book one it tells you about frogmen.

Maxine: How to make it?

Matthew: Not how to make 'em.

Teacher: What's the difference between frogmen and deep-sea divers?

Matthew: 'Cos deep-sea divers aren't like frogmen—deep-sea divers haven't got flippers and —

Teacher [turning to answer a child in another part of the room, then turning back to Matthew]: Sorry!

Matthew: — and they have different kinds of—frogmen don't have helmets but deep-sea divers do. [Pause, while teacher answers another child.] So frogmen are quite different, 'cos they haven't got helmets.

(Wells, 1985, pp 112–3)

Wells has cited a number of instances of teachers who are so preoccupied with their own subject-matter or with keeping the work of other children going that the needs of the child immediately in hand are neglected. Here he comments:

Perhaps what is most striking about this teacher is the quality of her listening. It is noticeable, in the above text, that even when she has to break off for a moment to respond to another child, she keeps her arm around Matthew, thereby signaling to him that it is only a temporary interruption, and on both occasions, when she turns back, Matthew continues where he had left off.

By listening attentively in this way, giving the children her full attention, she indicates that what they have to say is important—that they have expertise that is of value. When she asks questions, it is in order to be further informed, not to check that the child's answer is in conformity with her knowledge about the topic. And by inviting other children to listen and ask questions in the same way, she builds up in each child a feeling of self-respect and confidence in what he or she knows and can do and, at the same time, a feeling of respect for others as well. (*ibid* p. 113)

The unexpectedness of Wells' choice of the teacher's *listening* is the mark of the knowledge, understanding and skills that teachers need, that will generate real standards instead of the fictitious notions of 'grammar' that inform much public discussion. There is an outstanding presentation of the same material in Donaldson (1978), but the best-known advocate of the teacher as listener and generator of learning by talk is of course Joan Tough (1977). Other sources are Wells (1985) and Halliday (1975).

The Needs of Initial Training

It is necessary to answer the question as to what kind of knowledge is being suggested for inclusion in initial training. Certainly we should not be looking for a course in academic linguistics: it is changing too rapidly and is too enmeshed in its own highly abstract formulations to be useful as an enabling discipline. Nor should we allow the need for disciplined language study to be precluded by allegations from the literature lobby that the work is either covert linguistics or inherently unnecessary. The disciplined study of language would have five components, and the order given them here does not imply an order of importance:

1 Language acquisition and development, up to and including the process of learning to write.
2 The descriptive grammar of modern English, treated on the kind of level exemplified in the first eighty pages of Perera (1984). This and other components require a basic acquaintance with phonetics.
3 Language variety—variations in speech-form, differences between speech and written language, linkages between intonation and meaning, relationship to audience.
4 The nature of written text, its texture and patterning (including spelling and punctuation); error interpretation.

5   The roles of speech in classrooms and schools, including the language and learning problems of ethnic minorities.

These elements do not add up to a course in linguistics, but they cannot be competently taught at initial-training level without lecturers who themselves are graduates in that field. The same requirement for specialist expertise exists in the teaching of reading, but in the programme of college amalgamations and closures in the 1970s many institutions made their reading specialists redundant. The tradition of higher education and its staff appointment practices have militated against the establishment of appropriately qualified teaching of language study. It will be argued that a course of this kind cannot be accommodated within a three-year or even a four-year first degree course, still less within the thirty-six weeks of the normal postgraduate certificate, and the evidence of continental experience suggests that it is unreasonable to expect what we now do of primary and secondary teachers without giving them a two-year training period. Even with our existing very limited postgraduate training, however, it is inexcusable that teachers are expected to start work with primary-age children with virtually no perception of how their language competence develops after the age of three or four, how to interpret the signs of growth, and how to foster successful learning. At the same time a majority of teachers who train as specialists in English are overtly encouraged to take a dismissive view of language and its educational role that can only be described as obscurantist.

The Labours of HMI

HMI do not merely inspect schools. They recruit and maintain a high order of expertise; they influence the placement and use of funds for research and inquiry; and they oversee the writing and publication of a considerable range of documents. In the language sphere they have inherited the situation outlined above, with some telling differences. Close observation of many schools reveals to them the flaw in the creativity and literature school that dominates secondary English practice: it reflects its origins in bourgeois culture in being good for the able and limiting for the below-average. HMI maintain a level of training and reading that gives many of them a working command of disciplined language study. The nature of their inspection discipline (*cf*. Pearce, 1986, chapter 6) gives them a cross-curricular perspective. So when they responded to the demand for a series of short pamphlets entitled *Curriculum Matters*, the English HMI had to address a peculiarly controversial area. The first of the series, *English from 5–16* (DES, 1984), set down thirty-three objectives for pupils aged 7; fifty-six objectives for 11-year-olds; and expressed many of them in terms of language performance. Moreover, in a pamphlet of twenty-two pages room was not found for a section headed literature. The English literature lobby responded with its characteristic passionate intensity and ensured a hostile bias in the comment and responses that HMI invited. These replies were summarized, answered and, in some cases, corrected in a second pamphlet (DES, 1986), which re-cast the objectives as a set of examples of how statements of objectives could and should be used in English teaching. Under 'Expectations at the age of 7' we find this about *Writing*:

> By the age of 7 all children should have been led to see writing as an important, purposeful, interesting and enjoyable process, to view themselves as capable of communicating on paper and to regard revision as a normal and unthreatening aspect of the writing process.

Under *The spoken word* the corresponding section says this:

> With appropriate support if necessary, most children should be able to vary pitch, intonation and enunciation and non-verbal features to deliver their meanings clearly.

Not all, perhaps not many, of the later pamphlet's readers will recognize that *pitch* and *intonation* are technical terms with precise meanings. Not all, to judge from the ignorance and misreading of the earlier pamphlet's responses, will have the comprehension skills to grasp the full measure of what is being set out in those quotations alone as the agenda of the infant school.

HMI are not being merely prescriptive: they, too, have read their Wells and have grasped the significance of the work of the Assessment of Performance Unit's Language team. In HMI's 1986 pamphlet we read of *children encouraged to talk and listen to their peers and adults ... in pairs, small groups of varying size ... answering questions, giving and receiving explanations.* We see, in my earlier quotations from Wells, a teacher seeking to develop Matthew's *powers of attention and grasp of turn-taking* and *purposeful use of powers of prediction and recall*, and much else in HMI's list of objectives. More important, perhaps, is the way in which HMI's objectives encourage the teacher who has never heard of Wells or Halliday or Trudgill but knows intuitively that purposive talk is the prime route to growth in command over meaning and to all school learning. (*cf.* Wells and Nicholls, 1985.)

For it is plain in this and many other HMI publications, as it is in a great quantity of research, that language is not a school subject but the medium for all school activity (*eg.* APU, 1978ff; Southgate *et al.*, 1981; Stubbs, 1976; Thornton, 1986). The detail of what children 'are taught', of lesson content in the narrow sense, is trivial compared with the language awareness the teacher brings to structuring and managing her pupils' experience. My example from Wells (above) reflects the priority that such awareness gives to listening. Barnes (1969, 1986) was the first to expose how lethal is the teacher's often habitual reluctance to listen to pupils. Yet every teacher complains that many pupils can only hear rather than listen. Not all of us can match Mrs M's skill in reinforcing good listening in Maxine and Amanda by the deft timing of her questions, but we are all going to have to try. For these interpersonal language skills are given a sharp prominence in the objectives of the new GCSE examination courses: suddenly the objectives set out in the 1986 *English 5–16* pamphlet from HMI have to come down from the mountain and establish themselves in every classroom, primary and secondary alike.

The implication for in-service training of teachers is also awkward. Little has happened since the Bullock Report's abortive recommendation 15 pushed language to the top of the training agenda, not of English specialists only but of all teachers. Teachers remain largely unaware of the distorting spectacles through which they perceive language, and quite naturally resent the suggestion that anything is in any degree wrong with their perception. They will share the layman's faith in a return to 'grammar', but they do not have the knowledge to handle a misconceived prescription let alone a sound one. The public policy dilemma remains: the way to improve language-learning and language competence in schools is through a radical improvement in teacher-training, but there is nothing at present to persuade initial trainees or most serving teachers that they stand in need of any such improvement. Worse still, there are no votes to be gained in this field except by imposing a classroom regime that every reliable source of expertise in this field knows to be counter-productive. [It must be added, alas, that professors of literature do not necessarily possess the grasp of language-learning they may sometimes claim.] I have included grammar in my list of what teachers should know, but it is not a grammar that is known in schools: there is a world of difference between traditional school-book clauses and an informed understanding of how English structures work. Nor, on the research evidence, is it a grammar that needs to be taught in schools, for it does not directly generate competence in writing or speaking.

No adult who uses language skills in a job can attribute those skills to a school education: we learn too much on the job for that to be honest or realistic. The argument from schoolroom grammar to adult language competence is a series of false inferences. Those who make this claim are hankering for a lost era, the bourgeois days when people knew the place their accents gave them. Why should language be the only part of the curriculum where children are taught on the basis of the ill-remembered misconceptions of laymen? Would we tolerate such a situation in mathematics? In an era when the microcomputer allows children to draft and edit and revise their meanings and writings, what business have we thinking that the technology should be used to instruct children in what self-appointed censors choose inaccurately to describe as 'grammar'?

References

ASSESSMENT OF PERFORMANCE UNIT (1978) *Language Performance*, Department of Education and Science.

ASSESSMENT OF PERFORMANCE UNIT (1981) *Language Performance in Schools: Primary Survey Report no 1*, HMSO.

ASSESSMENT OF PERFORMANCE UNIT (1982) *Language Performance in Schools: Primary Survey Report No 2*, HMSO.

ASSESSMENT OF PERFORMANCE UNIT (1984) *Language Performance in Schools: 1982 Primary Survey Report*, Department of Education and Science.

ASSESSMENT OF PERFORMANCE UNIT (1986) *Language Performance in Schools: A Review of Language Monitoring 1979–1983*, Department of Education and Science.

BARNES, D., BRITTON, J. and ROSEN, H. (1969) *Language, the Learner and the School*, Penguin Books.

BARNES, D., BRITTON J. and TORBE, M. (1986) *Language, the Learner and the School*, (New edn.) Penguin Books.

BENTON, M. and FOX, G. (1985) *Teaching Literature—Nine to Fourteen*, Oxford University Press.

DEPARTMENT OF EDUCATION AND SCIENCE (1975) *A Language for Life* (The Bullock Report), HMSO.

DEPARTMENT OF EDUCATION AND SCIENCE (1978). *Primary Education in England: A Survey of HM Inspectors of Schools*, [The 'Primary Survey'], HMSO.

DEPARTMENT OF EDUCATION AND SCIENCE (1984). *English from 5 to 16: Curriculum Matters 1*, HMSO.

DEPARTMENT OF EDUCATION AND SCIENCE (1985) *GCSE: The National Criteria*, HMSO.

DEPARTMENT OF EDUCATION AND SCIENCE (1986) *English from 5 to 16: The Responses to Curriculum Matters 1*, HMSO.

DONALDSON, M. (1978) *Children's Minds*, Fontana.

DOUGHTY, P., PEARCE, J. and THORNTON, G. (1972) *Exploring Language*, Edward Arnold.

GREGORY, R. L. (1970) *The Intelligent Eye*, Weidenfeld.

HALLIDAY, M. A. K. (1975) *Learning How to Mean*, Edward Arnold.

MACLURE, M. and HARGREAVES, M. (1986) *Speaking and Listening: Assessment at Age 11*, NFER/Nelson.

MEEK, M., WARLOW, A. and BARTON, G. (1977) *The Cool Web: The Pattern of Children's Reading*, Bodley Head.

PEARCE, J. (1985) *The Heart of English—Nine to Fourteen*, Oxford University Press.

PEARCE, J. (1986) *Standards and the LEA: The Accountability of Schools*, NFER/Nelson.

PERERA, K. (1984) *Children's Writing and Reading: Analysing Classroom Language*, Basil Blackwell.

SOUTHGATE, V., ARNOLD, H. and JOHNSON, S. (1981) *Extending Beginning Reading*, Heinemann Educational.

STUBBS, M. (1976) *Language, Schools and Classrooms*, Methuen.

THORNTON, G. M. (1974) *Language, Experience and School*, Edward Arnold.

THORNTON, G. M. (1986) *APU Language Testing 1979–1983: An Independent Appraisal of the Findings*, Department of Education and Science.

TOUGH, J. (1977) *The Development of Meaning*, Allen and Unwin.

TRUDGILL, P. (1975) *Accent, Dialect and the School*, Edward Arnold.

TRUDGILL, P. (Ed.) (1984) *Language in the British Isles*, Cambridge University Press.

WELLS, G. C. (1985) *Language Development in the Pre-school Years*, Cambridge University Press.

WELLS, G. C. (1986) *The Meaning Makers: Children Learning Language and Using Language to Learn*. Heinemann.

WELLS, G. and NICHOLLS, J. (1985) *Language and Learning: An Interactional Perspective*, Falmer Press.

WHITE, J. (1986) *The Assessment of Writing: Pupils aged 11 and 15*, NFER/Nelson.

Primary Science—The Hidden Challenge

Michael Day

Developments in the 1980s

In 1985 science was the subject of the first curriculum policy statement published by the government—*Science 5–16: A Statement of Policy* (DES 1985c). This document (hereafter referred to as the Science Policy) is the culmination of several central initiatives since 1980 and must be seen as an outcome of the declared aim of the government to get broad agreement on the objectives and content of the school curriculum (DES, 1981, 1984c, 1985a). Inevitably, with its almost doctrinal status it will have a major influence on curriculum planning in primary schools for the remainder of the decade. In general most of its major recommendations have been accepted (ASE, 1986) and reinforce the trends in primary science since 1978 which have led to significant moves on both the curriculum and pedagogical fronts.

Curriculum Shift

The position of science within the primary curriculum has altered markedly from 1978 when only a minority of schools had an effective programme of work (DES, 1978). Recent surveys (APU, 1984a, 1985) found 90 per cent of the schools covered included science activities in their curriculum. A further significant finding was that over half had a staff member responsible for science. Although only half had a written scheme or policy document with more than broad guidelines, this proportion has steadily increased since 1978 and reflects, in part, the increased emphasis on accountability in the 1980s. This in turn has prompted greater clarification of science concepts, processes and attitudes at the primary level. The Progress in Learning Project which led to Match and Mismatch (Harlen *et al*, 1977) identified several processes and attitudes which have been used as a reference in many science schemes. As part of its monitoring brief the APU has developed an assessment framework in which it has defined operationally scientific skills and processes. This framework and the major findings of the APU are available in a useful series for teachers distributed by the ASE (APU, 1984b). Further guidance is available in the Science Skills Booklet produced by the School Natural Science Society (1984).

Significantly, the Science Policy firmly grasps the 'nettle' of content. Although acknowledging the importance of science processes, the message that children need to gain progressively deeper understandings of some central concepts in science is emphatically declared. Teachers are expected to ensure pupils 'meet and grasp certain fundamental facts' and 'need to be clear about which concepts are to be used or developed'. These concepts should be linked with experiences of living things, materials, forces and energy. The Policy is understandably coy about which concepts are fundamental. Harlen (1978) offers some guidance which might be a little overwhelming and the APU gives a list of ideas which it would expect primary children to have met by the age of 11 (APU, 1984b). Unfortunately it is a rather confusing mixture of facts and generalisations. Barber *et al.* (1985) suggest a more straightforward 'concept sheet' in which a few salient concepts are directly linked to the areas of experience outlined in the Policy.

Promoting stronger curriculum links with the community and industry has been a constant theme in recent years and has led to a broader curriculum base for primary science. Indeed these links feature in two criteria for selecting content listed in the Policy: one refers to the pupils' role as citizens of the future, another to technology. Technology figures again when the Policy states that 'science and technology in the primary school should form, and be experienced as a continuum' and 'pupils should also use their science in technological activities which pose realistic problems to be solved and involve designing and making'. Some impetus in that direction has been provided by the increased popularity of science fairs, which typically involve pupils in technological problems. In a more institutionalized manner, the Standing Conference of Schools Science and Technology (SCSST) and the Science and Technology Regional Organizations (SATRO) have coordinated several initiatives. Conference reports of the SCSST and its joint publication with the Engineering Council, 'Problem-solving; science and technology in primary schools' (1985) are significant contributions to the current discussion on primary science and technology. The advent of the microcomputer, a powerful piece of technology in itself, has led to the emergence of quite sophisticated control-technology in primary schools (MEP, 1985). Many activities described in each of these initiatives embrace scientific problem-solving skills and clearly demonstrate the science-technology continuum advocated in the Science Policy document.

Curriculum material to support these developments has become more widely available and varied over the past five years. APU (1984a) list fifteen different schemes being used in one survey population. Eleven of these had pupil material making up the main part of the package which is in marked contrast to the earlier teacher orientated Nuffield Junior Science and Science 5–13 schemes. This may be a response to the need for structuring pupil activities that teachers have voiced over the years. A balance of biological and physical science is found in most schemes and this is probably linked with reports that science programmed for 11-year-olds no longer shows the strong bias towards biology that seemed to be the case in the 1978 HMI survey (APU, 1984a). Interestingly, bearing in mind the Policy's emphasis, in the more recent schemes content has a higher profile than hitherto.

Pedagogical Shift

The approach to primary teaching has been strongly influenced by Piaget's developmental view of learning. However in recent years research into the learning of science has increasingly used Ausubel's theory of meaningful learning (McClelland, 1982). Here the focus is on cognitive 'readiness' in the sense that for meaningful learning, a learner must be able to relate a new idea to previously acquired concepts. What children already believe or 'know', therefore, will critically affect both their acceptance and interpretation of ideas. This would account for the ability of very young children, unexpected on Piagetian developmental grounds, to cope with quite formal reasoning in contexts with which they are familiar and have had adequate cognitive preparation. How children build up their own versions of scientific concepts has been intensively investigated. The results suggest we learn by actively constructing meanings from reading, talking and sharing experiences. Driver and Bell (1986) summarize this constructivist view of learning as having these premises: learning outcomes are related to both the learning environment and the knowledge of the learner; learning involves the construction of the meanings which may not be the teacher's intention; learners have the final responsibility for learning and that there are patterns in the types of meanings shared by pupils. The interaction of language and learning is critical in this context with personal experiences and everyday language reinforcing the development of concepts.

This work immediately raises the question of how we can get pupils to relate their private 'alternative frameworks' to the public versions of knowledge exemplified by school science. Accepting the importance of the child's version of science concepts has implications for the teaching style and feedback the teacher adopts. To begin with teachers will need advice on ways of discovering what these 'alternative frameworks' might be within normal classroom constraints. If the findings of research into the patterns of meaning shared by pupils could be made accessible to teachers this would be a useful first step. Secondly, the required cognitive preparation can be provided through a variety of learning experiences, from didactic demonstration to open enquiry depending on the learning outcome intended (Summers, 1982). An interesting example of applying this

Ausubelian approach to a science programme is outlined by McClelland (*op cit*). Although currently this shift in pedagogy is largely theoretical, the emergence of concept development as a major aim of primary science will make it increasingly pertinent to the classroom.

In-Service Implications

To ensure implementation of the Science Policy schools are expected to monitor their programmes of work, to have consultant teachers available and to have all their teachers including some science in their teaching. In addition outside support should be available at the advisory or training-institution level. To encourage and sustain this level of teacher involvement and support will demand in-service initiatives at all levels.

The DES have made grants available to LEAs to support in-service training for primary science coordinators (DES, 1984b) and primary science is also one of the designated curriculum areas to receive Education Support Grants (DES, 1984a). Financing the appointment of a science advisory teacher to work alongside teachers in their classrooms has been one of the most promising developments. This continues a school-based trend clearly seen where LEA and Higher Education centres have combined to mount courses incorporating substantial classroom practice (Brown, 1981; Day, 1985). A review of LEA initiatives providing resources in the form of working party papers, guidelines, trial material, directories etc gives a picture of immense energy and richness of response (Raper and Stringer, 1984). Other in-service programmes have focussed on involving teachers in the design and production of their own science equipment (Day, 1983). An interesting alternative source of income is the use of DIS grants to boost primary science and technology (Hussey, 1985). To what extent these initiatives can be sustained and provide the recommended in-service viz. to consolidate scientific knowledge, practice of scientific skills and post-course support in the present educational climate is debatable. Part of the answer will be in the hands of the LEAs, who will have a major voice in deciding which direction in-service takes from 1987 (DES, 1986).

A Quality Plateau?

Since 1980, then, science has become more firmly established in the primary curriculum with the training of curriculum leaders, school policies no longer the exception, curriculum materials increasing in number and diversity and an emerging, albeit limited, in-service programme. At several levels it appears to be a healthier scene than the late seventies. However, reports on practice still show a disappointing level of performance by pupils in science-specific skills (APU, 1984a). Generally the prescribed nature of the practical work prevents genuine experimentation, speculation and problem-solving (DES, 1985b) and pupils are given insufficient responsibility for pursuing their own enquiries and deciding how to tackle their work (DES 1985a). Primary science appears to have progressed quantitatively but seems stuck on a plateau qualitatively. Even allowing for the normal lag between curriculum policy and implementation progress seems exasperatingly slow. Perhaps we are underestimating just how challenging investigative science may be to many primary teachers. I feel we must focus much more clearly on the nature of this challenge.

Although the literature provides a far from consistent definition of primary science (Brophy 1985) and philosophically, science and science education are a matter of continuous debate (Chalmers 1982; Hodson 1985) it is expected that children should be engaged in investigations using certain procedures in order to test ideas in a practical way. Furthermore, it is recommended that such investigations should as far as possible be based on the curiosity, interests and experiences of the children (DES, 1985c; ASE, 1986). Developing the learning context to support such an approach to science raises curriculum and teacher-pupil issues which many teachers may find difficult to resolve. This becomes clearer when we look at the underlying structure of investigation.

Typically investigations, experiments and problem-solving have certain procedural stages in common *viz.*

— the identification or representation of a question, hypothesis or problem;
— the designing of some strategy to get answers to or test the validity of the question, problem or hypothesis;
— the carrying out of the strategy using certain techniques and equipment;
— the recording and interpreting of the data collected;
— evaluating both the information gained and the approach adopted.

Although presented in a linear form it is not suggested that this represents an invariable sequence. Sometimes the strategy and solution is half developed from the start and certainly will be continually redefined as the investigation or experiment proceeds. Analogous stages have been described in contexts as widespread as control technology (MEP, 1985), science performance categories (APU, 1984b), problem solving in mathematics (Burton, 1984), mathematics across the curriculum (OUP, 1980), science and technology in primary schools (SCSST, 1985) and later re-emerge at the secondary level in the GCSE science criteria.

To engage fully in these procedures, children need to be discussing and sharing ideas, co-operating in designing and performing tasks, making decisions and critically reviewing their experiences. If they are to approach this level of initiative, independence and creativity, learning contexts must be planned which provide opportunity for choice and, above all, sufficient time on task to allow children to think as well as do. Clearly this assumes an approach to teaching which gives a high status to encouraging pupil autonomy.

But classroom observations suggest that children have few opportunities to discuss, argue or reflect (DES, 1985a, 1985b), rarely make decisions about their own activity or collaborate (Galton *et al*, 1980), are seldom asked to apply skills in new context or expected to be accountable for their own learning (Bennett *et al*, 1984) and that certain investigative skills are relatively poorly developed by the age of 11 (APU, 1984a). Such a low incidence of activities seen to be valuable right across the curriculum must reflect deep-seated problems. These I contend rest in the perception some teachers have of teaching.

Teachers' Perceptions as a Key Factor

Many curriculum developers emphasize teacher perception as being just as critical to curriculum development as the so-called objective realities of staffing and resources (Campbell, 1985). Primary teachers have a dominant role in assessing children's needs, organizing their curriculum experience and evaluating their performance. Their views on the curriculum, the nature of knowledge, children's learning and classroom management will strongly shape their response to any curriculum change.

Alexander (1984) proposes an interesting division of the curriculum as perceived by primary teachers. One category, the 'basics', is seen as having a high priority and time allocation, a knowledge content which is received and rationalist, codified into categories and hierarchies, amenable to objective evaluation and generally having a teacher-directed pedagogy. The remaining 'non-basics' have the quite different characteristics of child centredness, empirical views of knowledge, heuristic pedagogy and relatively subjective evaluation. Alexander emphasizes that this model is a generalization but is inferred from many reports on classroom practice and teacher intentions. A further feature of primary teachers perception is the anti-subject bias traditionally part of primary ideology. Subjects represent 'facts to be learned' and are therefore alien to a child-based process dominated curriculum. That such a curriculum is largely a myth has been commented on by Simon (1981) and this gap between rhetoric and practice has been substantiated by numerous surveys.

However, should a large proportion of teachers perceive the curriculum in this way then science presents a confusing picture. The offending subject image of science was well recognized in early attempts to establish science when Nuffield Junior Science and Science 5–13 were presented as largely investigative; thus being high in process and low in structure. This softer image was reinforced by encouraging teachers to do science within their own projects, a context which is still seen very much in the 'non-basic' category by teachers (SCDC, 1985). In that position investigative science would have low priority and by implication a reduced allocation of time: hardly favourable conditions for development.

On the other hand, with the intensive lobbying and curriculum development over the past ten years, primary science has become more codified with content, structure and monitoring expected. The Science Policy clearly sees science as a basic subject even sounding warnings against losing its identity in thematic work. If in its promotion to 'basic' status science also takes on the attributes of a teacher directed pedagogy and received views of knowledge this could militate against promoting the investigative procedures outlined earlier. The current 'neo-basic' status of science is a classic 'Catch–22 situation', with either a perceived low priority when in its non-basic guise or a possible undermining of the investigational core when seen as a 'basic'. Ambivalence at this level must confuse and slow down implementation.

Any proposed curriculum change affecting classroom management must also take into account teachers' perceptions of their role in the classroom. Too often we forget that teachers have interests at the personal as well as the professional level. Workload, health, enjoyment and autonomy are legitimate concerns. Sociologically, teaching styles have been seen as coping strategies which attempt to reconcile a teacher's personal needs with professional demands (Pollard, 1985). It may be that some teachers focus on class control and adopt a relatively didactic instructional style as a strategy to reduce management stress. Clearly, genuine enquiry, with its divergent activity, negotiation and collaboration could be perceived as undermining such a strategy. Should control in a prescriptive sense be central to a significant number of teachers' perceptions of their role, then it not surprising that learning contexts emphasizing pupil autonomy appear to be uncommon in primary classrooms.

However, even where teachers include scientific processes involving pupil-choice in their list of teaching priorities, it is sometimes found that in practice these processes had a much lower profile than was intended (APU, 1984a). Whilst to some extent this might be due to lack of teacher expertise, it might also reflect a 'perception-gap'. Galton (1983) suggests this could arise from a teacher's beliefs and values conflicting with a professional 'self-image' in which competence, busy-ness, discipline and voluminous end-products are publically demonstrated to one's colleagues. Although valuing investigative work, teachers at the same time could see it giving the appearance of less control and organization as well as producing fewer end-products; thereby threatening their self-image. According to Galton's thesis, where there is this mismatch between beliefs and self-image, the psychological outcome might be a 'perception-gap' with teachers not recognizing the degree to which they are exerting control despite striving for pupil-initiated activities. Interestingly, in the APU report referred to above, it was found that typical control activities like writing and recording, figured higher in practice than was intended.

Furthermore, at a more general level, any pressure to re-examine teaching styles carries with it an implied criticism of current practice and the philosophy informing it. To very experienced teachers this could be seen as a personal affront and a threat different in kind to the stress of adding another 'subject' onto the curriculum.

Some implications of investigative science have been examined in the context of teacher's perceptions of the curriculum, their practice and self-image. It is suggested that the hidden challenge of science lies in its core of enquiry-based teaching requiring a learning context which conflicts with the views many teachers hold at both ideological and perceptual levels. If this hypothesis is true then primary science enthusiasts inside and outside the schools must provide ways of encouraging, and above all protecting innovative teachers who may be exposed to these pressures resisting change. In-service education will need to clarify the nature of investigative science, advise on ways of negotiating the time for developing the required learning context and raising its curriculum status. Some ways forward are suggested in the next section.

Encouraging Investigative Work in Science

A Progressive introduction of investigative work

Managing enquiry-based science is clearly a complex task. Teachers would benefit from guidance on ways of gradually introducing this to their classroom especially if their pupils are facing it for the first time. There is a need for curriculum developers to build up a range of progressively 'pupil-dominated' science packs which would offer teachers short term sustainable alternatives to supplement the more global schemes currently available. To gradually reduce 'teacher-dependence', pupils could initially undertake quite structured programmes of 'discovery' within which there are specific opportunities for decision-making. Modified primary versions of the flow-chart system of Rotheram (1984) might be helpful here. Many self-contained problem-solving exercises in mathematics (Burton, 1984) could also be used to introduce pupils to certain procedural skills without threatening teachers with whole class practicals from the start.

Perhaps a major disservice to teachers in the past has been judgments on teaching 'styles' which imply that only wholesale adoption of one type is acceptable. More important is that teachers should feel free to use the style which fits the learning outcomes intended. The work of Mosston and Ashworth (1986) and of Ausubel (Summers, 1982) support this more liberal approach. Employing a range of teaching materials which have varying degrees of pupil-choice would seem to be a sensible strategy when weaning children from what might be a strongly teacher dominated curriculum towards one which encourages pupil-autonomy.

A procedural framework

Earlier it was pointed out that certain procedures are common to enquiry and problem-solving. These could form the basis of a planning strategy which teachers could use to predict in broad process terms the development of an investigation. If, say, it is recognized that children must have the opportunity to identify or formulate questions in terms meaningful to them, then the teacher knows that a context for that learning to take place must be built into the teaching scheme. Whether visits, initial discussion or just handling materials are part of this procedure will depend on the particular investigation. Similarly, the other investigational procedures can be seen as an identifiable sequence of stages through which the children need to pass as an investigation proceeds. In this way a procedural framework provides both a planning strategy and, moreover, a rationale for defending the time and resources needed for each stage.

It is also easy to see how teachers might be apprehensive when faced by the daunting list of process skills and attitudes they are expected to handle. Part of the problem is that these lists often give the impression that each skill must be taught as a separate item. Within an investigation, however, any one process skill, observation for example, can contribute to several different procedures and should not be seen as an isolated activity. Similarly certain attitudes are not the preserve of one procedure. Each investigative procedure, therefore, can be seen as really a cluster of skills and attitudes. Certain procedures predictably provide opportunities to practise particular processes or call for specific attitudes e.g. looking for patterns when examining data or being critical when evaluating. What is important is that teachers can identify them when they occur or are pertinent; the SNNS Skills Booklet (1984) might be useful here. Adopting a procedural framework could give coherence to planning and increase the likelihood of pupils practising process skills in a purposeful context.

Combining concept development and investigation

Teachers are expected to ensure pupils 'meet and grasp certain fundamental facts' (Science Policy). This immediately raises the dilemma of how one avoids programming out genuine enquiry by overstucturing in order to establish specific concepts. Hawkins (1974) in his essay 'Messing about in Science' presents a model which goes some way towards a synthesis of process, content and views on children's learning. He sees investigation at three levels. In the first phase there is free exploration in a selected area, e.g. materials or minibeasts, followed by a second more structured exploration based on questions and activities arising from the children's responses in the earlier phase. Only after these two stages, would attempts be made to elicit or introduce higher order concepts or generalizations such as adaptation. The second phase's structured approach could encompass the 'cognitive preparation' and active 'construction' of concepts associated with Ausubel's view of learning whereas the earlier free exploration preserves pupil contribution and reflects Piagetian ideas of concrete experience. Hawkins' model might be a way of developing specific concepts without violating the notion of child-based investigation.

Providing a context for free discussion and pupil contribution

Enquiry in the classroom is only likely to flourish if the teacher builds up a learning environment sufficiently relaxed to encourage unsolicited contributions. Hinton (1985) describes an observation schedule for primary science in which pupil contributions are categorised as volunteering facts or principles; identifying or suggesting a problem; volunteering an inference or hypothesis; or suggesting an experimental procedure. In a pilot study all categories except that of suggesting a problem were observed. Identifying a spectrum of pupil contributions would be a first step towards designing a strategy to promote them.

If contributions from pupils are vital then we need to be aware of potential constraints. Teachers on the Ford Teaching Project (Elliot, 1976) explored various constraint-removing strategies. When focussing on how the teachers themselves restrict pupil contribution they itemized a range of potential constraints. A questioning strategy which asked for consensus, responded positively to predetermined outcomes, suggested there was a single correct answer or inordinately enthused over a useful suggestion was considered likely to restrict free discussion of problems, ideas and evidence. Other constraints identified were too early a recourse to secondary sources, especially books; emphasis on written work of a relatively passive recording type and excessive status accorded to adult experts. Research on 'wait time', (pause-length after a teacher's question or pupil's response) suggests that teachers seldom wait for more than one second and find it almost impossible to wait for more than two seconds. When wait times were increased to three seconds or more responses altered in directions that encouraged enquiry, eg responses were longer, more frequent, more speculative and explanations more varied (Rowe, 1978).

Free discussion and debate, perhaps, should be seen just as much part of practical science as the equipment (Science Policy: para. 28) and are essential if we wish to nurture positive pupil contribution.

Formulating productive questions

Questions which arise from the class could clearly influence the direction an investigation takes. At the same time they acquire immediate status in the eyes of the pupils which in turn is likely to encourage further contributions. However, it is important to distinguish between productive and non-productive questions and to have strategies for converting the latter into the former.

Those questions which are not easily answered by first hand evidence of the type that primary age children can generate are non-operational or unproductive as starting points. 'Why' questions, for example, usually require explanations beyond the level of children's understanding or are not amenable to simple tests or observations, e.g. 'Why do birds sing?' or 'Why do aeroplanes stay up?' These questions do little for teachers unsure about their scientific knowledge and unfortunately reinforce the notion that science teachers should know the answers. More productive are 'where', 'when' and 'how many' type questions which are useful starters and can lead to observational and recording activities suitable for any age group or ability range. Data collected from such questions can be the basis for generating researchable or operational enquiry questions, with the added advantage of encouraging children to use their own information. These researchable questions characteristically involve altering variables by elimination, substitution or manipulating them quantitatively (Allison and Shringley 1986). It often helps to structure the question in the form—what happens to X if I alter Y—with X frequently being some property of an object (living or non-living). Both X and Y need to be defined operationally before the investigation becomes a practical proposition. If X, say was the cooling of water and Y the thickness of the insulating straw layer: then operationally X could be the time for 500 cm to cool from $80°C$ to room temperature; and Y, the varying thicknesses of straw. If these factors arose from a discussion of how to test a suggestion that 'straw keeps things warm', one is halfway to designing an investigation. The feasibility or validity of that design can be part of another discussion at the appropriate time.

Teachers intuitively use starter questions but often have had little experience or training in formulating operational questions from observations. Developing this skill should be central to any in-service claiming to support scientific investigation in the classroom. At the heart of such initiatives we should be encouraging teachers to see questions from children not as a demand for explanation but the first step towards investigation.

Freeing time for investigations to develop by using science to develop and apply basic skills

In the first half of this decade we have seen a noticeable shift towards the notion of a primary core curriculum. This has already raised the spectre of a curriculum overcrowded with subjects. On the other hand teachers are being asked to ensure pupils have the time to design, discuss and communicate in order to consolidate their experiences throughout the curriculum (DES, 1985a). Congestion seems inevitable unless some 'subject' sharing of the curriculum is accepted. One way forward might be to capitalise on the constant plea in curriculum documents since the 1978

Survey for the basic skills to be practised in a variety of contexts rather than in isolated timetable slots.

Examples of the powerful interaction between science and language are provided by Carre and Howett (1983) and Tunnicliffe (1986). Mathematical links with science at the data collection, processing and interpreting levels are readily made. If science is seen as a context for the purposeful application of language and mathematical skills a significant amount of time on the curriculum could be shared.

Scientific investigation itself relies on basic skills other than the more science-specific ones of recognizing variables or designing ways of testing a simple hypothesis. Pupils need to have had some experience in independent and unsupervised working, simple information retrieval, observing social conventions appropriate to group activity, assembling and presenting information as well as rudimentary skills in debate and discussion. None of these activities are exclusive to any 'subject' and their development could be part of a broadly conceived science programme which would benefit all areas of the curriculum.

We also need to recognize that, inherently, science has an expressive dimension in the sense that pupils should be asked to explore, defer or focus on ideas and issues that are of personal interest and importance (Calouste Gulbenkian, 1984). This is clearly built into the 'real' investigation model. Pupils communicating the questions posed, ways of answering them, their findings and, equally important, their feelings would provide a natural link between science and the expressive arts. Of particular value would be taking advantage of the ubiquitous classroom display. Portraying the development of an investigation with all its struggles, *cul-de-sacs* and revisions as well as its products could help preserve the personal and creative element of investigative science. In this way, too, the enormous amount of time and energy expended on display might become identified with a wider range of curriculum objectives than is sometimes the case.

Real investigations as common ground for science and technology

Investigations which appear real to children usually retain their interest. Real problems share some of the following characteristics (OUP, 1980):

— the problem has been initiated by the children themselves or has been reconstructed into a form which is theirs
— there is no answer in the 'book'
— solving it would be useful to someone else other than themselves
— it has applications in adult life
— it involves designing and making something

Technology projects have as their focus the production of a useful artefact and therefore almost automatically qualify as real problems. They also have the advantage that the design process involves hypothesizing, problem-solving, and testing; all vital scientific processes. Although science is primarily concerned with developing ideas useful in understanding the world around us, these ideas are widely exploited in technology as are the technological artefacts in science. Clearly the distinction can easily become blurred and certainly, at primary level, technology is a valuable opportunity for children to practice science investigative skills in a self-evidently purposeful context.

Providing status through record-keeping

The Science Policy clearly expects each school to 'develop programmes of work and ... monitor its own progress in putting its aims into effect'. Record-keeping is notoriously demanding and must be more than a cosmetic accountability exercise. At the same time it underwrites the priority of those items being monitored. Collecting 'curriculum' data is a legitimate and necessary first step to establish the presence of specific activities and overall curriculum balance. However, even at this level scientific investigation has a low profile. In one survey of primary school record-keeping (Clift *et al*, 1981) less than 20 per cent of schools included scientific skills or experience in their reports. This reflects the low priority given to investigative skills in teacher intentions and practice reported elsewhere (APU, 1984a).

Match and Mismatch (Harlen *et al.*, 1977) is a well known attempt to provide a check-list and scales of progression for science process skills, concepts and attitudes. This work comprehensively covers the clusters of skills making up investigative procedures. However in an unmodified form it is probably unrealistic in the classroom (Shipman, 1983). A more 'digestible' translation for teachers is provided by Davis (1983). Little is available in the way of progressive scales for concepts although some steps towards this might emerge from ideas in Squires (1980), McClelland (*op. cit.*) and the build up of information on pupils 'alternative frameworks'.

Hilton (1984) describes a skills profiling system which could be modified and applied to the more structured type of science exercises. An interesting system is suggested in a Topic Work Project (SCDC, 1985) where tasks are analyzed in terms of cognitive 'levels' such as procedures, facts, skills, concepts and principles. As a further refinement, a matrix is proposed in which one dimension is the cognitive one just described and the other is using the appropriateness of task analysis of Bennett *et al* (1984) in their Quality of Pupils Learning research.

However, these schemes are largely at the fine tuning level and it may be that more general appraisals would be useful starting points. One example would be to see progression as a movement from a qualitative, descriptive level towards a more quantitative stance. Some form of measuring often leads to a greater clarification of variables, a more purposeful collection of data and wider use of data processing skills.

Alternatively, an insight into how well pupils understand an experiment as a whole, can be inferred from their answers to the question 'What would you change if you were doing this again?'. Seeing whether they can refine the method used, extend the observations, recognize the importance of sample size or restate the initial results would also give feedback on their ability to criticize investigative procedures (Evans, 1985).

Summary

Research and in-service must focus more intensively on ways of translating into practice the levels of enquiry, concept development and record-keeping clearly expected for primary science in the 1980s. The need to fully appreciate the demands of investigative work have been outlined here. Examplars of recommended practice are rare and those teachers meeting the expectations need to be identified and encouraged to share their expertise. HMI is currently collecting examples of good practice in a variety of curricular areas (DES, 1985a) which could establish patterns for guidance. Unless the advice is packaged in ways which allow progressive implementation and are clearly sustainable in today's classrooms we may find the picture of primary science in 1990 strikingly similar in quality to that of 1985.

Even should progress be achieved in meeting some of these demands primary science has other problems ahead which may affect its future development.

Which Way Forward?

The Science Policy has been used as the touchstone for current thinking in primary science and there has been general acceptance of its major recommendations. However any government intervention raises questions over whose values are to inform classroom practice. The general issues arising from this are considered elsewhere in this book but there are other questions which leave primary science standing at the curriculum crossroads.

Teachers are now expected to balance and combine the priorities of teaching concepts and process skills and it will be difficult to avoid a content led trend which could increasingly isolate science from an investigative context. Once on the road to a subject based curriculum, fragment-ation is an ever present danger. This could be compounded by the unequivocal support for specialist strength and posts of curriculum responsibility by HMI (DES, 1978, 1983). Will the training of these specialists be broad enough to include an awareness of the implications of children's learning theory for pedagogy, the position of science in the whole curriculum and the required skills of leadership to ensure curriculum consultancy is not just the provision of specialist activities? (Morrison, 1985). Here one is asking for continuous collaboration inside the staffroom as well as in the classroom. Yet the prevailing view is that primary schools are individualistic rather than collegial in endeavour, although Campbell (1985) is less pessimistic.

Currently, record-keeping is a feature of curriculum development but it can dominate if interpreted as the narrow testing of concepts and performance of process skills. Will LEA and school monitoring guidelines provide enough space on the recording 'sheet' to ensure real investigation has its place on the time-table? Heads and their science postholders will need to handle APU material and its derivatives sensitively to head off a drift towards a simplistic curriculum objectives model.

A particularly unfortunate aspect of the Science Policy (not shared by the ASE Policy, 1986) is the fleeting, insubstantial reference to science in the context of the whole curriculum and learning theory. There is no case made for science as an expressive or creative activity. A generally, unproblematic, instrumental and utilitarian view pervades the document which could drive science further into isolation from the expressive areas of the curriculum. No intimation either, of the limitations of scientific method and that by its very genesis scientific knowledge is tentative (Royal Society, 1985). Are we ignoring the personal dimension and presenting science as received fixed knowledge? At the very least we should be encouraging teachers to see scientific dispute as a celebration than a failure of scientific method.

Perhaps one of the most interesting developments has been the gradual emergence of primary technology. This young curriculum cousin of science is very much part of the utilitarian thrust of current government thinking. Could it be that technology is a safer curriculum bet to safeguard practical investigation by children? It has the qualifications: the inescapable design core, hypothesizing in an immediately purposeful context and allows easy integration of arts, science and humanities. Much unrecognized technology is already part of teachers experience embedded in their DIY activities in the garden, in the house and on the car. Perhaps the continuous struggle to sustain and develop science investigation will result in some science/technology chimera or will technology eventually squeeze science out of the curriculum? Finally, staying with biological metaphors, how should we respond to the question posed by Black (1980) as to whether the primary science plant needs just more light, air, and water or should we look again at its roots? The conditions necessary for investigative science to grow have been explored here. Certainly it is a stronger specimen in the mid-80s. Perhaps the question should be rephrased—has the pure strain sufficient vigour or will we need to graft it onto a technology stock?

References

ALEXANDER, R. J. (1984) *Primary Teaching*, Holt, Rinehart and Wilson.

ALLISON, A. and SHRIGLEY, R. (1986) 'Teaching children to ask operational questions' *Science Education*, 70, 1, pp. 73–80.

APU (1984a) *Science in Schools Age 11: Report No. 3*, HMSO.

APU (1984b) *The APU Assessment Framework for Science at Age 11* (one of a series of APU digests for teachers distributed by A.S.E. Hatfield).

APU (1985) *Science in Schools Age 11: Report No. 4*, HMSO.

ASE (1986) 'Primary science—A statement of policy' *Education in Science*, April, 13, 1.

BARBER, B. and JACKSON, D. *et al*, (1985) 'Primary science concepts', *Teaching Science*, 3,3, pp. 8–9.

BENNETT, N. *et al*, (1984) *The Quality of Pupil Learning Experiences*, Lawrence Elbaum Associates.

BLACK, P. (1980) 'Why hasn't it worked?' *Times Educational Supplement*, 3 October.

BROPHY, M. (1985) 'Primary science: Some contradictions', *School Science Review*, 234,67, pp. 534–8.

BROWN, C (1981) 'Sandwich course for primary science', *School Science Review*, 223,63, pp. 342–3.

BURTON, L. (1984) *Thinking Things Through—Problem-solving in Mathematics*, Blackwell.

CALOUSTE GULBENKIAN FOUNDATION (1982) *The Arts in Schools*, Oyez Press.

CAMPBELL, R. (1985) *Developing the Primary School Curriculum*, Holt, Rinehart and Winston.

CARRE, C. and HOWETT, B. (1983) 'Science education through personal language: an integrated approach in a primary school', *Educational Review*, 35,3, pp. 243–57.

CHALMERS, A. (1982) *What is this Thing Called Science?* Open University Press.

CLIFT, P. *et al.*, (1981) *Record Keeping in the Primary School*, Macmillan Educational.

DAVIS, B. (1983) 'How can children's progress in science be monitored, recorded and evaluated?' in RICHARDS, C. and HOLFORD, D (Eds) *Teaching of Primary Science: Policy and Practice*, Falmer Press.

DAY, M. (1983) *In-service and Teacher Produced Resources for Science*, Curriculum and Resources Series No. 2 School of Education, Exeter University.

DAY, M. (1985) 'A resource-based in-service model for primary science', *British Journal of In-Service Education*, 12,1, pp. 29–34

DEPARTMENT OF EDUCATION AND SCIENCE (1978) *Primary Education in England: A Survey by HMI*, HMSO.

DEPARTMENT OF EDUCATION AND SCIENCE (1981) *The School Curriculum*, HMSO.

DEPARTMENT OF EDUCATION AND SCIENCE (1983) *Science in Primary Schools*, HMSO.

DEPARTMENT OF EDUCATION AND SCIENCE (1984a) *Education Support Grants*, Circular 6/84, HMSO.

DEPARTMENT OF EDUCATION AND SCIENCE (1984b) *In-Service Teacher Training Grants*, Circular 4/84, HMSO.

DEPARTMENT OF EDUCATION AND SCIENCE (1984c) *The Organisation and Content of the 5–16 Curriculum: A Discussion Paper*, HMSO.

DEPARTMENT OF EDUCATION AND SCIENCE (1985a) *Better Schools*, HMSO.

DEPARTMENT OF EDUCATION AND SCIENCE (1985b) *Education 8–12 in Combined and Middle Schools*, HMSO.

DEPARTMENT OF EDUCATION AND SCIENCE (1985c) *Science 5–16: A Statement of Policy*, HMSO.

DEPARTMENT OF EDUCATION AND SCIENCE (1986) *The New Specific Grant Scheme for In-Service Training*: Circular 3/86, HMSO.

DRIVER, R. and BELL, B. (1986) 'Student's thinking and the learning of science: A constructivist view' *School Science Review*, 240, 67, pp. 443–56.

ELLIOTT, J. (1976) *Implementing the Principles of Inquiry/Discovery Teaching: Some Hypotheses*, Unit 3, Ford Teaching Project, Centre for Applied Research, University of East Anglia.

EVANS, J. (1985) 'Criticising the experiment in a junior school', *School Science Review*, 238,67, pp. 142–3.

GALTON, M. (1983) 'Teaching and learning in the classroom' in GALTON, M. and WILLCOCKS, J. (Eds) *Moving from the Primary Classroom*, Routledge and Kegan Paul.

GALTON, M., SIMON, B. and CROLL, P. (1980) *Inside the Primary Classroom*, Routledge and Kegan Paul.

HARLEN, W. *et al.* (1977) *Finding Answers: Match and Mismatch*, Oliver and Boyd.

HARLEN, W. (1978) 'Does content matter in primary science?' *School Science Review*, 59, pp. 614–25.

HAWKINS, D. (1974) *The Informed Vision*, Agathon Press.

HILTON, R. (1984) 'Profiling skills in science', *Education in Science*, April, pp. 32–4.

HINTON, R. (1985) 'The observation schedule in primary science classes', *Journal of Education for Teaching*,11,3, pp. 290–4.

HODSON, D. (1985) 'Philosophy of science, science and science education', *Studies in Science Education*, 12, pp. 25–57.

HUSSEY, D. (1985) 'Department of Industry boosts primary science and technology on the Isle of Wight', *School Science Review* 238,67, pp. 15–17.

MCCLELLAND, G. (1982) 'Ausubels's theory and its application to introductory science', *School Science Review*, 227,63, pp. 353–7.

MEP (1985) *Primary Control Technology Micro-electronics Project*.

MORRISON, K. (1985) 'Tensions in subject specialist teaching in primary schools', *Curriculum*, 6,2, pp. 24–9.

MOSSTON, M. and ASHWORTH, S. (1986) *Teaching Physical Education*, Merrill Publishing Co.

OUP (1980) *Mathematics Across the Curriculum*, PME 233, Unit 5 Open University Press.

POLLARD, A. (1985) *The Social World of the Primary School*, Holt, Rinehart and Wilson.

RAPER, and STRINGER, J. (1984) 'LEA initiatives in primary school science', *School Science Review* 235,66, pp. 384–7.

ROTHERAM, K. (1984) 'Guided exploration using flowcharts', *School Science Review*, 233,65, pp. 655–69.

ROWE, M. (1978) *Teaching Science as a Continuous Inquiry*, McGraw–Hill.

ROYAL SOCIETY (1985) 'The public understanding of science', *Education in Science*, April, 13–14.

SCDC (1985) *A Topic Work Project*, School Curriculum Development Committee.

SCSST and ENGINEERING COUNCIL (1985) *Problem-solving; Science and Technology in Primary Schools.*

SCHOOL NATURAL SCIENCE SOCIETY (1984) *Primary Science Skills,* (distributed by ASE Hatfield).

SHIPMAN, M. (1983) *Assessment in Primary and Middle Schools,* Croom Helm.

SIMON, B. (1981) 'The primary school revolution: Myth or reality' in SIMON B. and WILLCOCKS J. (Eds) *Research and Practice in the Primary School,* Routledge and Kegan 1981.

SQUIRES, A. (1980) 'What is science for primary school children?' *Education 3–13,* 8,1, pp. 9–12.

SUMMERS, M. (1982) 'Science education and meaningful learning', *School Science Review,* 226, 64, pp. 361–4.

TUNNICLIFFE, S. (1986) 'Thinking and writing in primary science', *School Science Review,* 240,67, pp. 602–7.

Microcomputing—Backwards into the Future?

André Wagstaff

My father was an enthusiastic rather than expert gardener; for most of his life he planted and hoed in a succession of pocket-handkerchief sized gardens. Every so often he would tell us of his plans for an ideal garden. We thought they were just pipe dreams, but to my father they were Plans for the Future (you could almost see the capital letters when he spoke). One day he came home with a fistful of paper from an estate agent. A bungalow was up for sale—with a huge garden. It had everything, two greenhouses, a grape vine, an apple orchard, a cage for growing soft fruits, an enormous vegetable garden, lawns, shrubs and even a plantation of young Christmas trees! My mother, comfortable in the house we had lived in for the past five years, sounded a note of realism. 'How', she asked insistently, 'Do you propose to keep all that going—it would need a full time gardener, and we could never afford that.'

For a moment my father looked downcast, then he brightened. 'Simple,' he said. 'We shall buy one of those thingumyjigs.' And that's what we did. It was a very splendid machine which chugged along on two wheels. You steered it by yanking on its handles. On its own it could do nothing. But by bolting on various attachments you could plough, hoe, dig potatoes, plant seed, cut grass, spray weeds, spread fertiliser and a perform a myriad of other horticultural tasks. Of course my father bought the lot. Each attachment came with a comprehensive manual. It all looked as if it was going to be easy. But it wasn't. There were four factors we had not foreseen.

First of all, each attachment required the mastery of different skills in order to use them properly. The shop that sold it did not know how it was to be used. Certainly there were no training courses we could go to. We had to fall back on the manuals which were often confusing and unhelpful. Sometimes we got over this by trial and error—sometimes we just gave up and put the appliance in question to the back of the toolshed. Very often this meant that we failed to use the most powerful of the attachments, and were left using the inconsequential ones. Secondly, there were times when a machine dedicated to the task in hand proved superior to the thingumyjig plus attachment; for instance, a proper lawn mower did a far better job of cutting the grass, was quicker and did not need any elaborate setting up or training in its use. Thirdly, it proved incapable of doing two jobs at once; there were arguments over who was going to use it. Whenever two people wished to use it the compromise was often that neither used it. Then we would feel guilty and start using it for trivial purposes, more suited to a hand tool. Ideally we should have had one thingumyjig for each member of the family, but they were just too expensive to allow this as a solution.

Finally, it suffered from obsolescence. A year after we bought it our next door neighbour got the newer model—the one you could sit on. Three years later spares became a problem and after five years our thingumyjig sat forlornly in a corner of the garden, rusting quietly away. 'You know,' said my father, 'it's almost been as expensive as employing a gardener.' My mother's reply does not bear repeating!

The Last Five Years

This salutory story has uncomfortable parallels with the recent introduction of micros into primary schools. During the last five years thingumyjigs in the shape of computers, together with accompanying attachments in the form of computer programs have appeared in most primary schools. Their potential contribution to the education of our children has been overshadowed by problems of training shortages, failure to understand when the micro is an appropriate device to use, worries about what to do with one computer and 200 children, and a growing awareness that the micro is no educational panacea.

The MEP (Microelectronics Education Programme) was set up by the government in 1980. Its aim was to help 'schools to prepare children for life in a society in which devices and systems based on microelectronics are commonplace and pervasive'. Its efforts were complementary to a Department of Industry funding scheme which helped subsidize every secondary school who wished to purchase one computer system. In 1982 this programme was extended to provide cassette-based computer equipment for primary schools. By 1985 nearly all the 27,000 schools who wished to take advantage of this offer had taken delivery of their hardware. MEP had commissioned a Microprimer Pack which contained distance learning materials to help teacher training and a selection of computer programs. Every LEA was supposed to undertake a certain amount of in-service training. Specifically this meant running two day courses which were to be attended by two members of each school, one of whom was to be the head.

Almost immediately problems began to arise, some trivial, others fundamental. It is easy to be wise after the event, but many of the errors arose due either to a failure to think things through, or to a reliance on the great British tradition of muddling through. For a start, many LEAs were unable to deliver the necessary training courses. This was not due to any ill-will—the funding was often just not there. The two day courses were supposed to be the forerunners of a whole series of courses which would be necessary to help all primary school teachers to set this exciting new classroom resource into a proper curricular context.

By 1985 a survey by Pauline Bleach revealed that of the 536 primary schools sampled, only 16 per cent said that all members of staff were familiar with the machine. This presumably implies that a fair number of primary teachers are either not using micros at all, or are only allowing them in the classroom under the supervision of another teacher. More disturbingly, 13 per cent of primary schools said that not even the DTI required two day courses had been provided for them and 64 per cent said that only the DTI course had been provided for them.

Denied the sort of support which any other profession would regard as a necessity, the primary schools have had to fall back on their own resources. The initial programs provided in the Microprimer Pack proved less than inspiring. Some lacked educational substance—ANAGRAMS gives practice in the sort of activity previously indulged in on a wet Friday afternoon or on the last day of term. Others had little educational validity—SHAPESHOOTER came in for some stiff criticism from the Mathematics Association as being misleading and based on some shaky underlying concepts. And some seemed to be an expensive way of duplicating the type of thing which could be done using pencil and paper or apparatus—FARMER used a few graphics to thinly disguise a well-known problem, DIET was a secondary school program, with small modifications in an attempt to make it suitable for primary schools. Some of the programs were, for the time, of real interest—CRASH required planning and forecasting skills, MQUIZ provided an opportunity for a child to construct quizzes, ANIMAL encouraged children to use language with precision and could stimulate purposeful debate. It would be nice to think that teachers were quickly able to sort out the educational gold from the dross, but this has simply not happened. Nor have most schools moved away from the Microprimer programs. Whilst more than 83 per cent of primary schools now have the Microprimer materials, for 60 per cent of primary schools this is more than half of the software in the school (Survey of 536 Primary Schools).

Of course, these programs might be argued to have been intended as a stop gap. Indeed, MEP set up a National Primary Project in 1983 with a brief to establish what support was needed for the training of teachers and then to produce suitable support materials. Part of the support materials which were provided consisted of software which could be used in the primary classroom. But it has not yet filtered through. Anita Straker, Director of the Project noted in 1986:

There are certainly a few schools where the micro is used to extend the opportunities for children to undertake investigations or to solve problems, but the majority have still not moved on from the use of drill and practice games.

During the last three years the programs contained in the Microprimer Packs have been succeeded, but not supplanted, by an enormous flood of computer software; some has been simple, some extremely complex, all have somehow had to be sifted, evaluated, accepted or rejected by primary schools. The Bleach survey points to the evidence: in 30 per cent of the schools surveyed the Microprimer programs BRICK UP, ANAGRAMS or BOX CLEVER, were amongst the three most commonly used. Only 13 per cent included GRANNY'S GARDEN and a mere 4 per cent placed DEVELOPING TRAY amongst their top three programs. Sadly, the incidence of use of a particular piece of software seems to be in inverse proportion to its educational worth. A program like ANAGRAMS offers a fairly trivial activity which can be done better using pencil and paper whilst TRAY is an excellent program for fostering language development at many levels. What possible reasons could there be to account for these cheerless statistics?

One plausible reason is the acute lack of funds to purchase good software. Indeed, 40 per cent of the primary schools surveyed said that they never bought software, a further 30 per cent said that they spent up to £50 annually, and the remainder said that their teachers or parents wrote their software. Yet this cannot be a sufficient reason. A considerable range of free software has been available to primary schools for some time— DEVELOPING TRAY for example, was included in the MEP National Primary Project's Language Pack and may be used freely in all educational institutions.

It is also possible that the sheer rate at which the micro has been introduced to primary classrooms has proven too fast for normal educational support structures, and that schools have either not known where to turn for advice or have had insufficient guidance about what constitutes educationally valid software. For example, no proper report on the use of microcomputers in primary education has yet been published by HMI. It is reasonable to suppose that one must be in the course of preparation and it should prove interesting reading. For the moment, teachers may have been alerted to the importance of the micro:

> The implications of current technology are so extensive that it is difficult to present a balanced appraisal without seeming to exaggerate. No doubt further developments are still to come, but whatever changes microcomputers may make to mathematical education in the future we may say, beyond doubt, that some of the changes which they have made already are so big that we lack

any previous standard by which to measure them. (Fletcher, 1983)

But they have as yet received no clear guidelines as to how the micro can best be integrated with existing primary practice.

It is also very possible that the choice of software is simply a reflection of a philosophy in primary schools which is still all too common:

> The vast majority of junior school teachers are firmly in control of their classrooms. They determine what activities their pupils will undertake; they prefer a didactic approach rather than a reliance on discovery methods; they are making increasing use of class teaching. (Barker Lunn, 1984)

A fundamental lack of resources is another possibility. Programs such as word processors or information retrieval packages require the use of disk drives and printers. Yet comparatively few schools have acquired these. The Bleach survey indicates that in 1985 40 per cent of primary schools still lacked a disk drive and 75 per cent have still to acquire a printer. Many primary schools had to struggle hard to find the funds for the basic DTI offer micro; at no time was it made obvious to them that a micro lacking this extra hardware lost much of its potential.

Another factor may have been the disruption of both LEA and school based teacher training during 1985/86. During this period many local authorities had extreme difficulty in running any courses at all, and most have at best been postponed, at worst cancelled indefinitely. A few local authorities put on no courses at all. Throughout the country, primary schools, institutions which quintessentially thrive on the ad hoc meeting and the incidental exchange of view, limped along as staff fulfilled only their minimal contractual obligations. Some school's managed to cope; for the majority there was an abandonment of staff meetings, both formal and informal; school based curriculum development simply ground to a halt.

The consequences of this disruption of courses and the lack of time for curriculum development have been severe. Their absence has led to teachers only using micros in a narrow way; some of the most exciting and educationally worthwhile computer applications have been widely ignored. To understand why this has happened we need to look at the main types of software available for use in primary schools.

Main Types of Software

The nature of computers and the purposes to which they may be put have been discussed by both Turkle (1983) and O'Shea and Self (1983). Their approaches and interests differ, but they agree on the protean nature of the computer itself. The O'Shea and Self stance is:

> ... the fact is that a computer is an exceptionally flexible device .... Developments in microelectronics have now made computers so cheap and reliable that there will be no shortage of people attempting to realise their own vision of computer assisted learning.

Turkle shares the same insight:

> The computer is evocative not only because of its holding power, but because holding power creates the condition for these different things to happen. An analogy captures the first of these: the computer, like a Rorschach inkblot test, is a powerful projective medium. Unlike stereotypes of a machine with which there is only one way of relating—stereotypes built from images of workers following the rhythm of a computer-controlled machine tool or children sitting at computers that administer maths problems for drill—we shall see the computer as a partner in a great diversity of relationships.

So computers are tools, tools which can be put to use in an incredibly wide range of situations. And in each case there is a tendency for the micro to merge with the background. As I type this I don't really think about using a computer—I am using a word processor. And children who are using a computer to control the motors and lights on some model they have built look to the model, not the micro. Most teachers of primary children are happy with this. There would appear to be a general concensus that for education the importance of micros lies not in what they are, but in what they can do; and that brings us to the consideration of the types of software available. Whilst software abounds and individual reviews are readily available, usefully classifying it is more problematical.

Thomson in Chandler and Marcus (1985) perceives four categories of program—the electronic blackboard, simulations, data bases, and word processing. Jones (1985) proposes a slightly different four category model which sees the computer being used for structured reinforcement, problem structuring and solving, and information technology. Although both these models are more sophisticated than the programming, problem solving, information handling one offered by Wayth (1983), they all fail to take into consideration the differential demands placed on teachers who attempt to introduce the micro into their classroom.

If we begin by thinking about the purposes and expectations in the mind of the program writer and the role envisaged for the teacher, we may arrive at a model which can explain much of the present impasse. Figure 1 shows one such possible way of classifying computer programs.

187

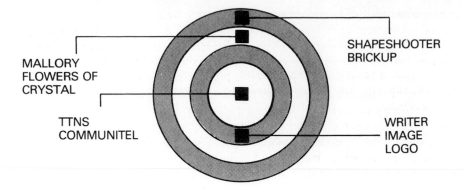

MALLORY
FLOWERS OF
CRYSTAL

SHAPESHOOTER
BRICKUP

TTNS
COMMUNITEL

WRITER
IMAGE
LOGO

The Outer Ring

In the outer circle can be found the programs written to practise specific skills or convey specific information. The authors knew exactly what route the child would take through the program and the desired end. The content of such programs is usually fixed and they are very easy for teachers to use. Literally all that is required is the ability to load the program into the machine. Examples of these are programs such as SHAPESHOOTER or BRICK UP. Programs such as these pose the question and provide the answer. It would be a mistake to dismiss all such programs as an inappropriate use of a scarce resource; there will always be a case for a program which accomplishes some limited educational end or offers practice in some skill to a child who would benefit from such practice. But unfortunately, because they are fairly easy to write, their quality is not always of the highest; they lend themselves perfectly to entire classes of children being seated in front of the micro, two by two like some electronic parody of Noah's Ark, to imbibe their dose of computing.

The First Inner Ring

In an inner circle of Figure 1 are the programs which were written with a definite goal for the user but which leave considerable latitude for the route taken to that goal. The content of such programs is often fixed, although some do allow for its variation through the creation of data files. This sort of program is exemplified by adventure programs such as MALLORY or FLOWERS OF CRYSTAL and simulations such as SUBURBAN FOX or POLICE. The role of the teacher in simulations is, as always, crucial. It is perfectly possible to use simulations in an extremely prescriptive and didactic fashion. The authors of a simulation package may have spent a lot of time and effort in trying to make it exciting, challenging, and thought provoking. But it will have none of these results unless the teacher encourages children to use their initiative, to consider the decisions which can be taken, and to reflect on their experience. All of this imposes a heavy load on the classroom teacher. It is not enough to be able to load a program such as this, one must also be able to interweave it with a whole host of other classroom activities most of which will involve small groups and probably children of mixed ability. What can these programs offer by way of improvement on those in the outer circle?

Firstly, they give children access to experiences which would otherwise be denied them. This denial might be on the grounds of safety—few heads would be prepared to have a real grand prix race held in a classroom. It might be because of cost, since conjecture in the real world can be quite expensive in terms of materials consumed; in simulations the only major cost is time. It might even be on the grounds of sheer impracticability; after all whoever heard of primary children salvaging a man of war? With the aid of the classroom micro children can be survivors on a desert island, try their hand at running a small business, be the first explorers in a new world, or try to survive in a city suburb as a fox. Of course, the experience will never be identical to the real thing—nor perhaps should we wish it. Yet experience gained in this manner can be as valid in its own right as any other. It may not be first hand experience yet it can produce as indelible a mark in the mind as a well-written book; we have yet to see literature condemned on the grounds of not offering first hand experience. It is the quality and educational value of an experience, not just its nature, which should be of concern to us.

The second argument for introducing computer simulations is their ability to act as a focus and a catalyst for other work in the classroom. Seen in this light, a micro does much more than offer children further practice in the sort of work which is already going on. It is, in fact, operating to extend the powers of the teacher, facilitating the setting up of circumstances in which equal appeal is made to children's imagination and to the skills and knowledge which they already possess. Computer simulations should not conjure up visions of hunched backs bowed before a flickering monitor. Rather should they make one think of children coming in to school carrying books they have borrowed from home, and eagerly showing the others the information they have discovered which will help them. Drama, dance, model making, creative writing, art, music and discussion are all activities which can be sparked off as consequence of a class embarking on a simulation. These activities then echo back to the work on the micro, giving it greater depth and enhancing its value.

Thirdly, simulations are worthwhile as a vehicle for the fostering of social skills. They provide an opportunity for children to work in small groups under conditions which call for genuine co-operation. This makes a welcome change from the all too frequent pitting of one child against another. A good simulation or adventure will provide the opportunity for each child to feel that a valuable contribution has been made to the group's success. Adventures and simulations give a chance for children to engage in negotiation and purposeful debate with their peers. Many of these programs demand that the children engage in role-play and some do this to great effect: empathy is not something which develops easily in the young. A program such as Suburban Fox helps children see that your view of the world varies according to who you happen to be.

The final point to make is that our environment is changing very rapidly. The world for which we are attempting to equip our children will change radically during their lifetime. The possession of a store of facts is no longer the hallmark of an educated mind. Instead, the skills of researching, arranging and interpreting facts become of much greater importance. In short, we need to do what we can to give children the ability not just to think, but to reason. The setting of goals, making of plans, carrying out and refining of these plans are all things which we as teachers need to nurture and encourage. Simulations and adventures offer us one possible route to achieving this.

It would, of course, be a mistake to see this sort of program as an educational philosopher's stone. Simulations are not good in all circumstances; indeed not all simulations are good. Consider, as an example, the program THE YELLOW RIVER KINGDOM GAME which came on the BBC Welcome tape. It is a crude simulation of the problems of running an agricultural community. Decisions have to be made as to how best to employ scarce resources of labour according to the season of the year. Now it is extremely unlikely that anyone would gain much from using this program, since the relationship between actions taken and later effects seem to be largely random and are not explained, nor can they be inferred. And yet it would be equally hard to deny the great interest which this program initially generates. So we must be careful to look beyond the superficial appearance of a simulation: there is little educational gold to be won in the Yellow River. Other simulations are extremely well executed, yet lack educational worth if used as a substitute for real experience. Look for example at programs like the Dudley GROWING A PLANT program. Here you have to try and grow a plant by finding out which factors determine growth. Technically the program is marvellous; educationally it is wholly inappropriate, unless its use is preceded by children having the opportunity to grow real plants. Consider how cheap it is to use real seeds, grown in real soils, under real climatic conditions and how much more likely it is that practical work such as this will lead on to other investigations.

The Schools Council Report noted as recently as 1981, 'In educational development, the privileged are those whose experiences stimulate their imagination, extend their use of language, demand thought and illustrate new concepts'. Properly used simulations on a micro can go a fair way towards helping all our children to become privileged.

It is obvious then, that teachers need a fair amount of both skill and commitment to use these programs, since much of their educational worth is lost if they are not used as part of some larger theme or topic, or if children are not actively encouraged to build on the experiences these programs provide. These sorts of programs provide the questions and many ways of finding the answer—sometimes there are many answers.

The Second Inner Ring

Within a further inner circle of Figure 1 lies software which exists to be used as a tool. Unlike the simulations and adventures which provide questions, and leave children to find answers, the tool software will provide answers, but the children will need to determine the questions.

Writers of such software know only the broad purposes for which they may be used and are ignorant of the goals which may be pursued by the user. These are information retrieval programs like GRASS, word processors like WRITER, graphics programs such as IMAGE, computer languages like LOGO or specialised extensions to computer languages like CONTROLLER.

The use of these programs places a heavy load on the teacher. Not only do they require a varying expertise in their use—word processors are fairly easy but LOGO is hard—but they provide no 'answer' to work towards. It is up to the teacher to decide where and when they can profitably be used. It is up to the teacher to decide on how children should be taught to use these powerful tools, and to what purposes they should be put. Children often have difficulty coming to grips with powerful tools like these.

Teachers need to think hard before introducing them into the classroom. What sort of prior experiences should their children have had? How much previous practice should children have at storing and sorting information on a conventional card index system before being introduced to an information retrieval program? In order to answer questions like these teachers need to have an awareness of the power and limitations of computer software of this type.

There has been much glib talk of teachers not needing to understand computers in order to use them. Or of teachers only being half a step ahead of the children. This may well be true up to a point: but when it comes to using software tools that point has been passed. To pursue the tools analogy—would we feel happy to see a teacher allowing children to use powered equipment in a woodwork class in ignorance of the purpose of the equipment, or of its mode of operation? Somehow one doubts it. Software tools can only be used to aid in the production of an answer—the user must both determine the questions and decide whether or not the answer is both satisfactory and reasonable. The posing of appropriate questions is never an easy task.

The Hub

Finally we come to software which lies in the innermost circle of Figure 1. Here is to be found the sort of software which is just a bridge for the extension of a computer's powers. Communications software such as that offered by COMMUNITEL or TTNS falls into this category; so do some utility programs. Communication programs enable the user to send information from one micro to another; the information flows down the telephone lines and distance becomes irrelevant. Utility programs increase the power of other programs; for example, they might enable children's writing to be printed out in a variety of forms or allow the easy transfer of data files between different computer programs.

These programs may be easy to use, indeed they depend upon being easy to use, but they make the heaviest of demands upon teachers. If proper use is to be made of them then it is likely that upon their backs will ride the use of complex pieces of other computer softwares such as word processors, many of the computer languages and information retrieval programs. Communications software is particularly compelling; it enables schools to communicate with other schools. The work done will not just be inter curricular but intra curricular. Used to their best advantage good communications software can do much to enhance existing good primary practice and more to encourage its spread.

The model in Figure 1 of concentric rings of software illustrates a load upon the teacher which increases in step with the educational worth of programs. It goes a long way towards explaining why teachers are still using the most trivial of the programs. It highlights the need for long term strategies for in-service and pre-service education, extending to all teachers, not just a select few. Computer enthusiasts must also shoulder some of the responsibility for the lack of progression towards the inner hub—it was they who were so assiduous in cultivating the impression that computers could do anything. This resulted in most class teachers first hopelessly overestimating the powers of a micro, then relegating it to a sideshow, a modern day raree box which, if it did no good, at least did little harm.

The Next Five Years

By now it should be clear that many of the problems and issues raised by the introduction of the micro are identical to those found when examining other aspects of the primary curriculum. We constantly need to remind ourselves of the processes by which children learn and how we can set about providing the necessary environment for that learning to take place. The computer should be used as a resource for learning, not something which children study as an end in itself.

Teachers are constantly reappraising their methods and strategies; they need encouragement to extend this critical approach to their use of computers. And just as its use in the classroom demands a rigorous scrutiny, so does its use throughout the school demand an examination of both policy and record-keeping. At present the average primary school has just under two machines—there is no way in which any really useful work can be done if the use of these is spread evenly throughout the school. One micro between two classes seems to be an irreducable minimum with the ideal being several per class. But we have to make do with what we have. Teachers will need to take a cool look at the range of possible uses of this scarce resource, and to choose which uses they will put the micro to in their school.

We need a greater awareness of the support adults require when faced with the sort of curriculum innovation which the use of a micro should imply. It is often thought that this support is only needed by staff; parents have a significant role to play in their child's education and there is a consequent need to look at the sort of support and information which they and the larger community require. The professional development needs of staff deserves close study—the requirements of a probationary teacher are very different from one close to retirement. Whilst establishing posts of responsibility for computers has an attraction, we need further debate. Such appointments could lead to other post holders assuming that anything that involved the use of a micro lay outside their curriculum area. And if this occurred, computers would continue to be used in isolation rather than as an integral part of the classroom.

The role played by local authorities will necessarily vary according to financial constraints and differences in educational viewpoints. Consideration needs to be given to the value of computer centres and software resource libraries. Advisory teachers are becoming more numerous and might well be significant sources of support for securing a proper role for the micro in the classroom. Much thought should be given to the type of courses provided. There seems to be a general concensus that courses which attempt to teach BASIC programing skills are wholly inappropriate. There is, however, as yet no clear agreement as to the most suitable form of replacement. One possibility is that teachers should attend courses of fairly long duration, with each section interspersed with periods during which the newly won skills are used in the classroom; ideally with the aid of advisory teachers.

There is a need for the investigation of sorts of information available to teachers and the channels of communication down which that information flows. At present this is too often confined to computer journals and magazines which are read only by the enthusiast.

Finally, there is an overriding and urgent requirement for a close scrutiny of the role played by the headteachers of our primary schools. They have always been recognized as pivotal points for effecting change. Their active support cannot, of course, ensure that the computer will take its proper place in the resources of their school; on the other hand the lack of that support is pretty well guaranteed to block all change. Staff attitudes are very often modelled on those of the head; in many primary schools the head is also a class teacher; their teaching style is a strong influence on others. It is headteachers who have the main responsibility for liaising with parents, governors and others schools. Their views on the educational worth of the micro help mould opinion and attitudes far beyond the walls of their school. It is headteachers who have a major say in determining school priorities for action both in the short and the long term. And of course, it is they who almost always control the purse strings.

Peering into the future, particularly with computers, is often unrewarding and frequently dangerous. The new 16 bit machines with their huge memory stores and enhanced graphic capabilities, the CD–Rom devices with their promise of vast files of information, the windows, icons and mice operating environments which accord much better with how most of us would choose to interact with a computer, the rapidly expanding world of electronic mail which could spell the end of isolation for our primary schools—all these will doubtless have a role to play. And whilst this new technology should necessarily interest us, it is not sufficient. It is not sufficient because we have not yet satisfactorily introduced the micro into the primary classroom. It is perhaps not going too far to say that 1988 may well be seen as a watershed for computers in primary schools—it is possible that this will be the year in which primary teachers begin to put this powerful resource in its proper perspective and use it to enhance children's learning experiences; it is equally possible that this will be the year in which the machines start to break down, class teachers place them at the back of the resources cupboard and put the experience behind them. Some educationalists would see this as no great tragedy, but this view would not be shared by all those who believe that we are now preparing children for life in the twenty-first century and should be doing so with the resources of today rather than those of fifty years ago. The computer, above all else is a device for communicating ideas—and the communication of ideas lies at the roots of all education.

References

BARKER LUNN, J. (1984) 'Junior school teachers: Their method and practices', *Educational Research*, November.

BLEACH, P. (1900) *The Use of Microcomputers in Primary Schools*, University of Reading School of Education, Reading and Language Information Centre.

CHANDLER, D. and MARCUS, S. (1985) *Computers and Literacy*, Open University Press.

FLETCHER, T. J. (1983) *Microcomputers and Mathematics in Schools: A Discussion Paper*, HMSO.

JONES, R. (Ed) (1985) *Micros in the Classroom*, Edward Arnold.

O'SHEA, T. and SELF, J. (1983) *Learning and Teaching with Computers*, Harvester Press.

SCHOOLS COUNCIL (1981) *The Practical Curriculum*, Methuen Educational for the Schools Council.

STRAKER, A. (1986) 'A sorry state of affairs', *Times Educational Supplement*, 9 May.

TURKLE, S. (1983) *The Second Self: Computers and the Human Spirit*, Granada.

WAYTH, P. J. (1983) *Using Microcomputers in the Primary School*, Gower.

The Arts in Primary Schools

The Calouste Gulbenkian Foundation

65   In General

We begin with three general observations. First, although we are discussing the value of the arts for all children, not all children will be interested in all the arts. The task is to provide adequate opportunities for different interests to show themselves and to develop. This calls for flexible provision.

Second, patterns of provision, necessarily, will be different according to the varying needs, interests and aspirations of pupils, the demands of different art forms and the circumstances of different schools. Consequently, we are thinking here only of general guidelines.

Third, many factors influence provision in schools—the availability of staff, buildings, materials and so on. In addition, there are the many problems being caused by falling rolls and by cuts in public spending. Some problems result from a lack of resources; others are due to existing attitudes in schools which give the arts a poor share of the resources which are available.

There are many schools where the arts flourish. In every case the headteacher and other staff appreciate and support them. In those schools where headteachers think the arts are marginal, they suffer, whatever the economic circumstances.

Token provision for the arts can be useless—and there is a vicious circle here. Where the arts are poorly provided for in schools, children will not benefit from them in the ways we have described. Consequently, other members of staff, parents and governors will not see their real value. As a result, they will continue to be poorly provided for. The Schools Council Project on Drama Teaching: 10–16 (1977) described this as a 'cycle of constraint'. In everything we say, therefore, we must assume a willingness, among headteachers in particular, to break this cycle and give the arts a realistic chance of success.

196

66   From Primary to Secondary

We are looking separately at primary and secondary schools, for two reasons. First, because the kinds of provision they need and the problems involved are different. Where the curriculum of the primary school is teacher-based, that of the secondary school is teachers-based. This involves more complicated patterns of organization.

Second, because there are shifts of emphasis in arts teaching between primary and secondary schools ... Although we are separating them here, we see a pressing need to develop more thorough methods of co-ordination and liaison between primary and secondary schools—as much in the arts as elsewhere.

The arts are *natural* forms of expression and communication. Part of the job of education is to develop these natural capacities into practical capabilities. This should begin in the primary school—if not before, in infant education—and be extended through the secondary school, as a continuous process. Too often, for reasons we will consider, there is almost no continuity here. As a result, there can be a considerable waste of time, resources and opportunity.

67   The Arts in Primary Schools

We share the view of HMI (1978) that work in the arts in many primary schools is disappointing. In some cases children do very little work in the arts. This may be because some teachers, as one survey has argued, do not put a high priority on creative work (1978). In some schools, where there is arts provision, children are working too far within their own capabilities—those in the top of the primary school still doing work of which they were capable much earlier. Sometimes this is because teachers' expectations of them are too low and the work lacks direction. At other times, it is because the work is over-directed and gives children little room to exercise their creative powers ... There is often, for example in the visual arts, a repetitious series of exercises or filling in of collage outlines supplied by the teacher.

In looking at the arts in primary schools we will consider four questions:

(a)   What should be aimed at?
(b)   What provision is needed?
(c)   What are the problems?
(d)   What solutions are there?

68   What should be aimed at?

Primary teachers have two broad responsibilities in the arts. The first is to establish them, as soon as possible, as part of the daily habit of education. Young children have a natural interest and pleasure in movement and rhythm, in shapes and colours, in making sounds, in imitation and in talk.

These are the beginnings of the arts. From the first, children should be encouraged to see these interests as important parts of the school day.

Second, the teacher must promote increasing confidence and competence in these activities ... As children develop it becomes important for them to control the media of the various forms of expression and to deepen their understanding of the processes involved. Exploring the potential of materials and the freedom of spontaneous expression are important stages in the development of artistic competence and enjoyment. There comes a point, however, when the ability to control these processes to chosen ends becomes equally important if they are not to breed a sense of incompetence and eventually of frustration. Elliot Eisner has noted, of development in the visual arts, for example, that from the ages of two to thirteen there seems to be a regular and predictable development in the way children create the illusion of space in their drawings. Beyond thirteen, these graphic skills seem to reach a plateau of competence so that those who have no instruction tend to develop further skills at a very slow rate. As a result,

> ... the drawings of most adults cannot be easily differentiated from those of young adolescents. It is not surprising that this should be true. Drawing and painting are, after all, the products of complex skills and, like most complex skills, they do not develop from simple maturation ... Since most adolescents do no formal work in the visual arts ... here is no reason to expect them to develop highly sophisticated graphic and painting techniques on their own. (Eisner, 1976, p 12)

Primary school teachers work with young children during their most formative years when they have an enormous capacity to absorb new experiences. But they do not develop the complex skills of any of the arts 'from simple maturation'. The natural pleasure and versatility which children have in learning, at this stage, give teachers the opportunity and, we think, the responsibility both to produce work of a high standard throughout the primary school and to give a firm foundation of attitudes, skills and understanding for all subsequent work in the arts. What this involves will vary between the arts. We can take as two examples, the visual arts in general, and music.

69 Visual Arts

In the visual arts, the curriculum from 5–11 should enable children to:

(a) experiment with different media—watercolour, crayon, paper, cloth, clay etc.;

(b) explore different techniques, tools and modes of manipulation in each—modelling, brush-work etc.;

(c) understand the basic ideas of, for example, tone, colour, texture and contrast, and, eventually, of more complicated ideas of, for example, balance, focus and proportion;

(d) begin to respond to a variety of styles and forms of visual art, including differences between cultural forms (eg Western, Oriental, African) and between historical periods (eg primitive, ancient, medieval, modern);

(e) develop an awareness of the use of visual symbols to convey ideas and feelings;

(f) develop an awareness of design—the relationships between materials, forms and functions of objects and constructions;

(g) develop powers of observation and description.

70   Music

An overall aim of music in the curriculum from 5–11 is to enable children to use and to understand sound as a medium of expression and communication. This will include enabling them to:

(a) experiment with, and develop skills in, producing sounds with:
— the voice
— a variety of musical instruments
— other means of sound production;

(b) work in a variety of groupings, large and small, using all of these;

(c) discriminate and use timbre, pitch, intensity, rhythm and duration, with increasing accuracy;

(d) use conventional and accepted musical forms and styles as well as experimenting with others;

(e) begin to repond to a variety of styles and forms of composition—Western and non-Western—and to appreciate their use and appropriateness in different situations;

(f) develop individual interests and abilities in making and appreciating music.

71   Other Arts

Similar lists could be drawn up for each of the arts in the primary school. Among them all, as between these two, there will be considerable overlap. There are two common emphases: to give children a broad introduction to the rich variety of media, techniques and forms of expressive and creative activity, and to aim continually to raise their levels of competence and attainment in using and understanding them.

72   What Provision is Needed?

In primary schools, children work for most of the day with the same teacher. Unlike work in secondary schools—except where certain spaces, such as the hall, are needed—there is no organizational need to establish fixed periods of time for the arts. Certainly, there is no educational need to do so. Indeed, separate timetabling can place artificial boundaries around activities which, with young children especially, should be seen as an integrated part of day-to-day experience. The most important need is for teachers themselves to recognize and respond to the opportunities for expressive and creative work which continually arise in the primary school. There are two central questions here: those of integration and of resources.

73   Integration

The arts in the primary school need to be conceived of, and organized, as an integral part of every school day. The fact that one teacher is concerned with almost the whole of the child's daily curriculum makes this a real possibility. There are three aspects to this.

First, the arts have to be defined very generally at this stage to embrace a wide range of expressive activity in movement, painting, music, dramatic playing and so on. A major value of these activities, from the earliest days of education, is in promoting the use of imagination, orginality, curiosity and a sheer pleasure in doing and learning.

Second, ... the aesthetic and creative mode ... embraces more than the arts. Looking through a microscope at an insect's wing; examining shells and fossils, plants and the local environment can be rich sources of aesthetic experience. The arts are the characteristic ways in which we record and reflect upon these experiences. Aesthetic experience, like creativity, should be fostered throughout the curriculum, as well as in the arts.

The third point stems from this. It is to emphasize the inter-disciplinary nature of the primary school curriculum—work in one mode of activity stimulating, and being stimulated by, work in another. The value in talking of modes of activity and understanding rather than of separate subjects, is partly in underlining that the same things can be seen and understood in a variety of ways, geographically, biologically, historically—aesthetically. Work in drama or dance is as likely to lead to a use of reference books as to further work in other art forms: for example, to exploring topics related to ritual, festivals, other civilizations. This may lead in turn to poetry or music.

In inter-disciplinary work, there is always a danger of sacrificing depth for variety. We will return to this later. We want to emphasize here that good primary school practice is based on teachers recognizing the opportunities to fertilize work in one part of the curriculum with work in another. The unifying and integrating aspects of the arts, give them a particular value in this respect.

74   Resources

There is a tendency to think of resources in terms of expensive equipment—projectors, video, hi-fi etc. Although these can enhance good arts teaching, they are not essential to it. In thinking about resources for the visual arts in the primary school, the Art Committee of the Schools Council make the central point that we should be conscious both of the scale of the child's world and of his/her relationship to it. The child, for whom everything is new and to be explored, becomes absorbed in things that adults have come to overlook or take for granted:

> Watch a young child playing in a rain-filled gutter, looking in a pond, studying a grasshopper or dissecting a plant ... often of most importance to the child is what is possible for him or her to hold in a cupped hand. (Schools Council, 1981, p 9)

In schools where there is work of quality, teachers are always sensitive to the nature of this relationship between the child and the world and to the need to create an environment which feeds curiosity:

> ... an environment where rocks and shells, creatures and bones, grasses and earth are considered together with the vast range of man-made things which surround and fascinate the child as fundamental resources for learning. (*ibid*, p 10)

In all of the arts, these 'fundamental resources for learning' are of two sorts: first, objects and experiences which excite the imagination and act as a stimulus for learning; and, second, the media through which children can formulate and express their responses to them ...

76 *Accessibility: The Ethos of School*

If such things are available, they must also be accessible to children. Display is an important factor here—including the display of children's own work as a resource for each other. The way in which work and other material is displayed and arranged in a school is more than a matter of convenience: it is a reflection of the atmosphere and attitudes which prevail there.

> Whatever the type of school and wherever resource material is displayed, it needs to be presented in a way that will encourage children to stop and think. It should be exciting, unexpected and stimulating ... it should be presented with as much visual sensitivity as the staff of a school can provide, and ... provide ... an ever-changing environment in which to work. (*ibid*, p 30)

In these respects, the arts and the provision of resources for them are to do with the whole ethos of a school.

77 *Expressive Media*

Resources to stimulate learning and enquiry can be distinguished from the media—paint, clay, sound, movement—through which children formulate and express their responses in the arts. Different arts use different media to address different modes of perception: visual, aural, tactile, kinaesthetic. Three requirements in provision here are for *variety*, *quality* and *adequacy*.

78 Variety

The case for variety of provision is implicit in our general argument ... it does not follow that because a person is creative in one realm of activity he or she is equally, or at all, creative in others. We all tend to show creative abilities in relation to particular problems or types of activity which engage our curiosity and for which we have a 'feel'. The creative musician is not necessarily a creative painter or dancer and need not find these other arts personally rewarding. The person who is 'at home' working with clay may feel awkward working with paint and so on.

It is common, however, to hear some children described as having no imagination or creative ability. We find this a pessimistic and despairing attitude. It is unlikely that any child is actually bereft of these things. It is far more likely that he or she has not found—and has not been helped to find—the areas in which his/her own creative abilities lie. This is not surprising in schools where the curriculum treads a narrow path of 'basic skills'. If schools are concerned with developing the full variety of human intelligence and capabilities, they must provide for the many ways in which this is likely to show itself from one child to the next. Providing for one art form in the belief that one does as well as another is not enough.

79 Quality

All work is improved by good tools and materials. Resources need not be expensive but that does not mean that materials—paint, paper, clay, instruments etc—need only be second rate. High standards of achievement in the arts will be encouraged when children work—as adults would wish to—with media that enhance rather than inhibit their attempts at expression and communication.

80 Adequacy

Although there is no need to prescribe the amounts of time to be spent on the arts in primary schools, it is essential that the time allowed is adequate for the task in hand. The performing arts—music, dance and drama—are key examples here.

Unlike, say, painting and modelling, the performing arts only exist as events in time. When the music, the dance or the drama ends, there is no object left to see or touch. To be seen or heard again, it must be done again. Time is thus one of the central media of the performing arts. The way in which is it used in a piece of work is crucial both to its meaning and its aesthetic qualities. This applies equally, in dance and drama, to the use of space.

Giving *some* time to the arts, or *some* space, is not necessarily enough. Provision must be sensitive to the particular ways in which the creative process makes use of these things, and to the need for work to develop both within the school day and from one day to the next.

81   Resourcefulness
To summarize, the effective teaching of the arts in primary schools depends upon:

(a) the active encouragement of expressive and creative activity in all areas of the curriculum;
(b) a stimulating classroom environment and a ready supply of interesting resources;
(c) the availability of suitable materials for the task in hand;
(d) the careful use of space and time to allow for the development of a variety of activities by individuals and by groups;
(e) careful preparation of work and the expectation of high standards of attainment within the capabilities of each child;
(f) co-operation and co-ordination between staff.

The most important resource of any school is its teachers: the most important quality of any teacher is resourcefulness. There are very few organizational problems in developing the arts in primary schools. Their success or otherwise leans heavily on the attitudes and resourcefulness of the class and the headteacher. It is important to comment on some of the problems which arise in relation to this.

82   What are the Problems?
The most common obstacle to effective arts teaching in the primary school is a lack of confidence among teachers, combined with—or resulting from—a feeling that they themselves are not 'artistic'. Of the many possible reasons for this, we will consider two: the influence of teachers' own education at school and the deficiencies of initial training courses.

83   A Vicious Circle
Teachers are themselves a product of the educational processes whose imbalance we have been criticizing. If they feel ill at ease in the arts and unable to organize these essential experiences for children, it may be because they were denied them as children. This strengthens our argument about the long-term dangers of lop-sided educational priorities. For the cycle is self-perpetuating. Teachers are among the successes of the education system. It is not surprising that they tend to maintain the practices which nurtured their success and to limit their involvement in the areas which they themselves were educated to neglect.

84   Initial Training
Initial training for primary school teachers is often deficient in two ways: either it includes no compulsory arts element at all, or students only

practise the arts at their own level, with little guidance in applying them to work with specific age groups. Educational theory tends to compose a separate part of the course. The new patterns of degree courses have now brought an even greater emphasis on theory. This is leading to a further neglect of practical and applied courses, despite the obvious need for balance. This makes the current outlook bleak for improving the arts in primary schools through existing initial training courses. While teachers themselves have little experience, low expectations and even less confidence in the arts, these will continue to be passed on to children.

85   What are Possible Solutions?

(a) the inclusion of a compulsory arts element in all initial training courses for primary school teachers;
(b) the appointment of teachers with specialist arts training in primary schools;
(c) the development of school-based in-service training in the arts.

87   The Need for Specialists

The insistent problem with specialist training is that the relatedness of the various parts of the curriculum, and the possibilities for interdisciplinary work, are easily overlooked. Nevertheless, the inadequacy of a good deal of arts teaching in primary schools does call for more teachers with specialised knowledge and skills to be appointed. This would certainly help to raise the quality of work in individual classrooms. What of the quality of work in the school as a whole?

88   The Advisory Service

We have emphasized the high quality of work in many schools and authorities. The work of the advisory service has always played a key role here. The adviser provides a vital means of communication between schools and between the different sectors of education across an authority. This is essential for the co-ordination of resources and policies and also for the provision of appropriate in-service training ... We believe that a strong advisory service is both the most effective and least expensive way of improving the quality of teaching. We strongly urge that the maintenance, and wherever possible the development, of the advisory service should be seen as an essential safeguard for the future of the arts in schools.

89   Staff Consultants

The two main ways in which the quality of the arts in primary schools —and we maintain, of the curriculum as a whole—can be improved are by:

(a) raising the general levels of teachers' competence and confidence in the arts;

(b) pursuing opportunities for interdisciplinary work.

Some schools are attempting to do this by designating teachers as consultants, who pass on specialist skills and knowledge to the rest of the staff. This role should be seen as complementary to, rather than instead of, the work of the advisers. The teacher in the school can help other members of staff on a day-to-day basis on matters affecting work with their own classes. This can be done through:

(a) advice:
   offering ideas on how to develop particular schemes of work through the arts, and how to extend, and deepen the quality of, arts activities already in hand;
(b) assistance:
   working alongside colleagues for specific lessons or activities;
(c) courses:
   organizing short practical sessions for staff on aspects of their own specialism—use of materials, basic concepts, etc.

Such teachers can also provide an element of more specialised activity with older children in the primary school who are ready for more demanding work in the arts.

Two further points should be made. First, although we are thinking particularly of the arts, specialists in any area of work could fulfil such a role for colleagues. Arts specialists have much to gain from other disciplines.

Second, there are obvious difficulties in the management of such an arrangement. Apart from those which might arise from teachers working with other classes, other staff may find it hard to accept a colleague in such a role.

There are, however, as we have suggested, many possible benefits which make such schemes worth supporting—certainly as an area of experiment. A benefit worth mentioning is the valuable experience this can give teacher/consultants themselves, not least as a preparation for further responsibility. It can provide an important means of professional development and the appearance of those with arts backgrounds in positions of responsibility in primary schools is a development we would very much welcome.

References

DEPARTMENT OF EDUCATION AND SCIENCE (1978) *Primary Education in England*, HMSO.
EISNER, E. (Ed) (1976) *The Arts, Human Development and Education*, McCutchan Publishing Corporation.

MACGREGOR, L., TATE, M. and ROBINSON, K. (1977) *Learning Through Drama*, Heinemann.

PRIMARY SCHOOLS RESEARCH AND DEVELOPMENT (1978) *Primary School Teachers' Attitudes to Issues Raised in the Great Debate*, Faculty of Education, University of Birmingham.

SCHOOLS COUNCIL (1981) *Resources for Visual Education*, Schools Council Art Committee.

The Social Subjects

Alistair Ross

On one level, there appears to have been little significant change in the teaching of the social subjects in primary schools over the past sixteen years. Lawton and his colleagues (1971, pp. 206–7) observed that:

> little social science based work appears to be going on. ... This is ... the result of uncertainty about what sort of social understandings should be encouraged, some underestimation of what children are capable of understanding about society, and a lack of knowledge about source materials and subject matter.

Seven years later, Her Majesty's Inspectorate (DES, 1978) were critical of 'the lack of progression and the amount of repetition in the work in geography and history' (para 8.26), which they felt probably resulted from a lack of planning. The study of the past was found in 60 per cent of 7-year-old classes, 90 per cent of 9-year-old classes, and almost 100 per cent of 11-year-old classes: but in some 80 per cent of all these 'the work was superficial. In many cases it involved little more than copying from reference books' (para 5.127). Geographical work was found in 60 per cent of 8-year-old classes, rising to 90 per cent with 9 and 11-year-olds: but again, 'much of the work tended to be superficial and there was often little evidence of progression' (para 5.135).

A small-scale survey by HMI of social sciences in primary schools six years later reported (Anglesey and Hennessey, 1984) that the HMI Social Science Committee was 'acutely aware of the need to assess [social science] work in primary schools', and observed that none of the schools that they had visited 'really had a clearly defined social science policy as such. Rather, individual social sciences were tapped from time to time in social studies or environmental studies programmes'.

These examples of apparent stagnation mask both some confusion over what constitute 'the social subjects', and a variety of local and relatively small-scale initiatives in this area not reflected in the national surveys.

Children and Their Primary Schools (CACE, 1967) was critical of subject divisions, but nevertheless identified history and geography as the two social areas in the curriculum. As Vincent Rogers (1968) pointed out, it omitted any reference to any social science. The HMI survey (DES, 1978, p. 70) identified 'social studies', which had only three elements within it (religious education, history and geography); but the HMI schedules of inspection, on which the report was based, apparently confuse this curriculum area with 'social abilities' (p. 216). Such blurring of the boundaries between social science and socialization is also common in primary schools (Anglesey and Hennessey, 1984, p. 84).

The next HMI survey of schools within the primary age range, *Education 5 to 9* (DES, 1982, p. 28) categorized a curriculum area as 'learning about people', including subheadings 'Themselves', 'Others', 'The locality', 'More distant places' and 'People in other times'. A year later, in *9–13 Middle Schools* (DES, 1983, p. 105), HMI simply lumped the subjects together under the heading 'History, Geography and Religious Education'. Meanwhile HMI's *A View of the Curriculum* (DES, 1980), the DES *The School Curriculum* (1981), the Schools Council's *The Practical Curriculum* (1981) and its successor *Primary Practice* (1983) were all referring to two areas of the primary curriculum: 'history and social studies' and 'geography'.

The White Paper *Better Schools* (Des 1985, para. 61) distinguishes the social area in two ways: primary schools should, *inter alia*:

> lay the foundation of understanding in religious education, history and geography, and the nature and values of British society;

> give pupils some insights into the adult world, including how people earn their living.

The curriculum document published by HMI (DES, 1985b) in their Curriculum Matters series refreshingly breaks away from this over-worn litany of subjects. This refers to 'areas of learning and experience', 'elements of learning' and 'essential issues not necessarily included within subjects but which need to be included in the curriculum (paras 25–26). Human and social areas are more carefully defined here in five paragraphs (41–45) to include the political, environmental, historical, economic and geographic areas of learning, linking each of these very clearly to children's experience, and ending with the caveat that 'in social matters how one learns is as important as what one learns'. The section on elements of learning is less specific, referring in broad terms to knowledge, skills, concepts and attitudes. 'Essential issues' include political education, education in economic understanding, preparation for the world of work ('progressively through the primary and secondary years') and the provision of equal opportunities for boys and girls.

The working definition that will be used in this chapter is derived from several of these. I will be referring to the social sciences—particularly sociology, economics and anthropology—to history, and to social geography. These may satisfactorily be linked in the primary school curriculum, employing a range of related skills and sharing many of each others' important organizing concepts.

The Schools Council Initiative: A Synthesizing Approach

The move to enhance the rigour of teaching in primary schools of the social subjects can be traced back at least as far as the Plowden Report (CACE, 1967). From its recommendation that four-year middle schools be introduced to replace the existing pattern of primary/secondary school division came a conference held by the Schools Council at Warwick on the curriculum for 8–13 year olds. Three papers considered the place of social studies, and one of these (Lawton, 1969) was followed by a more detailed survey funded by the Schools Council (Lawton *et al*, 1971). This suggested the development of a sequential curriculum based on core social concepts, using Bruner's model of a spiral curriculum.

From this came the curriculum development project funded by the Schools Council that was variously known as 'Place, Time and Society', 'Social Studies, History and Geography 8–13' or 'The Blyth Project', after the Director, Professor W. A. L. Blyth. They produced a core planning book (Blyth *et al*, 1976), a set of ancillary booklets, and a limited number of teaching packs, intended as exemplars to the profession. As Blenkin and Kelly (1981, p. 80) have pointed out, the planning by objectives model adopted by the project presented many difficulties to classroom practitioners: their aims in practice are constantly being modified as a project unfolds with a class. Aims cannot be rigidly enshrined in a discrete set, fixed in advance by curriculum planners from outside. Blyth (1974) accepted this when he suggested that all their objectives should be seen as provisional.

Blyth's team identified a set of core concepts, skills and attitudes around which they mapped out various ways that local authorities and schools might map out a rigorous social subjects curriculum. Their scheme integrated traditional social subjects such as history and geography into an all-embracing curriculum area of social studies, and provided a coherence and rationale for such a synthesis. Thirteen LEAs were involved in the project's diffusion processes, which included the trial of the teaching strategies suggested by the project and the developing of materials. The project's list of concepts in particular was derived from similar work in the United States, particularly that of Hilda Taba: they suggested core concepts of communication, power, values and beliefs, conflict/consensus, similarity/difference, continuity/change and causality.

The project packs that followed the teachers' materials were not adopted widely: the project put more emphasis on urging local authorities to disseminate ideas about how the social areas might be planned in primary and middle schools. It was argued that each LEA should support the needs of the social subjects 'in terms of both rethinking and of resources'. The project, however, received minimal support from such important curriculum legitimators as HMI. One of the project team has compared their lack of support in this area with the enthusiasm of Sir Keith Joseph and the Department of Industry for primary children to study wealth creation (Derricott, 1984). It may also fairly be pointed out that the Schools Council itself, in its final phase of operation from the reorganization and re-emphases of programme areas in 1979 paid scant attention to the work of the project, as witnessed by the rather weak definitions of the social subjects in *The Practical Curriculum* (1981) and its primary school sequel (1983).

Local Authority Responses

The challenge of the social subjects has been taken up by a number of LEAs in the late 1970s and 1980s. Three particular examples will be considered here, which show some of the range of responses.

Merton, an authority not involved in the Schools Council project, responded by concentrating on the issue of continuity and development of the social subjects across the first, middle and high school phases of education. Groups of teachers were given the task of reviewing existing development work, and then to 'synthesize, simplify and apply it' (London Borough of Merton/Schools Council, 1981). The groups were based variously on a phase basis (eg. first school teachers meeting together) and on an area basis (feeder first schools meeting with their middle and high school counterparts). The meetings, over a period of nearly three years, did much for the development of the schools involved in the project, but perhaps had less continuing impact than was hoped for across all the schools in the authority (Harries, 1984). The report, *The New Approach to the Social Studies*, concluded that both first and middle schools needed subject coordinators, one of whose most important tasks would be to coordinate the provision of resources. The outline schemes of work produced, for example for the middle school range, were ambitious in their breadth but might be criticized for using relatively few local social issues as a focus for study.

One of the great distractions for teachers in social studies is to encourage children to study things rather than people: a bias towards the safe and the uncontroversial that will be returned to later in this chapter.

By way of contrast, the Inner London Education Authority had been involved in the work of the Schools Council project. Some of the teachers involved were brought together and given the task of developing an 8 to

11 social studies curriculum to be disseminated through the Authority's schools. The inquiry model of learning that they proposed, and their list of eight core concepts (power and authority, conflict, change, tradition, cooperation, the division of labour, interdependence and social control) owed much to the work of Blyth and Lawton (ILEA, 1980b). They also felt that exemplar curriculum materials were needed, and Sue Wagstaff was seconded to produce the *People Around Us* set of teaching packs, that took *Families*, *Friends*, and *Work* as their themes (ILEA, 1978, 1979, 1980a). Each pack was supposed to supplement the use in school of children's own experiences of the social world. The materials have been criticized for too accurately reflecting the world as it is (including its discriminatory patterns based on gender, race and class), although the intention of the materials was that such issues should be thrown up for discussion. The processes of dissemination here can be seen as teacher meetings leading to the centralized preparation and production of materials, followed by local dissemination and adaptation (a periphery-centre-periphery model) (Ross, 1982). The materials were circulated and modified widely in the authority's schools, and were accompanied by the publication of a guidelines document that probably remains one of the best succinct statements of this approach (ILEA, 1980b).

Northamptonshire were not originally involved in the diffusion of the Schools Council project, but the local inspectorate took on the task of promoting the materials (Driscoll, 1986). Unlike Merton's policy of establishing groups of teachers on both a phase and a locality basis, and working a policy from this, and ILEA's periphery-centre-periphery model, Northamptonshire adopted a 'top-down' model of dissemination. *Humanities Curriculum Guidelines for the Middle Years* was written by the authority's inspectorate and used as the basis for in-service education. The document urges a broadening of the traditional humanities subjects of history and geography to include relevant aspects of the social sciences, and particularly emphasizes a skills-based approach, drawing heavily upon the skills suggested in the Schools Council project.

The Social Sciences or the Social Subjects?

At least at an anecdotal level, there is clearly much confusion in teacher's minds about 'subjects' and their boundaries. While the majority of primary teachers accept the notion of an integrated approach to early learning (even if they do not fully implement such an approach themselves), there still appears to be a notional hierarchy of the appropriate content appropriate for the primary school, and this definition is implicitly defined in terms of traditional subjects. Thus, for example, geographical aspects are often introduced to the upper infant age range, and historical ideas begin in the lower to mid-juniors. The subject matter more usually associated with the social sciences—sociology, politics, economics and anthropology, for example—is often not deemed appropriate for inclusion in an integrated scheme. However, it could be argued that much of the material studied in such disciplines is closer to the direct experience of the young child than the content matter of many schemes with a strong and 'pure' geographical or historical basis. Other teachers resist attempts to include history and certain aspects of geography in the curriculum, as being distant from children's experience, but not substitute any other material than that eclectically drawn from the immediate locality. Anglesey and Hennessey (1984) have pointed out that primary schools tend to draw on the social sciences for either social studies or environmental studies:

> ... The difference in nomenclature is possibly significant. Schools referring to their syllabuses as 'Environmental Studies' tended to relate to work in the natural sciences (particularly biology) and to instrumental aspects of life. Courses referred to as 'Social Studies' were more likely to be vehicles for history and geography and to general social education, often of a kind which leaned towards socialization.

One reason for such attitudes probably stems from teachers' own education, and from their views of what the disciplines are: they seem to be often regarded as discrete bodies of knowledge, rather than as procedures for enquiry. This can be seen clearly in the typology of subjects used by the primary HMI in their schedules of enquiry used in the various primary surveys, outlined above (DES; 1978, 1982, 1983).

This need not be so. There have been some serious efforts to demonstrate the interdependence of the social sciences and the traditional subjects of history and geography. Braudel (1985, p. 333) has argued for comparative cultural studies that are both synchronic (comparing disparate cultures that occur at the same time) and diachronic (comparing changes in cultures over time): both require the development of a sense of contemporary society. Burke's attempt (1980) to demonstrate the integrity of history with the social sciences may ring true to those currently engaged in historical research, but has alarmed further those teachers of history who see their subject as under threat of erosion from integrated humanities, particularly in the secondary schools.

The confusion over what constitute the social subjects is greater in the primary school for two principal reasons. Firstly, there are few teachers with a specialist background in any of the social subjects. While a number of primary BEd courses offer some major specialism in the traditional social subjects of history and geography, there are very few that offer any social science based course. Those with social science degrees are actively discouraged from entering primary education by the PGCE route: degrees in politics, economics, philosophy and the like are categorized by the DES as 'not relevant' to the primary curriculum (*THES*, 1983). Secondly, in the curriculum studies undertaken as the generalist part of their course by all primary student teachers, there is rarely a cohesive view put forward of the social subjects as a necessary and coherent element within the primary curriculum. Students either pass through a collection of discrete subject studies, each necessarily brief and superficial; or have an integrated course that frequently fails to distinguish the unique contributions of the disciplines. Both routes result in students devaluing the curriculum area as being less than central to the 'real' work of the primary school.

The result of these two tendencies is that there are few teachers able to offer specialist leadership in social subjects in primary schools, and even were there such teachers, there is not a strongly defined notion of the curriculum area amongst other, non-specialist primary teachers.

There have been attempts to change this: the distinctive contribution initiated by the Schools Council has already been described. This might be categorized as a *synthesizing* approach to the social subjects: an attempt to provide an over-arching definition of the curriculum area into which examples of good practice might be fitted. Two other similar approaches will be reviewed here—that of the Association for the Teaching of the Social Sciences (the ATSS) and that of what is sometimes called the 'Topic' school.

Two other categories of approach to the social subjects will also be defined: the *restructuralists* those who attempt to deny the social subjects as a legitimate area for study, and to relocate some of their subject matter into more traditional and 'safe' subjects; and the *particularists*—those who accept the synthesizers' structures, but seek to exemplify these structures through specific curriculum contexts that might seem more familiar to primary teachers (such as world studies, multiculturalism, or industry education).

The Synthesizers

The Schools Council project and its successor provided a framework for the social subjects in primary education, based on a particular methodology that children could use to investigate social issues, the development of particular skills of social understanding, and, most particularly, a clear notion of conceptual development. Two other sets of educationalists might be considered under this category.

The ATSS are a subject association of teachers—almost all in secondary or further education—concerned with the social sciences. In this they are similar to the two other social science subject associations, the Economics Association and the Politics Association; but unlike these the ATSS have made some determined efforts to involve themselves in primary school social studies. Two issues of their journal, *The Social Science Teacher*, have been devoted exclusively to work in primary education (ATSS, 1980, 1984), and between these there have been a fairly regular stream of articles from primary and middle schools (eg. Wagstaff and North, 1980). These contributions have on the whole been within the synthesizing tradition of the Schools Council project, echoing the concerns of the secondary teacher membership with a concepts/skills approach (Mountain and Brownlie, 1984).

Links with language development have also been particularly stressed by those in the synthesizing school. In particular, oral discussions have been emphasized by several writers as an important way of groups of children collaborating on the definition of developing concepts (Tarrant, 1984; Ross, 1983).

The second synthesizing approach has sprung from primary school roots, or at least from primary teacher-training roots. The work at Trent Polytechnic of Stella and Dennis Gunning and of Jack Wilson has built on the popular 'topic' teaching approach found in many primary schools (1981). Their focus on topic work firmly identifies it as social science, history and geography, and demands that primary teachers adopt a fairly rigorous concept-based approach. Detailed examples of children's work and conversation demonstrate the depth of the approach they advocate (Wilson and Gunning, 1980, 1983; Kerry, 1983, 1984; Lavender, 1983; Miles, 1984).

The Restructuralists

Under this category I include all those who apparently seek to deny the validity of any grouping of 'the social subjects' in the primary curriculum. They generally do this by reasserting the primacy of the traditional subjects, particularly history and geography, claiming that their traditional values allow skill and knowledge development that is both necessary and sufficient for primary children's development (Reeves, 1980). Some members of the Historical Association (through not those associated with the education committee) have been particularly associated with this movement (*The Times*, 1985), and have been encouraged in this by speeches of the former Secretary of State (*TES*, 1984a, 1984b).

This is not to suggest that all enthusiasts of history fall into the category of those dismissing the other social subjects. Joan Blyth has managed to successfully proselytize the cause of history (1982) as well as history and geography (1984) without detracting from the importance of the social sciences. The guidelines issued by the ILEA, *History in the Primary School* (1980c) were carefully designed to complement the simultaneously published *Social Studies in the Primary School*. (This overlap was not true, however, of the ILEA's geographical/environmental guidelines. *The Study of Places in the Primary School* (ILEA, 1981), which only bear a superficial similarity to the History and Social Studies documents.) The more recent HMI booklet *History in the Primary and Secondary Years: An HMI View* (DES, 1985a) is particularly careful to advocate a social science concepts/skills approach. One particular aspect of history that has developed in primary schools has been oral history, where children collect and assess evidence directly from participants (Purkis, 1980; Ross, 1984), and this has obvious links with the oral skills developed through the social sciences referred to above. But it is in areas such as history that the tyranny of the 'safe' can take over: there is something rather like Gresham's Law at work here, where in any given social studies project the uncontroversial will drive out the potential for exploring uncomfortable issues. This may be true also for such areas as environmental studies, where Anglesey and Hennessey (1984) observed environmental studies being used by schools to define the study of the physical surroundings, while those (fewer) schools using the term social studies had a greater emphasis on human activities and issues. A more potent restructuralist threat comes from those who attempt to redefine the social subjects as social education (*ibid*, 84). The Thomas Report on improving ILEA primary schools (ILEA, 1985) falls into this category. Certain important social skills—such as the development of self-esteem, the ability to work in groups, etc.—are identified as the core reasons for work in the social areas of the curriculum: this has the effect of shifting the process of social studies learning to being a process of social development *per se*. Social studies become merely a vehicle for personal development, and the subject's own validity as a process of social understanding and investigation are consequently devalued.

The Particularists

This third group are defined as those who seek to link particular issues or areas to the work of the social science/social studies synthesisers. This approach has the advantage of giving particular content and significance to the area of the social subjects. This seems to meet an important need for many non-specialist primary teachers who find the approach of the synthesisers diffuse, content-free and difficult to use as a basis for planning.

The world studies movement, led by a Schools Council/Rowntree Trust project organised by Fisher and Hicks (1984; and Hicks, 1980), aims to develop knowledge, skills, attitudes and concepts relevant to living in both a multicultural society and an interdependent world. Much of the approach is based on the synthesized social sciences approach: the introduction of controversial issues, concepts such as conflict, interdependence, cooperation, peace and human rights; and the links between children's everyday experience and the wider world. The world studies movement has not been without its critics. It has been claimed by Sturman (1986) that it remains a Eurocentric approach, 'us' studying 'them'. Fisher and Hicks, it is said, tend to use only the experience of white indigenous children as a reference point in the classroom, and to discount the experiences of children of other cultures—in particular, the bilingual experience of many children.

Similar criticisms have been made of much of the more recent multi-cutural materials for primary school children appearing on the commercial market. Klein (1986) has commented on the changing approaches in series such as *Beans* (A & C Black), which use detailed case studies of different cultures (as advocated by many of the synthesizing group of social science educators), which focus on particular concepts such as change, cooper-ation, tradition and conflict, and yet in some instances remain voyeuristic and patronizing.

The growth of multicultural and anti-racist studies in primary schools has accelerated over the past decade, particularly in the urban areas; and it has a clear base both in teachers' concerns with the issues affecting all the children that they teach and in the skills/concepts approach of the social science educators. However, it seems fair to claim that the links between multicultural/anti-racist teaching and the social sciences are less clear to primary teachers than are the links with the more discrete World Studies movement: multicultural and anti-racist teaching very often is seen as social education rather than social studies education, whereas the world studies movement can perhaps combine its more distant perspective with a more defined curriculum focus.

The primary schools-industry developments over the past five years have also shown a certain ambivalence in their relationship with the social sciences, though several writers have made the link explicit (eg Ross and Smith, 1985). W. A. L. Blyth—who has become associated with this schools-industry work since 1982—has pointed out that there are two distinct strands in this area of work—firstly, a social science/social subjects strand, which focusses on social organization in the workplace, and social interaction in classroom activities and, secondly, a technological/science strand, which uses industry (and particularly, though not exclusively, the technological manufacturing industries) as a focus for studying the applica-tion of modern technology (1987, forthcoming). Blyth has also drawn useful distinctions between education for industry, education about indus-try, and education *through* industry (1984). What teachers aim to achieve through such work can also vary quite sharply, between those who see the area in an instrumental way, where children acquire key information about the country's economic system that informs their opinions on the value of industry and manufacture, to those who share a process view of the curriculum, who use industry as an interesting vehicle to develop particular social science skills and attitudes (Ross, 1985).

The principal initiative for primary schools-industry work has come from the Schools Curriculum Industry Project (SCIP), which developed a process learning model about industry for secondary school pupils in the late 1970s. In 1981 they began to coordinate the work of several primary school groups in the country, notably the work at Edge Hill College of Higher Education, and also that in the ILEA, and in Gwent and Clwyd (Jamieson, 1984). In primary schools, work has followed one of two patterns: there have been detailed case studies of particular work places, with usually much emphasis on children working with adults other than teachers—either at the workplace or visiting school; and there have been school-based mini-enterprises, where children organize, produce and market some product or service. Both patterns stress the active involvement of children in processes of enquiry and learning. There is usually a strong skills/concepts thrust to the work, and there is a congruence between many of the concepts in Ross and Smith (1985) and those in the earlier integrationist sources, such as Blyth (1978) and ILEA (1980b).

Conclusions

Despite the apparent lack of development on a national scale noted at the beginning of this chapter, there has been a considerable development of relatively small scale developments in the social subjects. These appear to fall into a pattern, as has been suggested here. The pioneering work of Lawton and Blyth's teams in the 1970s, sponsored by the Schools Council, synthesized an integrated framework for the development of the curriculum area. This was adopted in a variety of ways in a not inconsiderable number of local authorities. But the initiative also provoked a series of rejoinders, both from those who sought to reassert the primacy of traditional subject divisions, and from those who wanted to redefine the social subjects as a convenient way of developing social skills. As yet, these reconstructionists are ill-coordinated and have not put forward any strongly argued and practical counter-proposals: but there probably would be a fair-sized body of primary teachers who would respond to a call to reintroduce the traditional subjects, taught in a traditional manner, into the junior school. A second response to the original initiatives has been from a variety of special interest groups, who have sought—often very successfully—to define their curriculum concerns in a manner that links them to the social sciences. This approach has strengthened the social science movement, inasmuch as it has provided a variety of concrete examples of how the concepts and skills of the social sciences might be practically developed in the primary classroom.

There are a number of possible developments in the social subjects. It could well happen that the "restructuralists" consolidate their forces and provide a more solid rejoinder to the social scientists than hitherto. This would, one suspects, strike a receptive chord from a large proportion of parents, many school governors, and from not a few teachers. If successful, the results might be—particularly in the junior age range—a move away from using children's own social experiences towards a greater reliance on text and topic books; a definition of the curriculum in terms of content rather than skills and concepts; and an overall weakening of children's understandings of the links between the social subjects.

A more likely development is the growth of the particularist groups. There are a number of possible groups who would find it relatively simple to define their concerns in a social sciences skills/concepts framework. As well as the groups considered above, those concerned with issues of gender, with human rights, with environmental and pollution concerns, with third world development, with minorities, with planning and development, with local community issues—all could find a secure place in the curriculum under a social subject umbrella.

A third development could be that the original synthesis is redefined and projected in some more forceful way, with legitimizing support from the local authorities and the HMI. This outcome seems a less likely possibility, given the relative weakness of the School Curriculum Development Committee compared to the Schools Council, the lack of enthusiasm shown by HMI as a whole, and the lack of interest and knowledge shown by most local authority advisers. But it could yet provide an important force for integration, perhaps particularly between the environmental education movement and the social subjects. If the development of the social subjects is left to the particularist interest groups, then there is a possibility that the integrated framework on which they are building may become submerged under their weight. It will be important that primary teachers can clearly see a synthesis between the social subjects, and that they are able to maintain a relatively simple concepts/skills model of the curriculum area on which to hang the particular social issues and concerns that arise from their children's experiences and interests.

References

ANGLESEY, K. J. and HENNESSEY, R. A. S. (1984) 'Social sciences in primary schools', *The Social Science Teacher*, 13, 3, pp. 83–4.

ASSOCIATION FOR THE TEACHING OF THE SOCIAL SCIENCES (ATSS) (1980) *The Social Science Teacher*, 9, 4–5.

ASSOCIATION FOR THE TEACHING OF THE SOCIAL SCIENCES (1984) *The Social Science Teacher*, 13, 3.

BLENKIN, G. M. and KELLY, A. V. (1981) *The Primary Curriculum*, Harper and Row.

BLYTH, J. E. (1982) *History in Primary Schools: A Practical Approach for Teachers of 5–11 year old Children*, McGraw-Hill.

BLYTH J. E. (1984) *Place and Time with Children Five to Nine*, Croom Helm.

BLYTH W. A. L. (1974) 'One development project's awkward thinking about objectives', *Journal of Curriculum Studies*, 6, pp. 99–111.

BLYTH, W. A. L. *et al* (1976) *Place, Time and Society 8–13: Curriculum Planning in History, Geography and Social Science*, Collins/ESL.

BLYTH, W. A. L. (1984) 'Industry education: Case studies from the north west' in

JAMIESON, I. (Ed) *'We Make Kettles': Studying Industry in the Primary School*, Longman.

BLYTH, W. A. L. (1987 forthcoming) 'Appraising and assessing young children's understanding of industry' in SMITH, D. *Primary Children and Industry*, Falmer Press.

BRAUDEL, F. (1985) *Civilisation and Capitalism 15th–18th Century; Vol 1: The Structures of Everyday Life*, Collins.

BURKE, P. (1980) *Sociology and History*, Allen & Unwin

CENTRAL ADVISORY COUNCIL FOR EDUCATION (ENGLAND), (1967) *Children and their Primary Schools* (The Plowden Report), HMSO

DEPARTMENT OF EDUCATION AND SCIENCE (1978) *Primary Education in England: A Survey by HM Inspectors of Schools*, HMSO.

DEPARTMENT OF EDUCATION AND SCIENCE (1980) *A View of the Curriculum*, (HMI Series: Matters for Discussion, 11), HMSO.

DEPARTMENT OF EDUCATION AND SCIENCE (1981) *The School Curriculum*, HMSO.

DEPARTMENT OF EDUCATION AND SCIENCE (1982) *Education 5 to 9: An Illustrative Survey of 80 First Schools in England*, HMSO.

DEPARTMENT OF EDUCATION AND SCIENCE (1983) *9–13 Middle Schools: An Illustrative Survey*, HMSO.

DEPARTMENT OF EDUCATION AND SCIENCE (1985a) *History in the Primary and Secondary Years: An HMI view*, HMSO.

DEPARTMENT OF EDUCATION AND SCIENCE (1985b) *The Curriculum from 5 to 16*, (Curriculum Matters 2: an HMI series), HMSO

DEPARTMENT OF EDUCATION AND SCIENCE (1985c) *Better Schools*, Cmnd 9469, HMSO

DERRICOTT, R. (1984) 'Place, time and society 8–13: Retrospect and prospect', *The Social Science Teacher*, 13, 3, pp. 81–3.

DRISCOLL, K. J., (1986) *Humanities Curriculum Guidelines for the Middle and Secondary Years*, Falmer Press.

FISHER, S, and HICKS D. (1984) *World Studies 8–13: A Teacher's Handbook*, Oliver & Boyd.

GUNNING, S., GUNNING, D. and WILSON, J. (1981) *Topic Teaching in the Primary School: Teaching about Society through Topic Work*, Croom Helm.

HARRIES, E., (1984) 'Social sciences 7–13: The view and the role of the local authority', *The Social Science Teacher*, 13, 3, pp. 71–3.

HICKS, D. (1980) 'Teaching about other people: how biased are school books?', *Education 3–13*, 9, 2, pp. 14–19.

INNER LONDON EDUCATION AUTHORITY (1978) *People Around Us: Unit 1: Families*, ILEA and A & C Black

INNER LONDON EDUCATION AUTHORITY (1979) *People Around Us: Unit 2: Friends*, ILEA and A & C Black

INNER LONDON EDUCATION AUTHORITY (1980a) *People Around Us: Unit 3: Work*, ILEA

INNER LONDON EDUCATION AUTHORITY (1980b) *Social Studies in the Primary School*, ILEA.

INNER LONDON EDUCATION AUTHORITY (1980c) *History in the Primary School*, ILEA.

INNER LONDON EDUCATION AUTHORITY (1981) *The Study of Places in the Primary School*, ILEA.

INNER LONDON EDUCATION AUTHORITY (1985) *Improving Primary Schools: Report of the Committee on Primary Education* [*The Thomas Report*], ILEA

JAMIESON, I. (Ed) (1984) '*We Make Kettles': Studying Industry in the Primary School*, Longman.

KERRY, T. (1983) 'Developing pupil's thinking through topic work', *Education 3–13*, 11, 2, pp. 4–7.

KERRY, T. (1984) 'Effective training for topic teaching', *Education 3–13*, 12, 1, pp. 33–7.

KLEIN, G. (1986) *Reading into Racism*, Routledge.

LAVENDER, R. (1983) 'Children using information books', *Education 3–13*, 11, 1, pp. 8–12.

LAWTON, D (1969) 'Social Studies 8–13' in Schools Council Working Paper 22, *The Middle Years of Schooling*, HMSO.

LAWTON, D., CAMPBELL, J. and BURKITT. V. (1971) *Social Studies 8–13* (*Schools Council Working Paper 39*), London, Evans/Methuen Educational

LONDON BOROUGH OF MERTON/SCHOOLS COUNCIL (1981) *The New Approach to the Social Studies: Continuity and Development in Children's Learning through First, Middle and High School*, Schools Council.

MILES, A (1984) 'A closer look: A case study of topic work in the classroom' *Education 3–13*, 12, 1, pp. 22–7.

MOUNTAIN, P. and BROWNLIE, A. (1984) 'Primary-secondary school links—correspondence' in *The Social Science Teacher*, 13, 3, pp. 78–9.

PURKIS, S. (1980) *Oral History in Schools*, Oral History Society.

REEVES, M. (1980) *Why History?*, Longman.

ROGERS, V. (1968) *The Social Studies in English Education*, Heinemann.

ROSS, A. (1981) 'Human rights education: Perspectives and problems in the primary school', *World Studies Journal*, 2, 3, pp. 13–16.

ROSS, A. (1982) 'In-service and curriculum development: A case study of social studies in primary schools in the ILEA', *British Journal of In-Service Education*, 9, 2, pp. 126–36.

ROSS, A. (1983) 'The bottle-stopper factory: Talking all together' *The English Magazine*, 11, pp. 14–18.

ROSS, A. (1984) 'Children becoming historians: An oral history project in a primary school' *Oral History*, 12, 2, pp. 21–31.

ROSS, A. (1985) 'Primary school teachers' aims in introducing industry into the classroom' *Curriculum*, 6, 3, pp. 20–8.

ROSS, A. and SMITH, D. (1985) *Schools and Industry 5–13: Looking at the World of Work—Questions Teachers Ask*, Schools Curriculum Industry Project.

SCHOOLS COUNCIL (1981) *The Practical Curriculum* (Schools Council Working Paper 70), London, Methuen Educational.

SCHOOLS COUNCIL (1983) *Primary Practice: A sequel to 'The Practical Curriculum'* (Schools Council Working Paper 75), Methuen Educational.

STURMAN, E. (1986) 'Who studies world studies?', *Issues in Race and Education*, 48, Summer 1986.

TARRANT, G. (1984) 'Social studies in the primary school: The place of discussion', *Social Science Teacher*, 13, 3, pp. 63–6.

The Times (1985) 25 October.

The Times Educational Supplement (1984a), 17 February.

The Times Educational Supplement (1984b), 24 August.

The Times Higher Educational Supplement (1983) 16 September.

WAGSTAFF, S. and NORTH, P. (1980) 'Social studies in the primary school', *The Social Science Teacher*, 9, 4/5, pp. 122–7.

WILSON, J. and GUNNING, D. (1980) 'Focussing ideas in junior school topic work' *Education 3–13*, 8, 1, pp. 33–6.

WILSON, J. and GUNNING, D (1983) 'Catering for a range of abilities in topic work', *Education 3–13*, 11, 2, pp. 8–11.

Important Publications Since 1980

ANGLESEY, K. J. and HENNESSEY, R. A. S. (1984) 'Social sciences in primary schools', *The Social Science Teacher*, 13, 3, pp. 83–4.

BLYTH J. E. (1984) *Place and Time with Children Five to Nine*, Croom Helm.

DEPARTMENT OF EDUCATION AND SCIENCE (1985) *History in the Primary and Secondary Years: An HMI view*, HMSO.

DEPARTMENT OF EDUCATION AND SCIENCE (1985) *The Curriculum from 5 to 16 (Curriculum Matters 2: An HMI series)*, London, HMSO.

DERRICOTT, R. (1984) 'Place, time and society 8–13: Retrospect and prospect', *The Social Science Teacher*, 13, 3, pp. 81–83.

FISHER, S. and D. HICKS (1985) *World Studies 8–13*: A Teacher's Handbook, Oliver & Boyd.

GUNNING, S., GUNNING, D. and WILSON, J. (1981) *Topic Teaching in the Primary School: Teaching about Society through Topic Work*, Croom Helm.

INNER LONDON EDUCATION AUTHORITY (1980a) *Social Studies in the Primary School*, ILEA.

INNER LONDON EDUCATION AUTHORITY (1980b) *History in the Primary School*, ILEA.

INNER LONDON EDUCATION AUTHORITY (1981) *The Study of Places in the Primary School*, ILEA.

JAMIESON, I. (Ed) (1984) *'We Make Kettles': Studying Industry in the Primary School*, Longman.

LONDON BOROUGH OF MERTON/SCHOOLS COUNCIL (1981) *The New Approach to the Social Studies: Continuity and Development in Children's Learning through First, Middle and High School*, London, Schools Council.

MEHLINGER, H. D. (Ed) (1981) *UNESCO Handbook for the Teaching of Social Studies*, Croom Helm.

ROSS, A. (1982) 'In-service and curriculum development: a case study of social studies in primary schools in the ILEA', *British Journal of In-Service Education*, 9, 2, pp. 126–36.

ROSS, A. and SMITH D. (1985) *Schools and Industry 5–13: Looking at the World of Work—Questions Teachers Ask*, Schools Curriculum Industry Project.

SCHOOLS COUNCIL (1983) *Primary Practice: A sequel to 'The Practical Curriculum'* (Schools Council Working Paper 75), Methuen Educational.

WAGSTAFF, S. and NORTH, P. (1980) 'Social studies in the primary school', *The Social Science Teacher*, 9, 4/5, pp. 122–7.

4
Developing Professional Effectiveness

Introduction

As the introductory paragraph in Colin Richards' first paper points out, the notion of 'development' has played an important part in primary education, especially since the Second World War. Often, perhaps too often, the notion has been used as part of the persuasive use of language associated with a 'liberal romantic' view of primary education (p. 11); 'the development of the whole child', 'the development of children's potential', 'the development of children's imagination and creativity' are examples of such usage. 'Development' has also a place in the academic discourse of education, particularly writing and research associated with child development, though in some aspects of this work it is difficult to separate out the descriptive and analytical from the prescriptive and ideological elements (Dearden, 1968). As a focus of academic interest, child development was particularly prominent in the forties and fifties, and though it has continued to be an important element in the education of teachers and, to a lesser extent, in educational research, it has tended to be over-shadowed by a series of successive emphases (some would say 'slogans') reflecting other kinds of development.

Curriculum development was a major motif for educational enquiry in the sixties and early seventies; as a result of the work of the Schools Council and a variety of other agencies at national, local and, more rarely, regional levels, a large number of proposals for new courses of study or patterns of educational experience were produced (Taylor and Richards, 1985). As a major motif, curriculum development has continued into the eighties, as illustrated by the work outlined in the third section of this book. As a slogan, it gave ground in the seventies to the idea of 'teacher development': a view that educational change comes about, not merely from the production of new curricular materials, but from the interaction between such materials and teachers' enhanced awareness of, and receptivity to, the processes of teaching and learning in their classrooms, particularly the epistemological and pedagogic principles underlying the transaction of the curriculum. The continuing importance of the 'teacher development' tradition or motif is exemplified, in part, by the contributions of Michael Golby and Howard Bradley in this volume.

The eighties have witnessed the rise to prominence of the twin notions of staff and school development. Through the former, the interests, experience and capabilities of individual teachers are harnessed and developed for the professional benefit not only of the individuals concerned but also of the school as a whole. Such staff development is seen as an important way in which the school can meet the ever-increasing demands being made upon it through releasing and developing the curricular and pedagogic expertise previously 'locked' inside individual classrooms. School development is an allied notion involving the pursuit by the staff as a whole of aims, objectives or aspirations collectively agreed as an agenda for action for a particular period of time (ILEA, 1985). Staff and school development are means of improving the professional effectiveness of teachers in institutional contexts.

The White Paper, *Better Schools* (DES, 1985) recognizes both the taxing nature of contemporary teaching and the need to strengthen teacher professionalism: 'The teacher's job has always been a demanding one. The policies for the curriculum present the schools with a difficult and challenging task which will require the full use of teachers' intellectual, physical and emotional resources. The work can rarely, perhaps never, be accomplished as well as its performer and others would wish. The teacher's professionalism represents his constant attempt to achieve that ideal' (paragraph 132). The Paper outlines a number of policy directions aimed at improving 'teacher quality': the reform of initial teacher training, revised INSET arrangements, management development for heads, teacher appraisal and more effective patterns of staff deployment. The papers in this section of the book address these themes and the notions of staff and school development; some take the White Paper's agenda as one focus but do so critically. Others discuss the implications of research for the future development of professional effectiveness.

Dan Wicksteed and Derek Sharples develop a sharply argued critique of current policy on initial teacher education set against the backcloth of likely demographic, economic and political prospects. They see great dangers in 'the clear and marked shift in policy towards increased central control' manifest particularly in teacher education by CATE (the Council for the Accreditation of Teacher Education). They trace the implications of current trends for college size, ethos, student experience and relationships with primary schools. Fundamentally they are critical of the underlying model of society into which they believe it is intended to induct students: a society which they characterise as essentially determined and closed rather than problematic and open. They raise the key question: 'To what extent can colleges maintain a critical awareness amongst students in the face of social determinism?

Howard Bradley sees many possibilities in the new developments likely to follow from the introduction of grant-related in-service training (GRIST). In particular, through INSET more directly geared to the needs of particular schools, it should be possible to bring together staff develop-ment and school development in a reinforcing, enriching way. He envis-ages much greater demand for INSET and greater need for its evaluation in the light of moves towards teacher appraisal (see pp. 277–86). His paper is based on the premiss that 'staff development and INSET hold the keys to the quality of the education we offer to pupils in the primary schools of the future'. He finishes on a challenging note, arguing that a choice has to made between INSET which minimizes teachers' fallibility and that which maximizes their creativity. It is clear where he stands on this issue.

Whilst agreeing with *Better Schools* on the importance of management development, Alan Coulson is critical of most current approaches, which he characterizes as based on the false assumption that 'leadership can be trained into people, that it can be equated with a role which can successfully be assumed and performed'. He argues that too much attention has been paid to the role requirements of primary headship and not enough to heads' personality. He proposes an alternative 'person-centred' approach to management development based on 'the belief that in primary headship the role and the person are so closely identified that professional and personal growth are inseparable' (p253). In his view, management development for heads and deputies needs to be seen as an integral part of a systematic LEA wide management development policy for the teaching profession as a whole. For him, notions of 'growth' and 'development' are central to increasing the effectiveness of primary headteachers and, necessarily along with that, their levels of professional and personal satisfaction.

Perhaps the most contentious of current proposals to increase profes-sional effectiveness is that related to teacher (including headteacher) appraisal. *Better Schools* comments: 'the regular and formal appraisal of the performance of all teachers is necessary if LEAs are to have the reliable, comprehensive and up-to-date information necessary for the systematic and effective provision of professional support and development and the deployment of staff to best advantage'. The fourth extract in this section is taken from the summary of an influential study on appraisal undertaken by a team from Suffolk LEA. It discusses the aims and objectives of appraisal, the responsibilities of various parties, the processes involved and the training and resource implications. Three fundamental questions need to be posed in relation to the Suffolk proposal and to any others that may emerge in the next few years: (i) Why is there concern about teacher appraisal?; (ii) What function or functions is appraisal expected to perform?; (iii) What is appraisal aimed at? Answers to such questions will indicate how far a proposal fosters or runs counter to the kinds of staff and school develop-ment outlined earlier in this editorial introduction.

Drawing on trends emerging from his own research and that of others,

Jim Campbell projects an image of the 'collegial' primary school where teachers collectively develop and review school-wide policies and practices for the curriculum. He is anxious to assert that this is an image, not yet a reality, except in a minority of schools. He is realistic enough to discuss two aspects of contemporary schooling which could hinder the development of collegiality: role relationships between teachers and the conditions under which teachers work. Nevertheless, his analysis leads to essentially optimistic conclusions. School development along collegial lines would help schools meet the demands of their various constituencies and if developed on a wide scale would be a counter-weight to what some contributors in this book fear, ie an undue degree of central control.

The sixth paper draws on the enormously influential national primary survey report which, once published in 1978, set the agenda for discussion and action in primary education for virtually a decade. The extract raises the vexed issue of class and specialist teaching and argues for a re-examination of the way staff are deployed in primary schools. It is careful not to suggest blanket solutions but it does question the confidence placed in class teaching as the sole mode of deployment. Almost ten years on, HMI's view of the primary curriculum is now couched in terms of areas of learning and experience (p56) but their essential challenge remains: can class teachers manage to provide children with access to all nine areas of learning and experience? 'If not, what must be done to help them to manage satisfactorily and in a way that is, on balance, advantageous?'

The last extract is taken from a summary of the ILEA Junior School Project which examined the progress of 2000 children in fifty primary schools over the four years of their junior schooling. As a result of this longitudinal study the researchers claim that some schools are considerably more effective than others in terms of children's educational outcomes. They identify two sets of factors contributing to primary schools' effectiveness: (i) 'givens' (ie less flexible characteristics of schools), eg age range, legal status, size, and (ii) 'policy factors' within the control of heads and teachers, eg purposeful leadership by heads, teacher involvement in curriculum planning and consistency in teaching approaches. Such findings would seem to provide empirical support for the notion of school policy-making and collective decision-taking advocated in the contributions of Jim Campbell, Alan Coulson and Colin Richards.

References

DEARDEN, R. (1968) *The Philosophy of Primary Education*, Routledge and Kegan Paul.
DEPARTMENT OF EDUCATION AND SCIENCE (1985) *Better Schools*, HMSO.
ILEA (1985) *Improving Primary Schools*, ILEA.
TAYLOR, P. and RICHARDS, C. (1985), *An Introduction to Curriculum Studies*, Second Edition, NFER.

Primary Teacher Education: Pre-service

Derek Sharples and Dan Wicksteed

Competing Perceptions

Panoramas of teacher education differ dramatically from viewpoint to viewpoint. For each the foreground can be starkly drawn, the features of the middle distance can be sketched in, but the perspectives of the late 1990s are emerging at the far reaches of our present vision, in the deepest of prospective blues.

In this picture of teacher education the size of canvas is dictated by the dimensions of demography and the economy. Its form is shaped by current policies for society and for education, its colour is derived from considerations of the kind of student experience which students will have in colleges of teacher education* in the coming years. Our portrayal focusses upon each prospect in turn.

Demographic Prospects

It is predicted that the number of primary age children will increase from 3953 thousand in 1984 to 4212 thousand in 1994 (DES, 1985). This is an increase of some 7 per cent. At the same time the number of secondary school pupils, including sixth formers, will decline from 3877 thousand to 3089 thousand. This is a decrease of over 20 per cent. So it will be that an increase in the number of students required to train for primary school teaching will occur at the same time as a considerable decline in the number of sixth formers seeking higher education or qualified to enter into training.

---

* The word 'college' is used throughout this article to indicate all institutions providing courses of teacher education, undergraduate or postgraduate, including university departments of education, colleges of higher education and polytechnics.

The proportion of the school-leaving cohort required to enter teaching will be considerably greater than has been previously achieved.

Given present staffing levels this demographic shift will give rise to a requirement for over 10,500 new primary teachers at the same time as LEAs seek to displace nearly 40,000 secondary teachers.

It is not unreasonable to predict from this that there will be a crisis of provision although it is not easy to predict the response to it. One possible scenario is that there will be dramatically worsened pupil-teacher ratios in primary schools. Another is the growth of a new training route, with large numbers of secondary teachers being retrained in preparation for teaching in primary schools. Almost certainly the pattern of provision for higher education will be one which will steer many students into teacher education as being the only available higher education opportunity. Such students will embark on teacher education courses without a strong commitment to teaching, and it is unlikely that the current concern for 'appropriate' features of personality and attitude amongst candidates will be able to be sustained.

Against this scenario it has to be admitted that through many vagaries of policy and provision the student feed to colleges has remained relatively constant in its characteristics. Most students expressing interest in primary education are modestly qualified young people, moderate in conduct, politics and values. Most are applying for entry end-on to secondary education and have an A-level background in humanities. The large majority are women. These characteristics describe a substantial pool of students which will continue to be available and will be predominate in the student cohorts applying for teacher education courses: but it is not the case that all of such students are those which in the event become effective primary teachers. Nevertheless teacher education in the 1990s must discover ways to foster that effectiveness from amongst them.

So far we have taken a view of pupils and students, but looking towards school staff we can see that another feature which may affect teacher education is the stability and age profile of the profession in teaching. Since the mid 1970s relatively small proportions of the teacher force each year have been probationers. At the other end of the age range older teachers have often taken early retirement to ease the problems of falling rolls. The net result has been both an aging of the profession and a peaking of its age profile. By 1990 some 60 per cent of primary teachers will be over 40 years of age and almost three-quarters (73 per cent) between 30 and 50*. Surveying this prospect imaginatively it could be speculated that as these teachers get older they will tend to find the younger children more exhausting. In our experience teachers not uncommonly move upwards to older age groups as they themselves age. It is common to find young

---

*Extrapolated from DES (1984) *Statistics of Education Teachers in Science in England and Wales.*

teachers and probationers being appointed to teach younger age groups. The ageing profile of teachers, the increasing numbers of school age children, together with any tendency for vacancies to occur with younger age groups could well lead to colleges attempting to meet substantial demands for probationary teachers to work with the younger age groups. They could be driven to provide more courses for the preparation of teachers of the youngest pupil groups.

Another feature of schools worthy of note is their size. Half of all primary schools have fewer than 175 pupils, justifying some seven staff. Current notions of primary 'specialism' will always have to take account of this. The increase in pupil roll is unlikely to be associated with a disproportionate growth in school size and the demand for the teacher who is required to behave as a polymath is likely to endure. The final demographic feature we might mention is the age profile of college staff. This has a very similar pattern to that already described for primary teachers. Whilst large numbers of primary teachers joined colleges in the 1960s, they are now in their mid to late fifties and already the object of critical comments on the ageing of their experience. Growth in primary teacher training is unlikely to be effected without substantial movement amongst these staff and an influx of tutors new to the field of training.

Economic Considerations

This is no place for a detailed look at the economy—but education, like all social services, is operating both in a climate of raised expectations and demands and also in a time of restricted expenditure and declining resources. Whatever policies are adopted by a future government this economic scenario seems likely to continue. Declining North Sea oil revenue, erosion of the economic contribution arising from manufacturing and an increasing percentage of the population receiving state pensions are just some of the factors which will continue to make for continuing moderate expenditure on education, and render overall improvement in the level of resourcing unlikely.

Political Policy

In the middleground of our view of the 1990s lie the policies and practices which are likely to colour the ideology of teacher education and its context. For all that ideological considerations will have some influence on the distribution of the public purse, other pragmatic issues will strongly influence the resources available for education.

Current policies have a commitment to reducing both taxes and expenditure, and to the fostering of an 'enterprise' economy. Such economic values can sharply affect both the structure and the style of education—the talk of loans and vouchers for education, the increasing expenditure on MSC programmes as against investment in curriculum development, the demand for initiatives in higher education based on a market bidding approach; all these are instances of that. A policy to direct such economic patterns in education would be likely to be characterized by concerns for centralized sponsorship and for direction of the curriculum, by impermanence of teacher employment contracts and by resourcing practices in which the chief aim will be to keep costs down.

Alternative ideologies would be likely to stress the 'social wage', or social entitlements more highly. Health Services, Education, Social and Employment Services would receive higher priority even if in principle this involved higher taxes. Central direction of provision might be less intense, criteria of effectiveness less dependent on production and more concerned with the processes of Education. The dominant ideology of the 1990s will influence the education of teachers both through the principles on which it is resourced and through the social and professional climate which those values give rise to and within which the students of the time will prepare for and enter teaching.

Whatever the dominant ideology there is always a dilemma for education in deciding what level of influence upon pupils and society it should exert. Contrary to the protestations of teachers, and certainly in contradiction to many political statements, there remains a hidden optimism concerning the potential contribution of education to personal, community and national development. Even a cursory review of the press over the last twelve months would show that in popular opinion 'the schools' could resolve social 'problems' such as drug abuse, road safety, negative attitudes to nuclear energy, itinerancy, aptitude for employment, conduct of tourists in Spain, spellings in letters of application, performance of cricketers in the West Indies or tolerance towards ethnic minorities in inner cities. Too loud a protest from teachers, or *a-fortiori* lecturers, that a particular-demand is expecting too much usually leads to the syphoning off of resources to temporary commissioned groups with little understanding of the intractability of the issues to processes of instruction.

Unfortunately those statements that appear to acknowledge the potential/achievement of education are usually expressed so as to stress, paradoxically, the inadequacies of education. At several levels of national debate on crucial issues involving institutional or collective conduct there is an easy scapegoating of education. It is and will remain the one social agency which has contact with all members of the community, it is the largest single object of local rate expenditure, its activities are distributed throughout the community giving it high visibility, and as all have experienced it all are experts on it.

Teacher education of the 1990s is unlikely to avoid the problems of over expectation and under provision which appear differentially as common features of whatever policy.

Education Policy

There has been a clear and marked shift in policy towards increasing central control, which has occurred under successive governments of all persuasions. Such central control is an inevitable corollary of the demand for control in times of declining resources and also has appeal for those wishing to effect rapid curriculum change through the employment of centre-periphery models. Whatever the cause, centralized control reveals itself in curriculum guidance, through increasing control of resource allocation and the setting of narrowly defined student, staffing and expenditure targets in the education service. Educational institutions are experiencing centralist pressures on the curriculum through publications, through examination reform, through explicit direction of governing bodies, through increased inspectoral activity and so on. Centralization is just as evident in teacher education. From 1986 onwards any student seeking to qualify as a primary teacher will have to embark on a course approved by the Secretary of State through the Council for the Accreditation of Teacher Education (CATE), which is an advisory body established by and answerable to him. The vast majority of teacher education courses will have had to be considerably remodelled to satisfy the criteria derived from the White Paper *Teaching Quality*. Courses will have much greater commonality of content than heretofore and the diversity of provision will be much restricted.

Current policies for primary schooling seem to derive from a new and clearly different perception of the task of primary teaching. Notions of 'natural' learning in the early years of childhood, and propositions concerning the integrity of the developing child, have been overwhelmed by an insistence upon a primary curriculum which serves the subject and skills curriculum of the secondary school much more directly. The primary curriculum appears to have been regarded as preparatory and elementary in recent publications of DES and HMI; it has been given little self-justification but rather a dependency upon reference to the subsequent secondary curriculum and to the external 'needs' of the economy, commerce and social order. Such would seem to be perception upon which current policy is insisting. Concern for the extent and level of subjects in the primary curriculum relates to a concern for the extent and level of subject study in teacher education courses. Teachers preparing for such a curriculum will be required by central direction to spend more time in the acquisition of particular subject content and in addressing issues of the nature of knowledge and skills. They will spend less time than has been the general practice on the thinking and development of pupils, more time in looking at the demands subjects make on young pupils; less time on the needs of young pupils for activities in various areas, more on considerations of the demands of disciplines and performances for constituent knowledge and skills.

The fear that primary schools act to prolong infancy rather than develop stated skills may be reinforced not because of any objective data, but because of the prevailing ideology and the background of the people in the system who make these decisions. The trend is not predominantly a political one but emerges from Elizabeth House. This change of policy, symbolized by CATE, has been seen to signal a lack of confidence in the institutions themselves and has placed decisions concerning the structure of teacher education in the hands of those only indirectly involved in effecting those decisions. It is hardly surprising that a group of tutors responsible for running such courses combined to form an unusually unanimous but largely ineffective protest group attempting to defend the autonomy of Undergraduate Primary Teacher Education Courses. (UPTEC). CATE signalled criticism of the principles and ideology of many colleges in terms of their over commitment to professional studies. No longer were these viewed as contributing to the academic quality of courses, they were to be judged by the 'recent and relevant' experience in schools of those teaching the courses. It did not go unnoticed that recent, relevant and extensive experience of teaching in colleges was discounted. In summary the operation of central accreditation through CATE was to effectively restrict a substantial area of professional autonomy. Those involved in planning and teaching the courses were no longer free to determine solutions for course design based on experience, principle or educational argument, but had to conform to patterns of external criteria. It can be taken that the model teacher education courses over the next five to ten years will have a conformity across the country that has not heretofore been the case.

It is not only the curriculum of colleges that is increasingly being centralized but also their level and pattern of resourcing and the dimension of student intake. The number of teacher education students that may be admitted to a college is now closely specified by the age range they will be trained to teach, the pattern of the award—BEd or PGCE—they will follow and the subjects they will study. This last criterion presently operates only for secondary courses: in the context of continuing concern over some curriculum areas of the primary school, the continuing shortage of specialist recruitment to teacher education courses, and a continuing national commitment to the value of mathematics, technology and science, it seems not unlikely that some allocation of primary students to subject courses could well be envisaged in the near future. It would appear too that the basis and mechanisms for funding will be less and less under LEA control and more and more responsive to central direction in relation to current policy and market demands.

Whether an alternative political ideology would permit any return of the previous autonomy is hard to estimate. Once power is acquired it is rarely given up and it is likely that education in the 1990s will be more carefully directed from the centre than has ever been the case, and that the procedures to achieve this will be seen to have been established in the 1980s.

Against this background to what extent will the next few years be characterized by a persistent, if not perhaps consistent, attempt to subvert central policies and reclaim something of lost autonomies?

The Nature of the Colleges

The term 'colleges' has been used so far to denote all the institutions which provide initial teacher education. However in this section it is at times necessary to distinguish between them.

The nature of colleges will continue to be a crucial issue in the 1990s. Over the past twenty years attempts to place the professional education of primary teachers in diversified institutions have not prospered. During the 1970s concern for the breadth of students' curriculum, for its depth and resourcing, together with a regard for the ambience achieved by a wide mix of courses and students in a 'multi-technic' context, led to strong central support for placing teacher education in polytechnics and larger diversified colleges, and urging the diversification of the monotechnic teacher education colleges. Course models which involved primary students studying alongside those with other academic and professional interests were explored. It was thought that this would make available more rigorous and challenging opportunities for students and might resolve the 'isolation' of the former colleges of education. In the event this did not prove to be the case. In a number of instances teacher education was taken over by larger and more diverse institutions, only to fade and wither—in part by falling recruitment, in part by resourcing decisions within those institutions and, in part, by a reversal of policy decisions. In contrast the growth of primary teacher education in university depart-ments has recently been dramatic, and has moved the balance of training substantially towards a PGCE model. Alongside this has gone a progress-ive movement towards four-year undergraduate programmes as the normal pattern for the BEd route into primary teaching.

It may be that the lack of success in establishing strong units for primary education in larger diversified colleges stems from the nature of the student population from which candidates are drawn. These might be characterized as having a preference for less radical, moderate, small-scale institutions with a reputation for having a humane ambience. It is our experience that most would-be primary teachers are attracted by those factors which characterized the erstwhile colleges of education.

However, in the light of declining numbers of students and of changing national resource priorities, current trends in higher education policies towards teacher education still appear to be directed towards strengthening larger institutions, reducing the number of smaller colleges by closure of courses, and associating monotechnic colleges with universities once more in order to gain academic support for subject studies.

Current policies appear to have the effect of providing resources in the light of student demand, and it may be that the smaller monotechnic colleges will remain attractive to students and hence viable. However, it is likely that demands for association between institutions will continue. In order to maintain a place for the smaller colleges it is currently being proposed that their students should spend one or more years as students at a local university. This is unlikely to be an effective solution in the light of previous experience. Students have been resistant to so dividing their courses, and previous experiments with courses of this kind would suggest that either the larger will seek to absorb the smaller, or the smaller will seek autonomy by another route. In either event the colleges will have to change in character in order to survive, and those changes are likely to move them away from the qualities of size, ambience, ethos and course focus which have been of attraction to students heretofore.

Small colleges in the 1990s are likely to be larger than the small of the 1970s, and many of the institutional qualities currently attractive to primary students are likely to be less evident in the colleges of the next decade.

College Ethos and Student Experience

We must now look towards more distant horizons and consider how these colleges may appear to, and be experienced by, the students who enter them. A national policy which emphasizes instrumentality and the primacy of the needs of employers will inevitably affect colleges' ethos. It is likely the first effects will be to harden the contractual nature of engagement in college and to reduce the significance of the less formal, more personal dimensions of college work. In schools the changes of emphases from process to product, from activity to conduct, from levels of engagement to standards of achievement, will in turn affect the nature of the engagement of higher education students. As already mentioned there may at this same time be an increasing number of students for whom teacher education is not so much a first preference in higher education as a last chance, the inevitable outcome of dramatic reductions of sixth form leavers coupled with more dramatic increases in the demand for primary teachers.

For these students an instrumental engagement with a clear 'product' model of the task may well prove effective, more so perhaps than the more personally inflected, supportive, individualistic and individualized climate of many of the present colleges. Such experience would, in turn, communicate different understandings of primary teaching to students—losing something of its supportiveness and individuality to the demands of normative expectations of performance and greater objectivity and instrumentalism in instruction.

So much for the potential effects of emergent policies on ethos. Another source of pressure on students will arise from conflicts of social expectation, with teachers continuing to be held responsible for many if not all the failings of society, and at the same time being expected to resolve them. The directness of such popular assumptions may lead to a harder 'product' emphasis in courses and put further at risk the provisional, intangible nature of much primary curriculum work which is widely valued amongst primary students and practitioners at present. There is further a continued but unexamined, assumption that the sector will continue to deliver general social skills, sensitivities and the ability to apply learning even when the curriculum is pressed toward the specificities of particular technologies and knowledge.

Yet another factor which will probably affect student experience of colleges is their institutional health. Colleges, like schools, are experiencing a crisis of confidence. The importance of the CATE accreditation procedures already mentioned has had a number of deleterious effects. Sensible as many of these 'external' criteria may be they nevertheless imply a lack of confidence in the colleges—indeed the more sensible the criteria are the more they imply lack of confidence. Do colleges really have to be told their courses should include substantial periods of teaching in schools, or that their students should have personal qualities suited for teaching—for example? Moreover, the style of delivery of accreditation is antipathetic to the tradition of the sector, with imposed criteria supervised by hierarchical review bodies using crude quantitative time data to determine curriculum balance. Indeed by implication determining quality as well. The intention of the procedure may be laudable but one of its effects is to dramatically reduce the confidence of those for whom these decisions have previously been a crucial part of their professional work. Students will increasingly be taught by tutors whose credibility has been very publicly challenged.

How will tutors react? Adopting common criteria will have effects going far beyond the approval of various programmes. It will almost certainly give rise to a counter ideology in which the distinctiveness and idiosyncrasy of individual courses and institutions will emerge by other means than the selection of content in the professional area, the balance of studies or the distribution of professional experience.

A further source of colleges' anxiety has been the continuing uncertainties of their own futures. Changes in higher education since 1970 have repeatedly demanded change in terms of institutional size, shape and in the level and conspectus of courses. Staff have adapted and requalified to teach in new courses, often meeting substantial demands for retraining, for research and publication, and for moving outside the field of teacher education. This has often been at the cost of the tutors' personal development and security, and yet employers have shown wide diversity and inconsistency in their response to the problem through retraining, redeployment and redundancy arrangements. Current resourcing proposals are likely to differentially affect many of the colleges in ways which will require another round of adaptation. Many college staff have a sense of powerlessness in the face of the sequence of demands for change and the relentness of the implied criticism of what (indeed whatever) they did before. Students in the 1990s will taught in a continuing context of uncertainty and insecurity.

Those features will also be present in the schools which students will visit during their training, for the schools are also experiencing a crisis of confidence. Many of the ideological pressures already described affect them too. Present indications are that the primary curriculum will be more controlled, there will be greater individual and collective accountability, more concern for management and direction, wider use of economic and budgetary controls at local and school level. This will on the one hand generate more autonomy and responsibility for the school, but that will be paid for from central funds to support nationally approved priorities. These will almost inevitably reinforce a subject curriculum with a continuing stress on science, mathematics, CDT and industrial apprenticeship—they may also feed teachers' feelings of inadequacy. Students joining the profession will have to be educated in a style that requires them to think of themselves as some sort of subject specialist or curriculum advisor; able to carry out that role in schools where self confidence will be even more variable than now. They will have to be prepared to meet deeper levels of hostility than at present, as their very qualification and training could be seen as devaluing the ideology behind their colleagues' experience and qualifications. The attempt to improve teacher education through raising subject content rigor in the context of specified pupil norms and close professional and community scrutiny could turn out to be a prescription for setting the profession against itself. Alternatively, the next generation may be welcomed as allies in addressing the new demands, and new entrants are likely to meet high expectations to act as sources of insight and skill in the instigation of the emergent professionality.

Changes in professional roles are likely as primary schools experience an intensified pressure for larger classes to be run more cheaply. New supervisory roles could well emerge if some para-professional staff have to be recruited to support fully qualified teachers in order to provide adequate adult cover in increasingly large classes, should the mismatch between teacher supply and pupil numbers be unresolved for example, it is possible that there could be a return to the Plowden concept of aides—analogous to nursery nurses and minimally trained to help primary teachers run large classes of forty or fifty children. Many classes will be staffed by teachers redeployed from other sectors and requiring higher levels of support than their general professional maturity might indicate. These trends will be differential in the intensity of their effect as between areas. The growth in pupil numbers is predicted to be geographically specific. Thus in areas of deprivation large classes with sub-professional staff support could become the norm, whilst areas of less deprivation are likely to have to call upon unpaid volunteer helpers, enabling teachers to cope with such growth in class size as occurs in these areas. Teacher education will have to attend to such a variety of professional support, and develop in them some appropriate skills of management and direct professional relationships. Newly qualified teachers after all go disproportionately to deprived areas, and it will be there that there will be the sharpest call to cope with other adults in school. This might in turn serve to enhance the self confidence of the profession of course. It could also lead to a greater awareness of the experience of low paid work which might provide a new source for radicalism amongst teachers.

So we foresee a range of factors which will affect not only the average size of the colleges but also deleteriously affect their ambience, the size of student groups, the supportiveness of the schools they experience, and also the amount of grant they receive whilst on course. On balance, over the next ten years students are likely to begin teaching in institutions where the affective climate is neither as congenial nor supportive as it has been. Students of the 1990s will have to be prepared for uncertainty and for dealing with a wide range of demands and expectations. These will arise from the heightened expectations of all social service professions, including those in education. There will be a requirement for starting teachers who have developed the ability to justify and argue for their own thought-out personal and professional values, able to appraise and determine their personal professional development and contribute to the institutional growth and development of their school. They will need the integrity to make judgments about the proper balance between personal values and social expectations and to have a developed autonomy and objectivity of professional evaluation. None of these qualities is as yet amongst the objectives identified amongst the new national criteria.

However, not all the features of the landscape are overcast or for the worst. The increased similarity of initial teacher education courses across all colleges might have some interesting and beneficial effects. It might facilitate a much clearer targeting of resources for such courses, enable the design of more materials for publication, provide a clear general provision for staff development, facilitate the mobility of students between programmes, enable comparisons between the performance of students from different colleges, and so on. The criteria certainly define a minimal position for teacher education.

The Match of Output and Demand?

Whilst it is possible to predict some of the features of teacher education in the 1990s it is less easy to predict that schools will be seeking the qualities being developed in the accredited courses. College courses will increasingly emphasize the specialist features of the primary teacher's role.

However, the schools and their appointing panels, the headteachers and advisers, will generally have experienced and have been educated in generalist practice and philosophy. In defining new teaching posts and in seeking new appointments they are likely to value those teachers who most closely conform to their expectations. In short the providers and the employers are likely to hold competing perceptions of what is required.

There is a far more important kind of match however. Colleges are preparing teachers who will reach a stage of relative professional maturity and influence in the mid-1990s. In the context of the current curriculum debates this is a challenging task. It demands a measure of prediction of the future role of the teacher and an appreciation of the skills for which they are being trained. Much current thinking worries us intensely. It is clearly informed by models which stress production and processing, and both schools and colleges are becoming over-burdened with competing advice, directives and demands. Teachers, student teachers and lecturers will require a range of skills to handle these external pressures and to resolve them with invention and integrity.

Until recently students might have been prepared to develop an understanding of education as a process for realizing individual autonomy in a context of mutual responsibility in society, and to perceive the ends of education as the realization of a process whereby members of society would have the knowledge and skills to bring about the communities they desired. This no longer seems the case. The argument is not currently conceived as a problematic one but has a strong deterministic flavour; the nature of the desirable community is seen as determined; its achievement is more a matter of directed prognostics than establishing ideals; its attainment is seen as being assured through particular technological and economic procedures and structures. The curriculum is increasingly considered as a means of inducting pupils into accepted societal models, and of developing in pupils the technological and economic skills and understanding which, it assumes, will enable them to be productively active in society. It is the confidence in a particular social model and its mechanisms that is most worrying. Whilst such an objective and procedural view of the curriculum endures, then its servicing and development is also seen as unproblematic. Colleges will be expected to prepare students able to teach basic skills of fluency and effectiveness in selected areas of social, communication and economic activity. Increasing emphasis in teacher education will be given to such issues as preparation for work, capability skills, demonstrated responsibility, technological capability and social conformity. The problematic nature of what is being learned in relation to the open democracy of social ideals has heretofore been a protection of schooling and higher education against indoctrination. Reviewing present policies for teacher training it is less clear what emphasis is to be given to the alternative, provisional imagination of society. To what extent can colleges maintain a critical awareness amongst students in the face of social determinism? Is the power of colleges to subvert central intentions our best guarantee of intellectual and eventually other freedoms? These are heady questions, but the landscape of the 1990s will conform to their formulation. The schools and society of the 2000s will depend on their effective resolution.

For us those horizons whilst admittedly hazy are definitely blue.

Suggestions for Further Reading

ALEXANDER, R., CRAFT, M. and LYNCH, J. (Eds) (1984) *Change in Teacher Education : Context and Provision*, Holt, Rinehart and Winston.

DEPARTMENT OF EDUCATION AND SCIENCE (1982) *Better Schools*, HMSO.

DEPARTMENT OF EDUCATION AND SCIENCE (1983) *Teaching Quality*, HMSO.

SHARPLES, D. and WICKSTEED, D. (1981) 'Public sector teacher education in the 1990s: Diagnosis, prognosis and prescription', *Educational Review*, 332, pp. 115–21.

Staff Development and INSET

Howard Bradley

Staff Development and School Development

This chapter explores the relationship between three interrelated activities —change in schools, the professional development of individuals and the in-service education and training of teachers (INSET). Each pair of these activities is related and the relationship can be in either direction, for example:

> professional development can lead to change in schools, change in schools can lead to professional development.

It would be a mistake, however, to believe that one activity always leads to another; very often they do not. Even if teachers do develop professionally, they may not be able to change their schools because circumstances or personalities stand in the way of change. Conversely, sometimes when a school changes, say to a new approach to part of the curriculum, a group of teachers may not change with it but will stick doggedly to their previous methods and goals.

From the James Report of 1972 onwards, INSET has been seen as the key to change and the instrument by which professional development is stimulated and change in schools encouraged. The task for those involved in INSET—the teachers themselves, the headteachers who support them within the school and those, such as advisers and teacher trainers, who offer help from outside—is to seek to understand the mechanisms involved, and to use them effectively. How can we maximize the impact on INSET on both individuals and schools?

It may be a good starting point to ask why good teachers, working hard and successfully, seek to commit yet more of their valuable time by becoming involved in these three activities. Why do teachers risk insecurity, uncertainty and even failure by becoming involved in innovation?

Two reasons suggest themselves:

(i) becoming involved in such activities, solving problems and over-coming challenges give the teacher continuing job satisfaction;
(ii) engaging in these activities enhances the teacher's prospects of career development.

These two needs seen by individual teachers—job satisfaction and career development—are driving factors which we must not ignore. If it is those needs which bring teachers to INSET, then the activities provided must be seen by teachers to meet those needs.

However, not only the teacher has needs. The school has its concerns. It needs:

(i) to strengthen its present performance;
(ii) to prepare itself to meet future demands on it. Increasingly, the demands of a changing economy or a changing technology put the school under pressure to change. Sometimes this impetus for change comes from changing ideology about education, sometimes it comes from the dissatisfaction of consumers—children, parents, employers or society in general.

These two groups of needs—the individual's and the school's—are often very different, yet INSET, if it is to be successful, must serve both. It is vital, therefore, to bring the needs of the school and those of the individual closer together. In addition to helping teachers develop ways of changing the school, INSET must also assist the school to find ways of actively helping its teachers to develop.

Establishing a Climate for Effective Staff Development

Are there organizational features of a school which make a positive contribution to the individual's development? Recent research suggests that there are. One such feature Charles Handy (1984) calls 'a bias for action'. In his study, Handy found that successful institutions laid an emphasis on problem-seeking, even more than problem-solving. They encouraged many leaders rather than relying on a single person. Another factor which Handy feels contributes to a bias for action is what he describes as control after the event rather than before it—'try it and we'll see if it works' rather than 'ask permission before you do anything'.

Other studies of effective schools point to a second feature which is often associated with success. This is that responsibilities are delegated and with them the power to take action. In these schools delegation is accompanied by participation. They are characterized by an openness in discussing issues, by the teachers within them feeling that they share the ownership of both problems and solutions. Characteristically, teachers in these schools see themselves as part of a team.

A third feature of schools which enhances individual development is an atmosphere of consistency and trust. The arguments for this feature are often best illustrated in schools where it does not exist. If school leaders exhibit inconsistent responses to effort and initiative, teachers soon learn to avoid negative responses by taking no initiatives. Equally, if leaders betray a lack of trust that subordinates can fulfil the tasks allotted them, constantly interfering with the process to ensure that it is being done as they wish, the subordinates soon learn that it is simplest to leave it all to the leader.

A fourth and final feature of the school as a work place which aids the development of the individual is the institution's attitude to evaluation. Where evaluation is seen as essential and non-threatening, where there is always an expectation that things can be improved, where there is an expectation that mistakes will be made and that such events are normal, then individuals blossom.

Most of us know schools where these precepts are seen in practice but too many fall short of these desirable conditions. It follows that INSET must be aimed in part at changing the system if it is to give the individuals their chance to bring about change.

The Headteacher's Role in Establishing Effective Staff Development

Clearly the achievement of excellence cannot emerge overnight, it calls for continuing good management over a lengthy period. Nevertheless, we can begin to identify priority areas and some goals. The organization development movement in the USA tends to blind us with jargon but we can learn from some of its strategies, in particular:

(i)   clarify communication;
(ii)   seek approval and commitment of all involved;
(iii) work from a good base of fact;
(iv) improve group procedures;
(v)   broaden the base of decision-making;
(vi) have a plan for problem-solving;
(vii) evaluate.

To establish this collaborative and participative team approach must be the first point of attack and responsibility for it lies firmly at the headteacher's door.

The second point of attack is to get the school organization right in the sense that maximum use is made of the talents of every member of staff. The focus of this attack must be on creating an efficient structure of responsibilities within the school and then on delegating effectively. David Trethowan (1983) in his booklet on delegation written for 'Education for Industrial Society' talks of the three As of delegation:

(i)   Area of responsibility clearly defined;
(ii)   Authority to carry out the job;
(iii) Accountability with certainty.

Trethowan says that in defining the area of responsibility we should make clear its purpose and its limits and how success will be judged. He believes that giving authority means giving the teachers room to do the job their way, giving them clear powers to control other adults and allowing them to take decisions without reference back.

The third point of attack is to consider what actions will actively encourage staff to take responsibility for their own development. Perhaps this can be approached most easily by posing three questions for head-teachers to ask:

(i)   what motivates my staff to continue learning?
(ii)   how many of these motivating factors can I influence positively?
(iii) what can I do to the organization of the school which will maximize the influence of those factors?

The Surrey Inspectorate's booklet *Professional Development* suggests ways in which headteachers can, through their organization of the school, increase the quality and volume of staff development. The booklet makes an important distinction between the opportunities provided by everyday experience and those designed specifically. It is vital not to ignore the former, particularly:

(i)   encouraging teachers to study their own teaching performance;
(ii)   involving teachers in sharing activities with other teachers. This need not necessarily mean team teaching, though the benefits of that are considerable, for the value of joint planning and evaluating are enormous in staff development terms. One of the major values of involving the school in some experimental development is the spin-off that it has for staff development;
(iii) involvement in management, particularly participating in decisions, exercising responsibility and leading other adults.

In the category of specific arrangements the Surrey booklet draws our attention to:

(i)   encouragement to read, by providing the material and by creating real reasons for reading it, for example by asking members of staff to keep the rest up to date on specific curricular areas;
(ii)   encouraging discussion and debate. Some schools find it useful to set up seminars on major issues, separate from the routine matters which tend to dominate normal staff meetings;
(iii) involvement in purposeful visits, to each other and to other schools;
(iv) encouragement to join courses, both school based and external; and
(v)   involvement in research and development.

What Kinds of Courses? INSET Which Brings Together School Development and Staff Development

Until a few years ago, INSET was something individual teachers decided to do in order to meet their own needs or pursue their own interests; schools, although they felt it right to encourage teachers who wanted to be involved in INSET, usually had little expectation of direct benefit for them as a result. The fact that mobility in the profession was then high often meant that teachers engaged in long courses changed schools at the end of their courses and this then made it difficult to work towards making an impact in the school. This has now changed and school staffs are no longer disrupted by rapid turnover. At the same time the growth of interest in making INSET school-focussed has enabled schools and those who provide them with INSET support—adviser, teachers' centres and the training institutions—to experiment with activities which address the school's development as well as the teacher's.

Making INSET school-focussed is not simply a question of making it school-based; indeed, the question of whether it should take place on or off the premises if often a distraction from the real questions of what are the appropriate goals for the activity, who needs to be involved and what support and commitment do they need from the school. Significantly, perhaps, many of the new and effective forms of INSET which have been developed have elements of school-based work combined with other elements which take place off the premises. Experience with them suggests that the staff of a primary school contemplating INSET should start by making their needs quite specific and then seek the best combination of INSET methods and activities to help them satisfy these goals. For example, development of the school's approach to topic work may require a term of data-collecting—observing each other teach, collecting children's work etc.—followed by a day's conference for staff attended by an external consultant, complemented by one teacher being released to attend a twenty-day course on topic work. This might get the staff to the point where they are able to commence the planning of a new scheme. There still remains the implementation and evaluation stages, both of which may need supporting INSET. We have to view INSET as a long-term process if it is to be linked with school improvement. The one-off event is almost certainly doomed to failure in terms of bringing about change in schools.

When we start to plan an INSET activity we need to ask ourselves a series of questions. Is it an eye-opening, awareness-raising exercise? If so, are the staff already receptive to discussion of the issue? If they are not their response is likely to be either that the discussion is not appropriate to their situation or that they already have a suitable system. If the staff is not yet aware of the problem, then another form of INSET exercise involving analysis of their own situation is called for. The initial development of this would be some action research, but are the skills required already available in the staff or must someone acquire them? Does somebody in the school already have the theoretical and practical knowledge necessary to help the school solve the problem, or does that too need to be sought? What sort of INSET activity will successfully bring observed data and theory together?

Experience suggests that it is sensible to start on the assumption that the staff of a school will have far fewer shared perceptions than might have been hoped. Almost always staff discussion reveals perceptions which differ about what the problem is and how it should be addressed, so the first act very often needs to be some sort of data gathering which leads individuals to a shared understanding of the issue, so helping the school but also developing the individual by enhancing his or her view of reality. In schools which are accustomed to problem-solving we can start with the expectation that teachers like to seek out and solve problems, for others this could be a situation of threat and worry. Similarly, teachers in innovative schools usually like to work together in an ordered, task-orientated way. In other schools the suggestion of collaboration would itself be a major innovation.

One of the major questions in planning school-focussed INSET is that of leadership of the activity. Should leadership come from within the staff group? Is that acceptable to other members of staff? If the head takes the lead does that inhibit the contributions of other staff? If the leader comes from outside the school, has he or she the credibility the job requires? Teachers like to feel they are led by someone who knows the problem thoroughly, whom they can trust to understand the staff group dynamics and who is devoted to helping them achieve their goals rather than 'selling' them his or her own solution.

Very often, if teachers become involved in INSET on this scale they see part of the benefit for them in gaining further qualifications. Experience at the Cambridge Institute of Education has demonstrated that award-bearing courses can be married successfully with school development. There are, however, some conditions which must be fulfilled. It is not enough simply to build school-focussed research and development into the course or even to do that and win commitment to it from teachers who are the students. To do so only leads to professional frustration in those teachers because they develop personally to the point where they can identify problems but are unable to bring about the appropriate change in the school. This may be because they lack the status in the school, the time to undertake what is often a considerable task or sometimes it is because they are untrained in the skills of bringing about change in a group of adults. In addition to building a research element into the course, the provider also has to negotiate a commitment from the school. The school must have an expectation that the involvement of one or some of its staff in the exercise will give rise to change. For some, the course may lead to changes inside the teacher's classroom and the impact upon other teachers need not be challenging or dramatic. However, many issues which are

chosen for investigation by teachers and their schools have direct consequences for many staff and often for the school's relationship with the
community. A teacher investigating how effectively the school deals with
the continuity and progression of children's experience is likely to produce
findings which involve all teachers and potentially will affect all teachers.
Questions then arise which the staff as a group and the provider must
foresee. One set of questions concerns the ownership of what is often very
sensitive data about what happens in the schools. Who decides what to do
with it and who should have access to it can become very important. A
second set of questions arises from the involvement in the school development of many teachers beyond those involved in the course and sometimes
this can place great demands on the other teachers. It emphasizes the need
for the project to be something recognized by all the staff as important, so
that involvement gives some reward to them as well as to the teachers
principally concerned.

The negotiation of this kind of activity is undeniably more strenuous and
demanding than the preparation for most courses, yet the rewards are
considerable when it is carried through successfully. It not only enhances
the confidence and the skills of the individual but also increases the
performance of the school and the confidence of its staff in each other.
Dadds (1986) says of the outcomes of an action research study group she
works with at the Cambridge Institute:

> There is little doubt that self-evaluation, especially in a supportive
> action research group, is demanding. Not only are members
> acquiring classroom research skills, they also need multiple skills
> for clarifying and communicating their findings. In addition,
> membership demands a range of skills and sensitivities for func-
> tioning effectively in a self-managed group. Evidence shows that
> the pay-off is well worth the effort over a sustained period. The
> knowledge members gain about their own and each other's
> practice feeds back into the craft of teaching. A new attitude, more
> constructive and optimistic, seems to develop. Being an action-
> researcher becomes an integral, indispensable part of one's profes-
> sional role and self-image. After talking to a group of headteachers
> about her research, one of our members was asked why, after such
> difficulties and hard work she continued her commitment. She was
> clear that, for her, it meant the difference between fulfilment in her
> work and sterility, between growth and stagnation. Such self-
> directed teacher development holds great potential for classroom
> and school improvement. Research, curriculum development and
> teacher development become inextricably bound.

A New Shape for INSET

It is fortunate that experiments like those at the Cambridge Institute have been taking place throughout the country for the changes now emerging in the funding and organization of INSET are likely to increase the demand for activities of this kind. The whole tenor of the new proposals suggests that priority will be given much more in future to INSET directly geared to the needs of a particular school. There is more than a suggestion that this may be at the expense of long award-bearing courses. Both schools and teachers should view this with some concern for in the teachers' case the opportunity of a lengthy period for self-appraisal is as useful as the qualification which emerges at the end and in the schools' case the timescale of change is often more in tune with longer courses than it is with shorter activities. Most providing institutions are now modifying their programmes to meet this trend by introducing the concept of a modular programme, each element of which carries credit towards an award. In many cases one of the modules will be a supervised research or development commissioned by the school or by a local education authority, so the impact of the courses of school development will hopefully not be lost.

In many LEAs the new regulations will enable an individual school, or a consortium of schools, to identify the need for a course provided solely for its staff, or a defined group within the staff who share a common concern or responsibility. They will then be able to seek appropriate collaboration from people outside the school. This collaboration is unlikely to be restricted simply to courses and we are likely to see a rapid expansion of consultancy services of many kinds which will enable members of the staff of training institutions to work in schools alongside their school colleagues in their development programmes. Some of the most immediate developments will be:

(i) schools buying 'off-the-shelf' courses from institutions providing INSET which will take place on the school premises or nearby and will be staged specifically for the staff concerned;

(ii) schools buying the time of a group of staff from an institution to plan and provide a course designed specifically for the school, to act as consultants for some development within the school or to form an evaluation team for a development. In effect, this enables the two groups of staff to become one working group with a clear focus and goal:

(iii) schools and LEAs sending one or more teachers on a short-term attachment to an institution where, together with staff from the institution, they will carry out a specific brief on behalf of their colleagues in school. This might be to produce a programme of development for the school, to carry out the evaluation of a project the school is developing or to design a course of INSET for their colleagues.

In many cases, individual teachers will be able to use their development work in schools as the basis of work which will lead to further qualifications. This is already happening successfully as a result of collaboration between institutions and LEAs involved in TVEI-related in-service training (TRIST) and Education Support Grant initiatives.

One factor underpins all these opportunities for developing INSET to serve both teachers and the school itself and that is the importance of a coherent and accepted school policy for staff development. This has been accepted conventional wisdom since the (ACSTT, 1978) booklet *Making INSET Work* but it now becomes essential that schools should consider their present position, make clear statements of both the needs of the school and those of individuals and put them in some order of priority. They must then plan equally specifically how those priorities will be met and having implemented the plans, go on to evaluate their success in meeting their goals.

The Impact of Teacher Appraisal on Staff Development and INSET

At the same time that INSET is changing fundamentally, there has been a meteoric growth of interest in teacher appraisal and it is now accepted in most areas of the education service that systems of appraisal will be established within the next year or two. Although early debate was distinguished by some very divergent views of the goals of teacher appraisal, most people now accept that its greatest value will be as part of the school's approach to staff development. Regular appraisal interviews will provide a valuable tool in the process of need establishment already noted as central to successful staff development. Because appraisal also involves the agreement of goals by the teacher and the management, both will inevitably look to INSET as a means of fulfilling their side of the agreement and this will create a pressure for INSET on a scale much greater than at present. Indeed, if support through INSET and in other ways is not forthcoming, any system of teacher appraisal will soon fall into disrepute for its credibility will depend upon action following upon the agreement of goals. An observed lack of commitment on the part of the management of the school at that point will rapidly ensure that the system is relegated to the back of teachers' minds.

There are important short term consequences of the introduction of teacher appraisal for INSET because there will be an immediate need for training in the skills needed for one-to-one interviewing, and these skills are needed by the appraised teacher as much as by the appraiser. Equally necessary are the skills of classroom observation and other data-collecting techniques which will ensure that the factual basis upon which the appraisal discussion takes place is as reliable as possible. Finally the skills involved in devising INSET activities which will help to achieve goals may also need reinforcing.

Nevertheless, the short term consequences for INSET are small compared with the longer term, for if every teacher is being regularly appraised and each appraisal leads to some agreed points of development, then almost everyone of these is likely to demand INSET support of one kind or another, though not all of those INSET activities will be conventional courses.

Evaluating INSET

Despite the developments described in earlier sections it would still not be far from the truth to describe much of the INSET currently provided, whether by institutions or LEAs, as a contract largely between the individual teacher and the provider. The teacher decides to take part in the INSET activity for his or her own reasons; the school's needs may, and often are, the source of those reasons but if the school's needs are involved, they are mediated through the perceptions of the teacher. Not surprisingly therefore the provider sees the teacher as the immediate client, who defines the needs which should be met by the activity. It follows from this that in evaluation it is the teacher's satisfaction with the activity which has been the yardstick. Some long way behind has come the evaluation of the impact of the activity on the teacher's performance and where this has been considered it has again often been mediated through the perceptions of the teacher. We should not be surprised at this because almost always no one else was party to the contract or was aware of the goals of the activity. Evaluation of the impact of an INSET activity on the practice of the school is even rarer in current practice and is likely to be a frustrating exercise when attempted until there is a much more general, overt and active sharing by schools of the responsibility for getting something from the INSET undertaken by an individual within the staff. The recent developments in the funding of INSET have had as one of their aims to increase the impact of INSET on the schools. In doing so they demand that we look again at how we might evaluate activities when not only the teacher is the client, but also the school and the LEA. The new scheme will demand much more than the evaluation of the individual INSET activities. Schools will need to evaluate how well they handle their responsibility for an INSET programme and so will LEAs. Most LEAs will put as their first INSET priority raising the performance of schools through the development of more effective curricula and by helping teachers to deliver those curricula more efficiently. The role of evaluation in this process is clear and essential though by no means simple. There are, however, other roles fulfilled by INSET which must now become part of LEAs' priorities. INSET has been a means of creating and maintaining job satisfaction for teachers and it has also been a means of preparing tomorrow's leaders. It will be essential to evaluate how successfully LEAs continue to achieve these goals under the new system. Concentration on training to raise the basic level of competence at the expense of the education and development of the leaders of the future would not be in the interests of our children in the longer term. Activities leading to professional development suitable for tomorrow's teachers are more difficult to evaluate than simple 'train and test performance' activities but it is essential that this nettle be grasped.

Within this wider and more demanding context, how is the evaluation of individual activities or programmes likely to change? It is certain that the scope of the evaluation must be much broader, encompassing preparation and planning, follow-up and impact as well as the actual execution. It will need to focus not only on the provider of the activity but also upon the school and the LEA. The kinds of question which will need to be addressed include:

(i) *Preparation*

Was the process of identification of need accurate? Was there consensus about the need among all the people concerned—teacher, colleagues, school and LEA?

Could the INSET activity concentrate on that single need or was there a multiplicity of needs among the participants in the activity?

Had the school done the necessary preparatory work (a) to enable the teachers taking part to obtain maximum benefit, (b) to enable other staff to benefit from their experience?

Did the teachers taking part accept 'ownership' of the INSET activity? Did the providing institution and its staff accept 'ownership' of the problem? In other words, was this a partnership in problem-solving? Were the skills of both utilized to the full in setting up the activity?

(ii) *Planning*

Did those who planned the activity have skills in the design of INSET activities?

Were the goals for the activity clearly defined? When change in attitude, teaching style or other fundamental factor was desired, was this made clear or was it hidden behind a facade of content, allowing participants to miss the point of the exercise? Were the goals shared by the participants in the activity?

Was the methodology appropriate to the goals? Was it appropriate for adult learners?

(iii) *Execution*

Did the activity in practice match the ideal which was planned?

Did the participants recognize the purpose and value of constituent parts of the activity?

Did the participants in fact share common purposes and goals or were there 'hidden curricula' which impeded group coherence?

Did the participants enjoy the process?
Did they find it of value to themselves professionally?
Did they feel it equipped them to help their colleagues?

(iv) *Follow-up*

Did the school welcome feedback from the participants?
Did the school facilitate debate as a result of the activity and encourage change?
Did the school and the LEA make resources available to enable change to be made?

(v) *Impact*

Was the school willing to change?
Did the INSET activity result in a change?
Was that change evaluated?
Was the change effective and in line with the needs and the priorities of the school?
Was the change in line with LEA goals?
Was the change supported by all those whose support was needed—senior staff, LEA and the community?
Was the change permanent?
Was the appropriate feedback and recognition given to the participants, the rest of the staff and the provider of the INSET activity?

Whether we shall be able to evaluate substantially all INSET activities is doubtful; it seems more likely that some activities—the radical, the fundamental—will be explored in depth while others will have much more limited evaluation, perhaps concentrating on particular aspects. If evaluation moves in this direction it is bound to be more expensive and certainly time-consuming. There will be a need to build the cost of evaluation into the activity as a matter of course, it will no longer be possible to regard evaluation as an optional extra. One benefit of this ought to be a growing recognition that evaluation is not a peripheral activity but one that is central to further development.

If evaluation does become more central to INSET we shall need to explore whether we need a race of independent specialist evaluators or whether the evaluation can be better carried out by the providers and participants as an integral part of the activity. Whichever course is chosen, we can assume with confidence that over the next few years there will be a considerable demand for evaluation skills within the profession on a much broader scale than ever before.

An Issue for the Future

There is little doubt that staff development and INSET hold the keys to the quality of the education we offer to pupils in the primary schools of the future. How their influence will be brought to bear remains to be seen. One view links quality with accountability and value for money. Such arguments tend to emphasize a common curriculum and the achievement of agreed standards. If this view prevails, good teaching will be seen as delivering the agreed curriculum adequately and helping children to achieve the desired standards. It follows that staff development and INSET will be needed to ensure that all teachers are able to achieve these goals. INSET activities could be expected therefore to be closely related to knowledge and methodology goals. A different view sees the teacher as innovator, decision-maker and evaluator. Again staff development and INSET are important but the goals in this case are very different—they are related to the processes of innovation and evaluation. Whereas the first model sees the teacher's training needs as akin to those of the worker on a production line, the second sees the teacher more in the role of manager or design team member.

These two conflicting views of the teacher's role pose considerable problems for staff development and INSET because they demand such different outcomes. Whereas one expects INSET to minimize teachers' fallibility, the other sets out to maximize their creativity. Until we can reach agreement on what we require of teachers it will be very difficult to make judgements about the effectiveness of staff development.

References

ADVISORY COMMITTEE on the SUPPLY and TRAINING of TEACHERS (ACSTT) (1978) *Making INSET Work*, HMSO.

DADDS, M. (1986) 'Group support for self-directed teacher research' *Forum*, 28 February.

HANDY, C. (1984) *Taken for Granted: The Organization of School*, Schools Council.

SURREY INSPECTORATE, (1980) *Professional Development*, Surrey LEA.

TRETHOWAN, D. (1983) *Delegation*, Education for Industrial Society.

An Approach to Headship Development Through Personal and Professional Growth

Alan A. Coulson

Introduction

Most courses for heads are rooted in a logical-rational planning model of thought and action which emphasizes analysis of school requirements, the systematic formulation of strategies to meet them, and the head's part in bringing all this about. The viewpoint taken in this chapter is that until now management courses have paid too much attention to the role requirements of headship and not enough to the head's personality, even though this is widely recognized as the most important determinant of the style and quality of the school. Further, it is argued that too much emphasis has been given to heads as authority figures and decision-makers and too little to the ways in which successful heads shape their schools through personal influence and their relationships with others, especially their teacher colleagues. Finally, it is held that, in order to convert into improved practice in schools the increased awareness and understanding which may be gained from courses, much greater support at school level is needed. Central to the approach to school management put forward here is the belief that in primary headship the role and the person are so closely identified that professional and personal growth are inseparable. The term 'personal growth' is here used to denote what happens when someone with no obvious problems in functioning normally in social life or at work pursues a process of self-exploration for greater self-understanding in order to become more effective, more creative and more self-fulfilled in all aspects of life.

The approach to management outlined in this chapter rests on the belief that human beings have an innate drive or formative tendency to become more fully-functioning (Rogers, 1980) or 'self-actualizing' (Goldstein, 1939; Maslow, 1970). Thus education, including headship development, should always be fundamentally concerned with the encouragement of this process as much as with attempts to respond to contemporary social and political demands.

Until the 1970s little interest was shown in the management of schools. Occasional short courses and summer schools provided channels for the transmission of established 'good' practice from one generation of heads to the next or for those ambitious for headship to learn the ropes from those already in post. Throughout the 1970s, however, there was a noticeable growth in course provision (Pennington and Bell, 1982) and by the end of the decade a large number of universities and colleges had established qualifications in education management. A national survey of education management courses (Hughes, Carter and Fidler, 1981) was commissioned by the DES. This was followed by the establishment of the National Development Centre for School Management Training (NDCSMT) in 1983. This official recognition of the importance of school management stimulated a further growth of activity, particularly in the provision of short courses for senior staff, many of which have since 1983 been the subject of special government funding.

As well as the further proliferation of courses, the 1980s have seen a broadening of concerns in school management, marked by the expansion of research activities and a growing quantity of published writing. They have also witnessed a reawakening of interest among educationists in scrutinizing the practice of management development in industry for possible pointers to development among heads (e.g. Everard, 1983; Everard and Morris, 1985). Central to, or underlying, the view of school management which has so far been prevalent is the assumption shared by teachers, heads, local education officers, and Her Majesty's Inspectorate that more than anything else the quality of the school depends heavily upon the personal calibre of the head:

> What matters above all is the quality, character and personality of the headteacher; upon that individual man or woman depends the ethos of the school, its standards, the example set by the staff, and the expectations that the staff have of the children... we know the power for good that a fine head can be. (Joseph, 1983)

School headship is not at root about skills, rules or procedures but hinges upon the personality of heads and their relationships with others, especially their capacity to lead by example and the capacity to embody key values (Coulson, 1986). Despite this, most courses devote the bulk of their time to ways of dealing with the environmental demands made on the school, and to organizational matters and contemporary problem issues. Attention is given to the formal or overt aspects of school management, which might typically include goal-setting, relations with the community, organizational structures, curriculum development and change, financial and resource management, and theories of leadership, decision-making and motivation. The allegedly all-important character and personality of heads, their ways of being and relating are rarely, if ever, the central focus of attention.

The principal supposition of the following account is that in the primary school progress towards more effective headship or more widespread practice of 'good' headship will more probably result from an understanding of, and subsequent improvement upon, the prevailing 'personal influence' pattern of management than from the attempted implantation of more quasi-objective, cognitive-logical strategies or skills which emanate from a culturally alien 'managerialism'.

Training or Development?

The designation, 'training', as in 'headship training', reflects a perspective in which it is implied that one person, who knows how heads should behave, teaches another person 'how to do it'. This is in contrast with the approach represented by the broader terms 'development' or 'education', which implies a greater degree of critical thinking and reflectiveness, and an emphasis on the learner's growing abilities to think and act for himself. Thus headship *development*, not training, would place the personal and professional growth of the head at the heart of the programme rather than at the periphery. It would concentrate on fostering the personal and interpersonal qualities of the head which aid success in school management. The contributions of intuition and creativity deserve greater acknowledgement, as do the increasingly crucial and complex diplomatic functions which heads have to undertake in linking their schools to the community they serve. Further, the whole headship development enterprise is unlikely to bring long term or widespread benefit unless it is set within the context of a broader and more far-reaching local or regional school management development policy (McMahon, 1984; Bolam, 1986). It needs also to be informed by an adult learning psychology which treats heads holistically as evolving persons as well as attempting to help them to tackle their pressing, but often transient, problems of the moment. A development approach would dwell as much on process as on content, as much on ways of being and relating as on skills to be acquired and practised, and as much on heads as people as on their role and responsibilities.

In the next section the centrality in primary school management of the notion of the head as 'leading professional' is indicated, and consideration is given to the ways in which tradition and the established norms and practices of heads and teachers shape the patterns of influence (or 'management') available to heads. A summary of the factors contributing to successful headship follows; these are interpreted principally in terms of heads' personal influence and professional leadership rather than their managerial knowledge, skills and techniques.

Figure 1:

Summary of the Head's Managerial Roles

CHIEF EXECUTIVE ROLES

Role	Description	Representative Activities
INTERPERSONAL		
Figurehead	Symbolic head, performing routine legal or social duties.	Assembly: signing reports and authorization.
Leader/Supervisor	Responsible for the motivation and coordination of subordinates' work.	Embodied in virtually all managerial activities involving subordinates: classroom visits, discussions, etc.
Liaison	Maintenance of network of outside contacts.	Correspondence; external committee work: links with LEA people and governors.
INFORMATIONAL		
Monitor	Seeks and receives wide variety of information to develop understanding of organization and environment: emerges as nerve centre of internal and external information.	Handling mail and contacts concerned primarily with receiving information (e.g. observational tours of school: LEA and government circulars and memoranda).
Disseminator	Transmits information to members of staff: some information factual, some involving interpretation and integration of diverse value positions from outsiders.	Directing mail and other material to teachers for informational purposes, verbal contacts involving information flow to subordinates.
Spokesman	Transmits information to outsiders on school's plans, policies, actions, results, etc: serves as education ''expert'' to general public.	Governors' meetings: handling contacts involving transmission of information to outsiders.
DECISIONAL		
Entrepreneur	Searches school and its environment for opportunities to initiate change through 'improvement projects'.	Reviews of curriculum and policy involving initiation of 'improvement projects'.
Disturbance Handler	Responsible for corrective action when school faces unexpected disturbances.	*Ad hoc* coping with breakdown of school facilities, unwelcome visitors: discipline.
Resources	Responsible for the allocation of school resources of all kinds—in effect the making or approval of all significant decisions.	Distribution of human and material resources in accordance with head's ''philosophy'' and scale of priorities, timetabling, budgeting.
Negotiator	Representing the school at negotiations	Promoting or defending the interests of the school.

LEADING PROFESSIONAL ROLES

Role	Description	Representative Activities
Goal Setter and Evaluator	Determining the overall character of the school and overseeing progress towards this as a goal.	Shaping curriculum and organization; formulating statements of aims (e.g. in school prospectus); school self-evaluation.
Curriculum Co-ordinator and Developer	Making final decisions as to emphases to be given among curriculum subjects and materials.	Keeping informed of curriculum developments, chairing meetings, allocating posts of responsibility for curriculum areas, choice and purchase of materials. Classroom supervision of teachers.
Teacher	The head's time in classrooms; personal teaching or working alongside teacher colleagues.	Scheduled teaching of classes or groups; covering for absent teachers.
Exemplar of Professional Values	Displaying behaviours valued by teachers and seen by them as exemplifying "professionalism".	Willingness to teach; 'commitment' to school; reliability, efficiency, concern for children and teachers. Solidarity with teachers' interests.

Primary Headship

The Head as Leading Professional

The head may be seen as the *chief executive* of an organization whose staff define themselves as professionals and also as its *leading professional* (Hughes, 1976). A central task of school management is the achievement of an accommodation between the professional values and perspectives heads share with other teachers and their needs as *chief executives* to meet external demands and pursue organizational imperatives. As *leading professionals* the heads' range of management options is channelled and constrained by the professional conventions and expectations of teachers, by their own previous experience and socialization *as teachers*, by established notions of the practices appropriate to headship in general, and by the customs and expectations resulting from the previous heads' regimes in each particular school.

An analysis of the head's managerial work has been undertaken using the *chief executive/leading professional* conceptual framework (Coulson, 1986, see Fig. 1). Of course, all of the head's managerial functions merit consideration in the context of training and development; however, despite the head's clear function as the school's *chief executive*, it is argued here that effective headship rests as much, or more, upon the successful exercise of *professional* leadership. Therefore the discussion which follows concentrates upon the personal and professional influence elements of the head's work which lie at the heart of successful professional leadership.

Central to the notion of professional leadership in schools is the expectation that heads will embody certain key educational values and convey them to colleagues and pupils through personal precept and example. A variety of factors contributes to this concept of headship as 'leading or managing by example'. The tradition for each school to have autonomy, 'to be itself', has led to a situation in which heads have had a good deal of latitude to pursue their own educational priorities within the school: there is usually therefore a close correspondence between the head's personality and the character of the school. Moreover, the head's philosophy is disseminated mostly through direct personal influence and example, particularly by face-to-face interaction with individuals. Though heads have an executive function they retain the public- and self-image of teacher albeit *headteacher*; the most successful mode of managerial influence within the school is therefore more likely to be as a colleague, as *primus inter pares*, rather than through authority of status or the more overt employment of administrative or managerial strategies. Additionally, heads serve as personal links between the different parts of the school, and their co-ordinating efforts are frequently implicit and personal, revolving around their own personal presence and their involvement in every aspect of school operation.

As a result of the close identification between heads and their schools, the actions and attitudes of heads are expected by teachers to exemplify to a high degree the personal and organizational values associated with their own internalized rules of professional conduct. For example, Nias (1981) shows how teachers' concept of 'commitment' is used to evaluate heads according to their dedication ('to be a good head you have to be totally involved, totally committed') and their adherence to high personal standards ('he sets such a high standard that you feel you want to be equally committed'). The framework of teacher expectations, which is part of their occupational culture (Hargreaves, 1980), puts pressure on heads to legitimate their promotion and status by equalling or exceeding their colleagues in the observance of teachers' cultural norms. By doing so they maintain and build their credibility as *leading* professionals and *head*teachers. The heads' self-identification with teacher culture and the establishment and maintenance of a consensus on professional values between themselves and teachers serves to alleviate the concern felt by many teachers that on promotion heads may become 'administrators', and in the process lose touch with classroom needs and perspectives.

In the eyes of people within the educational community the image of 'good' or successful heads and expectations for their behaviour continue to stem from norms and beliefs embedded in the culture of schools and the occupational values of teachers-at-large rather than from more generalizable notions of what constitutes sound organizational management in other types of organization.

A recent study of primary school headship in England and Wales (Coulson, 1986) concludes that successful heads' managerial behaviour is integrated with, and serves the realization of, their particular educational and organizational vision. In other words, the successful head has the capacity to create and communicate a view of a desired state of affairs in the school that induces commitment and collaboration among those working there.

Primary school headship hinges less upon some*thing* called leadership or management than on the *process* of leading—of the head's exerting influence in the school setting. Through their personal influence heads attempt to create and nurture an organizational culture which is aligned with their vision for their particular school and which, at the same time, is in keeping with the norms and expectations of other interested parties—parents, local authority officials and, especially, teachers. These conclusions are broadly in keeping with the findings of investigations of principalship in the United States (e.g. Blumberg and Greenfield, 1980; Hall, Rutherford, Hord and Huling, 1984; Sergiovanni, 1984; Manasse, 1985). Despite the variety of variables and perspectives in these studies, it is possible tentatively to draw on them to hypothesize some of the characteristics of headteachers which are consistently associated with successful school management:

1 Successful heads are *goal-orientated* insofar as they have a vision of how they would like to see their schools develop. Thus they give the school a sense of direction and are capable of operationalizing their goals and values both through a long-term strategy and at the level of their day-to-day actions.

2 Successful heads show a high degree of *interpersonal competence*. Primary heads transmit policies and values largely through face-to-face interpersonal interaction with other participants in the school situation. More effective heads have greater ability to listen sensitively to and enter into constructive dialogue with teachers, parents and others.

3 Successful heads are *sensitive to the dynamics of power* inside and outside their schools. They are adept at seeking out sources of power and support through informal networking outside the school and at the same time sensitive to the informal codes of professional practice which govern expectations for relations among teachers and between teachers and head.

4 Successful heads enjoy a relatively high degree of *personal security* in that their sense of themselves as people enables them to tackle issues inside and outside the school without feeling unduly threatened.

5 Successful heads have a *high tolerance for ambiguity*. Heads whose

personal needs for structuring, continuity and stability are high can find frequent change and uncertainty a potent source of frustration and tension.

6 Successful heads tend to be *proactive* in confronting the internal and external demands of the school. They take hold of change by meeting it half way and they push at the boundaries of the system rather than being mainly reactive.

7 Successful heads behave in ways which enable them to be *in charge of the job and not let the job be in charge of them*. Thus, while having due regard to the constraints inside and outside their schools, they are still able to devote time and energy to the pursuit of activities in line with their own evolving visions. In doing so they infuse the tasks of teaching and managing with value beyond their immediate requirements.

8 Successful heads take a *holistic perspective* towards problem-solving. They bring to bear appropriate professional knowledge, experience and expertise; thus their approach to solving individual problems is rooted in an understanding of their meaning within the context of the overall operation of the school.

A head's management style, like other facets of interpersonal behaviour, is not an objective, rational, consistent and cognitive strategy external to, and detached from, the person, it is an integral part of that individual's way of being: an expression of underlying attitudes and values. Thus the means by which successful heads permeate their schools with their own educational and personal values and priorities without infringing the sensibilities and sense of professional autonomy of their staffs owes as much to the head's sensitivity to others and responsiveness to the dynamics of situations as to the pursuit of overt objectives and strategies or the application of specific skills.

The compatibility or otherwise between the temperament and value system of the individual and the culture of teachers and school is therefore a key consideration in determining the degree of success and satisfaction headship may offer. As Everett Hughes (cited in Hargreaves, 1980) has remarked, 'the culture of a profession appears in the individual as a set of personality traits'.

Any approach to improving headship which largely ignores the centrality of the psychology of the individual, as well as the conditions, demands, and constraints that give rise to and sustain the culture of teaching, is unlikely to prove fully effective.

The assumption underlying most existing school management courses seems to be that if heads acquire greater knowledge of the social and educational demands being placed upon them and learn certain skills the schools will become more effective. The next section argues that this kind of approach is inadequate because it amounts to an attempt to modify complex behaviour without addressing sufficiently the roots of headteachers' actions in their personal beliefs, values and feelings.

Headship Development

A Critique of the Orientation of Current School Management Courses

Role Learning

Through their experience of teaching, their socialization into the norms of schools, and their observation and evaluation of the ways of their predecessors, most heads and aspiring heads have developed firm expectations as to what headship involves. Informed opinion suggests that heads look to management courses to confirm their basic assumptions about headship. Typically course activities include hearing about theories of organization and management, receiving the advice and direction of experienced practitioners, inspectors and advisers, working on case studies or simulation exercises, and, increasingly, undertaking small scale investigations of current school problems and practices. All these are no doubt beneficial; however, they are usually dealt with in a fashion which suggests that the process of managing a school is only incidentally connected with the head as a *person*, as an individual. Individualism is often spoken of as a valued quality in headship but most courses, especially those directed by existing heads, appear to promote orthodoxy rather than encouraging a variety of approaches.

Many participants in these programmes seem to be seeking information and 'expert' guidance not only on current problems, but also on how to display certain behaviours which have come to be associated with school 'leadership'. In other words, the implicit assumption persists that leadership can be trained into people, that it can be equated with a role which can successfully be assumed and performed. Those taking this approach to learning about relations with colleagues tend to think in terms of shaping their behaviour in accordance with some kind of leadership 'model'; they seek to join the ranks of that section of the educational community which is seen as demonstrating proper leadership. Employing mainly traditional educational methods, such as lectures, discussions, and exercises, most courses seem to have carried two implications: first, that course participants are defined as recipients: they are the object, not the subject of the endeavour; second, that tactics, strategies, policies and practices can be discussed more or less independently of the persons involved. In other words, the focus remains upon the individual's professional role-facade.

Recently heads and schools have come under increasing pressure as a result of an uncomfortable combination of a deteriorating financial situation, falling enrolments, rapid social change, and the more controlling and constraining character of central and local government policies. One effect of this has been to open to question the traditional, received model of headship and to undermine heads' personal feelings of confidence in what they are doing. Thus, among the most vital needs to be met by in-service programmes of management development is the provision of support and reassurance for heads in order to increase their capacity to function satisfactorily within a context of more or less perpetual uncertainty and ambiguity. In an unstable context where pluralistic and conflicting demands are made upon schools, heads (and other colleagues) can no longer simply *perform*, they must continually *learn* and change. The situation disturbs established perceptions, values and practices and presents a challenge to each head *as a person*. The headship role can no longer merely be learned, it must be continually recreated by the individual. The critical outcome of a headship development programme '... is not particular new knowledge or behaviour, rather it is trust in the capacity to make new sense, to create new forms of action, and to take action in a context of doubt and uncertainty' (Jentz and Wofford, 1979). Thus management development has the task of integrating attempts to attend to the personal growth needs of individuals with efforts to increase their sense of professional competence and effectiveness.

Interpersonal Skills

As the movement to provide management education for school personnel has gathered momentum it has become clear that to a large extent it is interpersonal competence which differentiates more successful from less successful heads, at least in the eyes of teachers. As a consequence greater attention is being turned to what are customarily termed 'interpersonal skills'. The premise here seems to be that communicating, interpersonal relating or, indeed, headship can be broken down or defined in terms of specific behaviours or skills which can be acquired or enhanced through training. This view overlooks the fact that communication and interpersonal relating consist of behavioural expressions of the person's attitudes, values and feeling states, a high proportion of which may be non-verbal, not to mention unconscious. Two crucial questions arise from this. First, how feasible is it to attempt to develop interpersonal skills without simultaneously dealing with the underlying attitudes and values of which they are an expression? Second, assuming it is possible, how desirable is it for heads to learn and exercise skills which may not be congruent with their underlying values? Relating to others is not a step-by-step procedure whereby specific skills are utilized at appropriate times, it is a dynamic process which utilizes the 'self as an instrument' and depends not only upon the beliefs, attitudes and values of individuals but also on their underlying motivation and intent (Combs, Blume, Newman and Wass, 1974; Ivey, 1971). In other words, behaviour is an expression of the person's internal impressions or perceptions. Thus altering or trying to train complex behaviour without attending to the beliefs, values and feelings associated with it is not only ethically dubious, it is not likely to be effective. More important than teaching heads skills *as skills* is the creation of a learning climate of trust and security within which they will have opportunities to explore, through the actual processes of communication and interpersonal interaction, their values, their beliefs and their ways of being with others. Enhancement of interpersonal 'skills' may follow but it is salutary to remember that in school it is not the head's possession of 'skills' which is in itself significant, more important is the sensitivity with which their use is *controlled*, the *intentions* with which they are employed, and their *flexibility* or changeability.

Argyris (1976, 1982) has summarized the crucial difficulty of bringing about significant change among managers by a skills-learning approach. He concludes:

> Luckily, people judge the credibility of human skills by evaluating what values they serve. This means that those who learn the new skills as gimmicks and tricks will be discovered. It means further that those who wish to gain credibility not only must learn the new skills but also must internalize a new set of values.

Thus no amount of new knowledge-acquisition and skills-training will in themselves effect much difference in the practice of headship in schools. As well as imparting information and skills, management development also has the task of enabling heads to expose to scrutiny the values underlying their present practices and helping them to adopt values and develop relationships genuinely consonant with the managerial practices and processes they hope to instigate.

An Alternative: A Person-Centred Development Approach

Within the kind of approach advocated here several elements relatively neglected in existing programmes feature prominently. First, the learning pursued in the course is put into the context of the life and career of the individual participant as well as set within the context of current educational requirements. Heads are seen as learners, who bring their own experiences and capacities, aspirations and anxieties to the learning situation. Second, and related to the previous point, the promotion of self-knowledge and self-awareness as part of the development of the whole person are central concerns: consideration of intuition as well as logic, feelings as well as thoughts lays the foundations for better understanding of both self and others, especially colleagues. Third, particular emphasis is placed upon fostering an interpersonally sensitive but educationally pro-active stance towards individuals and agencies in the community as a means of generating a network of relationships supportive of the school.

Adult Learning and Change

An adult psychology is as necessary for continuing or teacher education (including headship development) as is an adolescent or child psychology for pupil learning in school (Mulford, 1984). Since psychological development and change continue in adult life, the concerns, emotions, needs, desires, aspirations and fears of the individual are inseparable from professional life. The person needs to be put back firmly into the professional picture. Consideration, for example, of stages of adult development (Loevinger, 1976; Adams, Hayes and Hopson, 1976; Levinson, Darrow, Klein, Levinson and McKee, 1978; Hopson and Scally, 1980) may help clarify the deeper motives and more fundamental purposes which underlie the career patterns of heads and teachers and influence the nature of their involvement in management development courses. It is as well to remind ourselves that the existential questions of meaning, purpose, vocation, social responsibility, dependence and human relationships continue to confront adults, headteachers included, and that these issues infuse and affect their professional as well as their private lives. Indeed the personal and professional are inseparable.

The fundamental process upon which both personal and professional growth depends is the modification of people's cognitive structure or organized pattern of thinking and feeling about themselves and their world. This change is difficult and for the mature individual often disturbing. Moreover, the kind of adult learning under consideration here, headship development, occurs only after individuals have been subject to a long period of professional socialization during which they will have expended considerable effort building what for them is a workable professional persona. The weight of past learning and accumulated expectations therefore powerfully affect the head's or would-be head's orientation towards the learning situation. Mulford (1984) reminds us that in these circumstances learning is concerned with modifying, transforming and reintegrating meanings, values, strategies and skills ('transforming'), rather than with forming and accumulating them as in childhood or at the commencement of learning in a quite new field ('forming'). In contrast to formations, transformations require more time and greater effort; they also require that established, taken-for-granted meanings and values be raised to a conscious level and exposed to critical scrutiny. In the process of 'transforming' it is important that any resulting new behaviours have a chance to be tested in 'safe' situations before being adopted. For many, the process of 'loosening' existing assumption and values, essential if real change is to occur, evokes defensiveness and resistance. While warning that students should be challenged but not 'bowled over', Mulford concludes that those responsible for the education of educators have the task of creating challenge, dissonance and discontinuity as necessary precursors to facilitating growth and change.

If change and development, as opposed to continuity and maintenance, are major goals of headship development, tutorial contributions from advisers, experienced heads and other practitioners firmly immersed in current orthodoxy need to be complemented by others from outside the immediate teacher culture and more equipped to facilitate personal growth and organization development. The familiar content- and problem-orientated in-service 'training' model needs to give way more and more to experiential workshop-type methodologies with an emphasis upon peer learning.

Self Knowledge and Development

Personal growth work involves the development of self-confidence, self-awareness and sensitivity to interpersonal processes. It necessitates two potentially threatening elements for some people: intensive feedback to individuals about how they are perceived and experienced by others, and the disturbance or de-structuring of each person's established assumptions and expectations in order to enable new perceptions and learning to occur. Because of sensitivity about these issues, development of the person is, as Evans (1983) comments in his report on School Leader Education in Sweden, the most challenging element of school management training. Many of the heads and teachers who in other ways show interest in management programmes seek to avoid the feelings of discomfort and insecurity which may be engendered by personal development work if this is introduced. However, continued neglect of this element will continue to dilute the potential of school management courses to have much real effect. After all, the less open to new experiences and to self-questioning people are, and the more defensive they tend to be of their present attitudes and practices, the less able they are to benefit from training (Gray and Coulson, 1982). Management development may assist individuals in identifying and activating those aspects of their work in which they are less competent and in learning to evoke all aspects in more appropriate configurations. Self-actualization of heads and their own openness to growth and change is a prerequisite to their being able to understand and facilitate development among others.

As has already been suggested, a substantial proportion of heads' managerial actions spring in a fairly spontaneous and *ad hoc* fashion from their way of being. Furthermore, most heads 'do more than they can say they do': much of the 'knowing by experience' or 'flying by the seat of the pants' elements of the head's work may remain unarticulated because they are outside verbal consciousness; they may in fact be interpreted as a form of cultivated intuition (Agor, 1984). A number of writers (e.g. Ornstein, 1977; Blakeslee, 1980; Agor, 1984; Zdenek, 1985) report research which shows that the left hemisphere of the brain clarifies, analyzes and categorizes in order to make meanings explicit whereas the right hemisphere unifies (or makes *Gestalts*), works in metaphors, and maintains sensed or implicit meanings. Most management courses have or so far been based on cognitive, rational models of thought and action (essentially left-brain activities). Lack of satisfaction is often expressed with the consequent tendency to present tidied-up, abstracted, and conceptualized formulations of school 'reality' ('theory'), and the inability of most courses to take adequate account of the untidy, rapid-paced immediacy of the 'reality' experienced by heads and teachers in schools ('practice'). In contrast to the systematic and reflective depictions of organizational management found in most management literature, Kotter (1982) has shown that effective managers work through informal and seemingly relatively disorganized networks of relationship, a process he calls 'the efficiency of seemingly inefficient behaviour'. This is consistent with Nugent's (1981) contention that 'many managers tend to be more at ease with the intuitive mode of thought in their everyday functioning, and this leads to their discomfort when they are forced into rational management science approaches'. It also fits closely with the situation of many heads and teachers on management courses. There is clearly a need for a synthesis of left and right brain faculties among managers and there can be little doubt that the outstanding heads are the ones who can couple effective right-brain processes—such as hunch, judgment, and synthesis with effective processes of the left—such as articulateness, logic and analysis (Huff, Lake and Schaalman, 1982). The left/right brain distinction may be oversimple and physiologically imprecise; nonetheless it can serve as a useful metaphor and a reminder of the need for balance and harmony between aspects of headship, one of which (the left, logical-rational one) has so far predominated in in-service programmes. For heads undergoing development, just as for learners in other spheres, 'significant learning combines the logical and the intuitive, the intellect and the feeling, the concept and the experience, the idea and the meaning. When we learn that way we are whole...' (Rogers, 1983a).

Relations with the Community
The previous careers of heads as classroom teachers is unlikely to have prepared them for much that they will need to do as heads—the schools' managers. Work with a variety of adults, both individually and in groups, within the loosely-organized context of the school and its environment calls for flexibility, a high tolerance of ambiguity, and a capacity to win the co-operation and support of people from different backgrounds and walks of life. Such work puts a premium on what Kaplan (1982) has called 'reticular competence' which he defines as the ability to work effectively in social networks—that is in settings larger than a group and considerably more complex and disconnected. It involves not only the possession of a diverse set of contacts in an inter-group network but also the knowledge of when to call upon them and in what configuration. It is through the development of a network of co-operative relationships, combined with a set of loosely connected goals and plans, that the head operates in the 'real'

world of the school as opposed to the well-organized one preferred by most management theorists and course providers.

In recent times much emphasis has been placed upon the need for heads and schools to become more responsive to external demands and constraints. However, the interaction between schools and the communities they serve is two-way. Thus, in addition to the reactive aspects of relations with the individuals and agencies who constitute the school's environment, courses could do more to help heads to become more proactive in relation to these same persons and groups. Research in the U.S.A. (e.g. Manasse, 1985) has shown that effective principals are proactive, using their daily interactions to gather information and monitor events, and gradually to move their schools toward their own vision of what the school should be. Professionally well-informed and personally secure heads who can gain and retain reciprocal trust and mutual confidence with the officers of their local authorities, parents, governors and other key figures can play a significant educational role external to the schools by creating the social and psychological climate in which they may flourish. In many of their managerial roles (see figure 1) heads have continual opportunities to adjust, influence and re-shape the framework of expectations held for the school by outsiders. In the process of doing so they can also interpret and negotiate their own version of the headship role with significant members of their role-set outside the school (among them governors, parents and LEA officers).

Also vital to heads is political competence to fathom the value-laden conflicts of interest in the loosely-organized system of the school and its environment, and to manage their own values and functions amidst these conflicts (Brown, 1980). Education in values clarification and assertiveness (e.g. Bolton, 1979; Back and Back, 1982) may prove valuable for the latter task. Provision for education likely to aid the development of reticular and political skills needs to be built into the design of headship development programmes. As McCall (1976) has pointed out in regard to leadership development in general, to be effective, training situations and simulations need to capture the important elements of the target organization, its environment and the management roles within it. Appropriate simulations and experiential learning situations are needed within which heads can be observed in action at first hand and from which they can receive intensive feedback from peers and tutors. The importance of establishing sound relationships with a variety of figures in the community again underlines the need for management development to concentrate on the head's ways of communicating and relating.

Course Organization
The character of person-centred headship development stems mostly from the values and personal qualities of the tutor. According to its originator, Carl Rogers (1983b, p. 88) a precondition of person-centred learning is that

the tutor 'is sufficiently secure within herself and in her relationships to others that she experiences an essential trust in the capacity of others to think for themselves, to learn for themselves'. The tutor fosters a learning climate of openness and genuineness and shares the responsibility for learning with the learners; resources are shared and learning is more and more provided by the learners for each other. Evaluation of the extent and significance of the learning is made principally by the learners themselves. Essentially the course members 'are regarded both as the agenda for the course and the context for learning' (Whitaker, 1986, p. 277).

Though tutors play a prominent part in establishing norms, a person-centred programme develops collaboratively. Scheduling is loose and open to revision by participants; work continues informally during breaks and sometimes spontaneously late into the evening. Workrooms usually have a busy, informal appearance with working papers and impromptu charts spilling over from tables onto floors and walls.

Often course members take turns to monitor the overall functioning of the group and observe individuals' ways of reacting and relating in response to a variety of situations. Extensive, often concurrent, feedback from participants and the use of video replay enables direct learning about each person's ways of being in the group and the responses they evoke in others. In some activities members adopt certain roles or follow specific procedures in order to directly encounter issues arising from differences of authority and status, communication problems or conflicting priorities and values. Undertaking less familiar roles within the group as well as those in which they practise familiar skills furthers participants' understanding of themselves and of interpersonal and group processes. Within a short period of time heads may, for example, address their assembled colleagues, be interviewers and interviewees in different situations, serve as leaders and subordinates in the same group, join a 'task force' solving a particular problem, and explore the feelings they experience under stress. Many sharing activities may be undertaken in pairs, giving participants opportunities to interact closely with different personalities and to explore working with people of varied experience. In the initial stages of a course fears are often expressed that the openness involved will prove threatening to heads by exposing them to the negative judgments of their peers. On the contrary, experience shows that once a climate of trust is established heads typically enjoy an unexpectedly high level of support and encouragement from their course colleagues, most of whom readily identify with the concerns and sentiments expressed by others. Feelings of uncertainty, anxiety and isolation are often alleviated, a common reaction being 'it's so good not to feel so alone'. After one session an experienced head commented, 'I rarely talk to anyone about my feelings; having done so I feel relieved and refreshed, more relaxed and confident'.

Though during the course emphasis is given to the head as a learner rather than to the discussion of past or future events in schools, there is probably more extensive discussion of the heads' real concerns and more widespread comparing of notes than on a more traditionally organized course. Throughout the programme heads are encouraged to share their learning with teacher colleagues back at school and to involve them fully in the planning and implementation of in-school development.

Implementation

Despite recent moves towards school-based and school-focussed in-service work, much provision for school management development continues to be in the form of courses. Participation in a course is often seen as an *event*—an experience outside everyday work rather than a *process* of learning, including practice in–post as an integral ongoing part of development. If successful, a course raises awareness, conveys skills and reviews school issues of concern to participants; little of this has so far been converted into actions at school level. The traditional autonomy of the individual head combines with the relative lack of attention and support given to implementation in effectively diluting the impact of courses upon schools.

Though there exists a considerable quantity of research and literature on planned change and the implementation of change, little effective use is made of this information in the planning of in-service work for heads and teachers. Three spheres in which fairly straightforward action might be taken to encourage greater implementation of managerial change in schools are briefly reviewed in the following sections.

Local Management Development Policies

Headship development, which has been the main focus of discussion here, suggests perhaps 'manager' development rather than the rather broader 'management' development. However, management is increasingly the concern of all who work in schools. Thus some form of preparation, support and development in this sphere eventually needs to be extended to all teachers. It is essential therefore for any courses in headship development to be an integral part of a systematic, overall local authority-wide management development policy for the teaching profession as a whole, with suitable programmes available to staff at different career stages and levels of seniority. The National Development Centre for School Management Training now recognizes the need for such policies and is encouraging all local education authorities to establish them:

> Each LEA and school should see its MD policy and programme as part of its overall human resource strategy. Such strategy should include its management recruitment and appointment procedures, its personnel system and its appraisal system; finally, the organizational structure of the LEAs and schools should be designed to

embrace these approaches in order to achieve policy goals. (Bolam, 1986, p. 3)

Education for positions within schools, including headship, would best precede teachers' appointment to managerial positions and prepare them for these posts; it might also be advantageous if it were linked to advancement procedures and provision of further support, guidance, and development after promotion. The need for all these issues to be integrated into a policy for teacher and headteacher recruitment and development is evident.

Since the success of any form of training must depend in large measure upon the quality of the trainees in the first place, no programme of headship development can proceed very far unless simultaneous improvements are also made in recruitment procedures. Morgan, Hall and Mackay (1983) have reported extensive research on the recruitment of secondary heads. They concluded that there are many major deficiencies in the procedures at present employed and suggest improvements. The centrality of the head in school effectiveness was universally accepted and the appointment of heads was acknowledged by local education authorities as the most important thing they do. Since these points apply with equal force at primary level, recommendations for improvement in the primitive and haphazard selection methods often in current use deserve the closest consideration. Though approaches specifically designed for the selection of primary heads are needed, the work of Morgan, Hall and Mackay (1983, 1984) points to one possibility for making the procedure more rigorous and systematic. Better matching between selection procedures and the nature of the post requires in-depth analysis of the head's job. One recent study (Coulson, 1986) has been undertaken but much more extensive and detailed work needs to be done, particularly on the qualities needed for successful headship in a context of change and uncertainty.

The recent increase in attention to school management improvement has so far focussed mainly on heads already in post (Bolam, 1986, p. 7). However, Fiedler (1967) Fiedler *et al* (1977) and others have for many years argued that since the leadership-styles and motivational patterns of leaders or managers are relatively stable characteristics of the individual, training based on modifying leadership behaviour (especially *after* appointment) may be of limited value. This argument applies with even greater force to a post, such as that of head, which carries with it a good deal of autonomy, since this situation results in unusually close ties between the manager's style and his personality (Hall, Rutherford, Hord and Huling, 1984, p. 27). According to Fiedler, what is likely to promote greater effectiveness is more careful matching of person to situation; in other words people are more likely to succeed when put into situations which call for their particular management styles. Adaptability in leadership and an increase in the capacity for change in schools might result if the traditional primary school management model, dependent as it is on the quality of a single individual, were in time to be modified by giving increased emphasis to group and organization development and moving towards the recruitment and development of teams of people who could contribute a range of complementary capacities and skills to the school's management.

The need for team building among teachers and for heads to become less paternalistic in their leadership is the subject of a later section.

Linking Development with In-School Performance

Wallace (1986a) has highlighted a number of obstacles to the implementation of managerial action as a consequence of out-of-school management courses. Participants come on courses for a variety of reasons and many certainly continue to associate attendance at a management course more with individual promotion than in-school development and change. An even more significant limiting factor has been the assumption that learning in one context (a course) can be transferred into practice in another (the school) without considerable further experimentation, feedback and support in-post.

Wallace suggests a number of ways in which the development taking place through courses could be more closely linked to managerial performance in the schools. Pre-course diagnosis of the needs of participants and their school situations could form the foundation of much of the work undertaken on the course. A 'sandwich' arrangement where participants alternate between school and other learning contexts can help links to be made. One way in which this is done is through action learning approaches in which participants establish a cycle of planning, implementation and evaluation of any modifications they wish to make in their managerial work or in some aspect of their organization. Important too is the establishment of on-going support of various kinds for individuals once a course has been completed. The establishment of peer-learning groups to extend course-initiated development within schools or to share experiences among personnel from different schools may be encouraged. These teacher-related activities would be additional to more formal follow-up to courses by tutors and advisers who would increasingly assume a facilitating function rather than the traditional instructional one.

All these strategies and other similar endeavours would best take place as part of a web of diverse but co-ordinated and mutually supportive activities, in short a management development policy of the kind referred to in the previous section.

The generation of a form of school organization which is continually evolving and flexible enough readily to accommodate to changing circumstances places more demands on heads than ever before. The increased need for heads to shed or share many of their traditional functions is the subject of the last section.

Teambuilding and Organization Development

Some years ago it was argued that for the sake of the organizational health of schools and the professional status of teachers, as well as for the welfare of heads themselves, it is desirable to modify the traditional paternal model of primary school headship (Coulson, 1980). The increased demands placed upon schools and their heads since then make this shift increasingly a necessity as well as a desirable state of affairs. Though the bulk of responsibility for the school remains with the head, less and less confidence can be placed in the capacity of a single individual to carry out adequately all the steadily proliferating tasks of school management.

The case for wider sharing of the duties normally associated with headship does not rest only upon the desirability of sparing conscientious heads from becoming overburdened and strained, but also upon the growing realization and acceptance among teachers that a team can produce more work and of a higher quality than an individual. An increasing number of teachers now wish to have a greater say in the running of their schools, and since the Primary Survey (DES, 1978) there has been official encouragement for more substantial delegation to post-holders and deputy heads, allowing them a greater contribution to the making of policy as well as its implementation. Many heads continue to take too much on themselves, reinforcing the paternalistic stereotype of the head as an all-provider and supreme authority. Help and encouragement is needed to enable heads to trust in and make better use of deputy heads (Coulson and Cox, 1975; Norfolk LEA, 1983) and postholders (DES, 1978; Rodger, 1983; Campbell, 1984, Morrison, 1986; Wallace, 1986b) and to develop teamwork.

In the present-day school situation any individuals, even heads, have, on their own, limited powers to effect change; their effectiveness will depend increasingly upon their success in building a staff team and providing it with acceptable professional leadership. The components of an effective team and the synergistic contribution which it can make to healthy organizational functioning have been demonstrated by Belbin (1981) and applied to education by Everard and Morris (1985). The relative isolation of primary classrooms from each other and the teachers' norm of individualism (Lortie, 1975) accentuate even more the need for team-building among teachers within a strategy for school management development. Moreover, a concept of headship which sees the head as a teambuilder and facilitator of the work of colleagues is more consistent with the emphasis given here to professional leadership and interpersonal proficiency than with the traditional paternalistic view of the head as a somewhat isolated authority figure and decision-maker. More widespread adoption of the facilitator view of headship might lead to the traditional institutionalized supremacy of the head giving way to the potentially much more exacting task of building, managing, and co-ordinating within the school a peer group of colleagues. Outside the school it would involve leading the colleague group in dialogue with the local authority and the public on the subject of their discharge of the school's responsibilities (Elliott, 1979).

Conclusion

The near future seems certain to be a period of radical social and cultural transformation which is likely to witness the emergence of a new paradigm of teaching and learning based on a greatly enlarged concept of human potential (Ferguson, 1982; Robertson, 1983; National Economic Development Council, 1986) In schools, changes in legislation, organization and curriculum tend to attract considerable attention when they are first introduced. Yet changes which at first seem major or dramatic often fade in significance as parts of them are assimilated into school operation or attention is diverted to newer concerns. Regardless of the changes the near future may bring, the central importance of the head as an exemplar of personal and professional qualities will remain. Since these qualities are fundamentally expressions of values, attitudes and feelings *within the person*, traditional in-service training approaches which concentrate on conveying new knowledge, imparting particular skills or prescribing certain patterns of behaviour are insufficient for headship development. To be successful, future education for headship will need to pay greater attention to the prime importance of the development and growth of heads *as persons*; it must therefore embrace consideration of their values and assumptions, their feelings and intuitions, and their relationships with others as much as their professional knowledge and teaching skills.

References

ADAMS, J., HAYES, J., and HOPSON, B. (1976) *Transition: Understanding and Managing Personal Change*, Martin Robertson.

AGOR, W. H. (1984) *Intuitive Management: Integrating Left and Right Brain Management Skills*, Prentice-Hall.

ARGYRIS, C. (1976) 'Theories of action that inhibit individual learning', *American Psychologist*, 31, 9, pp. 638–54.

ARGYRIS, C. (1982) 'The executive mind and double-loop learning', *Organisational Dynamics*, Autumn, pp. 5–22.

BACK, K. and BACK, K. (1982) *Assertiveness at Work*, McGraw-Hill.

BELBIN, M. (1981) *Management Teams: Why They Succeed or Fail*, Heinemann.

BLAKESLEE, T. R. (1980) *The Right Brain: A New Understanding of the Unconscious Mind and its Creative Powers*, Anchor Press/Doubleday.

BLUMBERG, A. and GREENFIELD, W. (1980) *The Effective School Principal: Perspectives on School Leadership*, Allyn and Bacon.

Alan A. Coulson

BOLAM, R. (1986) 'The first two years of the NDC: A progress report', *School Organization*, 6, 1, pp. 1–15.

BOLTON, R. (1979) *People Skills*, Prentice-Hall.

BROWN, L. D. (1980) 'Planned change in underorganized systems' in CUMMINGS, T. G. (Ed.), *Systems Theory for Organizational Development*, Wiley.

CAMPBELL, R. J. (1984) 'In-school development: The role of the curriculum postholder', *School Organization*, 4, 4, pp. 345–57.

COMBS, A. W., BLUME, R. A., NEWMAN, A. J. and WASS, H. L. (1974) *The Professional Education of Teachers*, Allyn and Bacon.

COULSON, A. A. (1980) 'The role of the primary head' in BUSH, T., GLATTER, R., GOODEY, J. and RICHES, C. (Eds.) *Approaches to School Management*, Harper and Row, pp. 274–82.

COULSON, A. A. (1986) *The Managerial Work of Primary School Headteachers*, Sheffield Papers in Education Management No. 48, Sheffield City Polytechnic.

COULSON, A. A. and COX, M. V. (1975) 'What do deputies do?', *Education 3–13*, 3, 2, pp. 100–3.

DEPARTMENT OF EDUCATION AND SCIENCE, (1978) *Primary Education in England*, HMSO.

ELLIOTT, J. (1979) 'The case for school self-evaluation', *Forum*, 22, 1, pp. 23–25.

EVANS, H. K. (1983) 'A Report on School Leader Education in Sweden (1976–83)', *School Organization*, 3, 2, pp. 191–204.

EVERARD, K. B. (1983) *Management in Comprehensive Schools—What Can be Learned from Industry?* 2nd ed., University of York, Centre for the Study of Comprehensive Schools.

EVERARD, K. B. and MORRIS, G. (1985) *Effective School Management*, Harper and Row.

FERGUSON, M. (1982) *The Aquarian Conspiracy: Personal and Social Transformation in the 1980s*, Granada.

FIEDLER, F. E. (1967) *A Theory of Leadership Effectiveness*, McGraw-Hill.

FIEDLER, F. E., CHEMERS, M. M. and MAKER, L. (1977) *Improving Leadership Effectiveness: The Leader Match Concept*, (rev. ed.), Wiley.

GOLDSTEIN, K. (1939) *The Organism*, American Book Co.

GRAY, H. L. and COULSON, A. A. (1982) 'Teacher education, management and the facilitation of change', *Educational Change and Development*, 4, 1, pp. 17–35.

HALL, G., RUTHERFORD, W. L., HORD, S. M. and HULING, L. L. (1984) 'Effects of three principal styles on school management', *Educational Leadership*, February.

HARGREAVES, D. H. (1980) 'The occupational culture of teachers', in WOODS, P., (Ed.) *Teacher Strategies: Explorations in the Sociology of the School*, Croom Helm, pp. 125–48.

HOPSON, B. and SCALLY, M. (1980) 'Change and development in adult life: implications for helpers', *British Journal of Guidance and Counselling*, 8, 2, pp. 175–85.

HUFF, S., LAKE, D. and SCHAALMAN, M. (1982) *Principal Differences: Excellence in School Leadership and Management*, McBer and Co.

HUGHES, M. G. (1976) 'The professional-as-administrator: The case of the secondary school head', in PETERS, R. S. (Ed.) *The Role of the Head*, Routledge and Kegan Paul, pp. 50–62.

HUGHES, M. G., CARTER, J. and FIDLER, B. (1981) *Professional Development Provision for Senior Staff in Schools and Colleges*, University of Birmingham.

IVEY, A. E. (1971) *Microcounselling*: *Innovations in Interview Training*, Charles C. Thomas.

JENTZ, B. C. and WOFFORD, J. W. (1979) *Leadership and Learning*: *Personal Change in a Professional Setting*, McGraw-Hill.

JOSEPH, K. (1983) 'Election platform', *Education*, 3 June, (161.22), p. 432.

KAPLAN, R. E. (1982) 'Intervention in a loosely organized system: an encounter with non-being', *Journal of Applied Behavioural Science*, 18, 4, pp. 425–32.

KNOWLES, M. (1974) 'Human resource development in OD', *Public Administration Review*, 34, 2.

KOTTER, J. (1982) *The General Managers*, Macmillan.

LEVINSON, D. J., DARROW, C. M., KLEIN, E. B., LEVINSON, M. H. and McKEE, B. (1978) *The Seasons of a Man's Life*, Alfred Knopf.

LOEVINGER, J. (1976) *Ego-Development*: *Conceptions and Theories*, Jossey-Bass.

LORTIE, D. L. (1975) *Schoolteacher*, University of Chicago Press.

McCALL, M. W. (1976) 'Leadership research: Choosing gods and devils on the run', *Journal of Occupational Psychology*, 49, pp. 138–53.

McMAHON, A. (1984) *The NDC's Project on Management Development in LEAs and Schools*, National Development Centre for School Management Training, November.

MANASSE, A. L. (1985) 'Improving conditions for principal effectiveness: Policy implications of research', *Elementary School Journal*, 85, 3, pp. 432–63.

MASLOW, A. (1970) *Motivation and Personality*, 2nd ed., Harper and Row.

MORGAN, C., HALL, V. and MACKAY, H. (1983) *The Selection of Secondary School Headteachers*, Open University Press.

MORGAN, C., HALL, V. and MACKAY, H. (1984) *A Handbook on Selecting Senior Staff for Schools*, Open University Press.

MORRISON, K. (1986) 'Primary school subject specialists as agents of school-based curriculum change', *School Organization*, 6, 2, pp. 175–83.

MULFORD, B. (1984) 'On teaching educational administration', *Journal of Educational Administration*, 22, 2, pp. 223–46.

NATIONAL ECONOMIC DEVELOPMENT COUNCIL (1986), Unpublished Study of Britain's Social and Economic Prospects till 2010, report in *The Guardian*, 7 February.

NIAS, J. (1981) '"Commitment" and motivation in primary school teachers', *Educational Review*, 33, 3, pp. 181–90.

NORFOLK LEA, (1983) 'The role of the deputy headteacher in the middle school', November.

NUGENT, P. S. (1981) 'Management and modes of thought', *Organizational Dynamics*, Spring, pp. 44–59.

ORNSTEIN, R. E. (1977) *The Psychology of Consciousness*, 2nd ed., Harcourt Brace Jovanovich.

PENNINGTON, R. C. and BELL, G. H. (1982) 'Headteacher education and training in England: A review of methods, techniques and possible new approaches', *Collected Original Research in Education* (CORE), 7, 1.

ROBERTSON, J. (1983) *The Sane Alternative*, revised edition, Turning Point.

RODGER, I. A. (1983) *Teachers with Posts of Responsibility in Primary Schools*, School of Education, University of Durham.

ROGERS, C. R. (1980) *A Way of Being*, Houghton Mifflin.

ROGERS, C. R. (1983a) 'Learning to be free', *The Times Educational Supplement*, 30 September, pp. 20–1.
ROGERS, C. R. (1983b) *Freedom to Learn in the 1980s*, Merrill.
SERGIOVANNI, T. J. (1984) 'Leadership and excellence in schooling', *Educational Leadership*, February, pp. 4–13.
TOFFLER, A. (1980) *The Third Wave*, Pan.
WALLACE, M. (1986a) 'Training and performance—A missing link?', *British Journal of In-Service Education*, 12, 2, pp. 68–72.
WALLACE, M. (1986b) 'The rise of scale posts as a management hierarchy in schools', *Educational Management and Administration*, 14, 3, pp. 203–12.
WHITAKER, P. (1986) 'A humanistic approach to teacher in-service education', *Self and Society*, 14, 6, pp. 276–81.
ZDENEK, M. (1985) *The Right Brain Experience*, Corgi.

Teacher Appraisal

Suffolk LEA

Main Summary and Conclusions

The cornerstone of appraisal schemes is the belief that teachers wish to improve their performance in order to enhance the education of pupils. Following from this is the assumption that appraisal systems should have a positive orientation: that is, the purpose should be to develop teachers professionally rather than to "get at" them. This developmental process should be characterized by negotiation and agreement about priorities and targets. There is little doubt that appraisal schemes operate more effectively where clear contractual obligations have been established.

The process should, then, be constructive, honest, professional and should not threaten the individuality or personality of the teacher. Teachers' creativity and spontaneity should not be inhibited by the process: on the contrary, idiosyncratic effectiveness should be encouraged. The process should be subject to external scrutiny and be capable of convincing and reassuring parents, ratepayers and taxpayers.

Aims and Objectives

As far as each school within an LEA is concerned, appraisal schemes should aim to:
  (a) improve learning opportunities for all pupils;
  (b) improve the management and support of the learning process;
  (c) improve the 'tone', or hidden curriculum, which influences all work in the school.
As far as the teacher is concerned, the process should:
  (a) recognize and support effective practice;
  (b) identify areas for development and improvement;
  (c) identify and develop potential.

Suffolk (1985) *Those Having Torches*, Suffolk Education Department.

Clearly, the appraisal process must assist teachers in their career development and can help them acquire the skills and experience to further their aspirations. These needs will differ according to the career stage of the teacher, just as 'whole school' development will be conditioned by the level of the abilities and skills of the teaching staff as a whole. The scheme must enable teachers whose performance falls below par to be identified so that steps can be taken by the school and LEA to rectify the situation, and, exceptionally, to terminate employment.

It is essential that:
- (a) teachers are supported in their efforts to increase effectiveness;
- (b) the process enhances the quality of learning of pupils;
- (c) some consideration of teacher career aspiration is accepted as part of the process.

Local Education Authorities have clear responsibilities in establishing appraisal schemes. These include:

(a) overall management of the scheme through its senior officers;

(b) initial work to establish aims and objectives; to determine local guidelines; to produce a manual or handbook for the LEA; to ensure an appropriate discretion in operation for individual schools and to use the scheme as a contribution to the positive and efficient management and deployment of the teaching force;

(c) to ensure that all staff understand the detail of the system;

(d) to establish criteria for classroom observation;

(e) to ensure regular consultation with professional associations;

(f) to provide appropriate documents for each phase of the appraisal process and to determine the limits of confidentiality and access;

(g) to set up training courses in appraisal skills; interviewing and classroom observation;

(h) to monitor the appraisal scheme, and ensure that its end product leads towards the achievement of its stated curricular aims and objectives;

(i) to moderate the scheme so as to ensure consistency of standards within and between schools;

(j) to evaluate the LEA system in order to make improvements after experience and feedback;

(k) to make arrangements to satisfy the resource implications in terms of appraisal time, training time for all personnel, and for the administrative support of the system.

The System

The process of appraisal can be broken down into distinct phases: Preparation; Classroom Observation; the Appraisal Interview; Results; Monitoring; Moderation; Evaluation. The process is a sequence in which each element depends upon the others.

Preparation

As far as the school is concerned, preparation will involve dissemination of the principles of the appraisal process, explanation so that all teachers understand the intention(s); agreement about the logistics of the scheme in that particular school.

Appraisers inevitably are constantly receiving information and forming impressions. Appraisal schemes must not disregard this 'data' but include it in the preparation procedures. Other preparation, common to teacher and appraiser, will be:

(a) gathering information;
(b) agreement about the priority areas to be discussed;
(c) re-evaluation of the teacher's job description.

The appraisal process should be positive, seeking to establish teachers' strengths, identifying areas for improvement, and career aspirations should be explored in a realistic way. Inhibitions on performance should be discussed.

Classroom Observation

Most teaching and much learning takes place in classrooms so, if the effectiveness of the teaching/learning process is to be appraised, classroom observation will offer the most practical procedure for collecting data about teacher performance. Because many teachers express unease about this, feeling that observers are an intrusion in the classroom, their very presence changing the situation, and because any one lesson may not typify the generality, observational data must be gathered with particular care and on more than one occasion. Teachers must have confidence in the fairness of the process. They are more ready to accept the recording of events than inferential judgments. The quality of the observation, the way in which appraisers collect and share data with teachers will be overall factors in the success and effectiveness of teacher appraisal.

Training will be essential to ensure that appraisers become skilled observers; it cannot be assumed that good teachers will necessarily be good observers. Teachers and appraisers need to see observation in a constructive way, as a cooperative venture between them leading to improved classroom performance.

Mutual agreement about the criteria on which observations are structured will be essential. Many lists, schedules and behaviourally anchored rating scales have been developed and would repay study to establish their appropriateness in particular LEA contexts.

The Interview

The appraiser should create a climate in which genuine dialogue can take place. The conditions for the interview should be comfortable, quiet and uninterrupted. Adequate time should be allocated for the interview and it should begin with the teacher's views of his/her performance during the past year. Attention should be focussed upon past successes and the data available should also be used to help indicate areas for improvement including ways by which this might be achieved. The teacher's interests and aspirations should be given attention, and the discussion should then move into a consideration of suitable targets for the following year. Above all, the focus should be on performance in the defined job rather than on personality.

Results
Teachers will expect practical results. Some results might be: a local course, a visit to another school, a change of role within the present school, working as a member of a team on a new project, taking part in team teaching. Targets could be as simple as an agreement to improve the quality of day to day administration or as complex as improved liaison with another department; they should be as specific and as realistic as possible. Some recommendations may not produce the intended results and other methods may have to be tried. The teacher's feedback on the outcome and his agreement about other approaches will be vital in maintaining or improving performance. Some targets may have to be 'recycled' for another effort—good teachers set themselves higher targets.

Monitoring
It is important that improvement is recognized. Appraisal can enhance staff development by recognition, encouragement and praise. Teachers have to be given the training and the time to achieve their targets. During this period, regular supervision, advice and support will be needed.

Moderation
The LEA will have to support a system of moderation to ensure as high a degree of consistency as possible within and between schools. Moderation needs to be undertaken by people who understand the LEA system and the schools' place within it, and, as a consequence, the moderating process should be undertaken by the deployment of officers, advisers, headteachers and senior teaching staff. There is a resource implication here; in addition, moderators will need training in supervision and observation skills.

Evaluation
There is some evidence to show that staff appraisal can degenerate into a paper exercise in which worthless reports are compiled and filed simply to comply with procedural instructions. To guard against this it will be necessary to evaluate the effectiveness of the system, on a regular basis, by finding ways to assess whether or not the stated aims are being met. A local review body comprised of professional personnel should be given respon-sibility for this task. They would need to identify, collect and collate

relevant data from appropriate sources in order to illuminate problem areas and to seek solutions.

It is important that:

- formal appraisal is seen to be only one stage in a continuous process;
- teachers understand the purposes of the appraisal process;
- classroom observation is seen to be central to the process;
- the appraisal interview is conducted in optimum physical conditions and stresses performance rather than personality;
- the results of the interview are practical, attainable and support to achieve them is forthcoming;
- time and encouragement are given for the attainment of targets;
- regular monitoring, moderating and evaluation take place.

Participation

Most performance appraisal systems appear to change over a period of time in response to the changed perceptions of the participants and the changing needs of the organization. Systems esteemed by participants have been developed cooperatively. They endeavour to accommodate the points of view of those affected by implementation and to take account of the local context. For example, in parts of North America the emphasis is, currently, on the development of the teachers' professional skills with the accountability factor largely confined to a simple 'satisfactory'/unsatisfactory' rating.

Local agreements should determine what is to be observed in classrooms and by what criteria it is to be assessed; what is an unsatisfactory teacher; what must be available to resource the system; and the procedures to support the 'failing' teacher must also be agreed. Differences have been noted from place to place in attitudes to self-appraisal, goal-setting, frequency of the appraisal cycle, etc., and all may be the subject of consultation and negotiation.

It has been noted that, in England and Wales, appraisal systems have frequently been changed in the light of experience and schools have been aware of this 'growth period' and the need for consultation about principles and procedures. The Service Children's Education Authority's scheme has evolved from close consultation between administrators, teachers and union representatives.

The following are considered important:

- consultation between central and local government and the teachers' associations to agree the aims of performance appraisal at nationwide level;
- local consultative groups/working parties committed to develop appraisal procedures which meet the agreed purposes and which are appropriate to the local context;

- such local groups to undertake regular reviews of all aspects of appraisal procedures.

Training

In order to establish and maintain a positive attitude towards appraisal, it will be necessary to ensure that all teachers are fully informed about both policy and procedures. Appraisers must have credibility and inspire the trust and confidence of the staff they appraise and, to this end, need to be trained in the skills and techniques of appraisal before the system is implemented. Time must be available to achieve this. Professional development days, a normal part of the North American school year, provide opportunities for both heads and teachers to undertake training to meet specific school or system needs. A similar provision of training time in schools in England and Wales would smooth the implementation of appraisal and persuade participants that, where developmental needs are identified, they will have the time to undertake any necessary training, be it school or system focussed.

The following are recommended:

- provision by the LEA of a manual detailing the philosophy and procedures for the appraisal process;
- training courses for appraisers in interviewing and classroom observation techniques;
- staff briefing by headteacher before each appraisal cycle begins;
- adjusting the school year by a sufficient number of days to allow adequate time for staff development.

Teachers in Difficulty

Appraisal schemes will not solve all the problems found in schools. They can, however, provide a systematic framework for ensuring that difficulties are registered and appropriate action is implemented to overcome weaknesses. Such teachers should be fully aware, through self-appraisal, the appraisal interview and written report, of the area of teaching which needs to be improved and should, through negotiation, be committed to accepting the appropriate support and training offered.

If the first approach fails to produce a significant change, other methods may have to be tried and regular monitoring will be essential. All advice and support should be written down both for the teacher and for a record of events. If, after two or three intensive support periods, performance is still unsatisfactory, it may then be necessary to move into more formal disciplinary procedures.

It is essential that:

- performance appraisal provide a framework for registering both strengths and weaknesses in teaching;
- the appraiser is positive and supportive at all times;
- the teacher is fully aware of and accepts the criteria by which areas of weakness are registered;
- the teacher is prepared to accept and adopt proposals for support and remediation.

Resources

The resources needed to sustain a rigorous, developmental system of teacher appraisal will be more accurately quantifiable after field trials. The broad implications are, however, clear enough.

Time will be required for lesson observation, inspection of pupils' work, the discussion of the teacher's lesson plans, etc.; for the preparation of the documents and other data prior to the interview itself. A follow-up review of progress towards goals will be needed at an agreed time after the main interview.

Training in appraisal interviewing skills will be required for all appraisers. Advisers/inspectors and officers will need similar training. Up-dating of these skills on a regular basis is recommended. School staffs will need an introductory training session about the appraisal system.

In-service As a result of the appraisal cycle, training needs must be satisfied, and support to ensure the attainment of goals must be available. Teachers experiencing difficulties will need enhanced help and support and more regular appraisal.

Administration There will be a clerical/typing commitment within schools and a need for higher administrative assistance to release appraisers for professional work. The LEA will incur costs in producing and printing the documents, and a further cost in the use of the adviser/inspector/officer time to monitor and to moderate the system. There will also be the cost of a commitment to evaluate the system....

General Conclusions

The evidence provided by this study leads us to the following conclusions:
- An appraisal scheme could strongly enhance the education service in England and Wales by:
  (a) recognizing and supporting good practice;
  (b) identifying areas for development and improvement;
  (c) identifying and developing potential;
  (d) improving overall professional performance.
- A national system could be designed so that all LEAs conformed to a general set of guidelines within which local variations were possible.

- The national guidelines should be the result of the fullest consultation between the DES, LEAs and the professional associations.
- The involvement of the professional associations in the implementation and continued evolution of appraisal schemes is essential.
- The approved guidelines should be published and made available to teachers and the general public.
- Some form of national and local moderation will be necessary.
- Field trials in a range of LEAs would provide closer estimates of the costs involved, as well as evidence of effective training methods.
- The appraisal scheme should apply to all personnel in the education service.
- Resources will be needed to provide training, moderation and, initially, for planning and organizing new schemes.
- Training will be required for all personnel involved.
- Expertise exists which could be used to enhance in-service training programmes in appraisal techniques.
- A properly planned evaluation could help to obtain the maximum benefit from field trials, indicating ways of improving appraisal methods and showing evidence of improvements in the education service.

The Appraisal of Headteachers

This would appear to be the nub of any scheme's credibility. It is, perhaps, worth drawing all threads together to make a coherent whole.

If the appraisal of headteachers is to be developmental and constructive then the headteacher's 'line-manager' must be clearly defined. 'Line-managers' are expected to be people who *know* the subordinate's work well and who are also intimately acquainted with the context in which that work is carried out. If this be so, as all the evidence suggests, then a 'visitation' of three (or even four) days from people generally unacquainted not only with the LEA system but also the school itself, is out of the question.

We need to remind ourselves that the formal appraisal cycle is one part of a continuous process. We have argued this for teachers; if it is true for teachers it must be true for headteachers. This, then, would suggest that the headteacher's appraiser should be aware of the work of the head and the school during the course of successive years, and not just for a limited period of days. We have made the point that the appraisal of the head and the appraisal of the school are complementary.

The appraiser should know, *by experience*, the work of the person appraised. If we argue, in large schools, that the head of mathematics is likely to know the work of mathematics teachers best, then the headteacher can only be appraised by *somebody who is, or has been, an experienced practitioner*. We would expect senior officers of the LEA to be involved with the appraiser in the process and, as with teachers, begin with self-appraisal by the headteacher.

We must draw attention once again to David Hancock's reference to a seconded or recently retired headteacher as appraiser, and to our experience of 'area supervisors' and 'area superintendents' in the USA and Canada. We say elsewhere in this study that the latter system has great attractions for us in England and Wales. We would not accept, however, that a retired headteacher or, indeed, a retired HMI would carry the degree of credibility necessary for a person operating in this crucial area. We would, however, assert quite definitely that the 'promotion' of experienced headteachers to fill this role is the only acceptable and logical way forward. Such postholders would be responsible for the appraisal of headteachers and for monitoring the general appraisal system in a clearly defined LEA area or over a clearly stated number of schools.

We would recommend:

(a) headteachers must be appraised;
(b) a clearly defined, realistic line of management must be established;
(c) in order to know the work of the head, the appraiser should be experienced in the task of headship;
(d) a level of 'promoted' head should be established for this work.

The implication of these recommendations is a radical review of the education system as a whole.

It is appreciated, for example, that each LEA's goal should, in logic, be so designed as to integrate into a national system which will ensure some uniformity of standards and content. This is in the interests of our pupils and their families and it need not imply an unacceptable degree of centralization.

Equally, if LEAs are to set their goals to meet national criteria they must be freed from many current constraints upon their actions, not least those arising from corporate management systems.

We have tentatively quantified the resources needed to implement our suggestions, and conclude that any appraisal system will afford an opportunity for the professionals in our schools to engage in a task of the utmost importance for the professional development of teachers. More secretarial and administrative assistance must be provided to free senior staff from relatively low-grade paper work.

A successful appraisal scheme should lead to an improvement in performance by many teachers. The logic suggests that improved performance deserves better reward. The teachers' associations might have to grasp the nettle of differentiated pay based upon merit at a later date but we stress that any system of merit pay should provide an incentive for the good teacher to remain in the classroom as an alternative to the present situation where any increase in status and salary more often than not means less time spent teaching.

The teaching profession is currently at a low ebb. Status, pay and public esteem are all perceived to be poor. We present our proposals, not as a further imposition on our sorely-tried colleagues, but as positive suggestions which, given the necessary resources and goodwill from all concerned to ensure their successful implementation, will bring considerable improvements to pupils, to teachers, and to the nation.

The 'Collegial' Primary School

Jim Campbell

An Image of the 'Collegial' Primary School

'The contemporary image of good practice' has a number of characteristic features. It shows small working groups of teachers reporting back recommendations for school-wide change to the collectivity of the whole staff meeting for decision-taking. These groups are led and organized by the curriculum postholders, who draw upon expertise from outside school as well as upon their own professional knowledge, in order to enable the staff to develop the curriculum as authoritatively as possible. Occasionally the postholder works alongside class teachers to illustrate ideas in practice, and to become aware of progress throughout the school. The skills involved in these processes are not only academic; considerable sensitivity, personal enthusiasm and charm are required in order to maintain good working relationships in schools where professional practice is being subjected to the scrutiny of colleagues. The teachers involved become used to tolerating uncertainty and working under pressure of time and conflicting demands. Supporting this collaborative effort is the headteacher who has committed himself or herself to developing responsibility to the staff group; servicing their activities by putting appropriate school facilities, and where possible his or her time, at their disposal.

The image also shows an atmosphere, ethos or climate distinctive to collegiality. The teachers exist in a school in which constructive and critical scrutiny of each other's practice and ideas is the normal expectation. There is a continuing commitment to professional development through in-service activities both within the school and outside it. Although the teachers are not insensitive to the implications of such involvement for their own career prospects, the major focus of in-service training is the

Reproduced from CAMPBELL, R. J. (1985) *Developing the Primary School Curriculum*, Holt, Rinehart and Winston.

whole school, and there is an open understanding that teachers will feed back into school implications they see for their the colleagues of off-site-in-service courses. The ethos is not created simply by encouraging teachers to feel solidarity with one another, but by deliberate strategies that make role expectations explicit to all staff, and by the head's involvement in school-based development in practical and supportive ways that do not undermine the authority of teachers with special expertise. The overt commitment to evaluate their initiative collectively accustoms the teachers to giving accounts to each other of the reasons and justifications for particular approaches to the curriculum, and so helps them to anticipate representing their subject or subject area to people outside the school, to parents, other teachers in feeder schools, to advisers, and governors and others. The school thus becomes collectively accountable for its curriculum. The teachers committed to collegiality see the atmosphere in the school as the element most critical to its maintenance, and derive strong personal and professional satisfactions from their involvement in, and contribution to, its continuance. They see the creation and maintenance of such an atmosphere as the responsibility not just of the headteacher, but of the whole staff group. Collegiality will survive the departure of the head.

It is obvious that the foregoing is a projection from empirical reality, not a description of it. It differs from previous images in one particular way: its dominant focus is upon teachers. In the foreground of this image is not the school's organization, or children's emotional adjustment, or community relationships, but working groups of teachers engaged in the process of developing school-wide policies and practices for the curriculum.

In-School Obstacles to the Development of Collegiality

Drawing an ideal picture, however helpful it is as an expression of values, nonetheless immediately raises questions, especially perhaps for teachers who find the values attractive. These questions are about obstacles to change, and the extent to which practice in contemporary primary schools may be hindered from moving to a better match with the image, if teachers become committed to the values it embodies.

Two features of the culture of contemporary primary schools may particularly hinder the development of collegiality; *role relationships* between teachers, and the *conditions* in which teachers work. The former has been seen in much of the literature as the overriding factor. Until very recently, the latter has been virtually ignored. I believe that the evidence for the problems associated with role relationships is rather insubstantial and to some extent dated, and that the major stumbling block for collegiality is no longer teacher relationships, but some of the conditions in which primary school-teachers have to work, which are not conducive to curriculum development of a school-based kind....

... The view of the professional culture of the primary school as massively oppositional to the development of more collegial relationships, needs to be questioned on two grounds; the nature of the evidence upon which it has been based, and some very recent studies that suggest that teacher roles, or at least teacher perceptions of their roles, may be changing in the direction whereby collegiality could become more feasible. ...

... These more recent studies suggest that primary school culture has begun to allow a little more flexibility than the somewhat tightly-prescribed roles discerned in the earlier studies, while others suggest that teachers' perceptions and beliefs about the legitimacy of intermediate authority roles, such as postholders, are undergoing change.

Bassey's (1978) survey of Nottinghamshire teachers included the responses of 114 heads to the question 'Who decides on the outline syllabus: head, a teacher with special responsibility for the subject, a group of staff or individual teachers?'. The replies are subject to the methodological problems associated with questionnaires, and there is the specific problem that what was meant by 'outline syllabus' probably varied from respondent to respondent, but 46 per cent of heads said that the mathematics syllabus was decided by groups of staff, and for other subjects the percentages for group decisions were: English 40 per cent, physical education 27 per cent, music 28 per cent. art/craft 21 per cent, and topic 20 per cent. Of Bassey's 281 infant teachers, 28 per cent had 'regular' assistance from another teacher in their classrooms, and around a third of junior and infant teachers 'meet with other staff' when their class is in assembly. What happens at these times is not specified. Although Bassey's survey provided evidence that was in a number of respects problematic and difficult to interpret, on the face of it his primary teachers appeared to operate in less isolated contexts, and his heads in less monopolistic decision-making worlds, than those envisaged in the previous studies.

A study sponsored by the Schools Council and the Primary Schools Research and Development Group at Birmingham University (1983) examined 'responsibility and the use of expertise' in primary schools using a range of methodologies, including questionnaires, interviews, discussion groups, free accounts and diaries, in order to obtain both range and depth in teacher perceptions and experience of the use of teacher expertise in schools. The study captured in a welcome and unusual way, a diverse and even contradictory range of teacher perceptions about the issues. It revealed teachers' unease about terms like 'expert' and even 'influence', whilst recording their readiness to seek advice from postholders, especially in informal ways. Non-postholders seemed more ready to acknowledge a distinctive role for 'experts' in school, at least in interview. Headteachers on the whole welcomed the idea of making fuller use of teacher expertise, with 80 per cent of the 65 heads who completed a questionnaire approving of the Primary Survey's suggestions to that effect (though they did not, ironically, seem to acknowledge their own self-interest, recognized by class teachers in interviews who felt the postholders were still seen as 'instruments of the head; to do his bidding, to realize his vision.') The heads also commented on the 'need for staff to be engaged in a common enterprise. To cooperate as a team, perhaps through small committees coordinated by staff with special curricular interests ...' The 465 teachers who responded to a questionnaire perceived as very or extremely important sources of their own professional development, 'help from colleagues with special knowledge and experience' (89.7 per cent), and 'help' from teachers with scale posts of responsibility' (82.6 per cent).

Paradoxically, although these teachers strongly supported the idea of school-based in-service activity, they did not expect teachers with posts of responsibility to be engaged in 'chairing a group of colleagues working in a curriculum area'. An important finding was that there were subject differences in the extent to which teachers would wish to draw upon subject expertise of colleagues, and in the kind of help that would be sought. There was more readiness to look for help in drawing-up schemes of work, than in teaching methods, resource management, and methods of assessment, possibly because the first area is seen as school policy, whereas the other three are seen as classroom practice. The teachers on the whole thought the wider use of teacher expertise would be mainly beneficial to the school, and judged that its effectiveness would depend to a great extent upon school-wide support. The ambivalent nature of support for the idea in general was summed up by the authors:

> One way teachers had of seeing the teacher expert was as an agent of change, alert to innovations in primary education and determined to make a contribution to the professional development of his colleagues. Another, as a quietly concerned colleague, ready to help if asked.
>
> In the main it was the last way of seeing the teacher expert that was most generally supported. The former found more support among teachers with posts of responsibility and among teachers who belong to a teaching association. But this support, though evident, was not strong. (Primary Schools Research and Development Group/Schools Council, 1983, p.98)

The evidence from the Birmingham study does not reveal a profession wholeheartedly committed to changing conventional authority roles and relationships; in many ways it could be used to demonstrate that teachers are divided about the consequences for in-school relationships of implementing the recommendations of the Primary Survey. I interpret it, tentatively, as a record of a profession at a transitional stage, aware of the potential benefit to a school of a shift in exercise of authority to teachers with subject expertise, but perceptive about the repercussions on the quality of staff relationships, and fearful of a loss of informality and reciprocity in professional exchanges. But the study cannot easily be used to argue that teacher perceptions of their roles are fixed in the immutable 'class–teacher–headteacher' division of earlier studies.

A study at Durham University by Rodger *et al.* (1983) comprised case studies of teachers with posts of responsibility built up collaboratively by the postholders and Rodger, by self-monitoring, triangulated interviews with the postholders and their headteachers, diaries, analysis of critical incidents and a questionnaire. The case studies are rich in personal detail and embedded in the contextual minutiae of postholders' working worlds, offering fascinating source material for examining the potential and problems associated with changing teacher roles in the contemporary primary school. There is naturally great variation in the case studies but the general picture gained from them supports the view of a professional culture being slowly and with difficulty modified in the direction of greater collegiality with some enlightened headteachers enabling postholders to attempt to influence the work of other class teachers, without challenging the principle of class teaching itself. The conclusion of Rodger's study noted the interdependence of the roles of postholder and head and the increase in 'corporate' approaches to managing aspects of the curriculum. He concluded, as the Birmingham study did, that postholders preferred informal 'consultant' roles to more directive ones, because they were uneasy at the prospect of being required to operate as a 'leader' in contexts where their colleagues felt themselves equally competent.

Finally, indirect supportive evidence for a shift in actual attitudes and role relationships has come from a very recent study at Sheffield Polytechnic by Gray (1984), in which headteachers reported that, in 'key' areas of language and mathematics, postholders were exercising a fully 'professional' role in their schools: this role included 'the broad oversight of one sector of the primary schools activities, requiring substantial delegation of powers from the headteacher' (p. 50). Furthermore, the heads identified, as their main criteria for promoting teachers, 'curricular knowledge and skills' and 'personal qualities and attitudes'. Gray quotes heads as explaining their priorities in the following terms (p. 57): 'It used to be for long service, but the climate is now right for curriculum posts' and, more directly, 'The postholders have been told that they've got to become curriculum experts and earn their money.'

All the recent studies are subject to limitations, especially in respect of how far their tentative findings may be generalizable. The Warwick (Campbell, 1985) and Durham studies were of small numbers of probably untypically committed postholders, and the Sheffield study is of what twenty-nine headteachers reported as happening. The multi-methodological Birmingham study used samples ranging from seven (the diaries kept by postholders) to 465 (the questionnaires from teachers), although the ways the samples were reported does not permit us to know what larger populations they were representative of, if any. Caution is necessary, given small, untypical samples, but all these recent studies have findings about role relationships in primary schools that point, albeit uncertainly, in the direction of collegiality and away from individualistic roles in private and autonomous classrooms.

A second obstacle to collegiality is a more practical one, and concerns the conditions in which teachers work. For the purposes of this analysis I am restricting the definition of working conditions to (a) the provision of *time*, and (b) access to *facilities* and *ideas* for in-school development.

The Use of Teacher Time

There is hardly any comparative evidence about the 'educationalist context' in primary schools, but it has been shown in (Campbell, 1985, chapter 3) that postholders in the inquiry schools were expected to deploy a wide range of curricular and interpersonal skills, many of which assumed that time was available for exercising such skills, over and above those required for the mainstream teaching. The major problem in adequately meeting these demands was identified by the teachers as a matter of the time available.

Likewise, Rodger *et al* (1983) comment of one of their postholders:

> *Organisation of non-contact time*. Fiona was never anything but totally dissatisfied with this aspect of her role. She either had no non-contact time due to circumstances in the school, or it was taken up with the remnants of her previous post, e.g. games and coaching. Accordingly she never felt able to devote enough time to her curricular leadership function. (p. 108)

In the conclusions of this study, Rodger indicated ways in which his postholders had 'won' time from other activities. These included such strategies as doubling up classes with another postholder and using hymn practices, assemblies, visits from outside speakers, etc., as well as team teaching and having the head teach classes (p. 136). Whatever their immediate effectiveness, such strategies required the teachers to remove themselves from school activities in which they would normally partici-pate. The assumptions about teacher time underlying curricular leadership activities thus appeared to clash with assumptions about teacher time underlying 'normal' teaching and teaching-related activities.

A fuller consideration of the issues raised by this kind of clash is offered below, where the use of teacher time is discussed under four headings, '*other contact*' time, '*group*' time, '*snatched*' time, and '*personal*' time.

'Other contact time'

The first kind of time is what is normally (and inappropriately) referred to as 'non-contact' time. This is time formally provided in the school to enable the teacher to be free of class teaching. It is the same time as secondary school teachers call 'free' time, although in primary schools staffing tends to be organized on the basis that teachers need, or should be allowed, less 'free' time than secondary school teachers. The basis for this distinction has not been articulated or justified, and a recent report from the National Association of Schoolmasters/Union of Women Teachers (1984) calls for up to 20 per cent of primary school teachers' time to be of this kind. It is perhaps unfortunate that this kind of time is most often seen as either a rest period or a period in which marking and preparation may be carried out. From the point of view of curriculum development, this time might most usefully serve two purposes, namely working alongside colleagues to develop ideas in practice or monitoring work through the school, and visiting other schools, or resource agencies in the LEA and elsewhere, in order to increase expertise. For these reasons it might be useful to designate it as 'other contact' time.

There are two points to make about the 'other contact' time. First, if the Warwick inquiry schools were even remotely typical, there is very little of it available for through-school and outside-school activities of this kind. Ignoring the head and the part-timer, the average time available to the other eight postholders was some 37 minutes per week, though there was great variation in individual schools. Four of the eight had no 'free' time at all.

The second point is that the non-contact time was a strangely inflexible arrangement since it meant that the postholder was free at a given time each week, whereas through-school development requires a much more flexible response. Some weeks there will be no need, from a curriculum development point of view, for postholders to be freed from teaching their classes. Some weeks they will need to work alongside teachers at quite different times from other weeks, and on occasions they will need to be out of school for a morning or a day. It is thus not merely shortage of time for this role that is the problem, but arrangements that are inappropriately inflexible to suit the curricular leadership function. 'Non-contact' time for marking and preparation is, or could be, adequately provided for by the current assumptions of how teachers' time should be organized, but through-school developments call for different, more flexible assumptions.

Group size
A second category is 'group time', i.e. time spent in working groups, of varying size, including both the smaller review and development groups producing guidelines, etc. and the whole staff groups which arrive at decisions about through-school policies. The current conditions mean that teachers have to organize these activities, obviously, outside the times when pupils are being taught. This means either at lunchtimes or after school, when most children have gone home, or on 'occasional' days given over to in-service training.

There are two problems with this use of time. First, many primary schoolteachers conventionally give time both over the lunch break and after school to pupils, for example by organizing clubs, music, sports and games coaching, extra reading and language work, etc. This means that curriculum working groups may interfere with these activities, or that some teachers, often the most committed ones, will be unable to participate in them, or will do so intermittently. Although this problem can be mitigated to some extent by advance planning, there would be understandable resistance among primary school teachers if in-school development was to be implemented at the expense of time devoted to these other kinds of professional activities. The other problem is to do with teacher perceptions. Group time is perceived as a voluntary activity, a 'moral' obligation, not a 'contractual' one, in Becher, Eraut and Knight's (1981) terminology. Because it is seen as voluntary, it is vulnerable both to the vagaries of industrial relations in education and differential levels of teacher involvement.

'Snatched' time.

A third time category is what can only be called 'snatched' time. Much school-based work involves informal discussion and consultation, and one part of the empirical picture of the postholder's role emerging from the Warwick inquiry is of brief and rushed consultations with other teachers, and with advisers and heads often at times such as lunch or coffee breaks. Such discussions also occurred whilst the postholder was actually engaged teaching a class. One postholder told me of being called out of her class to discuss the school scheme with an adviser whose help had been sought, whilst two others referred to discussions occurring in the classroom. No doubt this has to happen, given the time constraints upon both the advisory staff and primary teachers, and it is clear from both the Birmingham and the Durham studies that class teachers value very highly curricular leadership exercised informally, but the use of snatched time for considering curricular issues must look to outsiders as an amateurish way for professional affairs to be conducted. It is probably necessary to make distinctions according to the nature of such consultations; a brief word over coffee about how to start pupils off on using pastels may be sensible and desirable given the informal and friendly nature of most staffroom contacts, but discussion of possible problems and approaches in a suggested scheme of work needs a less harried, more thoughtful context than a school corridor or classroom.

In many ways the use of snatched time is not unexpected; it is how much time of primary teachers is used in the routine of school days—mending plugs for equipment, dealing with interruptions of lessons by requests for administrative information, going along the corridor to borrow work cards or teaching materials, helping children find things they have lost or mislaid, taking assembly at unavoidably short notice, and so on. But snatched time sits uneasily with a rhetoric about extended professional behaviour and raising the quality of in-school decision-making.

'Personal' time

The final category is 'personal time', i.e. time used by individuals for curriculum development, entirely out of school, either for reading, attending courses, and time used for discussion with external 'experts' such as university and college tutors. This was not a serious problem amongst the postholders in the Warwick inquiry, partly because of their history of involvement in such activities, and partly because it is the only time category under their own control. Moreover, they were unusually well-matched in terms of their initial training and the subject for which they held responsibility posts. In the situation where a postholder is required to acquire familiarity with a relatively new subject, as was the case in some of Rodger's postholders, much more personal time will be used up.

The Primary Survey noted that some time would have to be available in school if postholders were to influence the work in their subject throughout the school, and thus went a little way towards recognizing the need formally to allocate time for in-school development....

... By facilities and ideas for in-school development I mean access to secretarial help, to reprographic processes, and to ideas and materials relevant to a particular programme.

Facilities

In most primary schools provision of facilities for reproducing notes or minutes of working group meetings, to ensure distribution of them in time for proper consideration, is antediluvian. To struggle for half an hour to get an antiquated Banda machine to provide even rough and ready versions of a manuscript original is a common experience; to have a secretary to type out and photocopy such matter is 'like gold', as one postholder said.

Conventional assumptions about the work of primary school teachers are that they will teach—they will be the 'teacher as teacher', and for that role all they will need is teaching materials, felt-tip pens for their work cards, and a ready supply of chalk. However the 'teacher as educationalist' role requires of them that they produce working drafts, discussion papers, guidelines, and all the documentary trappings that flow from more collective forms of decision-making. In most of the schools in the Warwick inquiry, there had been cuts in the hours of the school secretary, and it was difficult to argue that priority should be given to the work of the postholder-led teacher groups over 'normal' administrative functions. The facilities in general were inadequate to cope with the kind of demands that in-school development has to make on secretarial and clerical services. For the purposes of my own inquiry I needed copies of working drafts, group papers, and guidelines etc., and in every case I had to have the material typed and copied at the University because it was not in a state that met normal reprographic standards. When I offered to make available to the schools some extra copies of their own schemes, typed and photocopied, I was made to feel like some modern version of a cargo cult carrier.

Ideas and Materials

A second problem is one of access to ideas and materials that can help in the curriculum development programme itself, and in the teachers' own professional development. Some schools were trying to build up staffroom copies of books, reports and materials relevant to a particular programme, but on the whole teachers do not have easy access to recent thinking, relevant research and reports of practice in other schools, or even to information about where such ideas might be available. The Schools Council (1983) has attempted to remedy the latter problem by identifying a list of twenty-six books for the staffroom—a kind of curricular version of 'Your 100 Best Tunes'—although the list seems somewhat arbitrary. The idea of a professional reference library in primary school staffrooms may sound a little pretentious, but easy access to major reports on the curriculum, together with teachers' handbooks on the major curriculum projects and materials in the normal curriculum areas, and subscription to one or two professionally-oriented journals might go some way towards reducing the professional isolation of primary school staff. Even if it only mildly dented the monopoly of the local authority job circular for teachers' attention in the staffroom, it would be worth it.

Teachers also need to access to specialized advice on ideas and materials from outside the school, from advisers, university staff and other people. At present time such access is difficult to arrange, mainly because it has not been given attention. It would be a considerable boost to schools involved in curriculum development if they knew that they could get access legitimately and quickly to the kinds of information and ideas necessary to its initiation and maintenance. At a time of reduced expenditure, discriminating advice at an early stage would help in decisions about priorities for spending what is available.

There is no single person, agency or institution that has a monopoly on specialized ideas and materials relevant to in-school development. LEA advisers, teachers' centres, other schools, publishing houses, university and college of education tutors, field centres and a number of other agencies are within the range of most teachers. What is required is that it should become normal, or expected, for teachers to have access to them. Without time and access to ideas, curriculum development will be less effective than it could be as Sutherland's (1981) comments on larger-scale projects reminded us.

Professional Accountability: A Model and a Practice

Up to this point, teacher role relationships and work conditions have been treated separately for purposes of analysis. But they are not independent of one another; in a collegial school they converge in the practice of 'professional accountability'—the delivery by postholders of 'curricular accounts' to their colleagues and the developing of such accounts with them. This kind of accountability to one's professional peers, includes providing statements justifying policies and practices, preparing material for discussion groups, recording and reporting their decisions, dealing with doubts and disagreements in staff meetings, handling inter-school liaison meetings, and representing the subject to advisers and others from outside the school. For most postholders this was a central, and to some extent stressful, aspect of their role, and to be effective it requires both appropriate working conditions and appropriate working relationships. There is in the literature both a model for and a report of professional accountability in practice.

A Mutual Accountability Model

A sustained analysis of this kind of accountability (in two institutions of higher education) by Adelman and Alexander (1982) characterized their 'mutual culpability', or mutual accountability, model as requiring that:

> all participants regardless of role or status, see themselves as equally accountable to each other for their particular contributions to the educational process. (p. 26)

Despite differences in the institutional contexts, Alexander (1984) has persuasively argued for the application of the mutual-accountability model to primary schools, pointing to its congruence with through-school curriculum development, and with the values that primary teachers hold up to their pupils.

> A 'whole curriculum' as we have considered it (i.e. as having a vertical dimension as well as the horizontal coherence) can exist only in a climate of mutuality, openness, sharing and comparing of ideas, dovetailing of schemes and practices. And if primary schools are serious in their commitment to educational goals for the child like co-operation, the development of empathy, interpersonal skills and so on, they need to acknowledge the force of the hidden curriculum in such matters whereby the behaviour of adults in the school towards each other is as significant a learning resource as, say, group work in the classroom. (p. 185)

Two points about the model shed light upon relationships in in-school development programmes. First, the model assumes an organisational style, stressing *flexibility* and 'organic' relationships rather than fixed roles and mechanistic relationships. It assumes that teachers are redefining their roles and relationships in order to cater for change. They render accounts to one another as equals, even though they may occupy different formal positions of authority. Second, it assumes relationships that are mutually *supportive*. This is because teachers opening up their professional practice to the professional scrutiny of their peers, are making both themselves potentially vulnerable, and the emergence of disagreement probable. For this to happen to the benefit of a school requires supportive, not corrosive, relationships between staff.

This was a point commonly made in the inquiry schools to explain why professional disagreement had not degenerated into dispute. As one head said:

> In another school, they would have quarrelled—the programme would have collapsed, because it was a serious disagreement they were having. They couldn't resolve it, they just disagreed about priorities. But they worked well as a team, they were very professional, and because their relationship was professional, they kept together as a team and saw it through.

Giving accounts to colleagues, therefore, is not just explaining and justifying educational policies in an educationalist discourse; it is a process embedded in, and simultaneously extending, relationships that permit what Alexander called 'intellectual autonomy' of individuals, but from a foundation of mutual support. Thus the mutual-accountability model translates at primary school level into a climate of relationships of *mutual responsibility*. Such a climate will need to be maintained not only by the head, though his role at the initial stages will be critical, but by the staff as a whole.

The model needs to be elaborated in two respects; one concerns the importance of personal characteristics, the other the importance of efficiency. First, professional accountability depends upon the personal, the idiosyncratic, the human qualities amongst staff. When teachers talked about the postholders' qualities it was these personal qualities that they stressed as much as anything—how well she had managed the meetings, how she had jollied them along, how interesting her style was in discussion groups, and so on. No management style can eradicate these unpredictable personal attributes from affecting a particular programme, any more than curriculum materials in centre-periphery projects were able to be teacher-proof. Conventional management techniques may see such unpredictability as a weakness, but the teachers in the schools saw it as a strength.

Second, for the climate to embody responsibility as well as mutuality, there is the need for efficiency, which does not sit easily with the long traditions of cosy informality in primary schools. The danger of unduly formalized staff meetings ought not to provide the excuse for unstructured and aimless meetings, which are neither informed by specialist advice nor managed and resourced effectively. This would lead to the legitimation of what Alexander (1984) has characterized as 'random chat'. His discussion of meetings show their potential and their pitfalls:

> Staff meetings can engender a sense of collective commitment; they can help teachers towards an understanding of and involvement in whole school concerns; open up the individual teacher to

alternative arguments and ideas; stimulate intellectual engagement; minimize curriculum incoherence and inconsistency: in short, staff meetings are potentially one way of realizing both the concept of a 'whole curriculum' ... and the notion of the (intellectually) autonomous teacher. Equally, staff meetings can consist of head-teacher monologues, aimless and trivial anecdote-swapping or opinion-parading, frustrating to staff and head alike.

... Obstacles to the full realization of collegiality in the professional life of primary schools have been examined in this chapter under the two headings of role relationships and working conditions. In the early 1970s it was the relationships between teachers that were seen as the major obstacle to change, whereas the working conditions of teachers were not given much attention. If the very recent studies prove reliable guides, problems of teacher relationships and teacher perceptions of their roles appear to be reducing (though by no means disappearing) as the profession responds to pressure from HMI and others, and begins to accord recognition to the intermediate authority of postholders.

Teacher working conditions however seem stuck on the anachronistic assumptions that there is no need to provide time, facilities and ideas for curriculum development. It is this aspect of primary school life that requires urgent reappraisal, especially in the light of findings of the most recent HMI surveys (DES 1983a, 1983b). At the present time expectations for school-based curriculum development of the kind called for in the stream of documents from the DES are probably only realisable in those schools that have a fortunate combination of an enlightened and supportive headteacher and unusually talented and hard-working postholders. What is now required is that such development should become routinized in the system; it should be translated from the pioneering schools into the normal ones. For this purpose the kinds of change in teacher working conditions hinted at earlier need to be implemented.

This is not the place for a full examination of what should happen to teacher working conditions, which are properly a matter of negotiation between employers' and teachers' representatives. There is, however, a basis for such negotiation. Teacher time as a problem could be alleviated by an additional allocation of a fixed (annual) amount of staff time to each school for in-school development, INSET, and other related activities, with the understanding that the school could decide in detail how the time should be used. Within the school the time might pass from one postholder to another in the light of school needs. This would provide for the desired flexibility in the use of postholders' time and give an extended professional role the symbolic recognition it needs. If this were done it might be easier to move to a position where teachers would accept that some of their working day after teaching could be rightly reserved for group planning of through-school practice.

Second, an additional element in the resource given to schools could be made available for flexible use of secretarial/clerical time, again to be used at the discretion of the individual school to service in-school development. Access to ideas and expertise also needs resourcing, and a small element of the school's budget for a professional library in the staffroom, or for teacher release to travel to appropriate agencies, could also be provided.

This is not a claim for more of everything in an indiscriminate way. It is a claim that in-school development has sufficient potential to make a fair bid for some of the budget nationally allocated for teacher INSET, and that what is required for using the resource wisely is a re-examination of the assumptions commonly made about the nature of primary school teachers' working conditions.

References

ADELMAN, C. and ALEXANDER, R. (1982) *The Self-evaluating Institution: Practices and Principles in the Management of Education Change*, Methuen.

ALEXANDER, R. (1984) *Primary Teaching*, Holt, Rinehart and Winston.

BASSEY, M. (1978) *Nine Hundred Primary School Teachers*, NFER.

BECHER, A., ERAUT, M. and KNIGHT, J. (1981) *Policies for Educational Accountability*, Heinemann.

DEPARTMENT OF EDUCATION AND SCIENCE (1983a) *9–13 Middle Schools*, HMSO.

DEPARTMENT OF EDUCATION AND SCIENCE (1983b) *Curriculum 11–16: Towards a Statement of Entitlement*, HMSO.

GRAY, L. (1984) *Resource Management in Primary Schools*, Sheffield Papers in Educational Management, Sheffield Polytechnic.

NATIONAL ASSOCIATION OF SCHOOLMASTERS/UNION OF WOMEN TEACHERS (NAS/UWT) (1984) 'Staffing standards in primary schools' quoted in *The Times Educational Supplement*, 9 March.

PRIMARY SCHOOL RESEARCH AND DEVELOPMENT GROUP/SCHOOLS COUNCIL (1983) *Curriculum Responsibility and the Use of Teacher Expertise in the Primary School*, Department of Curriculum Studies, University of Birmingham.

RODGER, I. *et al* (1983) *Teachers with Posts of Responsibility in Primary Schools*, Schools Council, University of Durham School of Education.

SCHOOLS COUNCIL (1983) *Primary Practice*, Methuen.

SUTHERLAND, A. (1981) *Curriculum Projects in Primary Schools: An Investigation on Projects Adoption and Implementation in 185 Northern Ireland Schools*, Northern Ireland Council for Educational Research.

Staff Deployment

Her Majesty's Inspectorate

Class and Specialist Teaching

8.40   Even when the curriculum is clearly defined and priorities are agreed upon, the range of work and the range of pupils present a formidable challenge to the knowledge and skill of an individual teacher. The older and the more able the children, the more obvious this difficulty is for the individual teacher. This is made plain by the present inclination in many schools to rely on one or two teachers for the teaching of music or French, and the poor showing of some subjects, including science and craft, which are commonly the responsibility of the class teacher. *A fuller use of teachers' particular strengths could make a useful contribution to the solution of this problem.*

8.41   *The traditional view has been that the one class to one teacher system should be maintained for nearly all of the work to be done. The class/teacher system has a number of potential advantages: the teacher can get to know the children well and to know their strengths and weaknesses; the one teacher concerned can readily adjust the daily programme to suit special circumstances; it is simpler for one teacher than for a group of teachers to ensure that the various parts of the curriculum are coordinated and also to reinforce work done in one part of the curriculum with work done in another. These advantages are not always exploited, as is shown particularly in the case of mathematics. Nevertheless potentially, and often in practice, these are important advantages and care should be taken to retain and use them.*

8.42   *They are not overriding advantages in all cases. When a teacher is unable to deal satisfactorily with an important aspect of the curriculum, other ways of making this provision have to be found. If a teacher is only a little unsure, advice and guidance from a specialist, probably another member of staff, may be enough. In other cases,*

Reproduced from DES (1978) *Primary Education in England*, HMSO, pp. 117–22.

more often with older than with younger children, and much more often in junior than in infant schools, it may be necessary for the specialist to teach either the whole class or a group of children for particular topics. In some cases, specialists may have to take full responsibility for the teaching of a class or classes other than their own in an area of the curriculum such as music, where expertise is short; perhaps more subjects, in particular science, should be added to the current list, at least for the older children.

8.43   A danger of specialist teaching is that the work done by a specialist may be too isolated from the rest of the children's programme, and this needs to be guarded against by thorough consultation between teachers. *The teacher responsible for the class may be the best placed to coordinate the whole programme of the class. Care needs to be taken to ensure that the programme of the specialist's own class is not too fragmented, and is arranged to utilize the complementary strengths of other teachers.* This may require more than a simple exchange of teachers between two classes. If specialist teaching is taken too far, the timetable becomes over-complex and does not allow variations in the arrangements which circumstances may require from time to time.

8.44   Some schools already adopt forms of cooperative or team teaching which allow teachers to work from their strengths. These arrangements can work well if areas of responsibility are clearly designated, though teams are rarely large enough to permit full coverage of the curriculum using the particular interests and abilities of teachers. No blanket solution is being suggested here. *The critical points are: can class teachers manage to provide all that is necessary for particular classes? If not, what must be done to help them to manage satisfactorily and in a way that is, on balance, advantageous?*

Posts of Special Responsibility

8.45   It is disappointing to find that the great majority of teachers with posts of special responsibility have little influence at present on the work of other teachers. *Consideration needs to be given to improving their standing, which is the product of the ways in which the teachers with special posts regard themselves and also of the attitudes that other teachers have towards them.*

8.46   *It is important that teachers with special responsibility for, say, mathematics should, in consultation with the head, other members of staff and teachers in neighbouring schools, draw up the scheme of work to be implemented in the school; give guidance and support to other members of staff; assist in teaching mathematics to other classes when necessary; and be responsible for the procurement, within the funds made available, of the necessary resources for teaching the subject. They should develop acceptable means of assessing the effectiveness of the guidance and resources they provide, and this may involve visiting other classes in the school to see the work in progress.*

8.47 *Teachers holding posts of responsibility require time to perform their duties, some of which must be carried out while the school is in session*; they also need to keep up to date with current knowledge and practices elsewhere, and this may take time outside normal school hours. The role of heads is rarely discussed specifically in this report because of the way in which the survey was arranged. In average sized and large schools the minor part of heads' time is usually spent in teaching, but this part is of considerable importance and should be safeguarded.

The Deployment of Teachers in Medium and Large Schools

8.48 *In schools of medium or large size, perhaps where the staff is eight or more strong, it may be possible to provide the necessary range and level of specialization from within the staff, especially if this requirement is taken into account when teaching appointments are made.*

8.49 Practice in the vast majority of schools, primary and secondary, makes it plain that criteria additional to class size are taken into account when deploying staff. Arrangements that are made either for freeing a teacher from teaching, or for enabling a teacher to teach groups smaller than a whole class, have the effect of increasing the size of the basic class unit; this is so whether small groups are withdrawn for special teaching or whether two teachers temporarily share the teaching of a class in one teaching area.

8.50 Considerations other than class size which are taken into account when deploying staff are: the ages and special needs of children; the expertise of individual teachers; and the need for teachers, especially the head, to undertake, in addition to teaching duties, administrative responsibilities and liaison on behalf of the school. *It is a matter of judgment in individual cases precisely how the criteria are balanced and how duties are allocated, but the survey evidence suggests that some shift in the deployment of teachers is worth considering.*

8.51 *After detailed analysis, the survey data led to the conclusion that differences in class sizes in classes of between about 25 and about 35 children made no difference to the children's scores on the NFER objective tests, or to the closeness of the match of the work to the children's abilities, or to the likelihood that a wide range of common items would be included in the curriculum. On the other hand, classes of these sizes performed worse in certain ways if they contained mixed rather than single age groups, the 7 and 11-year-olds were more likely to be given work that was too easy; the 9 and 11-year-olds scored less well on the NFER tests. This is probably because, for children of these ages and in classes of these sizes, the teacher's perception of the class as a whole masks the considerable differences between the children and especially the differences in their rates of progress. It is probably unreasonable to expect most teachers to work as effectively with mixed age classes of about 30 children as they would with single age classes of that size. Class size is only one factor to be taken into account when determining suitable staffing standards. The findings of this survey do not mean that staffing standards could safely be tightened, but rather that there are some ways of using teachers' time, including those described in the next paragraph, which could bring bigger benefits than simply minimizing class sizes.*

8.52 *Bearing in mind what has been said in the previous paragraph about class sizes and about classes with mixed age groups, heads and teachers could usefully consider how staff might be deployed in order to make the best uses of the strengths of individual teachers, to employ holders of posts of responsibility most effectively and to allow some time for the preparation of work. In large and some medium sized schools it might, within limits, be worth arranging for one or more teachers additional to the head to be free of full responsibility for a class, though in virtually full-time teaching contact with children. This would make registered class sizes larger than they would otherwise be, given the number of teachers. On different occasions these teachers could be used to teach their own specialism and to enable teachers with other curricular responsibilities to be freed to assess the extent to which modifications are needed in the programme of work in their subject; they, or the teachers they free, might be able to assist others in the course of their teaching; work with subdivisions of a class in order to meet the specific needs of individuals or groups of children; or undertake the teaching of other classes, particularly in areas of the curriculum where expertise is short. In schools of medium size, these arrangements may be possible only if staffing standards are particularly generous, except in so far as the head uses his own teaching timetable for these purposes.*

Special Responsibilities and Small Schools

8.53 *In small schools the number of teachers on the staff is likely to be too small to provide the necessary specialist knowledge in all parts of the curriculum. The teachers in a group of schools can profitably share their skills in planning programmes of work and a number of small schools (and large) have benefited from doing so as a result of their own enterprise, under the guidance of local authority advisers, through teachers' centres or with the help of Schools Council and other curricular projects.*

8.54 *Teachers in some small schools already make arrangements to exchange classes, for example for half a day a week during the summer term or from time to time. Some local authorities employ visiting teachers of sufficient status to be accepted as specialists by teachers, including heads, of the schools they visit. They are most commonly involved in remedial education and music, but in a few areas a range of specialist advice is provided and the visiting teacher works alongside the class teacher. This is a practice that might usefully be extended and avoids the danger, for which there is some tentative evidence in the survey, that peripatetic teaching directed solely at special groups of children, whether the most able in music or the least able in reading, has little carry over effect on the levels of work for the rest of the children.*

Factors Influencing Primary Schools' Effectiveness

ILEA

Key Factors for Effective Junior Schooling

[Through the research] ... a picture evolves of what constitutes effective junior schooling. This picture is not intended to be a 'blueprint' for success. Inevitably, many aspects of junior schooling could not be examined in the Junior School Project. Furthermore, schools are not static institutions. This survey was carried out between 1980 and 1984, and it has, therefore, not been possible to take full account of all the changes (particularly in approaches to the curriculum) that have taken place since that time. Nonetheless, this section identifies the key factors that were consistently related to effective junior schooling.

Initially, before examining factors over which schools and teachers can exercise direct control, consideration is given to less flexible characteristics of schools. It was found that certain of these 'given' features made it easier to create an effective school.

Schools that cover the entire primary age range (JMIs), where pupils do not have to transfer at age 7, appear to be at an advantage, as do voluntary-aided schools.[*] Smaller schools, with a junior roll of under 160 children, also appear to benefit their pupils. Class size is particularly relevant: smaller classes, with less than twenty-four pupils, had a positive impact upon pupil progress and development, especially in the early years.

Not surprisingly, a good physical environment, as reflected in the school's amenities, its decorative order, and its immediate surroundings, creates a positive situation in which progress and development can be fostered. Extended periods of disruption, due to building work and

Reproduced from ILEA (1986) *The Junior School Project: A Summary of the Main Report*, ILEA, pp. 33–8.
[*] On the whole, the latter tend to have more socio-economically advantaged intakes than county schools.

redecoration, can have a negative impact on pupils' progress. The stability of the school's teaching force is also an important factor. Changes of head and deputy headteacher, though inevitable, have an unsettling effect upon the pupils. It seems, therefore, that every effort should be made to reduce the potentially negative impact of such changes. Similarly, where there is an unavoidable change of class teacher, during the school year, careful planning will be needed to ensure an easy transition, and minimize disruption to the pupils. Where pupils experience continuity through the whole year, with one class teacher, progress is more likely to occur.

It is, however, not only continuity of staff that is important. Although major, or frequent changes tend to have negative effects, change can be used positively. Thus, where there had been no change of head for a long period of time, schools tended to be less effective. In the more effective schools, heads had usually been in post for between three and seven years.

It is clear, therefore, that some schools are more advantaged in terms of their size, status, environment and stability of teaching staff. Nonetheless, although these favourable 'given' characteristics contribute to effectiveness, they do not, by themselves, ensure it. They provide a supporting framework within which the head and teachers can work to promote pupil progress and development. The size of a school, for example, may facilitate certain modes of organization which benefit pupils. However, it is the factors *within* the control of the head and teachers that are crucial. These are the factors that can be changed and improved.

Twelve key factors of effectiveness have been identified.

The Twelve Factors

1   Purposeful leadership of the staff by the headteacher

'Purposeful leadership' occurred where the headteacher understood the needs of the school and was actively involved in the school's work, without exerting total control over the rest of the staff.

In effective schools, headteachers were involved in curriculum discussions and influenced the content of guidelines drawn up within the school, without taking total control. They also influenced the teaching style of teachers, but only selectively, where they judged it necessary. This leadership was demonstrated by an emphasis on monitoring pupils' progress through the keeping of individual records. Approaches varied— some schools kept written records; others passed on folders of pupils' work to their next teacher; some did both—but a systematic policy of record keeping was important.

With regard to in-service training, those heads exhibiting purposeful leadership did not allow teachers total freedom to attend *any* course: attendance was allowed for a good reason. Nonetheless, most teachers in these schools had attended in-service courses.

2 The involvement of the deputy head

The Junior School Project findings indicate that the deputy head can have a major role in the effectiveness of junior schools.

Where the deputy was frequently absent, or absent for a prolonged period (due to illness, attendance on long courses, or other commitments), this was detrimental to pupils' progress and development. Moreover, a change of deputy head tended to have negative effects.

The responsibilities undertaken by deputy heads also seemed to be important. Where the head generally involved the deputy in policy decisions, it was beneficial to the pupils. This was particularly true in terms of allocating teachers to classes. Thus, it appeared that a certain amount of delegation by the headteacher, and a sharing of responsibilities, promoted effectiveness.

3 The involvement of teachers

In successful schools, the teachers were involved in curriculum planning and played a major role in developing their own curriculum guidelines. As with the deputy head, teacher involvement in decisions concerning which classes they were to teach, was important. Similarly, consultation with teachers about decisions on spending, was important. It appeared that schools in which teachers were consulted on issues affecting school policy, as well as those affecting them directly, were more likely to be successful.

4 Consistency amongst teachers

It has already been shown that continuity of staffing had positive effects. Not only, however, do pupils benefit from teacher continuity, but it also appears that some kind of stability, or consistency, in teacher approach is important.

For example, in schools where all teachers followed guidelines in the same way (whether closely or selectively), the impact on progress was positive. Where there was variation between teachers in their usage of guidelines, this had a negative effect.

5 Structured sessions

The Project findings indicate that pupils benefitted when their school day was structured in some way. In effective schools, pupils' work was organized by the teacher, who ensured that there was always plenty for them to do. Positive effects were also noted when pupils were *not* given unlimited responsibility for planning their own programme of work, or for choosing work activities.

In general, teachers who organized a framework within which pupils could work, and yet allowed them some freedom within this structure, were more successful.

6 Intellectually challenging teaching

Unsurprisingly, the quality of teaching was very important in promoting pupil progress and development. The findings clearly show that, in classes where pupils were stimulated and challenged, progress was greater.

The content of teachers' communications was vitally important. Positive effects occurred where teachers used more 'higher-order' questions and statements, that is, where their communications encouraged pupils to use their creative imagination and powers of problem-solving. In classes where the teaching situation was challenging and stimulating, and where teachers communicated interest and enthusiasm to the children, greater pupil progress occurred. It appeared, in fact, that teachers who more frequently directed pupils' work, without discussing it or explaining its purpose, had a negative impact. Frequent monitoring and maintenance of work, in terms of asking pupils about their progress, was no more successful. What was crucial was the *level* of the communications between teacher and pupils.

Creating a challenge for pupils suggests that the teacher believes they are capable of responding to it. It was evident that such teachers had *high* expectations of their pupils. This is further seen in the effectiveness of teachers who encouraged their pupils to take independent control over the work they were currently doing. Some teachers only infrequently gave instructions to pupils concerning their work, yet everyone in the class knew exactly what they were supposed to be doing, and continued working without close supervision. This strategy improved pupil progress and development.

7   *Work-centred environment*

In schools, where teachers spent more of their time discussing the *content* of work with pupils, and less time on routine matters and the maintenance of work activity, the impact was positive. There was some indication that time devoted to giving pupils feedback about their work was also beneficial.

The work-centred environment was characterized by a high level of pupil industry in the classroom. Pupils appeared to enjoy their work and were eager to commence new tasks. The noise level was also low, although this is not to say that there was silence in the classroom. Furthermore, pupil movement around the classroom, was not excessive, and was generally work-related.

8   *Limited focus within sessions*

It appears that learning was facilitated when teachers devoted their energies to one particular curriculum area within a session. At times, work could be undertaken in two areas and also produce positive effects. However, where many sessions were organized such that three or more curriculum areas were concurrent, pupils' progress was marred. It is likely that this finding is related to other factors. For example, pupil industry was lower in classrooms where mixed activities occurred. Moreover, noise and pupil movement were greater, and teachers spent less time discussing work and more time on routine issues. More importantly, in mixed-activity sessions the opportunities for communication between teachers and pupils were reduced (as will be described later).

A focus upon one curriculum area did not imply that all the pupils were doing exactly the same work. There was some variation, both in terms of choice of topic and level of difficulty. Positive effects tended to occur where the teacher geared the level of work to pupils' needs.

9   *Maximum communication between teachers and pupils*

It was evident that pupils gained from having more communication with the teacher. Thus, those teachers who spent higher proportions of their time *not* interacting with the children were less successful in promoting progress and development.

The time teachers spent on communications with the whole class was also important. Most teachers devoted the majority of their attention to speaking with individuals. Each child, therefore, could only expect to receive a fairly small number of individual contacts with their teacher. When teachers spoke to the whole class, they increased the overall number of contacts with children. In particular, this enabled a greater number of 'higher-order' communications to be received by *all* pupils. Therefore, a balance of teacher contacts between individuals and the whole class was more beneficial than a total emphasis on communicating with individuals (or groups) alone.

Furthermore, where children worked in a single curriculum area within sessions, (even if they were engaged on individual or group tasks) it was easier for teachers to raise an intellectually challenging point with *all* pupils.

10   *Record keeping*

The value of record keeping has already been noted, in relation to the purposeful leadership of the headteacher. However, it was also an important aspect of teachers' planning and assessment. Where teachers reported that they kept written records of pupils' work progress, in addition to the Authority's Primary Yearly Record, the effect on the pupils was positive. The keeping of records concerning pupils' personal and social development was also found to be generally beneficial.

11   *Parental involvement*

The research found parental involvement to be a positive influence upon pupils' progress and development. This included help in classrooms and on educational visits, and attendance at meetings to discuss children's progress. The headteacher's accessibility to parents was also important, showing that schools with an informal, open-door policy were more effective. Parental involvement in pupils' educational development within the home was also beneficial. Parents who read to their children, heard them read, and provided them with access to books at home, had a positive effect upon their children's learning. One aspect of parental involvement was, however, not successful. Somewhat curiously, formal Parent-Teacher Associations (PTAs) were not found to be related to effective schooling. It could be that some parents found the formal structure of such a body to be intimidating.

Nonetheless, overall, parental involvement was beneficial to schools and their pupils.

12   *Positive climate*

The Junior School Project provides confirmation that an effective school has a positive ethos. Overall, the atmosphere was more pleasant in the effective schools, for a variety of reasons.

Both around the school and within the classroom, less emphasis on punishment and critical control, and a greater emphasis on praise and rewarding pupils, had a positive impact. Where teachers actively encouraged self-control on the part of pupils, rather than emphasizing the negative aspects of their behaviour, progress and development increased. What appeared to be important was firm but fair classroom management.

The teachers' attitude to their pupils was also important. Good effects resulted where teachers obviously enjoyed teaching their classes and communicated this to their pupils. Their interest in the children as individuals, and not just as pupils was also valuable. Those who devoted more time to non-school chat or 'small talk' increased pupils' progress and development. Outside the classroom, evidence of a positive climate included: the organization of lunchtime and after-school clubs for pupils; teachers eating their lunch at the same tables as the children; organization of trips and visits; and the use of the local environment as a learning resource.

The working conditions of teachers contributed to the creation of a positive school climate. Where teachers had non-teaching periods, the impact on pupil progress and development was positive. Thus, the climate created by the teachers for the pupils, and by the head for the teachers, was an important aspect of the school's effectiveness. This further appeared to be reflected in effective schools by happy, well-behaved pupils who were friendly towards each other and outsiders, and by the absence of graffiti around the school.

These are the twelve key factors that have been identified in the study. Some had a stronger effect than others on the cognitive and non-cognitive areas investigated, but all were positive.... these factors depend on specific behaviours and strategies employed by the headteacher and staff. It is essential to realize that the school and the classroom are in many ways interlocked. What the teacher can or cannot do depends, to a certain extent, on what is happening in the school as a whole.

Whilst these twelve factors do not constitute a 'recipe' for effective junior schooling, they can provide a framework within which the various partners in the life of the school—headteacher and staff, parents and pupils, and governors—can operate. Each of these partners has the capacity to foster the success of the school. When each participant plays a positive role, the result is an effective school.

5
Postscript

The pace of change alluded to in this book's *Foreword* and in the editorial introduction to Section 1 makes written comment on contemporary developments positively vulnerable. Such comment is too quickly overtaken, though not necessarily rendered irrelevant, by events. Since the preparation of papers for this book, the government has announced plans for the introduction of a national curriculum: such plans have a direct bearing on many of the issues raised here but with effects that are, as yet, unclear. This last extract published as a postscript, outlines the government's thinking about the main elements of a national curriculum and how they might operate in practice. Readers are asked to consider how far such proposals reinforce, run contra to, or are irrelevant to the issues emerging in this book.

Towards a National Curriculum

Department of Education and Science

B. The Components of the National Curriculum and Assessment Arrangements

11. This section sets out the Secretaries of State's thinking about the main elements of the national curriculum and how they will operate in practice. Section C sets out what will be included in legislation. What is required by statute—including the regulations that will be made over a period of time to secure full implementation of the national curriculum—will be determined by a process of discussion and development of the ideas in this document.

12. The non-statutory subject working groups which the Secretaries of State are appointing will play a key part in this process. They will make recommendations about attainment targets and programmes of work for each of the foundation subjects, which will be the basis for consultations about what is eventually set out in regulations about the curriculum.

(a) Foundation subjects

13. Maths, English and science will form the core of the curriculum, and first priority will be given to these subjects. They and other foundation subjects are to be followed by all pupils during compulsory schooling. The government has proposed that, in addition to English, maths and science, the foundation subjects should comprise a modern foreign language, technology, history, geography, art, music and physical education. The degree of definition in the requirements set out for each of these subjects will vary considerably, and will be greatest for the three core subjects. The place of Welsh in the national curriculum in Wales is dealt with below.

Reproduced from DES (1987) *The National Curriculum 5–16: A Consultative Document*, HMSO, paragraphs 11–18, 22–36 and 94–5 with the permission of the Controller of Her Majesty's Stationery Office

14. It is not proposed that a modern foreign language should be included in the foundation subjects for primary school children. The majority of curriculum time at primary level should be devoted to the core subjects.

15. During compulsory secondary schooling, it is proposed that all pupils should continue with some study of all the foundation subjects. As the table below shows, between 30–40 per cent of curriculum time should still be devoted to the three core subjects. Not all foundation subjects will necessarily be taken to examination level—though the Secretaries of State expect that most pupils should be able to take GCSEs covering seven or eight of the foundation subject areas, and all the core subjects should be taken. Pupils in the fourth and fifth years should be able to opt to study either combined sciences as a single subject or sciences leading to a double GCSE award; and to pursue a combined course covering art, music, drama and design. This should leave adequate time in the curriculum for choice of other examination subjects which are not among the foundation subjects. The table illustrates how this might be organized in England:

SECONDARY PHASE—YEARS 4 AND 5
ALLOCATIONS OF CURRICULUM TIME

Foundation subjects	%	Additional subjects eg for GCSE might include:	
English	10	Science	)
Maths	10	Second Modern Foreign Language	)
Combined Sciences	10–20	Classics	)
Technology	10	Home Economics	)
Modern Foreign Language	10	History	)
		Geography	)
History/Geography or History *or* Geography	10	Business Studies	) 10%
Art/Music/Drama/Design	10	Art	)
Physical Education	5	Music	)
		Drama	)
		Religious Studies	)

16. The Secretaries of State do not intend to prescribe in legislation how much time should be allocated to each subject area. But the foundation subjects commonly take up 80–90% of the curriculum in schools where there is good practice. The Secretaries of State will take that as their starting

point in issuing non-statutory guidance (separately for England and for Wales) about how much time should normally be spent on learning related to each subject at each phase of education, and the subject working groups will base their recommendations about programmes of study on this guidance.

17. Religious education is already required by statute, and must continue to form an essential part of the curriculum. There will be time available beyond that required for the foundation subjects for religious education, and also for other popular subjects, such as home economics, which are taught by many schools and will continue to be a valuable part of the curriculum for many pupils in the secondary as well as primary phase. LEAs and governing bodies of schools will determine the subjects to be taught additional to the foundation subjects.

18. In addition, there are a number of subjects or themes such as health education and use of information technology, which can be taught through other subjects. For example, biology can contribute to learning about health education, and the health theme will give an added dimension to teaching about biology. It is proposed that such subjects or themes should be taught through the foundation subjects, so that they can be accommodated within the curriculum but without crowding out the essential subjects.

22. The Secretaries of State believe it to be important that schools should also have flexibility about how they organize their teaching. The description of the national curriculum in terms of foundation subjects is not a description of how the school day should be organized and the curriculum delivered. The clear objectives for what pupils should be able to know, do and understand will be framed in subject terms. Schools will be able to organize their teaching in a variety of ways. This flexibility, together with the time available outside the foundation curriculum, ought to enable schools, while meeting the requirements of the national curriculum, to give special emphasis to particular subjects, such as science and technology in City Technology Colleges.

(b) Attainment targets

23. Attainment targets will be set for all three core subjects of maths, English and science. These will establish what children should normally be expected to know, understand and be able to do at around the ages of 7, 11, 14 and 16, and will enable the progress of each child to be measured against established national standards. They will reflect what pupils must achieve to progress in their education and to become thinking and informed people. The range of attainment targets should cater for the full ability

range and be sufficiently challenging *at all levels* to raise expectations, particularly of pupils of middling achievement who frequently are not challenged enough, as well as stretching and stimulating the most able. This is a proven and essential way towards raising standards of achievement. Targets must be sufficiently specific for pupils, teachers, parents and others to have a clear idea of what is expected, and to provide a sound basis for assessment.

24. There will also be attainment targets for other foundation subjects where appropriate, in Wales for the study of Welsh, and for the other themes and skills taught through each of the foundation subjects. For art, music and physical education there will be guidelines rather than specific attainment targets.

25. Attainment targets for age 16 can be expected to take account of GCSE criteria. But not all GCSE criteria are sufficiently specific, and not all pupils will study all foundation subjects for public examination, so there will be other attainment targets to build on what they have learnt up to age 14.

(c) Programmes of study

26. The programmes of study will also be based on recommendations from the subject working groups. They will reflect the attainment targets, and set out the overall content, knowledge, skills and processes relevant to today's needs which pupils should be taught in order to achieve them. They should also specify in more detail a minimum of common content, which all pupils should be taught, and set out any areas of learning in other subjects or themes that should be covered in each stage. Some GCSE syllabuses will have to be revised in due course to reflect the national curriculum attainment targets and programmes of study for age 16.

27. Within the programmes of study teachers will be free to determine the detail of what should be taught in order to ensure that pupils achieve appropriate levels of attainment. How teaching is organized and the teaching approaches used will be also for schools to determine. It is proposed that schools should set out schemes of work for teaching at various stages to improve coordination. The government intends that legislation should leave full scope for professional judgment and for schools to organize how the curriculum is delivered in the way best suited to the ages, circumstances, needs and abilities of the children in each classroom. This will for example allow curriculum development programmes such as the Technical and Vocational Education Initiative (TVEI) to build on the framework offered by the national curriculum and to take forward its objectives. There must be space to accommodate the enterprise of teachers, offering them sufficient flexibility in the choice of content to adapt what they teach to the needs of the individual pupil, to try out and develop new approaches, and to develop in pupils those personal qualities which cannot be written into a programme of study or attainment target.

(d) Assessment and examinations

28. The attainment targets will provide standards against which pupils' progress and performance can be assessed. The main purpose of such assessment will be to show what a pupil has learnt and mastered and to enable teachers and parents to ensure that he or she is making adequate progress. Where such progress is not made, it will be up to schools to make suitable arrangements to help the pupil.

29. The Secretaries of State envisage that much of the assessment at ages 7 (or thereabouts) 11 and 14, and at 16 in non-examined subjects, will be done by teachers as an integral part of normal classroom work. But at the heart of the assessment process there will be nationally prescribed tests done by all pupils to supplement the individual teachers' assessments. Teachers will administer and mark these, but their marking—and their assessments overall—will be externally moderated.

30. The Secretaries of State hope that the moderation of teachers' assessments and whatever arrangements are needed for administering nationally set tests will be undertaken by the five GCSE examining groups, under contract from a School Examinations and Assessment Council (see paras 53 below). The Department will be undertaking detailed discussion of this proposal, and of the kind of administrative and moderation arrangements needed, with the examining groups and others. The actual tests and other forms of assessment will be developed and piloted by various organizations on behalf of the government.

31. The precise basis for recording assessments will be considered by an expert Task Group on Assessment and Testing which the Secretaries of State will appoint shortly. It will make recommendations on the common elements of an assessment strategy to be used across all subjects and will be asked to report by Christmas.

32. The government aims to set in place by 1990 national arrangements for the introduction of records of achievement for school leavers. Such records, which are at present being piloted in a number of areas and on which an interim report will be made this autumn by the National Steering Committee, will have an important role in recording performance and profiling a pupil's achievements across and beyond the national curriculum.

33. At age 16, GCSE and other qualifications at equivalent level will provide the main means of assessment through examinations. But in order to ensure that the qualifications offered to pupils support or form part of the national curriculum's attainment targets and programmes of study, the government proposes to take powers to specify what qualifications may be offered to pupils during compulsory schooling. It also proposes to put onto a statutory footing the approval of syllabuses or courses leading to these qualifications, which is presently done by the non-statutory Secondary Examinations Council for GCE and GCSE examinations.

34. Because of the importance of steady progression from what is studied

pre-16 to the qualifications available post-16, and the need to ensure proper standards and coherence in what is offered, the government also proposes to take a reserve power similarly to regulate qualifications and courses offered to full-time 16–19-year-old pupils in schools and colleges—for use only if experience shows this to be necessary. This power would be exercised only after consultations with the National Council for Vocational Qualifications and other relevant examining and validating bodies responsible for qualifications offered to full-time 16–19-year-old pupils.

(e)   Availability of information

35. In order to raise standards, people must be aware of what is being achieved already and of the objectives set. This means that the legislation on the national curriculum must provide for all interested parties to have appropriate and readily digestible information, relevant to their interests, about what is being taught and achieved. The Secretaries of State are convinced that at every level of the service, the provision of more information will lead to a better understanding of how the education system is performing.

36. The Secretaries of State believe that it is essential that:

   (i) *Pupils and parents* should know what individual pupils are being taught in each year, and how that relates to the national curriculum attainment targets and programmes of study. Similar information would have been provided to parents under regulations made under Section 20 of the 1986 Education Act, which the legislation on the national curriculum will supersede. They also need to know how the individual pupil has performed against the attainment targets, and by comparison with the range of marks achieved by pupils in his or her class—for example 10 per cent got Grade 1, 20 per cent Grade 2, 30 per cent Grade 3.

  (ii) *Teachers* should know how individual pupils are progressing so that they can decide on appropriate next steps for their learning; and how pupils in their class overall are doing as compared with the attainment targets, with other similar classes in the school, and with other schools, particularly in the same LEA and with the national average.

 (iii) *Parents, governing bodies, employers and the local community* should know what a school's assessment and examination results indicate about performance and how they compare with those of other schools within the LEA or neighbourhood. In order to inform their choice of school parents also need to know about the curriculum followed in each school, and its schemes of work.

 (iv) *LEAs* should know about attainment in the schools they maintain, in comparison other LEAs, with grant-maintained schools in the locality, and with the national average; and

    (v) at the national level, *central government, Parliament and the public* should to be able to monitor national standards of attainment and improvement over time.

94. The proposals outlined in the document represent a major step forward towards the common aims for compulsory education which have emerged from the debate about the curriculum begun ten years ago and recorded in *Better Schools*. The challenge for the education service is to raise standards through the full and successful implementation of the national curriculum—to the point where every pupil is studying for, and being regularly assessed against, worthwhile attainment targets in all the essential foundation subjects, and where all members of the community with an interest in the country's education services are able to inform themselves properly about its objectives and achievements. There will be continuing and fruitful discussion throughout this process. That will influence the real substance of the work, which is to establish the national curriculum; legislation can only provide the framework.

95. The task ahead will not be done, nor done well, without the initiatives, efforts and commitment of the education profession, in particular teachers in the classroom. Their role will be enhanced rather than curtailed by a national curriculum. Theirs will be the responsibility for putting into practice an historic development which has widespread support, for realising the shared aims of the education service and its consumers alike in raising standards, and for injecting the quality and imagination into the arrangements which legislation cannot secure. The Secretaries of State hope that this document will help to stimulate debate and the thinking which will result in successful implementation of the national curriculum, as well as providing an opportunity for more immediate comment on the legislative framework proposed.

Notes on Contributors

Neville Bennett was Professor of Educational Research at the University of Lancaster until becoming Professor of Primary Education at the University of Exeter in 1985. His books include *Teaching Styles and Pupil Progress, Open Plan Schools* and *The Quality of Pupil Learning Experiences.*

Alan Blyth was Sydney Jones Professor of Education in the University of Liverpool and is now Honorary Senior Fellow there. His interests and publications have been in the field of primary education, and especially in the primary curriculum. At present he is completing a study of appraisal and assessment of Humanities in primary schools.

Howard Bradley is Director of the Cambridge Institute of Education and Fellow of Hughes Hall, Cambridge. He has carried out research into INSET needs and the induction year. His present work is in management courses for senior staff in schools. He is also Director of the Evaluation of the School Teacher Appraisal Pilot Study.

R. J. Campbell is currently Senior Lecturer in Education at the University of Warwick, and has taught in primary and comprehensive schools and in a tertiary college. His major research interests are in curriculum development, especially in primary and middle schools. His publications include *Developing the Primary School Curriculum*, Holt Rinehart and Winston (1985), and *The Routledge Compendium of Primary Education* (1987). He is currently writing a book on the ways children reconstruct ideas about society that they acquire in primary schools. He is editor of the journal *Education 3–13.*

Malcolm Clarkson was formerly Head of the Department of Primary Education at Brighton Polytechnic. He was co-editor of *The Changing Patterns of Teacher Education* (1976), *The Middle Years Curriculum* (1974) and *Teaching the 8–13's* (1976). He is now a full-time publisher being the Managing Director of Falmer Press and Books Director of Taylor & Francis Ltd.

Anne Cockburn is a Research Fellow at the University of East Anglia. After reading psychology at the University of St Andrews she went to Moray House College of Education and subsequently taught infant children in Edinburgh. Since then she has worked on a wide range of research projects in Strathclyde, Lancaster and Norwich. She is particularly interested in the education of young children and, among other things, is currently investigating the potential value of mathematical games in the infant classroom. She is co-author (with Charles Desforges) of *Understanding the Mathematics Teacher* (1987).

Alan Coulson is currently Senior Lecturer in Education Management at the North East Wales Institute of Higher Education where his main professional interest is the application of humanistic psychology in management development, especially among heads and teachers. He has taught in both primary and secondary schools and, part-time, in the prison service and three universities. His main publications discuss primary school management.

Michael Day taught in Canada, before returning to England as a member of staff at St Luke's, Exeter which later merged with the University of Exeter's School of Education. He is co-ordinator of the primary science studies at BA/BEd and PGCE level. Much of his in-service work has been exploring with teachers ways of encouraging investigative work throughout the curriculum. Currently he is developing the use of interactive video-discs as a resource for widening teachers' perceptions of enquiry and problem-solving in the classroom.

Joan Dean has worked as a teacher in primary and secondary schools and in further education, as lecturer in a college of education, as head of two primary schools, as Senior Adviser for Primary Education and for the past fifteen years as Chief Inspector for Surrey.

During this period she has written some twenty-four books, numerous articles for the education press, has broadcast and appeared on television and has contributed to a number of national committees. Her most recent books are *Organising Learning in the Primary School Classroom, Managing the Secondary School* and *Managing the Primary School*, all published by Croom Helm.

She was President of the National Association of Inspectors and Educational Advisers for the year 1971–2 and was awarded the OBE for her contribution to education in 1980.

Charles Desforges is currently Professor of Primary Education at the University of Exeter. He was a school teacher for ten years. Since then he has worked in several institutions in higher education, including the universities of Lancaster and East Anglia. He has carried out research into children's thinking and, more recently, into classroom processes. His publications include *The Quality of Pupils' Learning Experiences* (1984) and

Recent Advances in Classroom Reasearch (1985). He is co-author (with Anne Cockburn) of *Understanding the Mathematics Teacher* (1987).

Michael Golby is Senior Lecturer and Chair of Educational Studies at the University of Exeter School of Education. His research interests centre on the control of education and he directs a major research study sponsored by the Leverhulme Trust into school governorship. A member of both the Morris Minor and MG Owners' Clubs, he contends that these dual loyalties represent two aspects of an as yet unresolved personality conflict.

Harold Heller is currently director of the newly established Centre for Adviser and Inspector Development (CAID), located at Woolley Hall, Yorkshire, on secondment from the post of Chief Adviser, Cleveland. He has written widely in the fields of Educational Change and Management Development and has a particular interest in Group-work and counselling approaches to training.

Keith Kimberley is a lecturer in the Centre for Multicultural Education at the London University Institute of Education. Previously, he taught in ILEA secondary schools for 14 years. He is co-author, with Crispin Jones, of *Intercultural Education: Concept, Context, Curriculum Practice*, (1986), Council of Europe.

Ann Lewis is Lecturer in Education at the University of Warwick and is particularly involved with the professional preparation of infant/first school teachers. Her research interest is in talk between young children with learning difficulties and their classmates. She is joint editor of *Education 3–13* and has taught in primary and special schools.

John Pearce was one of the teacher members of the Schools Council Programme in Linguistics and English Teaching; shared in writing *Language in Use* and other books of wide influence; an LEA inspector in Cambridgeshire until recent retirement; now a consultant. Central interest: how to bridge the gulf between scholarly study and the work of classroom teachers and advisers.

Colin Richards is Staff Inspector (Curriculum), Her Majesty's Inspectorate.

Alistair Ross taught in London primary schools for nine years, including a period as ILEA advisory teacher for history and social studies in primary schools. Since 1985 he has been Principal Lecturer in Primary Education at the Polytechnic of North London, where he is Course Leader for the BEd(Hons) degree, editor of the journal *Primary Teaching Studies* and director of the Primary Schools and Industry Centre.

Hilary Shuard was formerly Deputy Principal of Homerton College, Cambridge. She is now Director of the SCDC Primary Initiative in Mathematics Education (PRIME) Project, and is on the Board of the Council for Educational Technology (CET), and the Microelectronics Education Support Unit (MESU).

Andre Wagstaff relinquished an established career as a chartered accountant to become a primary classroom teacher. He followed this with two years as Deputy Director of the MEP National Primary Project. He is now Primary Curriculum Coordinator with the Microelectronic Education Support Unit based at the University of Warwick.

Dan Wicksteed and **Derek Sharples** have worked and taught together for a number of years at Worcester College of HE. Both are experienced primary teachers who are now extensively involved in professional education and enquiry. Dan, whose background is in philosophy and science, leads the primary area of the College, whilst Derek, whose studies have been in psychology and humanities, is the Dean of Education there. They have published a number of papers in the fields of primary curriculum and teacher education.

Judith Byrne Whyte is author of *Beyond the Wendy House: Sex Role Stereotyping in Primary Schools* (1983) Schools Council/Longman, and *Girls Into Science and Technology* (1986) Routledge and Kegan Paul. She also edited *Girls Friendly Schooling* (1985) Methuen. She is now Head of Research and Policy at the Equal Opportunities Commission.

Index

Pages numbered in **bold** include tables. Pages numbered in *Italics* include figures.